The Marshall Cavendish Illustrated History of

POPULAR MUSIC

Volume 21

INDEX

MARSHALL CAVENDISH
NEW YORK, LONDON, TORONTO, SYDNEY

Reference Edition Published 1990

Published by Marshall Cavendish Corporation
147 West Merrick Road
Freeport, Long Island
N.Y. 11520

Printed and Bound in Italy by L.E.G.O. S.p.a. Vicenza.

Reference edition produced by DPM Services.

© Orbis Publishing Ltd.MCMLXXXIX
© Marshall Cavendish Ltd.MCMLXXXIX

Set ISBN 1-85436-015-3

Library of Congress Cataloging in Publication Data

The Marshall Cavendish history of popular music.
    p.   cm.
   Includes index.
   ISBN 1-85435-100-1 (vol. 21)
    1. Popular music – History and criticism. 2. Rock music – History
and Criticism. I. Marshall Cavendish Corporation. II. Title:
History of popular music.
ML 3470. M36 1988
784. 5' 009 – dc19
                    88-21076
                    CIP
                    MN

Editorial Staff

Editor	Ashley Brown
Executive Editors	Adrian Gilbert
	Michael Heatley
Consultant Editors	Richard Williams
	Peter Brookesmith
Editorial Director	Brian Innes

Reference Edition Staff

Reference Editor	Mark Dartford
Revision Editor	Fran Jones
Consultant Editor	Michael Heatley
Art Editor	Graham Beehag

CONTENTS

CONTENTS OF SET

VOLUME I

4   **1967 The Year It All Came Together**
Simon Frith

21   **Rock Around The Clock**
Adrian Gilbert

24   **The Haley Story**
Rob Finnis

29   **Rhythm and Blues**
Bill Millar

33   **Louis Jordan**
Cliff White

36   **The Drifting Cowboy**
John Collis

38   **Country Boogie**
Martin Hawkins

41   **Memphis, Tennessee**
Adrian Gilbert

44   **The Sun Story**
Martin Hawkins

48   **Elvis—The Early Years**
Peter Jones

55   **Music in the Air**
Tony Russell

59   **Charting Success**
Dick Bradley

61   **Black Voices**
Geoff Brown

64   **Chuck Berry**
Charles Shaar Murray

69   **Doo-Wop**
Geoff Brown

74   **Clyde McPhatter**
Bill Millar

76   **Teenage Tragedy**
Bill Millar

78   **Electrifying Music**
Charles Shaar Murray

81   **Rock Takes Over**
Peter Brooke Smith

84   **Rock '56**
Chris Welch

86   **Elvis Goes National**
Peter Jones

91   **Marketing a Million-Dollar Talent**
Peter Jones

94   **In the Studio and on the Road**
Geoff Brown

96   **'Love Me Tender'**
Jonathan Reed

98   **Cars and Sex and Rock'n'Roll**
Peter Brookesmith

101   **Rockabilly**
Bill Millar

104   **Gene Vincent**
Rob Finnis

109   **Blue Suede Shoes**
Colin Escott, Martin Hawkins

112   **In the Farms and on the Forecourts**
Bill Millar

114   **The Burnettes**
Bill Millar

116   **Cat Clothes and the Curtis Cut**
Robert Shelton

118   **From Blue Caps to Stray Cats**
Chris North

VOLUME 2

121 The UK Rocks
Ashley Brown

124 Lonnie Donegan & Skiffle
Karl Dallas

129 The Bermondsey Backbeat
Rob Finnis

132 Clubs and Coffee Bars
Brian Innes

135 The Elvis Followers
Rob Finnis

138 Rock around the Gaumont
Chris Welch

141 New Orleans Rock
Adrian Gilbert

144 The Fat Man
Clive Anderson

148 His Majesty
Michael Watts

153 Crescent City
Clive Anderson

156 Lloyd Price
Bill Millar

158 Gospel
Clive Anderson

161 Live and Kicking
Michael Heatley

164 Rock '57
Chris Welch

166 The Killer
Nick Tosches

173 Rock Shock Horror
Cliff White

176 Big Bopper
Martin Hawkins

178 Hammers and Keys
Clive Unger-Hamilton

181 Not Fade Away
Michael Heatley

184 Buddy Holly
John Beecher

190 New Mexico Music
John Beecher

192 The Happy Rockabilly
Bill Millar

194 They Died Young
Karl Dallas

196 Ritchie Valens
Martin Hawkins

198 Shaping the Sounds of Success
Chris Gardner

201 Rock Spreads Its Wings
Ashley Brown

204 Rock '58
Chris Welch

206 Rock at the Drive-in
Bob Woffinden

211 Presley on Film
Michael Heatley

215 Mr Rock'n'Roll
Bill Millar

218 DJs in Bribes Shock
Ashley Brown

221 A Romance with Rock
Ashley Brown

224 Don and Phil
Adam Komorowski

230 Country Tunesmiths
Clive Anderson

232 Nashville Cats
Martin Hawkins

235 At the Hop
Bill Millar

238 Sweetheart Years
Cynthia Rose

VOLUME 3

241   **From National to International**
       Adrian Gilbert

244   **Eddie Cochran**
       Clive Anderson

249   **Rocking' All Over The World**
       Peter Jones

252   **Bringing It All Back Home**
       Billy Altman

255   **G.I. Blues**
       Peter Jones

258   **Smalltown Dreamers**
       Billy Altman

261   **The Industry at Work**
       Ashley Brown

262   **Fight for Survival**
       Greg Shaw

267   **Calypso, Comedy and the Creep**
       Peter Jones

271   **Atlantic Crossover**
       Clive Anderson

276   **Cutting the Grooves**
       John Morrish

281   **The Alchemists**
       Ashley Brown

284   **Rock '59**
       Adian Gilbert

286   **Leiber and Stoller**
       Peter Guralnick

290   **Under The Boardwalk**
       Bill Millar

294   **At Smokey Joe's Cafe**
       Bill Millar

298   **Golden Platters**
       Bill Millar

301   **Girls and Boys**
       Ashley Brown

302   **Small-Screen Rocker**
       Phil Hardy

306   **My Way**
       Stephen Barnard

310   **Venus in Blue Jeans**
       John Pidgeon

313   **Rock top Religion**
       Stephen Barnard

316   **All-American Girl**
       Martin Hawkins

318   **Little Miss Dynamite**
       Martin Hawkins

321   **The Roots of Soul**
       Ashley Brown

323   **Brother Ray**
       Robin Katz

330   **Hot Gospel**
       Clive Richardson

333   **Twistin' The Night Away**
       Clive Anderson

336   **Free at Last**
       Bill Millar

338   **Music Unlimited**
       Tony Russell

341   **Philadelphia Pop**
       Adam White

344   **Dream Lover**
       John Pidgeon

348   **The Philly Teen Idols**
       Adam White

354   **Charlie Gracie**
       Bill Millar

356   **Mr Clean**
       Adam White

VOLUME 4

361　　The Age of the Heart-Throb
　　　　Rob Finnis

364　　Gee Whizz It's Cliff
　　　　Rob Finnis

370　　Adam Faith
　　　　John Pidgeon

374　　The Boy Next Door
　　　　Chris Welch

376　　BBC Blues
　　　　Bob Woffinden

378　　Hit or Miss?
　　　　Bob Woffinden

381　　Without a Voice
　　　　Greg Shaw

384　　The Shadows
　　　　Tony Bacon

389　　Sounds Worldwide
　　　　Greg Shaw

394　　Have Guitar. . .
　　　　Chris Gardner

396　　Stormy Weather
　　　　Bill Millar

398　　Purely Percussive
　　　　Chris Welch

401　　Shades of Pop
　　　　Stephen Barnard

404　　Rock '60
　　　　Adrian Gilbert, Jenny Dawson

406　　Poetry in Motion
　　　　Clive Anderson

408　　Street-corner Sounds
　　　　Angie Errigo

410　　The Rockin' Fifties

412　　Only the Lonely
　　　　Stephen Barnard

417　　The Runaway Returns
　　　　Graham Gardner, Bob Fisher

421　　Songs and Studios
　　　　Rob Finnis

424　　The Sound of Fury
　　　　John Pidgeon

429　　Celluloid Rock
　　　　Bob Woffinden

432　　Schoolgirl Chart-Topper
　　　　Stephen Barnard

434　　Shaking' All Over
　　　　Michael Heatley

436　　Genius of the Console
　　　　Rob Finnis

438　　It's Trad, Dad!
　　　　Brian Innes

441　　The Pop Factory
　　　　Greg Shaw

445　　Weavers of Dreams
　　　　Val Wilmer, Robin Kats, Greg Shaw

450　　The Songs of Sedaka
　　　　Phil Hardy

454　　Rock '61
　　　　Adrian Gilbert, Jenny Dawson

456　　Bouncing to Success
　　　　Clive Anderson

458　　Before Dawn
　　　　Bill Millar

460　　Paying Your Dues
　　　　Stephen Barnard

461　　From Star to Superstar
　　　　Ashley Brown

464　　Grand Master of the Blues
　　　　Tony Russell

468　　Rockabilly from Michigan
　　　　John Collis

470　　Motown Magician
　　　　Bill Millar

474　　The Miraculous Mr Robinson
　　　　Adam White

CONTENTS OF SET

VOLUME 5

481   **Dance, Dance, Dance**
Clive Anderson

484   **Let's Twist Again**
Stephen Barnard

488   **Babysitter Bop**
Clive Anderson

490   **Long-Term Investment**
Mick Brown

494   **The Midnight Man**
Cliff White

496   **Freddy Cannon**
Bob Woffinden

498   **Peppermint Pop**
Cynthia Rose

501   **The West Coast Scene**
Stephen Barnard

504   **Rock '62**
Adrian Gilbert, Jenny Dawson

506   **To Know Him Is To Love Him**
Greg Shaw

513   **Phil's Fillies**
Geoff Brown

516   **Blue-eyed Soul**
Clive Anderson

518   **Artists Anonymous**
Stephen Barnard

521   **Why Liverpool?**
Bill Harry

524   **Ferry Cross The Mersey**
Stephen Barnard

528   **From the Cavern to Cabaret**
Bob Woffinden

532   **The Epstein Stable**
Stephen Barnard

536   **Northern Lights**
Peter Jones

538   **Germany Calling**
Bill Harry

541   **The Beatles**
Stephen Barnard

544   **Beatles Diary**
Adrian Gilbert

546   **Ticket To Ride**
Ashley Brown

551   **Songwriters Supreme**
Michael Watts

554   **Brian Epstein**
Phil Hardy

556   **With The Beatles**
Bob Woffinden

558   **Beatlemania**
Stephen Barnard

561   **The Singer or the Song**
Greg Shaw

564   **Rock '63**
Adrian Gilbert, Jenny Dawson

566   **Leaders of the Pack**
Greg Shaw

570   **Valli's Evergreens**
Bob Fisher

574   **Raves from the Grave**
Cynthia Rose

576   **Sophisticated Lady**
Clive Anderson

578   **The Bacharach Sound**
Stephen Barnard

581   **Straight from the Heart**
Ashley Brown

583   **UK Blues**
John Pidgeon, Graeme Ewens

590   **Hey! Bo Diddley**
Val Wilmer

592   **Loud and Clear**
Tony Russell

594   **Gimme That Harp, Boy!**
John Broven

596   **Fame at the Flamingo**
John Pidgeon

VOLUME 6

601 **Beat rules UK?**
Stephen Barnard

604 **Hits in Harmony**
John Pidgeon

609 **Glad All Over**
Alan Clayson

612 **Manchester Dreamers**
Barbara Charone

615 **The Dagenham Sound**
Peter Jones

618 **Saturday Night Out**
Stephen Barnard

621 **Puppets on a String**
Mary Harron

624 **Rock '64**
Adrian Gilbert, Jenny Dawson

626 **Barefoot in the Charts**
Michael Watts

629 **Simply Cilla**
Stephen Barnard

632 **Pet Sounds**
Peter Jones

634 **Shout!**
Gary Herman

637 **The Martin Mix**
John Tobler

641 **Shapes of Things . . .**
Adrian Gilbert

644 **Mann Made Hits**
Bob Woffinden

650 **Flying High**
Brian Hogg

654 **Save the Wail!**
Michael Heatley

656 **Animal Tracks**
Tom Hibbert

661 **The Sounds of the Campus**
Dave Laing

666 **Johnny Appleseed**
Dave Laing

668 **Folk Goes Pop**
Robert Shelton

670 **Sad-eyed Lady**
Dave Laing

674 **Folk+Rock+Protest=Dollars**
Stephen Barnard

678 **From Cotton Field to Coffee Bar**
Peter Brookesmith

681 **Britain Invades the World**

684 **Into Something Good**
Stephen Barnard

688 **Time of the Zombies**
Pete Frame

692 **Brits on Broadway**
Stephen Barnard

696 **The Easybeats**
Tom Hibbert

698 **Rocking the Continent**
Demitri Argyropulo

701 **Tamla Hits the Top**
Ashley Brown

702 **What's Going On?**
Mick Brown

706 **Mary Wells**
Bill Millar

708 **Sax'n'Soul**
Clive Anderson

710 **Reach Out!**
Michael Heatley

714 **Hitsville USA**
Adam White

CONTENTS OF SET

VOLUME 7

721 **Still Going Solo**
Pete Fowler

724 **Rock '65**
Adrian Gilbert, Jenny Dawson

726 **Gene Pitney**
Bob Woffinden

730 **From Folk to Soul**
Chris North

734 **Baroque and Roll**
Ed Sparrow

736 **Mr Beefcake**
Phil Hardy

738 **Clubs and Cabaret**
Stephen Barnard

741 **Swinging London**
John Platt

744 **Piracy in the Air**
Stephen Barnard

748 **Carnaby Street**
Brian Innes

750 **Well Respected Men**
Phil Hardy

757 **Producers and Sessionmen**
Brian Hogg

761 **All Summer Long**
Johnny Rogan

764 **Surf's Up**
Barry Lazell

766 **Dead Man's Curve**
Bob Fisher

768 **Beach Boys Diary**
Mike Grant

770 **Good Vibrations**
Rob Mackie

774 **Breakaway**
John Morrish

778 **Heroes & Villians**
John Morrish

781 **Black and Proud**
David Morse

784 **The Memphis Machine**
Rob Mackie

793 **The Impressions**
Bob Fisher

796 **Clown Prince of Soul**
Peter Guralnick

798 **Bland and Blues**
Joe McEwen

801 **The Mod Generation**
Pete Fowler

804 **Rock '66**
Adrian Gilbert, Jenny Dawson

806 **Facing the Music**
John Pidgeon

810 **Funky Butt Live!**
John Pidgeon

812 **Jamaican Soul**
John Pidgeon

814 **Out of Time**
John Pidgeon

816 **Mod Managers**
Brian Hogg

818 **Where the Action Was**
Brian Hogg

821 **The Folk-Rock Explosion**
Dave Laing

824 **What's That Sound?**
Dave Laing

827 **Tambourines and Twelve-Strings**
Phil Hardy

832 **Paul Revere and the Raiders**
Tom Hibbert

834 **The Sound of Texas**
Phil Hardy

836 **I Got You, Babe**
Brian Hogg

838 **California Dreamin'**
Johnny Rogan

VOLUME 8

841   Rock on Show

844   Reeling & Rocking
       Graham Fuller

849   TV Rock
       Colin Shearman

854   A Hard Day's Night
       Bob Woffinden

858   The Age of Aquarius
       Stephen Barnard

861   Positively 4th Street
       Lenny Kaye

866   Summer Magic
       Dave Laing

870   Garage Bands
       Lenny Kaey

874   Groovin'
       Stephen Barnard

878   Crew Cuts to Granny Glasses
       Cynthia Rose

881   It's Only Rock'n'Roll
       Cliff Ash

884   Stones Diary
       Michael Heatley

886   Heart of Stone
       John Pidgeon

888   Through the Past Darkly
       Mark Williams

896   Everybody Needs Somebody
       Brian Hogg

898   Glimmer Twins
       David Sinclair

901   SF Fantasies
       John Platt

904   Long Strange Trip
       Ken Hunt

909   Airplanes and Starships
       Nick Ralph

914   Quicksilver Messengers
       Steve Burgess

916   Rocking East and West
       John Platt

918   Street Life
       John Platt

921   The Heyday of Soul
       Michael Heatley

923   Pain in my Heart
       Peter Guralnick

928   Stax
       Adam White, Cliue Anderson

934   King Solomon
       Peter Guralnick

936   Double Dynamite
       Rob Mackie

938   The Wicked Pickett
       Clive Anderson

941   Pop's Hall of Mirrors
       Gary Herman

944   The Troggs
       Tom Hibbert

947   Scots on the Rocks
       Fred Dellar

950   Zabadak to Xanadu
       Barry Lazell

952   Around Amen Corner
       Barry Lazell

954   Scene and Herd
       Barry Lazell

956   Brotherly Love
       Fred Dellar

958   JK All the Way
       Stephen Barnard

CONTENTS OF SET

VOLUME 9

961   **The Third World**
Chris May

964   **The Sound of Africa**
Chris May

968   **Osibisa**
Chris Schuler

970   **Toots and the Maytals**
Lindsay Wesker

972   **Aces High**
Lindsay Wesker

974   **Ska**
Nick Kimberley

978   **The Harder They Come**
Lindsay Wesker

981   **Pop for Profit**
Christopher North

984   **Rock '67**
Rom Hibbert, Jenny Dawson

986   **Daydream Believers**
Glen Baker

992   **Happy Together**
Tom Hibbert

994   **Crimson and Clover**
Barry Lazell

996   **Chewy Chewy**
Barry Lazell

1001   **The Blank Generation**
Cynthia Rose

1004   **The Velvet Underground**
Giovanni Dadomo

1009   **Strange Days**
David Prockter

1014   **Playing Around**
Tom Hibbert

1016   **Love**
Steve Burgess

1018   **High Times**
John Dennis

1021   **Guitar Gods and Other Divinities**
John Pidgeon

1024   **Wheels of Fire**
David Sinclair

1030   **Army or Airforce?**
David Sinclair

1032   **Jack Bruce**
Paul Henderson

1034   **Slowhand Solo**
John Pidgeon

1038   **Precision and Power**
Tony Bacon

1041   **Tamla: The New Generation**
Geoff Brown

1044   **The Supremes**
Adam White

1050   **On Cloud Nine**
Clive Anderson

1053   **Twist'n'Funk**
Geoff Brown

1056   **Masterpiece**
Adam White

1058   **Soul From the Windy City**
Robert Pruter

1061   **The Genius of Jimi**
Fred Frith

1064   **Hendrix**
David Sinclair

1070   **The Roots of Heavy Metal**
Brian Harrigan

1073   **Groupies**
John Dennis

1076   **Guitar Madness**
Tony Bacon

VOLUME 10

1081   **Flower Power or Money Power?**
Stephen Barnard

1086   **Procol Harum**
Paul Kendall

1090   **Where Have all the Flowers Gone?**
John Dennis

1092   **Business as Usual**
Greg Shaw

1096   **The Fish Cheer**
Marianne Ebertowski

1098   **Monterey Pop**
John Platt

1101   **Blues Power**
Neville Wiggins

1104   **Lightnin' Strikes**
Tony Russell

1106   **T-Bone Walker**
Tony Russell

1108   **King of the Blues**
Tony Russell

1112   **Steppin' Out**
David Sinclair

1116   **On the Road Again**
Christopher North

1118   **Fleetwood Mac—Take One**
David Sinclair

1121   **Times A-Changin'**
Stephen Barnard

1126   **Perfect Partners**
Dave Laing

1132   **Rock '68**
Tom Hibbert, Jenny Dawson

1134   **Donovan**
Steve Burgess

1138   **Folk or Forgery?**
Dave Laing

1141   **The Long and Winding Road**
Ashley Brown

1144   **Beatles Diary**
Michael Heatley

1146   **All Things Must Pass**
Paul Kendall

1152   **Classic Sounds, Northern Songs**
Stephen Barnard

1156   **Apple**
Gary Herman

1161   **Colour Me Soul**
Bill Millar

1164   **Rock '69**
Tom Hibbert, Jenny Dawson

1166   **Sheffield Steel**
Gary Herman

1170   **Pearl**
Ken Hunt

1174   **The Box Tops**
Tom Hibbert

1176   **South'n'Soul**
Paul Fryer

1178   **Chart Ryder**
Fred Dellar

1181   **Second City Sounds**
Michael Heatley

1182   **Music and Movement**
Gary Herman

1186   **Blues from Birmingham**
Ted Gibbons

1188   **Winwood**
Ken Hunt

1193   **Threshold of Success**
Brian Harrigan

1198   **Family Entertainment**
Barry Lazell

CONTENTS OF SET

VOLUME 11

1201   **Like A Rolling Stone**
Ashley Brown

1202   **Dylan**
P. L. Frankson

1214   **Conclusions on the Wall**
Peter Brookesmith

1218   **Bringing It All Back Home**
Patrick Humphries

1221   **Blues and More . . .**
Dave Walters

1224   **Space Cowboy**
Michael Heatley

1228   **Rough'n'Ready**
Tom Hibbert

1233   **Still Alive And Well**
David Sinclair

1236   **Taj Mahal**
Clive Anderson

1238   **Blues in Bloom**
Dave Walters

1241   **The Festive Generation**
Ashley Brown

1242   **Festivals Diary**
Dafydd Rees

1244   **Barefoot in the Park**
Colin Shearman

1249   **Woodstock**
Phil Hardy

1252   **The New Utopia**
Barry Lazell

1255   **Confessions of a Festival-Goer**
Tom Hibbert

1258   **The Dream Goes Sour**
Cliff Ash

1261   **Ready Steady Who!**
Michael Heatley

1262   **Who Diary**
Michael Heatley

1264   **Who's Who**
John Pidgeon

1274   **Mods and Rock Operas**
Ed Hanel

1276   **Track Record**
Brian Hogg

1278   **The Seeker**
Peter Clark

1281   **Sound and Vision**
Ashley Brown

1282   **Picture This . . .**
Robert Ellis

1289   **Art On Their Sleeves**
Phil Hardy

1296   **Pop Goes The Easel**
Johnathan Reed

1301   **In the Pink**
Tom Hibbert

1303   **Going Underground**
John Platt

1307   **Welcome to the Machine**
Peter Clark

1314   **Pink Floyd Diary**
Neville Wiggins

1316   **Celluloid Floyd**
John Gill

1318   **Crazy Diamond**
Tom Hibbert

VOLUME 12

1321   **Words and Music**
Ashley Brown

1322   **Rock Books**
Stephen Barnard

1326   **Mirroring the Melodies**
John Hunt

1329   **Paging the USA**
Jeff Tamarkin

1332   **Roll Away The Stone**
Bob Woffinden

1334   **The Press Gang**
Gary Herman

1338   **Fan Fare**
Phil Hardy

1341   **Single Images**
Tom Hibbert

1342   **Rock '70**
Tom Hibbert, Jenny Dawson

1344   **Both Sides of Joni**
Steve Clarke

1348   **Judy Collins**
Elizabeth M. Thomson

1350   **Songs From A Room**
Elizabeth M. Thomson

1353   **Day of the Cat**
Barry Lazell

1356   **Waxing Lyrical**
Colin Shearman

1361   **Hard Times**
Neville Wiggins

1362   **Precious Metal**
Paul Kendall

1369   **Children of the Grave**
Luke Crampton

1372   **Sympathy for the Devil**
Francis King

1374   **Ten Years After**
David Sinclair

1376   **Power to the Purple**
Brian Harrigan

1381   **Turn on, Tune in, Drop out**
Gary Herman

1384   **Generation Landslide**
Ian J. Knight

1388   **Psychedelic Wallflowers**
John Platt

1392   **Revolutions in Sound**
Ed Hanel

1396   **The Inner Light?**
Colin Shearman

1401   **Paint it Black**
Clive Anderson

1404   **Stoned Soul**
Geoff Brown

1408   **Hayes Fever**
Clive Anderson

1412   **Move On Up**
Ted Gibbons

1415   **La Belle with Love**
Clive Anderson

1418   **Putting On The Style**
Paul Fryer

1421   **All That Glitters**
Stephen Barnard

1424   **Rock '71**
Tom Hibbert, Jenny Dawson

1426   **Feel The Noize**
Tom Hibbert

1430   **Leader of the Gang**
Annette Kennerley

1434   **Feet First**
Frances Kennett

1436   **Born to Boogie**
Christopher North

CONTENTS OF SET

VOLUME 13

1441   Southern Comfort
        Gary Herman

1444   Leon Russell
        Stephen M Stroff

1448   Accept No Substitute
        Bob Woffinden

1450   Night Tripper
        Max Bell

1454   Sounds of the Swamp
        Bill Millar

1456   Travelin' Band
        Max Bell

1461   Rock Around the Maypole
        Dave Laing

1464   Fairport's Full House
        Patrick Humphries

1468   The Incredibles' Journey
        Luther Paisley

1471   Steeleye Span
        Dave Laing

1474   Rock On The Tyne
        Dave Laing

1476   Five-Star Folk
        Bob Woffinden

1478   Hats Off to Harper
        Steve Clarke

1481   Sounds of Subversion
        Tom Hibbert

1484   Unconditionally Guaranteed
        Luther Paisley

1488   MC5
        Tom Hibbert

1490   Zappa
        Miles

1497   Raw Power
        Peter Clark

1501   Gonna Make You a Star
        Paul Fryer

1504   Puppy Love
        Tom Hibbert

1507   Rock On
        John Stretton

1510   Rollermania!
        Colin Shearman

1514   Stardust Memories
        Patrick Humphries

1516   Darling David
        Tom Hibbert

1518   The Odd Couple
        Graham Fuller

1521   All That Jazz
        Ashley Brown

1524   Sounds Orchestral
        Hugh Hopper

1526   Chicago
        Bob Woffinden

1529   Miles Ahead
        Graham Collier

1532   Heavy Weather
        Hugh Hopper

1534   The Latin Quarter
        David Sinclair

1538   Blood, Sweat and Tears
        Bob Woffinden

1541   New Pioneers
        Ken Hunt

1544   Rock '72
        Tom Hibbert, Jenny Dawson

1546   The Best in the Land
        Mark Williams

1550   The Belfast Cowboy
        Michael Heatley

1554   Hello and Goodbye
        Max Bell

1556   GP
        Max Bell

1558   Cooder's Story
        Patrick Humphries

VOLUME 14

1561	Work in Progress Hugh Hopper	1616	The Guess Who Ed Hanel
1564	In the Court of King Crimson Adrian Gilbert	1618	The Beat Goes On Adrian Gilbert
1568	In Praise of Learning Julian Petley	1621	Ringing the Changes Chris Schüler
1570	Minstrel in the Gallery Annette Kennerley, Paul Roland	1624	Bowie Chris Charlesworth
1575	Air Conditioned Alan Kinsman	1632	Boys Keep Swinging Chris Schüler
1578	Soft Machine John Platt	1634	Growing Up In Public Luther Paisley
1581	Soul Satisfaction Michael Heatley	1638	Designs For Living Luther Paisley
1582	Young, Gifted and Black Sharon Davis	1641	Country Life Ilene Melish
1586	Gladys Knight and the Pips Graham Betts	1642	The Man in Black Ilene Melish
1588	White Unlimited Clive Anderson	1646	Outlaw Man Richard Wootton
1590	Diana Adam White	1648	Merle Haggard Tony Byworth
1594	Sweet Soul Music Clive Anderson	1650	To Beat The Devil Patrick Humphries
1596	TSOP: The Sound of Philadelphia Clive Richardson	1653	Honky Tonk Hero Tony Byworth
1601	Loud and Proud Tom Hibbert	1656	Steelin' Away Lenny Kaye
1602	Southern Fried Boogie David Sinclair	1658	Music City USA Richard Wootton
1606	Mountain Climbing David Sinclair	1661	One-Man Bands Michael Heatley
1609	We're An American Band Lenny Kaye	1663	Rocket Man Chris Charlesworth
1612	Rock'n'Roll Outlaws Ed Hanel	1670	Innervisions Graham Betts
1614	Spirit of California Max Bell	1678	Fame and Fortune Bob Woffinden

CONTENTS OF SET

VOLUME 15

1681	I Hear A Symphony ... Chris Schüler	1741	Pomp and Circumstance Derek Jewell
1684	Twice as Nice Mark Williams	1744	Rock '74 Jenny Dawson, Tom Hibbert
1690	Yes Peter Clark	1746	ELO Colin Shearman
1696	The Caped Crusader Chris Welch	1750	The Musical Box Graham Fuller
1698	Switched-On Keyboards Dave Crombie	1756	Peter Gabriel Ian J. Knight
1701	Me, Myself, I Stephen Barnard	1758	Indelibly Stamped Mike Hales
1704	Rock '73 Tom Hibbert, Jenny Dawson	1761	Hotel California Bob Woffinden
1706	Mr Melancholy Steve Clarke	1764	Triad Steve Clarke
1709	No Secrets Steve Clarke	1768	Staying Power Alastair Dougall
1712	Playin' Favourites Bob Woffinden	1772	Desperados Dave Walters
1714	Portrait of the Artiste Elizabeth M. Thompson	1776	America Michael Heatley
1716	Melanie Peter Clark	1778	For Everyman Patrick Humphries
1718	The Outsider Stephen Barnard	1781	Saints and Sinners Clive Anderson
1721	Rockin' the Seventies Tom Hibbert	1784	Green'n'Blues Graham Betts
1722	Rod Dave Morley	1788	Lady Soul Adam White
1728	Very 'eavy, Very 'umble Malcolm Dome	1792	One Happy Family Bob Woffinden
1730	Again and Again Neville Wiggins	1794	Nina Simone Chris Schüler
1736	Pilgrimage Barbara Charone	1796	Billy's Bag Sharon Davis
1738	Tons of Sobs David Sinclair	1798	Quiet Fire Clive Anderson

VOLUME 16

1801	**Oh! You Pretty Things**	Dave Rimmer
1804	**For Your Pleasure**	Graham Fuller
1812	**Sheer Chart Attack**	David Sinclair
1818	**All The Young Dudes**	David Sinclair
1821	**Teenage Rampage**	John Tobler
1824	**Rock '75**	Tom Hibbert, Jenny Dawson
1826	**Every One's A Winner**	Bob Woffinden
1829	**Suzi Q**	Tom Hibbert
1832	**The Midas Touch**	Steve Turner
1835	**Sweet Schizophrenia**	Christopher North
1838	**Cockney Rebel**	Graham Fuller
1841	**Stages and Stadia**	Michael Heatley
1842	**Nothin' Fancy**	Chris Charlesworth
1845	**Cry Tough**	Mark Williams
1848	**Rocks**	Peter Clark
1850	**Listen To The Music**	Dave Walters
1854	**Tres Hombres**	Chris Malcolm
1856	**Ballads and Bullets**	Bob Woffinden
1858	**Little Feat**	Max Bell

1861	**Shock Tactics**	Graham Fuller
1864	**Welcome To My Nightmare**	Ian J. Knight
1868	**Kiss**	Chris Charlesworth
1872	**Tubes**	Cliff Ash
1876	**House Of Horror**	Martin Sutton
1878	**Too Much Too Soon**	Miles
1881	**Cooling Down the Pace**	Nick Kimberley
1888	**Bob Marley**	Chris Salewicz
1894	**The Solo Singers**	Dave Hendley
1898	**Versions Galore**	Chris Lane
1901	**Mass Production**	Michael Heatley
1903	**The Hermit of Mink Hollow**	John Tobler
1906	**Sound Advice**	Ray Hammond
1908	**Getting It Taped**	Ray Hammond
1913	**The Original Soundtrack**	Chris Charlesworth
1916	**Mike Oldfield**	Derek Jewell
1918	**Steely Dan**	Max Bell

VOLUME 17

1921	**Back to the Bars** Nigel Cross	
1926	**Rock '76** Tom Hibbert, Jenny Dawson	
1928	**Dr Feelgood** Chris Malcolm	
1930	**Juke Box Jury** Rob Mackie	
1934	**Seconds Of Pleasure** Michael Heatley	
1936	**Heat Treatment** Trevor Dann	
1938	**The Stiff Story** Bert Muirhead	
1941	**Family Favourites** Stephen Barnard	
1943	**ABBA** Neville Wiggins	
1948	**Close To You** Christopher North	
1950	**Rock'n'Roll Juvenile** Steve Turner	
1954	**Songs For Europe** Stephen Barnard	
1958	**Sounds Of The Seventies** Stephen Barnard	
1961	**Tomorrow Never Knows** Bob Woffinden	
1962	**Baby You're A Rich Man** Patrick Humphries	
1967	**Dark Horse** Luther Paisley	

1970   **'I Don't Believe In Beatles'**   Colin Shearman

1975   **It Don't Come Easy**   Mike Hales

1978   **Beatles For Sale**   Rene Timmins

1981   **British Steel**   Chris Welch

1984   **Shades of Deep Purple**   Brian Harrigan

1988   **Nazareth**   Darren Crook

1990   **The Boys Are Back**   David Sinclair

1994   **Vambo Rools**   Chris Malcolm

1996   **In Search Of Space**   Julian Petley

1998   **Know Your Rites**   Malcolm Dome

2001   **The Bowery Beat**   Tom Hibbert

2006   **Prime Time**   Tom Hibbert

2009   **Ramones**   Jeff Tamarkin

2012   **Destiny Street**   Debbie Geller

2014   **Oh No! It's Devo**   Irving Klaw

2016   **Roadrunner**   Peter Clark

2018   **Smithereens**   Debbie Geller

2021   **Adults Only**   Stephen Barnard

2022   **Cross Country**   Bob Woffinden

2026   **Crisis—What Crisis?**   Steve Clarke

2028   **The Middle Man**   Dave Laing

2030   **Fleetwood Mac—Take Two**   Dave Walters

2033   **Behind A Painted Smile**   Dave Laing

2036   **Station To Station**   Stephen Bernard

2038   **The Face of '76**   Steve Clarke

VOLUME 18

2041 Anarchy in the UK
Chris Salewicz

2044 Sex Pistols
Giovanni Dadomo

2049 The Great Rock'n'Roll Swindle
Steve Turner

2052 The Punk Collection
Mick Mercer

2056 Rip It Up
Lindsay Shapero

2058 Going To A Pogo
Mick Mercer

2061 1977—Two Sevens Clash
Chris Salewicz

2064 Rock '77
Tom Hibbert, Jenny Dawson

2066 Combat Rockers
Penny Valentine

2070 Making Waves
Sue Stewart

2073 Buzzcocks
Chris Schüler

2076 John Peel
Trevor Dann

2078 Smash It Up
Luther Paisley

2081 Out In The Street
Cynthia Rose

2084 Hard Promises
Peter Clark

2087 Born To Run
Patrick Humphries

2092 Johnny Too Bad
Glenn A Baker

2094 King Of The Road
Alastair Dougall

2096 Rickie Lee Jones
Steve Clarke

2098 Words From The Wise?
Peter Brookesmith

2101 Disco Fever
Clive Anderson

2104 Children of the World
Steve Turner

2108 Kool and the Gang
Graham Betts

2110 Hot Stuff
Dave Hill

2113 C'est Chic
Dave Walters

2116 Natural High
Adam White

2118 The Munich Machine
Demitri Argyropulo

2121 Tunes Of Glory
Byron St Tugby

2122 American Gothic
Jay Williams

2125 Agents of Furtune
Peter Clark

2128 The Grand Illusion
Chris Collingwood

2130 Van Halen
Jay Williams

2132 Rock in Exile
Chris Malcolm

2134 Pat Benatar
Debbie Geller

2137 Turn It Up!
James Betteridge

2141 Children of the Revolution
Mick Mercer

2142 Rock '78
Jenny Dawson, Chris Schüler

2144 Borstal Breakout
Carol Clerk

2146 Tom Robinson Band
David Sinclair

2148 Siouxsie and the Banshees
Chris Schüler

2152 Angels with Dirty Faces
Carol Clerk

2155 Independents' Day
Phyllis Tyne

2158 The Politics of Punk
Chris Schüler

VOLUME 19

2161 Soul Spectrum — Michael Heatley	**2201** Coventry Calling — Allan Jones	**2241** Second Time Around — Nigel Cross
2162 Earth Wind & Fire — Clive Anderson	**2204** Special Delivery — Peter Clark	**2244** That's Entertainment — Colin Shearman
2166 Breezin' — Mark Lewisohn	**2208** The Birmingham Beat — Michael Heatley	**2249** Rat Trap — Mark Williams
2168 Cybernetic Soul — Stuart Cosgrove	**2210** One Step Beyond — Sally Payne	**2252** Talk of the Town — Allan Jones
2170 One Nation Under A Groove — Stuart Cosgrove	**2214** Signing Off — Mark Williams	**2254** Look Sharp! — Debbie Geller
2173 Unsung Heroes — Graham Betts	**2216** Reggae UK — Paul Bradshaw	**2256** Squeeze — John Voysey
2176 Rap It Up — David Toop	**2218** Celtic Soul — John Voysey	**2258** Yesterday Once More — Bob Woffinden
2178 Stars On Solar — Adam White	**2221** Men of Metal — David Sinclair	**2261** Hicks from the Sticks — Nigel Burnham
2181 Musicians Only — Michael Heatley	**2224** Rock '79 — Annette Kennerley, Jenny Dawson	**2264** Rock '80 — Annette Kennerley
2183 The Police — David Sinclair	**2226** High Voltage — Glenn A Baker	**2266** Unknown Pleasures — Mark Johnson
2188 The Stranglers — Graham Fuller	**2230** The Iron Age — Chris Collingwood	**2270** Songs of Praise — Steve Turner
2192 I'm Not Angry — Allan Jones	**2234** Rush — Brian Harrigan	**2272** Postcard from Scotland — Bert Muirhead
2196 Joan Alone — Alastair Dougall	**2236** Pyromania — Geoff Banks	**2276** Echo and the Bunnymen — John Wilde
2198 Sultans of Swing — Steve Clarke	**2238** White Line Fever — Luther Paisley	**2278** Eric's and After — Sally Payne

VOLUME 20

2281   Entertainment USA
Adam White

2282   Fear of Music
Chris Schüler

2286   Whammy!
Mark Ellen

2288   Shake Some Action
Tom Hibbert

2290   Blondie
Rob Mackie

2294   Kid Creole and the Coconuts
Headley Down

2298   Living My Life
Alastair Dougall

2301   Electronically Yours
Irving Klaw

2304   Rock '81
Annette Kennerley, Chris Schüler

2306   Who Dares Wins
Peter Clark

2310   Kraftwerk
Julian Petley

2313   Reach For The Sky
Bob Woffinden

2316   On Manoeuvres
Mike Nicholls

2318   In The Moog
Dave Crombie

2321   Seeing is Believing?
Michael Heatley

2322   Antmusic!
Tom Hibbert

2326   It's Only A Movie
Johnny Black

2330   The Kick Inside
Mark Lewisohn

2334   Toyah
Johnny Waller

2336   Song & Dance
Stephen Barnard

2338   Catch My Soul
Rennie Timmins

2341   A Fine Romance
Dave Hill

2344   Rock '82
Annette Kennerley, Chris Schüler

2346   Journeys To Glory
Rene Timmins

2350   Palace People
Mike Nicholls

2352   Ultravox
Johnny Waller

2355   Visions Of The Orient
Mark Williams

2358   Video Stars
Mike Heatley

2361   World Service
Demitri Argyropulo

2363   Life In Tokyo
Mark Williams

2366   New Europeans
John Gill, Alan Kinsman

2370   Wizards of Oz
Glenn A. Baker

2373   Many Rivers To Cross
Paul Bradshaw

2376   Back In The USSR
Peter Brookesmith

2378   African Children
Sue Steward

2381   Music For Chameleons
Reginald Stincuer

2382   Rock '83
Annette Kennerley

2384   Fantastic Days
Michael Heatley

2386   Sweet Dreams
Annette Kennerley

2388   Duran Duran
Colin Shearman

2392   Hitsville UK
Graham Betts

2395   The New Producers
Dave Hill

2398   Mad About The Boy
Steve Turner

2401   Two Faces of Rock
Chris Schüler

2402   Charity Rock
Phil Hardy/Michael Heatley

2406   Goint It Alone
Annette Kennerley

2410   Wham!
Annette Kennerley

2412   Madonna
Sheryl Garratt

2417   Bring on the Girls
Michael Heatley

2419   Frankie Say
John Gill

2420   Rock '84
Annette Kennerley

2421   Rock '85
Annette Kennerley

2422   The Charts
Paul Bursche

2425   Into a Digital Future
Michael Heatley

2427   New Country
Michael Heatley

2430   Michael Jackson
Michael Heatley

2432   U2
Michael Heatley

2434   Dire Straits
Michael Heatley

2436   Prince
Michael Heatley

2438   Rock '86
2439   Rock '87
2440   Rock '88
2441   Rock '89
Michael Heatley

CONTRIBUTORS

CLIVE ANDERSON

Co-author of *The Soul Book* and contributor to *Encyclopedia of Rock*, he has also written for *Black Music, Black Echoes, New Kommotion* and other magazines.

STEPHEN BARNARD

Has contributed to *Atlantic Rock, Melody Maker* and the *Rock Files* series. He also lectures at the City University, London.

DICK BRADLEY

Completed his PhD thesis on *British Popular Music in the Fifties* at the Centre of Contemporary Cultural Studies in Birmingham, England, and has also written articles for *Media, Culture & Society*.

JOHN BROVEN

Author of *Walking to New Orleans* and *South of Louisiana*, he has also contributed to *Nothing but the Blues* and *Encyclopedia of Rock*. He writes for *Blues Unlimited* and has also compiled several New Orleans rhythm and blues anthologies

ROB FINNIS

Author of *The Phil Spector Story* and *The Gene Vincent Story*, he has contributed to the major rock journals and runs a specialist record shop.

SIMON FRITH

A lecturer at the University of Warwick, England, he has built up a reputation over the last 15 years as one of the leading international commentators on rock music. He has co-edited the *Rock File* series, and written *The Sociology of Rock*.

PETER GURALNIK

Author of *Feel Like Going Home, Lost Highway* and *Nighthawk Blues*, his articles on blues, country and rock have appeared in *Rolling Stone*, the *Village Voice, Country Music, Living Blues*, the *New York Times* and the *Boston Phoenix*.

BILL HARRY

Founder member of UK's *Mersey Beat*, he later became news editor of *Record Mirror* and music columnist for *Weekend*. He is currently an independent PR for such artists as Suzi Quatro and Kim Wilde.

MARTIN HAWKINS

An acknowledged expert on the Sun era of rock'n'roll (author of *The Sun Story*), he writes for *Melody Maker, Time Barrier Express* and *Country Music*

BRIAN HOGG

Publisher of *Bam Balam*, which concentrates on US and UK bands of the Sixties, he has also written for such magazines as *New York Rocker* and *Record Collector*.

PETER JONES

Was editor of UK's *Record Mirror* from 1961 to 1969. He then became UK News editor of *Billboard* in 1977 and later UK and European Editor.

ROBIN KATZ

After 10 years in the Motown Press Office, she now writes freelance for *New Sound, New Styles, International Musician* and *Smash Hits*.

JOE McEWEN

An acknowledged authority on soul music, he has written for *Rolling Stone, Phonograph Record, Black Music*, the *Boston Phoenix* and Boston's *Real Paper*.

BILL MILLAR

As a freelance journalist he writes for *Melody Maker* and other rock papers. He is the author of *The Drifters* and *The Coasters*.

DAVID MORSE

Author of *Motown*, he lectures at the School of English and American Studies at Sussex University, England.

TONY RUSSELL

Editor of *Old Time Music* from 1971, he contributes regularly to *Blues Unlimited* and *Jazz Journal* and is the author of *Blacks, Whites and Blues*.

ROBERT SHELTON

Has written about blues, country and folk for the *New York Times*, London *Times, Listener, Time Out* and *Melody Maker*.

NICK TOSCHES

Author of *Hellfire*, a biography of Jerry Lee Lewis, he also writes for *New York Times* and *Village Voice*.

MICHAEL WATTS

Writes on popular arts for *The Los Angeles Times* and London *Times* and is rock columnist for *Records and Recording Magazine*.

ADAM WHITE

Has written about Motown for *Music Week* and *Black Echoes*, and scripted a six-hour documentary about the company and its music for US radio. Also worked as managing editor of *Billboard* magazine in New York.

BIBLIOGRAPHY

The Beach Boys: A Biography in Words and Pictures
Ken Barnes, Sire Books, 1976

The Beach Boys and the California Myth
David Leaf, Grosset & Dunlap, 1978

The Beach Boys,
Byron Preiss, Ballantine, 1979

The Beatles: The Authorized Biography
Hunter Davies, McGraw-Hill, 1968

The Beatles: The Real Story
Julius Fast, Putnam, 1968

The Beatles: A Hard Day's Night
J. Philip DiFranco (editor), Penguin, 1977/78

The David Bowie Story
George Tremlett, Futura, 1974

A Boy Named Cash
Albert Govoni, Lancer Books, 1970

Brother Ray: Ray Charles' Own Story
Ray Charles and David Ritz, Dial Press, 1978

Sam Cooke: A Biography in Words and Pictures
Joe McEwen, Sire Books, 1977

Billion Dollar Baby (Alice Cooper Biography)
Bob Greene, Atheneum, 1974

Inside Creedence
John Hallowell, Bantam Books, 1971

Jim Morrison and The Doors
Mike Jahn, Grosset & Dunlap, 1969

Bob Dylan: An Intimate Biography
Anthony Scaduto, Grosset & Dunlap, 1971

Fleetwood Mac: The Authorized History
Samuel Graham, Warner Books, 1978

The Dead Book: A Social History of The Grateful Dead
Hank Harrison, Link Books, 1973

Hendrix: A Biography
Chris Welch, Flash Books, 1973

Buddy Holly
Dave Laing, Studio Vista, 1971

Grace Slick: The Biography
Barbara Rowes, Doubleday, 1980

A Conversation With Elton John and Bernie Taupin
Paul Gambaccini, Flash Books, 1975

Buried Alive: The Biography of Janis Joplin
Myra Friedman, William Morrow, 1973

The Led Zeppelin Biography
Ritchie York, Metheun, 1976

Whole Lotta Shakin' Goin' On
Robert Cain, Dial Press, 1981

Bob Marley: Soul Rebel—Natural Mystic
Adrian Boot & Vivien Goldman, St. Martin's Press, 1982

Meet Elvis Presley
Favius Freidman, Scholastic Book Services, 1971

The Rolling Stones: The First 20 Years
David Dalton, Alfred A. Knopf, 1981

Cher!
Vicki Pellegrino, Ballantine Books, 1975

Rod Stewart
Richard Cromelin, Chappell & Co., 1976

The Who
Gary Herman, Studio Vista, 1971

The Story of Stevie Wonder
James Hoskins, Dell, 1976

No Commercial Potential: The Saga of Frank Zappa and The Mothers of Invention
David Walley, Outerbridge & Lazard, 1972

Rock, Roll & Remember
Dick Clark and Richard Robinson, Popular
Library, 1976

The Sound of Soul
Phyl Garland, Henry Regnery Co., 1969

**A Social History of Rock Music: From
the Greasers to Glitter Rock**
Lloyd Grossman, McKay, 1976

From Blues to Soul in Black America
Michael Haralambos, Drake Publishers,
1975

Rock: From Elvis to The Rolling Stones
Jerry Hopkins, Quadrangle/New York
Times Book Co., 1973

The Illustrated History of Rock Music
Jeremy Pascall, Galahad Books, 1978

**Honkers and Shouters: The Golden
Years of Rhythm and Blues**
Arnold Shaw, Macmillan, 1978

**Dick Clark's The First 25 Years of Rock
& Roll**
Michael Uslan & Bruce Solomon, Dell, 1981

An A—Z of Rock & Roll
Graham Wood, Studio Vista, 1971

**The Rolling Stone Encyclopedia of Rock
& Roll**
Jon Pareles & Patricia Romanowski
(editors), Rolling Stone Press/Summit
Books, 1983

Elvis & Gladys
Elaine Dundy, Dell, 1985

**Born To Run: The Bruce Springsteen
Story**
Dave Marsh, Dell, 1979

Lennon Remembers (The Rolling Stone
Interviews)
Jann Wenner, Rolling Stone Press, 1971

A Twist of Lennon
Cynthia Lennon, Star/W. H. Allen Co., 1978

**Survivor: The Authorized Biography of
Eric Clapton**
Ray Coleman, Futura, 1985

**Symphony For The Devil: The Rolling
Stones Story**
Philip Norman, Dell, 1984

**The True Adventures of The Rolling
Stones**
Stanley Booth, Vintage Books, 1985

Streisand: The Woman and The Legend
James Spada, Pocket Books, 1981

Is That It?
Bob Geldof, Penguin Books, 1986

**The Life and Times of Little Richard—
The Quasar of Rock**
Charles White, Harmony Books, 1984

Moon Walk
Michael Jackson, Doubleday, 1988

I, Tina
Tina Turner and Kurt Loder, Wm. Morrow
& Co., 1986

**Heroes & Villains: The True Story of The
Beach Boys**
Steven Gaines, New American Library, 1986

Divided Soul: The Life of Marvin Gaye
David Ritz, McGraw-Hill, 1985

Lennon
Ray Coleman, McGraw-Hill, 1984

**No Direction Home: The Life and Music
of Bob Dylan**
Robert Shelton, Beech Tree Books, 1986

California Dreamin'
Michelle Phillips, Warner Books, 1986

Dylan: A Biography
Bob Spitz, McGraw-Hill, 1989

Country: The Music and The Musicians
Paul Kingsbury and Alan Axelrod (editors),
Country Music Foundation and Abbeville
Press, 1989

**Surfin' Guitars: Instrumental Surf
Bands of the Sixties**
Robert J. Dalley, Surf Publications, 1989

The New Grove Dictionary of Jazz
Barry Kernfeld (editor), Grove's
Dictionaries of Music, 1989

U.S. HIT SINGLES

1955

JANUARY
1 THIS OLE HOUSE *Rosemary Clooney*
8 MR SANDMAN *Chordettes*
15 MR SANDMAN *Chordettes*
22 LET ME GO LOVER *Joan Weber*
29 LET ME GO LOVER *Joan Weber*

FEBRUARY
5 HEARTS OF STONE *Fontane Sisters*
12 SINCERELY *McGuire Sisters*
19 SINCERELY *McGuire Sisters*
26 SINCERELY *McGuire Sisters*

MARCH
5 SINCERELY *McGuire Sisters*
12 SINCERELY *McGuire Sisters*
19 SINCERELY *McGuire Sisters*
26 THE BALLAD OF DAVY CROCKETT
     Bill Hates

APRIL
2 THE BALLAD OF DAVY CROCKETT
     Bill Hates
9 THE BALLAD OF DAVY CROCKETT
     Bill Hates
16 THE BALLAD OF DAVY CROCKETT
     Bill Hates
23 THE BALLAD OF DAVY CROCKETT
     Bill Hates
30 CHERRY PINK AND APPLE BLOSSOM
     WHITE *Perez Prado*

MAY
7 CHERRY PINK AND APPLE BLOSSOM WHITE
     Perez Prado
14 CHERRY PINK AND APPLE BLOSSOM WHITE
     Perez Prado
21 CHERRY PINK AND APPLE BLOSSOM WHITE
     Perez Prado
28 CHERRY PINK AND APPLE BLOSSOM WHITE
     Perez Prado

JUNE
4 CHERRY PINK AND APPLE BLOSSOM WHITE
     Perez Prado
11 CHERRY PINK AND APPLE BLOSSOM WHITE
     Perez Prado
18 CHERRY PINK AND APPLE BLOSSOM WHITE
     Perez Prado
25 CHERRY PINK AND APPLE BLOSSOM WHITE
     Perez Prado

JULY
2 CHERRY PINK AND APPLE BLOSSOM WHITE
     Perez Prado
9 ROCK AROUND THE CLOCK *Bill Haley*
15 ROCK AROUND THE CLOCK *Bill Haley*
23 ROCK AROUND THE CLOCK *Bill Haley*
30 ROCK AROUND THE CLOCK *Bill Haley*

AUGUST
   ROCK AROUND THE CLOCK *Bill Haley*
13 ROCK AROUND THE CLOCK *Bill Haley*
20 ROCK AROUND THE CLOCK *Bill Haley*
27 ROCK AROUND THE CLOCK *Bill Haley*

SEPTEMBER
3 THE YELLOW ROSE OF TEXAS
     Mitch Miller
10 THE YELLOW ROSE OF TEXAS
     Mitch Miller
17 THE YELLOW ROSE OF TEXAS
     Mitch Miller
24 THE YELLOW ROSE OF TEXAS
     Mitch Miller

OCTOBER
1 THE YELLOW ROSE OF TEXAS
     Mitch Miller
8 LOVE IS A MANY SPLENDORED THING
     Four Aces
15 LOVE IS A MANY SPLENDORED THING
     Four Aces
22 THE YELLOW ROSE OF TEXAS
     Mitch Miller
29 AUTUMN LEAVES *Roger Williams*

NOVEMBER
5 AUTUMN LEAVES *Roger Williams*
12 AUTUMN LEAVES *Roger Williams*
19 AUTUMN LEAVES *Roger Williams*
26 SIXTEEN TONS *Tennessee Ernie Ford*

DECEMBER
3 SIXTEEN TONS *Tennessee Ernie Ford*
10 SIXTEEN TONS *Tennessee Ernie Ford*
17 SIXTEEN TONS *Tennessee Ernie Ford*
24 SIXTEEN TONS *Tennessee Ernie Ford*
31 SIXTEEN TONS *Tennessee Ernie Ford*

1956

JANUARY

7	SIXTEEN TONS	*Tennessee Ernie Ford*
14	MEMORIES ARE MADE OF THIS	
		Dean Martin
21	MEMORIES ARE MADE OF THIS	
28	MEMORIES ARE MADE OF THIS	
		Dean Martin

FEBRUARY

4	MEMORIES ARE MADE OF THIS	
		Dean Martin
11	MEMORIES ARE MADE OF THIS	
		Dean Martin
18	ROCK AND ROLL WALTZ	*Kay Starr*
25	LISBON ANTIGUA	*Nelson Riddle*

MARCH

3	LISBON ANTIGUA	*Nelson Riddle*
10	LISBON ANTIGUA	*Nelson Riddle*
17	LISBON ANTIGUA	*Nelson Riddle*
24	POOR PEOPLE OF PARIS	*Les Baxter*
31	POOR PEOPLE OF PARIS	*Les Baxter*

APRIL

7	POOR PEOPLE OF PARIS	*Les Baxter*
14	POOR PEOPLE OF PARIS	*Les Baxter*
21	HEARTBREAK HOTEL	*Elvis Presley*
28	HEARTBREAK HOTEL	*Elvis Presley*

MAY

5	HEARTBREAK HOTEL	*Elvis Presley*
12	HEARTBREAK HOTEL	*Elvis Presley*
19	HEARTBREAK HOTEL	*Elvis Presley*
26	HEARTBREAK HOTEL	*Elvis Presley*

JUNE

2	HEARTBREAK HOTEL	*Elvis Presley*
9	HEARTBREAK HOTEL	*Elvis Presley*
16	THE WAYWARD WIND	*Gogi Grant*
23	THE WAYWARD WIND	*Gogi Grant*
30	THE WAYWARD WIND	*Gogi Grant*

JULY

7	THE WAYWARD WIND	*Gogi Grant*
14	THE WAYWARD WIND	*Gogi Grant*
21	THE WAYWARD WIND	*Gogi Grant*
28	I WANT YOU I NEED YOU I LOVE YOU	
		Elvis Presley

AUGUST

4	MY PRAYER	*Platters*
11	MY PRAYER	*Platters*
18	DON'T BE CRUEL/HOUND DOG	
		Elvis Presley
25	DON'T BE CRUEL/HOUND DOG	
		Elvis Presley

SEPTEMBER

1	DON'T BE CRUEL/HOUND DOG	
		Elvis Presley
8	DON'T BE CRUEL/HOUND DOG	
		Elvis Presley
15	DON'T BE CRUEL/HOUND DOG	
		Elvis Presley
22	DON'T BE CRUEL/HOUND DOG	
		Elvis Presley
29	DON'T BE CRUEL/HOUND DOG	
		Elvis Presley

OCTOBER

6	DON'T BE CRUEL/HOUND DOG	
		Elvis Presley
13	DON'T BE CRUEL/HOUND DOG	
		Elvis Presley
20	DON'T BE CRUEL/HOUND DOG	
		Elvis Presley
27	DON'T BE CRUEL/HOUND DOG	
		Elvis Presley

NOVEMBER

3	LOVE ME TENDER	*Elvis Presley*
10	LOVE ME TENDER	*Elvis Presley*
17	LOVE ME TENDER	*Elvis Presley*
24	LOVE ME TENDER	*Elvis Presley*

DECEMBER

1	LOVE ME TENDER	*Elvis Presley*
8	SINGING THE BLUES	*Guy Mitchell*
15	SINGING THE BLUES	*Guy Mitchell*
22	SINGING THE BLUES	*Guy Mitchell*
29	SINGING THE BLUES	*Guy Mitchell*

1957

JANUARY

5	SINGING THE BLUES	*Guy Mitchell*
12	SINGING THE BLUES	*Guy Mitchell*
19	SINGING THE BLUES	*Guy Mitchell*
26	SINGING THE BLUES	*Guy Mitchell*

FEBRUARY

2	SINGING THE BLUES	*Guy Mitchell*
9	TOO MUCH	*Elvis Presley*
16	TOO MUCH	*Elvis Presley*
23	TOO MUCH	*Elvis Presley*

MARCH

2	YOUNG LOVE	*Tab Hunter*
9	YOUNG LOVE	*Tab Hunter*
16	YOUNG LOVE	*Tab Hunter*
23	YOUNG LOVE	*Tab Hunter*
30	PARTY DOLL	*Buddy Knox*

APRIL

6	ROUND AND ROUND	
13	ALL SHOOK UP	*Elvis Presley*
20	ALL SHOOK UP	*Elvis Presley*
27	ALL SHOOK UP	*Elvis Presley*

MAY

4	ALL SHOOK UP	*Elvis Presley*
11	ALL SHOOK UP	*Elvis Presley*
18	ALL SHOOK UP	*Elvis Presley*
25	ALL SHOOK UP	*Elvis Presley*

JUNE

1	ALL SHOOK UP	*Elvis Presley*
8	LOVE LETTERS IN THE SAND	*Pat Boone*
15	LOVE LETTERS IN THE SAND	*Pat Boone*
22	LOVE LETTERS IN THE SAND	*Pat Boone*
29	LOVE LETTERS IN THE SAND	*Pat Boone*

JULY

6	LOVE LETTERS IN THE SAND	*Pat Boone*
13	TEDDY BEAR	*Elvis Presley*
20	TEDDY BEAR	*Elvis Presley*
27	TEDDY BEAR	*Elvis Presley*

AUGUST

3	TEDDY BEAR	*Elvis Presley*
10	TEDDY BEAR	*Elvis Presley*
17	TEDDY BEAR	*Elvis Presley*
24	TEDDY BEAR	*Elvis Presley*
31	TAMMY	*Debbie Reynolds*

SEPTEMBER

7	TAMMY	*Debbie Reynolds*
14	DIANA	*Paul Anka*
21	TAMMY	*Debbie Reynolds*
28	THAT'LL BE THE DAY	*Crickets*

OCTOBER

5	HONEYCOMB	*Jimmy Rodgers*
12	HONEYCOMB	*Jimmy Rodgers*
19	WAKE UP LITTLE SUSIE	*Everly Brothers*
26	JAILHOUSE ROCK/TREAT ME NICE	*Elvis Presley*

NOVEMBER

2	JAILHOUSE ROCK/TREAT ME NICE	*Elvis Presley*
9	JAILHOUSE ROCK/TREAT ME NICE	*Elvis Presley*
16	JAILHOUSE ROCK/TREAT ME NICE	*Elvis Presley*
23	JAILHOUSE ROCK/TREAT ME NICE	*Elvis Presley*
30	JAILHOUSE ROCK/TREAT ME NICE	*Elvis Presley*

DECEMBER

7	YOU SEND ME	*Sam Cooke*
14	YOU SEND ME	*Sam Cooke*
21	YOU SEND ME	*Sam Cooke*
28	APRIL LOVE	*Pat Boone*

1958

JANUARY

4	APRIL LOVE	*Pat Boone*
11	AT THE HOP	*Danny and the Juniors*
18	AT THE HOP	*Danny and the Juniors*
25	AT THE HOP	*Danny and the Juniors*

FEBRUARY

1	AT THE HOP	*Danny and the Juniors*
8	AT THE HOP	*Danny and the Juniors*
15	DON'T/I BEG OF YOU	*Elvis Presley*
22	DON'T/I BEG OF YOU	*Elvis Presley*

MARCH

1	DON'T/I BEG OF YOU	*Elvis Presley*
8	DON'T/I BEG OF YOU	*Elvis Presley*
15	DON'T/I BEG OF YOU	*Elvis Presley*
22	TEQUILA	*Champs*
29	TEQUILA	*Champs*

APRIL

5	TEQUILA	*Champs*
12	TEQUILA	*Champs*
19	TEQUILA	*Champs*
26	TWILIGHT TIME	*Platters*

MAY

3	WITCH DOCTOR	*David Seville*
10	WITCH DOCTOR	*David Seville*
17	ALL I HAVE TO DO IS DREAM/CLAUDETTE	*Everly Brothers*
24	ALL I HAVE TO DO IS DREAM/CLAUDETTE	*Everly Brothers*
31	ALL I HAVE TO DO IS DREAM/CLAUDETTE	*Everly Brothers*

JUNE

7	ALL I HAVE TO DO IS DREAM/CLAUDETTE	*Everly Brothers*
14	THE PURPLE PEOPLE EATER	*Sheb Wooley*
21	THE PURPLE PEOPLE EATER	*Sheb Wooley*
28	THE PURPLE PEOPLE EATER	*Sheb Wooley*

JULY

5 THE PURPLE PEOPLE EATER *Sheb Wooley*
12 THE PURPLE PEOPLE EATER *Sheb Wooley*
19 THE PURPLE PEOPLE EATER *Sheb Wooley*
26 HARD HEADED WOMAN *Elvis Presley*

AUGUST

2 HARD HEADED WOMAN *Elvis Presley*
9 POOR LITTLE FOOL *Ricky Nelson*
16 POOR LITTLE FOOL *Ricky Nelson*
23 VOLARE *Domenico Modugno*
30 LITTLE STAR *Elegants*

SEPTEMBER

6 VOLARE *Domenico Modugno*
13 VOLARE *Domenico Modugno*
20 VOLARE *Domenico Modugno*
27 VOLARE *Domenico Modugno*

OCTOBER

4 IT'S ALL IN THE GAME *Tommy Edwards*
11 IT'S ALL IN THE GAME *Tommy Edwards*
18 IT'S ALL IN THE GAME *Tommy Edwards*
25 IT'S ALL IN THE GAME *Tommy Edwards*

NOVEMBER

1 IT'S ALL IN THE GAME *Tommy Edwards*
8 IT'S ALL IN THE GAME *Tommy Edwards*
15 IT'S ONLY MAKE BELIEVE
   Conway Twitty
22 TOM DOOLEY *Kingston Trio*
22 IT'S ONLY MAKE BELIEVE
   Conway Twitty

DECEMBER

6 TO KNOW HIM IS TO LOVE HIM
   Teddy Bears
13 TO KNOW HIM IS TO LOVE HIM
   Teddy Bears
20 TO KNOW HIM IS TO LOVE HIM
   Teddy Bears
27 THE CHIPMUNK SONG
   The Chipmunks with David Seville

1959

JANUARY

3 THE CHIPMUNK SONG
   The Chipmunks with David Seville
10 THE CHIPMUNK SONG
   The Chipmunks with David Seville
17 THE CHIPMUNK SONG
   The Chipmunks with David Seville
24 SMOKE GETS IN YOUR EYES *Platters*
31 SMOKE GETS IN YOUR EYES *Platters*

FEBRUARY

7 SMOKE GETS IN YOUR EYES *Platters*
14 STAGGER LEE *Lloyd Price*
21 STAGGER LEE *Lloyd Price*
28 STAGGER LEE *Lloyd Price*

MARCH

7 STAGGER LEE *Lloyd Price*
14 VENUS *Frankie Avalon*
21 VENUS *Frankie Avalon*
28 VENUS *Frankie Avalon*

APRIL

4 VENUS *Frankie Avalon*
11 VENUS *Frankie Avalon*
18 COME SOFTLY TO ME *Fleetwoods*
25 COME SOFTLY TO ME *Fleetwoods*

MAY

2 COME SOFTLY TO ME *Fleetwoods*
9 COME SOFTLY TO ME *Fleetwoods*
16 THE HAPPY ORGAN *Dave 'Baby' Cortez*
23 KANSAS CITY *Wilbert Harrison*
30 KANSAS CITY *Wilbert Harrison*

JUNE

6 THE BATTLE OF NEW ORLEANS
   Johnny Horton
13 THE BATTLE OF NEW ORLEANS
   Johnny Horton
20 THE BATTLE OF NEW ORLEANS
   Johnny Horton
27 THE BATTLE OF NEW ORLEANS
   Johnny Horton

JULY

4 THE BATTLE OF NEW ORLEANS
   Johnny Horton
11 THE BATTLE OF NEW ORLEANS
   Johnny Horton
18 LONELY BOY *Paul Anka*
25 LONELY BOY *Paul Anka*

AUGUST

1 LONELY BOY *Paul Anka*
8 LONELY BOY *Paul Anka*
15 BIG HUNK O' LOVE *Elvis Presley*
22 BIG HUNK O' LOVE *Elvis Presley*
29 THE THREE BELLS *Browns*

SEPTEMBER

5 THE THREE BELLS *Browns*
12 THE THREE BELLS *Browns*
19 THE THREE BELLS *Browns*
26 SLEEPWALK *Santo and Johnny*

OCTOBER

3	SLEEPWALK	*Santo and Johnny*
10	MACK THE KNIFE	*Bobby Darin*
17	MACK THE KNIFE	*Bobby Darin*
24	MACK THE KNIFE	*Bobby Darin*
31	MACK THE KNIFE	*Bobby Darin*

NOVEMBER

7	MACK THE KNIFE	*Bobby Darin*
14	MACK THE KNIFE	*Bobby Darin*
21	MR BLUE	*Fleetwoods*
28	MACK THE KNIFE	*Bobby Darin*

DECEMBER

5	MACK THE KNIFE	*Bobby Darin*
12	MACK THE KNIFE	*Bobby Darin*
19	HEARTACHES BY THE NUMBER *Guy Mitchell*	
26	HEARTACHES BY THE NUMBER *Guy Mitchell*	

1960

JANUARY

2	WHY	*Frankie Avalon*
9	EL PASO	*Marty Robbins*
16	EL PASO	*Marty Robbins*
23	RUNNING BEAR	*Johnny Preston*
30	RUNNING BEAR	*Johnny Preston*

FEBRUARY

6	RUNNING BEAR	*Johnny Preston*
13	TEEN ANGEL	*Mark Dinning*
20	TEEN ANGEL	*Mark Dinning*
27	THEME FROM *A SUMMER PLACE* *Percy Faith*	

MARCH

5	THEME FROM *A SUMMER PLACE* *Percy Faith*	
12	THEME FROM *A SUMMER PLACE* *Percy Faith*	
19	THEME FROM *A SUMMER PLACE* *Percy Faith*	
26	THEME FROM *A SUMMER PLACE* *Percy Faith*	

APRIL

2	THEME FROM *A SUMMER PLACE* *Percy Faith*	
9	THEME FROM *A SUMMER PLACE* *Percy Faith*	
16	THEME FROM *A SUMMER PLACE* *Percy Faith*	
23	THEME FROM *A SUMMER PLACE* *Percy Faith*	
30	STUCK ON YOU	*Elvis Presley*

MAY

7	STUCK ON YOU	*Elvis Presley*
14	STUCK ON YOU	*Elvis Presley*
21	STUCK ON YOU	*Elvis Presley*
28	CATHY'S CLOWN	*Everly Brothers*

JUNE

3	CATHY'S CLOWN	*Everly Brothers*
11	CATHY'S CLOWN	*Everly Brothers*
18	CATHY'S CLOWN	*Everly Brothers*
25	CATHY'S CLOWN	*Everly Brothers*

JULY

2	EVERYBODY'S SOMEBODY'S FOOL *Connie Francis*	
9	EVERYBODY'S SOMEBODY'S FOOL *Connie Francis*	
16	ALLEY-OOP	*Hollywood Argyles*
23	I'M SORRY	*Brenda Lee*
30	I'M SORRY	*Brenda Lee*

AUGUST

6	I'M SORRY	*Brenda Lee*
13	ITSY BITSY TEENY WEENY YELLOW POLKA DOT BIKINI	*Brian Hyland*
20	IT'S NOW OR NEVER	*Elvis Presley*
27	IT'S NOW OR NEVER	*Elvis Presley*

SEPTEMBER

3	IT'S NOW OR NEVER	*Elvis Presley*
10	IT'S NOW OR NEVER	*Elvis Presley*
17	IT'S NOW OR NEVER	*Elvis Presley*
24	THE TWIST	*Chubby Checker*

OCTOBER

1	MY HEART HAS A MIND OF ITS OWN *Connie Francis*	
8	MY HEART HAS A MIND OF ITS OWN *Connie Francis*	
15	MR CUSTER	*Larry Verne*
22	SAVE THE LAST DANCE FOR ME *Drifters*	
29	I WANT TO BE WANTED	*Brenda Lee*

NOVEMBER

5	SAVE THE LAST DANCE FOR ME *Drifters*	
12	SAVE THE LAST DANCE FOR ME *Drifters*	
19	GEORGIA ON MY MIND	*Ray Charles*
26	STAY	*Maurice Williams and the Zodiacs*

DECEMBER

3	ARE YOU LONESOME TONIGHT? *Elvis Presley*	
10	ARE YOU LONESOME TONIGHT? *Elvis Presley*	

17 ARE YOU LONESOME TONIGHT?
     Elvis Presley
24 ARE YOU LONESOME TONIGHT?
     Elvis Presley
31 ARE YOU LONESOME TONIGHT?
     Elvis Presley

1961

JANUARY

7   ARE YOU LONESOME TONIGHT?
     Elvis Presley
14 WONDERLAND BY NIGHT   *Bert Kaempfert*
21 WONDERLAND BY NIGHT   *Bert Kaempfert*
28 WONDERLAND BY NIGHT   *Bert Kaempfert*

FEBRUARY

4   WILL YOU LOVE ME TOMORROW?   *Shirelles*
11 WILL YOU LOVE ME TOMORROW?   *Shirelles*
18 CALCUTTA   *Lawrence Welk*
25 CALCUTTA   *Lawrence Welk*

MARCH

4   PONY TIME   *Chubby Checker*
11 PONY TIME   *Chubby Checker*
18 PONY TIME   *Chubby Checker*
25 SURRENDER   *Elvis Presley*

APRIL

1   SURRENDER   *Elvis Presley*
8   BLUE MOON   *Marcels*
15 BLUE MOON   *Marcels*
22 BLUE MOON   *Marcels*
29 RUNAWAY   *Del Shannon*

MAY

6   RUNAWAY   *Del Shannon*
13 RUNAWAY   *Del Shannon*
20 RUNAWAY   *Del Shannon*
27 MOTHER-IN-LAW   *Ernie K-Doe*

JUNE

3   TRAVELIN' MAN   *Ricky Nelson*
10 RUNNING SCARED   *Roy Orbison*
17 TRAVELIN' MAN   *Ricky Nelson*
24 MOODY RIVER   *Pat Boone*

JULY

1   QUARTER TO THREE   *Gary US Bonds*
8   QUARTER TO THREE   *Gary US Bonds*
15 TOSSIN' AND TURNIN'   *Bobby Lewis*
22 TOSSIN' AND TURNIN'   *Bobby Lewis*
29 TOSSIN' AND TURNIN'   *Bobby Lewis*

AUGUST

5   TOSSIN' AND TURNIN'   *Bobby Lewis*
12 TOSSIN' AND TURNIN'   *Bobby Lewis*

19 TOSSIN' AND TURNIN'   *Bobby Lewis*
26 TOSSIN' AND TURNIN'   *Bobby Lewis*

SEPTEMBER

2   WOODEN HEART   *Joe Dowell*
9   HIGHWAYMEN   *Michael*
16 HIGHWAYMEN   *Michael*
23 TAKE GOOD CARE OF MY BABY   *Bobby Vee*
30 TAKE GOOD CARE OF MY BABY   *Bobby Vee*

OCTOBER

7   TAKE GOOD CARE OF MY BABY   *Bobby Vee*
14 HIT THE ROAD JACK   *Ray Charles*
21 HIT THE ROAD JACK   *Ray Charles*
28 RUNAROUND SUE   *Dion*

NOVEMBER

4   RUNAROUND SUE   *Dion*
11 BIG BAD JOHN   *Jimmy Dean*
18 BIG BAD JOHN   *Jimmy Dean*
25 BIG BAD JOHN   *Jimmy Dean*

DECEMBER

2   BIG BAD JOHN   *Jimmy Dean*
9   BIG BAD JOHN   *Jimmy Dean*
16 PLEASE MR POSTMAN   *Marvelettes*
23 THE LION SLEEPS TONIGHT   *Tokens*
30 THE LION SLEEPS TONIGHT   *Tokens*

1962

JANUARY

6   THE LION SLEEPS TONIGHT   *Tokens*
13 THE TWIST   *Chubby Checker*
20 THE TWIST   *Chubby Checker*
27 PEPPERMINT TWIST
     Joey Dee and the Starlighters

FEBRUARY

3   PEPPERMINT TWIST
     Joey Dee and the Starlighters
10 PEPPERMINT TWIST
     Joey Dee and the Starlighters
17 DUKE OF EARL   *Gene Chandler*
24 DUKE OF EARL   *Gene Chandler*

MARCH

3   DUKE OF EARL   *Gene Chandler*
10 HEY! BABY   *Bruce Chanel*
17 HEY! BABY   *Bruce Chanel*
24 HEY! BABY   *Bruce Chanel*
31 DON'T BREAK THE HEART THAT LOVES YOU
     Connie Frances

APRIL

7   JOHNNY ANGEL   *Shelley Fabares*
14 JOHNNY ANGEL   *Shelley Fabares*

21	GOOD LUCK CHARM	*Elvis Presley*
28	GOOD LUCK CHARM	*Elvis Presley*

MAY

5	SOLDIER BOY	*Shirelles*
12	SOLDIER BOY	*Shirelles*
19	SOLDIER BOY	*Shirelles*
26	STRANGER ON THE SHORE	*Acker Bilk*

JUNE

2	I CAN'T STOP LOVING YOU	*Ray Charles*
9	I CAN'T STOP LOVING YOU	*Ray Charles*
16	I CAN'T STOP LOVING YOU	*Ray Charles*
23	I CAN'T STOP LOVING YOU	*Ray Charles*
30	I CAN'T STOP LOVING YOU	*Ray Charles*

JULY

7	THE STRIPPER	*David Rose*
14	ROSES ARE RED	*Bobby Vinton*
21	ROSES ARE RED	*Bobby Vinton*
28	ROSES ARE RED	*Bobby Vinton*

AUGUST

4	ROSES ARE RED	*Bobby Vinton*
11	BREAKING UP IS HARD TO DO *Neil Sedaka*	
18	BREAKING UP IS HARD TO DO *Neil Sedaka*	
25	THE LOCO-MOTION	*Little Eva*

SEPTEMBER

1	SHEILA	*Tommy Roe*
8	SHEILA	*Tommy Roe*
15	SHERRY	*Four Seasons*
22	SHERRY	*Four Seasons*
29	SHERRY	*Four Seasons*

OCTOBER

6	SHERRY	*Four Seasons*
13	SHERRY	*Four Seasons*
20	MONSTER MASH *Bobby 'Boris' Pickett/The Crypt Kickers*	
27	MONSTER MASH *Bobby 'Boris' Pickett/The Crypt Kickers*	

NOVEMBER

3	HE'S A REBEL	*Crystals*
10	HE'S A REBEL	*Crystals*
17	BIG GIRLS DON'T CRY	*Four Seasons*
24	BIG GIRLS DON'T CRY	*Four Seasons*

DECEMBER

1	BIG GIRLS DON'T CRY	*Four Seasons*
8	BIG GIRLS DON'T CRY	*Four Seasons*
15	BIG GIRLS DON'T CRY	*Four Seasons*
22	TELSTAR	*Tornados*
29	TELSTAR	*Tornados*

1963

JANUARY

5	TELSTAR	*Tornados*
12	GO AWAY LITTLE GIRL	*Steve Lawrence*
19	GO AWAY LITTLE GIRL	*Steve Lawrence*
26	WALK RIGHT IN	*Rooftop Singers*

FEBRUARY

2	WALK RIGHT IN	*Rooftop Singers*
9	HEY PAULA	*Paul and Paula*
16	HEY PAULA	*Paul and Paula*
23	HEY PAULA	*Paul and Paula*

MARCH

2	WALK LIKE A MAN	*Four Seasons*
9	WALK LIKE A MAN	*Four Seasons*
16	WALK LIKE A MAN	*Four Seasons*
23	OUR DAY WILL COME	*Ruby and the Romantics*
30	HE'S SO FINE	*Chiffons*

APRIL

6	HE'S SO FINE	*Chiffons*
13	HE'S SO FINE	*Chiffons*
20	HE'S SO FINE	*Chiffons*
27	I WILL FOLLOW HIM *Little Peggy March*	

MAY

4	I WILL FOLLOW HIM *Little Peggy March*	
11	I WILL FOLLOW HIM *Little Peggy March*	
18	IF YOU WANNA BE HAPPY	*Jimmy Soul*
25	IF YOU WANNA BE HAPPY	*Jimmy Soul*

JUNE

1	IT'S MY PARTY	*Lesley Gore*
8	IT'S MY PARTY	*Lesley Gore*
15	SUKIYAKI	*Kyu Sakamoto*
22	SUKIYAKI	*Kyu Sakamoto*
29	SUKIYAKI	*Kyu Sakamoto*

JULY

6	EASIER SAID THAN DONE	*Essex*
13	EASIER SAID THAN DONE	*Essex*
20	SURF CITY	*Jan and Dean*
27	SURF CITY	*Jan and Dean*

AUGUST

3	SO MUCH IN LOVE	*Tymes*
10	FINGERTIPS PT. II	*Stevie Wonder*
17	FINGERTIPS PT. II	*Stevie Wonder*
24	FINGERTIPS PT. II	*Stevie Wonder*
31	MY BOYFRIEND'S BACK	*Angels*

SEPTEMBER

7	MY BOYFRIEND'S BACK	*Angels*
14	MY BOYFRIEND'S BACK	*Angels*
21	BLUE VELVET	*Bobby Vinton*
28	BLUE VELVET	*Bobby Vinton*

OCTOBER

5	BLUE VELVET	*Bobby Vinton*
12	SUGAR SHACK	
	Jimmy Gilmer and the Fireballs	
19	SUGAR SHACK	
	Jimmy Gilmer and the Fireballs	
26	SUGAR SHACK	
	Jimmy Gilmer and the Fireballls	

NOVEMBER

2	SUGAR SHACK	
	Jimmy Gilmer and the Fireballs	
9	SUGAR SHACK	
	Jimmy Gilmer and the Fireballs	
16	DEEP PURPLE	
	Nino Temple and April Stevens	
23	I'M LEAVING IT UP TO YOU	
	Dale and Grace	
30	I'M LEAVING IT UP TO YOU	
	Dale and Grace	

DECEMBER

7	DOMINIQUE	*Singing Nun*
14	DOMINIQUE	*Singing Nun*
21	DOMINIQUE	*Singing Nun*

1964

JANUARY

4	THERE I'VE SAID IT AGAIN	
	Bobby Vinton	
11	THERE I'VE SAID IT AGAIN	
	Bobby Vinton	
18	THERE I'VE SAID IT AGAIN	
	Bobby Vinton	
25	THERE I'VE SAID IT AGAIN	
	Bobby Vinton	

FEBRUARY

1	I WANT TO HOLD YOUR HAND	*Beatles*
8	I WANT TO HOLD YOUR HAND	*Beatles*
15	I WANT TO HOLD YOUR HAND	*Beatles*
22	I WANT TO HOLD YOUR HAND	*Beatles*
29	I WANT TO HOLD YOUR HAND	*Beatles*

MARCH

7	I WANT TO HOLD YOUR HAND	*Beatles*
14	I WANT TO HOLD YOUR HAND	*Beatles*
21	SHE LOVES YOU	*Beatles*
28	SHE LOVES YOU	*Beatles*

APRIL

4	CAN'T BUY ME LOVE	*Beatles*
11	CAN'T BUY ME LOVE	*Beatles*
18	CAN'T BUY ME LOVE	*Beatles*
25	CAN'T BUY ME LOVE	*Beatles*

MAY

2	CAN'T BUY ME LOVE	*Beatles*
9	HELLO DOLLY	*Louis Armstrong*
16	MY GUY	*Mary Wells*
23	MY GUY	*Mary Wells*
30	LOVE ME DO	*Beatles*

JUNE

6	CHAPEL OF LOVE	*Dixie Cups*
13	CHAPEL OF LOVE	*Dixie Cups*
20	CHAPEL OF LOVE	*Dixie Cups*
27	A WORLD WITHOUT LOVE	
	Peter and Gordon	

JULY

4	I GET AROUND	*Beach Boys*
11	I GET AROUND	*Beach Boys*
18	RAG DOLL	*Four Seasons*
25	RAG DOLL	*Four Seasons*

AUGUST

1	A HARD DAY'S NIGHT	*Beatles*
8	A HARD DAY'S NIGHT	*Beatles*
15	EVERYBODY LOVES SOMEBODY	
	Dean Martin	
22	WHERE DID OUR LOVE GO?	*Supremes*
29	WHERE DID OUR LOVE GO?	*Supremes*

SEPTEMBER

5	HOUSE OF THE RISING SUN	*Animals*
12	HOUSE OF THE RISING SUN	*Animals*
19	HOUSE OF THE RISING SUN	*Animals*
26	OH, PRETTY WOMAN	*Roy Orbison*

OCTOBER

3	OH, PRETTY WOMAN	*Roy Orbison*
10	OH, PRETTY WOMAN	*Roy Orbison*
17	DO WAH DIDDY DIDDY	*Manfred Mann*
24	DO WAH DIDDY DIDDY	*Manfred Mann*
31	BABY LOVE	*Supremes*

NOVEMBER

7	BABY LOVE	*Supremes*
14	BABY LOVE	*Supremes*
21	BABY LOVE	*Supremes*
28	LEADER OF THE PACK	*Shangri-Las*

DECEMBER

5	RINGO	*Lorne Green*
12	MR LONELY	*Bobby Vinton*

19	COME SEE ABOUT ME	*Supremes*
26	I FEEL FINE	*Beatles*

1965

JANUARY

2	I FEEL FINE	*Beatles*
9	I FEEL FINE	*Beatles*
16	COME SEE ABOUT ME	*Supremes*
23	DOWN TOWN	*Petula Clark*
30	DOWN TOWN	*Petula Clark*

FEBRUARY

6	YOU'VE LOST THAT LOVIN' FEELIN'
	Righteous Brothers
13	YOU'VE LOST THAT LOVIN' FEELIN'
	Righteous Brothers
20	THIS DIAMOND RING
	Gary Lewis and the Playboys
27	THIS DIAMOND RING
	Gary Lewis and the Playboys

MARCH

6	MY GIRL	*Temptations*
13	EIGHT DAYS A WEEK	*Beatles*
20	EIGHT DAYS A WEEK	*Beatles*
27	STOP! IN THE NAME OF LOVE	*Supremes*

APRIL

3	STOP! IN THE NAME OF LOVE	*Supremes*
10	I'M TELLING YOU NOW	
	Freddie and the Dreamers	
17	I'M TELLING YOU NOW	
	Freddie and the Dreamers	
24	GAME OF LOVE	
	Wayne Fontana and the Mindbenders	

MAY

1	MRS BROWN YOU'VE GOT A LOVELY
	DAUGHTER *Herman's Hermits*
15	MRS BROWN YOU'VE GOT A LOVELY
	DAUGHTER *Herman's Hermits*
22	TICKET TO RIDE *Beatles*
29	HELP ME RHONDA *Beach Boys*

JUNE

5	HELP ME RHONDA	*Beach Boys*
12	BACK IN MY ARMS AGAIN	*Supremes*
19	I CAN'T HELP MYSELF	*Four Tops*
26	MR TAMBOURINE MAN	*Byrds*

JULY

3	I CAN'T HELP MYSELF	*Four Tops*
10	(I CAN'T GET NO) SATISFACTION	
	Rolling Stones	

17	(I CAN'T GET NO) SATISFACTION	
	Rolling Stones	
31	(I CAN'T GET NO) SATISFACTION	
	Rolling Stones	

AUGUST

7	I'M HENRY VIII I AM	
	Herman's Hermits	
14	I GOT YOU BABE	*Sonny and Cher*
21	I GOT YOU BABE	*Sonny and Cher*
28	I GOT YOU BABE	*Sonny and Cher*

SEPTEMBER

4	HELP	*Beatles*
11	HELP	*Beatles*
18	HELP	*Beatles*
25	EVE OF DESTRUCTION	*Barry McGuire*

OCTOBER

2	HANG ON SLOOPY	*McCoys*
9	YESTERDAY	*Beatles*
16	YESTERDAY	*Beatles*
23	YESTERDAY	*Beatles*
30	YESTERDAY	*Beatles*

NOVEMBER

6	GET OFF MY CLOUD	*Rolling Stones*
13	GET OFF MY CLOUD	*Rolling Stones*
20	I HEAR A SYMPHONY	*Supremes*
27	I HEAR A SYMPHONY	*Supremes*

DECEMBER

4	TURN! TURN! TURN!	*Byrds*
11	TURN! TURN! TURN!	*Byrds*
18	TURN! TURN! TURN!	*Byrds*
25	OVER AND OVER	*Dave Clark Five*

1966

JANUARY

1	SOUNDS OF SILENCE	
	Simon and Garfunkel	
8	WE CAN WORK IT OUT	*Beatles*
15	WE CAN WORK IT OUT	*Beatles*
22	SOUNDS OF SILENCE	
	Simon and Garfunkel	
29	WE CAN WORK IT OUT	*Beatles*

FEBRUARY

5	MY LOVE	*Petula Clark*
12	MY LOVE	*Petula Clark*
19	LIGHTNIN' STRIKES	*Lou Christie*
26	THESE BOOTS ARE MADE FOR WALKIN'	
	Nancy Sinatra	

MARCH

5 THE BALLAD OF THE GREEN BERETS
S/SGT. Barry Sadler

12 THE BALLAD OF THE GREEN BERETS
S/SGT. Barry Sadler

19 THE BALLAD OF THE GREEN BERETS
S/SGT. Barry Sadler

26 THE BALLAD OF THE GREEN BERETS
S/SGT. Barry Sadler

APRIL

2 THE BALLAD OF THE GREEN BERETS
S/SGT. Barry Sadler

9 YOU'RE MY SOUL AND INSPIRATION
Righteous Brothers

16 YOU'RE MY SOUL AND INSPIRATION
Righteous Brothers

23 YOU'RE MY SOUL AND INSPIRATION
Righteous Brothers

30 GOOD LOVIN'   *Young Rascals*

MAY

7 MONDAY MONDAY   *Mamas and Papas*

14 MONDAY MONDAY   *Mamas and Papas*

21 MONDAY MONDAY   *Mamas and Papas*

28 WHEN A MAN LOVES A WOMAN
Percy Sledge

JUNE

4 WHEN A MAN LOVES A WOMAN
Percy Sledge

11 PAINT IT BLACK   *Rolling Stones*

18 PAINT IT BLACK   *Rolling Stones*

25 PAPERBACK WRITER   *Beatles*

JULY

2 STRANGERS IN THE NIGHT
Frank Sinatra

9 PAPERBACK WRITER   *Beatles*

16 HANKY PANKY
Tommy James and the Shondells

23 HANKY PANKY
Tommy James and the Shondells

30 WILD THING   *Troggs*

AUGUST

6 WILD THING   *Troggs*

13 SUMMER IN THE CITY   *Lovin' Spoonful*

20 SUMMER IN THE CITY   *Lovin' Spoonful*

27 SUMMER IN THE CITY   *Lovin' Spoonful*

SEPTEMBER

3 SUNSHINE SUPERMAN   *Donovan*

10 YOU CAN'T HURRY LOVE   *Supremes*

17 YOU CAN'T HURRY LOVE   *Supremes*

24 CHERISH   *Association*

OCTOBER

1 CHERISH   *Association*

8 CHERISH   *Association*

15 REACH OUT I'LL BE THERE   *Four Tops*

22 REACH OUT I'LL BE THERE   *Four Tops*

29 96 TEARS   *Mysterians*

NOVEMBER

5 LAST TRAIN TO CLARKSVILLE   *Monkees*

12 POOR SIDE OF TOWN   *Johnny Rivers*

19 YOU KEEP ME HANGIN' ON   *Supremes*

26 YOU KEEP ME HANGIN' ON   *Supremes*

DECEMBER

3 WINCHESTER CATHEDRAL
New Vaudeville Band

10 GOOD VIBRATIONS   *Beach Boys*

17 WINCHESTER CATHEDRAL
New Vaudeville Band

24 WINCHESTER CATHEDRAL
New Vaudeville Band

31 I'M A BELIEVER   *Monkees*

1967

JANUARY

7 I'M A BELIEVER   *Monkees*

14 I'M A BELIEVER   *Monkees*

21 I'M A BELIEVER   *Monkees*

28 I'M A BELIEVER   *Monkees*

FEBRUARY

4 I'M A BELIEVER   *Monkees*

11 I'M A BELIEVER   *Monkees*

18 KIND OF DRAG   *Buckinghams*

25 KIND OF DRAG   *Buckinghams*

MARCH

4 RUBY TUESDAY   *Rolling Stones*

11 LOVE IS HERE AND NOW YOU'RE GONE
Supremes

18 PENNY LANE   *Beatles*

25 HAPPY TOGETHER   *Turtles*

APRIL

1 HAPPY TOGETHER   *Turtles*

8 HAPPY TOGETHER   *Turtles*

15 SOMETHIN' STUPID
Nancy and Frank Sinatra

22 SOMETHIN' STUPID
Nancy and Frank Sinatra

29 SOMETHIN' STUPID
Nancy and Frank Sinatra

MAY

6   SOMETHIN' STUPID
     Nancy and Frank Sinatra
13 THE HAPPENING   *Supremes*
20 GROOVIN'   *Young Rascals*
27 GROOVIN'   *Young Rascals*

JUNE

3   RESPECT   *Aretha Franklin*
10 RESPECT   *Aretha Franklin*
17 GROOVIN'   *Young Rascals*
24 GROOVIN'   *Young Rascals*

JULY

1   WINDY   *Association*
8   WINDY   *Association*
15 WINDY   *Association*
22 WINDY   *Association*
29 LIGHT MY FIRE   *Doors*

AUGUST

5   LIGHT MY FIRE   *Doors*
12 LIGHT MY FIRE   *Doors*
19 ALL YOU NEED IS LOVE   *Beatles*
26 ODE TO BILLY JOE   *Bobby Gentry*

SEPTEMBER

2   ODE TO BILLY JOE   *Bobby Gentry*
9   ODE TO BILLY JOE   *Bobby Gentry*
16 ODE TO BILLY JOE   *Bobby Gentry*
23 THE LETTER   *Box Tops*
30 THE LETTER   *Box Tops*

OCTOBER

7   THE LETTER   *Box Tops*
14 THE LETTER   *Box Tops*
21 TO SIR WITH LOVE   *Lulu*
28 TO SIR WITH LOVE   *Lulu*

NOVEMBER

4   TO SIR WITH LOVE   *Lulu*
11 TO SIR WITH LOVE   *Lulu*
18 TO SIR WITH LOVE   *Lulu*
25 INCENSE AND PEPPERMINTS
     Strawberry Alarm Clock

DECEMBER

2   DAYDREAMER BELIEVER   *Monkees*
9   DAYDREAMER BELIEVER   *Monkees*
16 DAYDREAMER BELIEVER   *Monkees*
23 DAYDREAMER BELIEVER   *Monkees*
30 HELLO GOODBYE   *Beatles*

1968

JANUARY

6   HELLO GOODBYE   *Beatles*
13 HELLO GOODBYE   *Beatles*
20 JUDY IN DISGUISE (WITH GLASSES)
     John/Fred Playboy Band
27 JUDY IN DISGUISE (WITH GLASSES)
     John/Fred Playboy Band

FEBRUARY

3   GREEN TAMBOURINE   *Lemon Pipers*
10 LOVE IS BLUE   *Paul Mauriat*
17 LOVE IS BLUE   *Paul Mauriat*
24 LOVE IS BLUE   *Paul Mauriat*

MARCH

2   LOVE IS BLUE   *Paul Mauriat*
9   LOVE IS BLUE   *Paul Mauriat*
16 (SITTIN' ON) THE DOCK OF THE BAY
     Otis Redding
23 (SITTIN' ON) THE DOCK OF THE BAY
     Otis Redding
30 (SITTIN' ON) THE DOCK OF THE BAY
     Otis Redding

APRIL

6   (SITTIN' ON) THE DOCK OF THE BAY
     Otis Redding
13 HONEY   *Bobby Goldsboro*
20 HONEY   *Bobby Goldsboro*
27 HONEY   *Bobby Goldsboro*

MAY

4   HONEY   *Bobby Goldsboro*
11 HONEY   *Bobby Goldsboro*
18 TIGHTEN UP
     Archie Bell and the Drells
25 TIGHTEN UP
     Archie Bell and the Drells

JUNE

1   MRS ROBINSON   *Simon and Garfunkel*
8   MRS ROBINSON   *Simon and Garfunkel*
15 MRS ROBINSON   *Simon and Garfunkel*
22 THIS GUY'S IN LOVE WITH YOU
     Herb Alpert
29 THIS GUY'S IN LOVE WITH YOU
     Herb Alpert

JULY

6   THIS GUY'S IN LOVE WITH YOU
     Herb Alpert
13 THIS GUY'S IN LOVE WITH YOU
     Herb Alpert
20 GRAZING IN THE GRASS   *Hugh Masekela*
27 GRAZING IN THE GRASS   *Hugh Masekela*

AUGUST

3   HELLO I LOVE YOU   *Doors*
10 HELLO I LOVE YOU   *Doors*
17 PEOPLE GOT TO BE FREE   *Rascals*
24 PEOPLE GOT TO BE FREE   *Rascals*
31 PEOPLE GOT TO BE FREE   *Rascals*

SEPTEMBER

7   PEOPLE GOT TO BE FREE   *Rascals*
14 PEOPLE GOT TO BE FREE   *Rascals*
21 HARPER VALLEY P.T.A.
    Jeannie C. Riley
28 HEY JUDE   *Beatles*

OCTOBER

5   HEY JUDE   *Beatles*
12 HEY JUDE   *Beatles*
19 HEY JUDE   *Beatles*
26 HEY JUDE   *Beatles*

NOVEMBER

2   HEY JUDE   *Beatles*
9   HEY JUDE   *Beatles*
16 HEY JUDE   *Beatles*
23 HEY JUDE   *Beatles*
30 LOVE CHILD
    Diana Ross and the Supremes

DECEMBER

7   LOVE CHILD
    Diana Ross and the Supremes
14 I HEARD IT THROUGH THE GRAPEVINE
    Marvin Gaye
21 I HEARD IT THROUGH THE GRAPEVINE
    Marvin Gaye
28 I HEARD IT THROUGH THE GRAPEVINE
    Marvin Gaye

1969

JANUARY

4   I HEARD IT THROUGH THE GRAPEVINE
    Marvin Gaye
11 I HEARD IT THROUGH THE GRAPEVINE
    Marvin Gaye
18 I HEARD IT THROUGH THE GRAPEVINE
    Marvin Gaye
25 I HEARD IT THROUGH THE GRAPEVINE
    Marvin Gaye

FEBRUARY

1   CRIMSON AND CLOVER
    Tommy James and the Shondells
8   CRIMSON AND CLOVER
    Tommy James and the Shondells

15 EVERYDAY PEOPLE
    Sly and the Family Stone
22 EVERYDAY PEOPLE
    Sly and the Family Stone

MARCH

1   EVERYDAY PEOPLE
    Sly and the Family Stone
8   EVERYDAY PEOPLE
    Sly and the Family Stone
15 DIZZY   *Tommy Roe*
22 DIZZY   *Tommy Roe*
29 DIZZY   *Tommy Roe*

APRIL

5   DIZZY   *Tommy Roe*
12 AQUARIUS/LET THE SUNSHINE IN
    Fifth Dimension
19 AQUARIUS/LET THE SUNSHINE IN
    Fifth Dimension
26 AQUARIUS/LET THE SUNSHINE IN
    Fifth Dimension

MAY

3   AQUARIUS/LET THE SUNSHINE IN
    Fifth Dimension
10 AQUARIUS/LET THE SUNSHINE IN
    Fifth Dimension
17 AQUARIUS/LET THE SUNSHINE IN
    Fifth Dimension
24 GET BACK   *Beatles*
31 GET BACK   *Beatles*

JUNE

7   GET BACK   *Beatles*
14 GET BACK   *Beatles*
21 GET BACK   *Beatles*
28 GET BACK   *Beatles*

JULY

5   LOVE THEME FROM *ROMEO AND JULIET*
    Henry Mancini
12 IN THE YEAR 2525   *Zager and Evans*
19 IN THE YEAR 2525   *Zager and Evans*
26 IN THE YEAR 2525   *Zager and Evans*

AUGUST

2   IN THE YEAR 2525   *Zager and Evans*
9   IN THE YEAR 2525   *Zager and Evans*
16 IN THE YEAR 2525   *Zager and Evans*
23 HONKY TONK WOMEN   *Rolling Stones*
30 HONKY TONK WOMEN   *Rolling Stones*

SEPTEMBER

6   HONKY TONK WOMEN   *Rolling Stones*
13 HONKY TONK WOMEN   *Rolling Stones*
20 SUGAR SUGAR   *Archies*
27 SUGAR SUGAR   *Archies*

OCTOBER

4 SUGAR SUGAR *Archies*
11 SUGAR SUGAR *Archies*
18 I CAN'T GET NEXT TO YOU
   Temptations
25 I CAN'T GET NEXT TO YOU
   Temptations

NOVEMBER

1 SUSPICIOUS MINDS *Elvis Presley*
8 WEDDING BELL BLUES *Fifth Dimension*
15 WEDDING BELL BLUES *Fifth Dimension*
22 WEDDING BELL BLUES *Fifth Dimension*
29 COME TOGETHER *Beatles*

DECEMBER

6 NA NA HEY HEY KISS HIM GOODBYE
   Steam
13 NA NA HEY HEY KISS HIM GOODBYE
   Steam
20 LEAVING ON A JET PLANE
   Peter Paul and Mary
27 SOMEDAY WE'LL BE TOGETHER
   Diana Ross and the Supremes

1970

JANUARY

3 RAINDROPS KEEP FALLIN' ON MY HEAD
   B.J. Thomas
10 RAINDROPS KEEP FALLIN' ON MY HEAD
   B.J. Thomas
17 RAINDROPS KEEP FALLIN' ON MY HEAD
   B.J. Thomas
24 RAINDROPS KEEP FALLIN' ON MY HEAD
   B.J. Thomas
31 I WANT YOU BACK *Jackson Five*

FEBRUARY

7 VENUS *Shocking Blue*
14 THANK YOU/EVERYBODY IS A STAR
   Sly and the Family Stone
21 THANK/YOU EVERYBODY IS A STAR
   Sly and the Family Stone
28 BRIDGE OVER TROUBLED WATER
   Simon and Garfunkel

MARCH

7 BRIDGE OVER TROUBLED WATER
   Simon and Garfunkel
14 BRIDGE OVER TROUBLED WATER
   Simon and Garfunkel
21 BRIDGE OVER TROUBLED WATER
   Simon and Garfunkel
28 BRIDGE OVER TROUBLED WATER
   Simon and Garfunkel

APRIL

4 BRIDGE OVER TROUBLED WATER
   Simon and Garfunkel
11 LET IT BE *Beatles*
18 LET IT BE *Beatles*
25 ABC *Jackson Five*

MAY

2 ABC *Jackson Five*
9 AMERICAN WOMAN/NO SUGAR TONIGHT
   Guess Who
16 AMERICAN WOMAN/NO SUGAR TONIGHT
   Guess Who
23 AMERICAN WOMAN/NO SUGAR TONIGHT
   Guess Who
30 EVERYTHING IS BEAUTIFUL
   Ray Stevens

JUNE

6 EVERYTHING IS BEAUTIFUL
   Ray Stevens
13 THE LONG AND WINDING ROAD/FOR YOU
   BLUE *Beatles*
20 THE LONG AND WINDING ROAD/FOR YOU
   BLUE *Beatles*
27 THE LOVE YOU SAVE *Jackson Five*

JULY

4 THE LOVE YOU SAVE *Jackson Five*
11 MAMA TOLD ME NOT TO COME
   Three Dog Night
18 MAMA TOLD ME NOT TO COME
   Three Dog Night
25 (THEY LONG TO BE) CLOSE TO YOU
   Carpenters

AUGUST

1 (THEY LONG TO BE) CLOSE TO YOU
   Carpenters
8 (THEY LONG TO BE) CLOSE TO YOU
   Carpenters
15 (THEY LONG TO BE) CLOSE TO YOU
   Carpenters
22 MAKE IT WITH YOU *Bread*
29 WAR *Edwin Starr*

SEPTEMBER

5 WAR *Edwin Starr*
12 WAR *Edwin Starr*
19 AIN'T NO MOUNTAIN HIGH ENOUGH
   Diana Ross
26 AIN'T NO MOUNTAIN HIGH ENOUGH
   Diana Ross

OCTOBER

3 AIN'T NO MOUNTAIN HIGH ENOUGH
   Diana Ross
10 CRACKLIN' ROSIE *Neil Diamond*

17 I'LL BE THERE   *Jackson Five*
24 I'LL BE THERE   *Jackson Five*
31 I'LL BE THERE   *Jackson Five*

NOVEMBER

7   I'LL BE THERE   *Jackson Five*
14 I'LL BE THERE   *Jackson Five*
21 I THINK I LOVE YOU
    Partridge Family
28 I THINK I LOVE YOU
    Partridge Family

DECEMBER

5   I THINK I LOVE YOU
    Partridge Family
12 TEARS OF A CLOWN
    Smokey Robinson and the Miracles
19 TEARS OF A CLOWN
    Smokey Robinson and the Miracles
26 MY SWEET LORD/ISN'T IT A PITY?
    George Harrison

1971

JANUARY

2   MY SWEET LORD/ISN'T IT A PITY?
    George Harrison
9   MY SWEET LORD/ISN'T IT A PITY?
    George Harrison
16 MY SWEET LORD/ISN'T IT A PITY?
    George Harrison
23 KNOCK THREE TIMES   *Dawn*
30 KNOCK THREE TIMES   *Dawn*

FEBRUARY

6   KNOCK THREE TIMES   *Dawn*
13 ONE BAD APPLE   *Osmonds*
20 ONE BAD APPLE   *Osmonds*
27 ONE BAD APPLE   *Osmonds*

MARCH

6   ONE BAD APPLE   *Osmonds*
13 ONE BAD APPLE   *Osmonds*
20 ME AND BOBBY McGEE   *Janis Joplin*
27 ME AND BOBBY McGEE   *Janis Joplin*

APRIL

3   JUST MY IMAGINATION   *Temptations*
10 JUST MY IMAGINATION   *Temptations*
17 JOY TO THE WORLD   *Three Dog Night*
24 JOY TO THE WORLD   *Three Dog Night*

MAY

1   JOY TO THE WORLD   *Three Dog Night*
8   JOY TO THE WORLD   *Three Dog Night*
15 JOY TO THE WORLD   *Three Dog Night*
22 JOY TO THE WORLD   *Three Dog Night*
29 BROWN SUGAR   *Rolling Stones*

JUNE

5   BROWN SUGAR   *Rolling Stones*
12 WANT ADS   *Honey Cone*
19 IT'S TOO LATE   *Carole King*
26 IT'S TOO LATE   *Carole King*

JULY

3   IT'S TOO LATE   *Carole King*
10 IT'S TOO LATE   *Carole King*
17 IT'S TOO LATE   *Carole King*
24 INDIAN RESERVATION   *Raiders*
31 YOU'VE GOT A FRIEND   *James Taylor*

AUGUST

7   HOW CAN YOU MEND A BROKEN HEART?
    Bee Gees
14 HOW CAN YOU MEND A BROKEN HEART?
    Bee Gees
21 HOW CAN YOU MEND A BROKEN HEART?
    Bee Gees
28 HOW CAN YOU MEND A BROKEN HEART?
    Bee Gees

SEPTEMBER

4   UNCLE ALBERT/ADMIRAL HALSEY
    Paul and Linda McCartney
11 GO AWAY LITTLE GIRL   *Donny Osmond*
18 GO AWAY LITTLE GIRL   *Donny Osmond*
25 GO AWAY LITTLE GIRL   *Donny Osmond*

OCTOBER

2   MAGGIE MAY   *Rod Stewart*
9   MAGGIE MAY   *Rod Stewart*
16 MAGGIE MAY   *Rod Stewart*
23 MAGGIE MAY   *Rod Stewart*
30 MAGGIE MAY   *Rod Stewart*

NOVEMBER

6   GYPSYS, TRAMPS AND THIEVES   *Cher*
13 GYPSYS, TRAMPS AND THIEVES   *Cher*
20 THEME FROM *SHAFT*   *Isaac Hayes*
27 THEME FROM *SHAFT*   *Isaac Hayes*

DECEMBER

4   FAMILY AFFAIR
    Sly and the Family Stone
11 FAMILY AFFAIR
    Sly and the Family Stone
18 FAMILY AFFAIR
    Sly and the Family Stone
25 BRAND NEW KEY   *Melanie*

1972

JANUARY

1 BRAND NEW KEY *Melanie*
8 BRAND NEW KEY *Melanie*
15 AMERICAN PIE *Don McLean*
22 AMERICAN PIE *Don McLean*
29 AMERICAN PIE *Don McLean*

FEBRUARY

5 AMERICAN PIE *Don McLean*
12 LET'S STAY TOGETHER *Al Green*
19 WITHOUT YOU *Nilsson*
26 WITHOUT YOU *Nilsson*

MARCH

4 WITHOUT YOU *Nilsson*
11 WITHOUT YOU *Nilsson*
18 HEART OF GOLD *Neil Young*
25 A HORSE WITH NO NAME *America*

APRIL

1 A HORSE WITH NO NAME *America*
8 A HORSE WITH NO NAME *America*
15 THE FIRST TIME EVER I SAW YOUR FACE
   Roberta Flack
22 THE FIRST TIME EVER I SAW YOUR FACE
   Roberta Flack
29 THE FIRST TIME EVER I SAW YOUR FACE
   Roberta Flack

MAY

6 THE FIRST TIME EVER I SAW YOUR FACE
   Roberta Flack
13 THE FIRST TIME EVER I SAW YOUR FACE
   Roberta Flack
20 THE FIRST TIME EVER I SAW YOUR FACE
   Roberta Flack
27 OH GIRL *Chi-Lites*

JUNE

3 I'LL TAKE YOU THERE *Staple Singers*
10 THE CANDY MAN *Sammy Davis*
17 THE CANDY MAN *Sammy Davis*
24 THE CANDY MAN *Sammy Davis*

JULY

1 SONG SUNG BLUE *Neil Diamond*
8 LEAN ON ME *Bill Withers*
15 LEAN ON ME *Bill Withers*
22 LEAN ON ME *Bill Withers*
29 ALONE AGAIN (NATURALLY)
   Gilbert O'Sullivan

AUGUST

5 ALONE AGAIN (NATURALLY)
   Gilbert O'Sullivan
12 ALONE AGAIN (NATURALLY)
   Gilbert O'Sullivan
19 ALONE AGAIN (NATURALLY)
   Gilbert O'Sullivan
26 BRANDY (YOU'RE A FINE GIRL)
   Looking Glass

SEPTEMBER

2 ALONE AGAIN (NATURALLY)
   Gilbert O'Sullivan
9 ALONE AGAIN (NATURALLY)
   Gilbert O'Sullivan
16 BLACK AND WHITE *Three Dog Night*
23 BABY DON'T GET HOOKED ON ME
   Mac Davis
30 BABY DON'T GET HOOKED ON ME
   Mac Davis

OCTOBER

7 BABY DON'T GET HOOKED ON ME
   Mac Davis
14 BEN *Michael Jackson*
21 MY DING-A-LING *Chuck Berry*
28 MY DING-A-LING *Chuck Berry*

NOVEMBER

4 I CAN SEE CLEARLY NOW *Johnny Nash*
11 I CAN SEE CLEARLY NOW *Johnny Nash*
18 I CAN SEE CLEARLY NOW *Johnny Nash*
25 I CAN SEE CLEARLY NOW *Johnny Nash*

DECEMBER

2 PAPA WAS A ROLLING STONE
   Temptations
9 I AM A WOMAN *Helen Reddy*
16 ME AND MRS JONES *Billy Paul*
23 ME AND MRS JONES *Billy Paul*
30 ME AND MRS JONES *Billy Paul*

1973

JANUARY

6 YOU'RE SO VAIN *Carly Simon*
13 YOU'RE SO VAIN *Carly Simon*
20 YOU'RE SO VAIN *Carly Simon*
27 SUPERSTITION *Stevie Wonder*

FEBRUARY

3 CROCODILE ROCK *Elton John*
10 CROCODILE ROCK *Elton John*
17 CROCODILE ROCK *Elton John*
24 KILLING ME SOFTLY WITH HIS SONG
   Roberta Flack

MARCH

3 KILLING ME SOFTLY WITH HIS SONG
Roberta Flack
10 KILLING ME SOFTLY WITH HIS SONG
Roberta Flack
17 KILLING ME SOFTLY WITH HIS SONG
Roberta Flack
24 LOVE TRAIN   *O'Jays*
31 KILLING ME SOFTLY WITH HIS SONG
Roberta Flack

APRIL

7 THE NIGHT THE LIGHTS WENT OUT IN
GEORGIA   *Vicky Lawrence*
14 THE NIGHT THE LIGHTS WENT OUT IN
GEORGIA   *Vicky Lawrence*
21 TIE A YELLOW RIBBON ROUND THE OLE
OAK TREE   *Dawn*
28 TIE A YELLOW RIBBON ROUND THE OLE
OAK TREE   *Dawn*

MAY

5 TIE A YELLOW RIBBON ROUND THE OLE
OAK TREE   *Dawn*
12 TIE A YELLOW RIBBON ROUND THE OLE
OAK TREE   *Dawn*
19 YOU ARE THE SUNSHINE OF MY LIFE
Stevie Wonder
26 FRANKENSTEIN   *Edgar Winter Group*

JUNE

2 MY LOVE   *Paul McCartney and Wings*
9 MY LOVE   *Paul McCartney and Wings*
16 MY LOVE   *Paul McCartney and Wings*
23 MY LOVE   *Paul McCartney and Wings*
30 GIVE ME LOVE GIVE ME PEACE ON
EARTH   *George Harrison*

JULY

7 WILL IT GO ROUND IN CIRCLES
Billy Preston
14 WILL IT GO ROUND IN CIRCLES
Billy Preston
21 BAD BAD LEROY BROWN   *Jim Croce*
28 BAD BAD LEROY BROWN   *Jim Croce*

AUGUST

4 THE MORNING AFTER   *Maureen McGovern*
11 THE MORNING AFTER   *Maureen McGovern*
18 TOUCH ME IN THE MORNING   *Diana Ross*
25 BROTHER LOUIE   *Stories*

SEPTEMBER

1 BROTHER LOUIE   *Stories*
8 LET'S GET IT ON   *Marvin Gaye*
15 DELTA DAWN   *Helen Reddy*
22 LET'S GET IT ON   *Marvin Gaye*
29 WE'RE AN AMERICAN BAND   *Grand Funk*

OCTOBER

6 HALF BREED   *Cher*
13 HALF BREED   *Cher*
20 ANGIE   *Rolling Stones*
27 MIDNIGHT TRAIN TO GEORGIA
Gladys Knight and the Pips

NOVEMBER

3 MIDNIGHT TRAIN TO GEORGIA
Gladys Knight and the Pips
10 KEEP ON TRUCKIN'   *Eddie Kendricks*
17 KEEP ON TRUCKIN'   *Eddie Kendricks*
24 PHOTOGRAPH   *Ringo Starr*

DECEMBER

1 TOP OF THE WORLD
Carpenters
8 TOP OF THE WORLD
Carpenters
15 THE MOST BEAUTIFUL GIRL
Charlie Rich
22 THE MOST BEAUTIFUL GIRL
Charlie Rich
29 TIME IN A BOTTLE   *Jim Croce*

1974

JANUARY

5 TIME IN A BOTTLE   *Jim Croce*
12 THE JOKER   *Steve Miller*
19 SHOW AND TELL   *Al Wilson*
26 YOU'RE SIXTEEN   *Ringo Starr*

FEBRUARY

2 THE WAY WE WERE   *Barbra Streisand*
9 LOVE'S THEME
Love Unlimited Orchestra
16 THE WAY WE WERE   *Barbra Streisand*
23 THE WAY WE WERE   *Barbra Streisand*

MARCH

2 SEASONS IN THE SUN   *Terry Jacks*
9 SEASONS IN THE SUN   *Terry Jacks*
16 SEASONS IN THE SUN   *Terry Jacks*
23 DARK LADY   *Cher*
30 SUNSHINE ON MY SHOULDERS
John Denver

APRIL

6 HOOKED ON A FEELING   *Blue Swede*
13 BENNIE AND THE JETS   *Elton John*
20 THE SOUND OF PHILADELPHIA
MFSB/The Three Degrees
27 THE SOUND OF PHILADELPHIA
MFSB/The Three Degrees

MAY

4 THE LOCO-MOTION *Grand Funk*
11 THE LOCO-MOTION *Grand Funk*
18 THE STREAK *Ray Stevens*
25 THE STREAK *Ray Stevens*

JUNE

1 THE STREAK *Ray Stevens*
8 BAND ON THE RUN
  Paul McCartney and Wings
15 BILLY DON'T BE A HERO
  Bo Donaldson and the Heywoods
22 BILLY DON'T BE A HERO
  Bo Donaldson and the Heywoods
29 SUNDOWN *Gordon Lightfoot*

JULY

6 ROCK THE BOAT *Hues Corporation*
13 ROCK YOUR BABY *George McCrae*
20 ROCK YOUR BABY *George McCrae*
27 ANNIE'S SONG *John Denver*

AUGUST

3 ANNIE'S SONG *John Denver*
10 FEEL LIKE MAKIN' LOVE
  Roberta Flack
17 THE NIGHT CHICAGO DIED
  Paper Lace
24 (YOU'RE) HAVING MY BABY
  Paul Anka with Odia Coates
31 (YOU'RE) HAVING MY BABY
  Paul Anka with Odia Coates

SEPTEMBER

7 (YOU'RE) HAVING MY BABY
  Paul Anka with Odia Coates
14 I SHOT THE SHERIFF *Eric Clapton*
21 CAN'T GET ENOUGH OF YOUR LOVE, BABE
  Barry White
28 ROCK ME GENTLY *Andy Kim*

OCTOBER

5 I HONESTLY LOVE YOU
  Olivia Newton-John
12 I HONESTLY LOVE YOU
  Olivia Newton-John
19 NOTHING FROM NOTHING
  Billy Preston
26 THEN CAME YOU
  Dionne Warwick and the Spinners

NOVEMBER

2 YOU HAVEN'T DONE NOTHIN'
  Stevie Wonder
9 YOU AIN' SEEN NOTHING YET
  Bachman-Turner Overdrive
16 WHATEVER GETS YOU THRU THE NIGHT
  John Lennon
23 I CAN HELP *Billy Swann*
30 I CAN HELP *Billy Swann*

DECEMBER

7 KUNG FU FIGHTING *Carl Douglas*
14 KUNG FU FIGHTING *Carl Douglas*
21 CAT'S IN THE CRADLE *Harry Chapin*
28 ANGIE BABY *Helen Reddy*

1975

JANUARY

4 LUCY IN THE SKY WITH DIAMONDS *Elton John*
11 LUCY IN THE SKY WITH DIAMONDS *Elton John*
18 MANDY *Barry Manilow*
25 PLEASE MR POSTMAN *Carpenters*

FEBRUARY

1 LAUGHTER IN THE RAIN *Neil Sedaka*
8 FIRE *Ohio Players*
15 YOU'RE NO GOOD *Linda Ronstadt*
22 PICK UP THE PIECES *Average White Band*

MARCH

1 BEST OF MY LOVE *Eagles*
8 HAVE YOU NEVER BEEN MELLOW *Olivia Newton-John*
15 BLACK WATER *Doobie Brothers*
22 MY EYES ADORED YOU *Franki Valli*
29 LADY MARMALADE *Labelle*

APRIL

5 LOVIN' YOU *Minnie Ripperton*
12 PHILADELPHIA FREEDOM *Elton John*
19 PHILADELPHIA FREEDOM *Elton John*
26 ANOTHER SOMEBODY DONE SOMEBODY WRONG SONG *B J Thomas*

MAY

3 HE DON'T LOVE YOU (LIKE I LOVE YOU)
  Tony Orlando/Dawn
10 HE DON'T LOVE YOU (LIKE I LOVE YOU)
  Tony Orlando/Dawn
17 HE DON'T LOVE YOU (LIKE I LOVE YOU)
  Tony Orlando/Dawn
24 SHINING STAR *Earth Wind and Fire*
31 BEFORE THE NEXT TEARDROP FALLS *Freddie Fender*

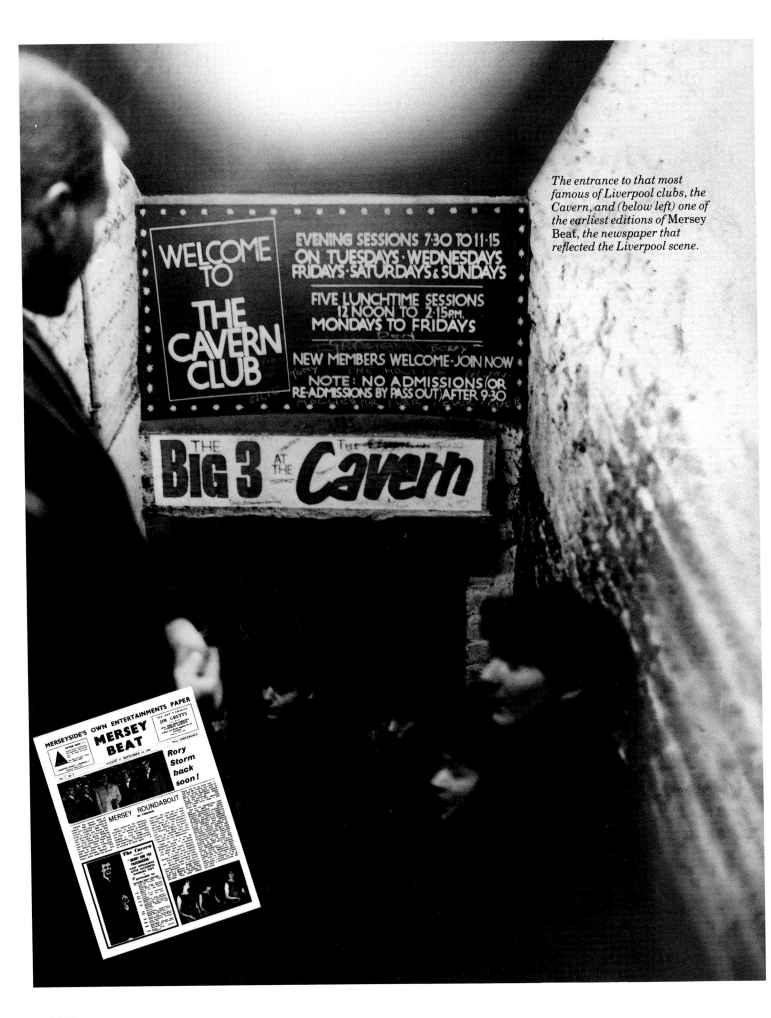

The entrance to that most famous of Liverpool clubs, the Cavern, and (below left) one of the earliest editions of Mersey Beat, the newspaper that reflected the Liverpool scene.

JUNE

7 THANK GOD I'M A COUNTRY BOY *John Denver*
14 SISTER GOLDEN HAIR *America*
21 LOVE WILL KEEP US TOGETHER *Captain and Tennille*
28 LOVE WILL KEEP US TOGETHER *Captain and Tennille*

JULY

5 LOVE WILL KEEP US TOGETHER *Captain and Tennille*
12 LOVE WILL KEEP US TOGETHER *Captain and Tennille*
19 LISTEN TO WHAT THE MAN SAID *Wings*
26 THE HUSTLE *Van McCoy and the Soul City Symphony*

AUGUST

2 ONE OF THESE NIGHTS *Eagles*
9 JIVE TALKIN' *Bee Gees*
16 JIVE TALKIN' *Bee Gees*
23 FALLIN' IN LOVE *Hamilton, Joe Frank and Reynolds*
30 GET DOWN TONIGHT *KC and the Sunshine Band*

SEPTEMBER

6 RHINESTONE COWBOY *Glen Campbell*
13 RHINESTONE COWBOY *Glen Campbell*
20 FAME *David Bowie*
27 I'M SORRY *John Denver*

OCTOBER

4 FAME *David Bowie*
11 BAD BLOOD *Neil Sedaka*
18 BAD BLOOD *Neil Sedaka*
25 BAD BLOOD *Neil Sedaka*

NOVEMBER

1 ISLAND GIRL *Elton John*
8 ISLAND GIRL *Elton John*
15 ISLAND GIRL *Elton John*
22 THAT'S THE WAY I LIKE IT *KC and the Sunshine Band*
29 FLY ROBIN FLY *Silver Convention*

DECEMBER

6 FLY ROBIN FLY *Silver Convention*
13 FLY ROBIN FLY *Silver Convention*
20 THAT'S THE WAY I LIKE IT *KC and the Sunshine Band*
27 LET'S DO IT AGAIN *Staple Singers*

1976

JANUARY

3 SATURDAY NIGHT *Bay City Rollers*
10 CONVOY *CW McCall*
17 I WRITE THE SONGS *Barry Manilow*
24 THEME FROM MAHOGANY *Diana Ross*
31 LOVE ROLLERCOASTER *Ohio Players*

FEBRUARY

7 50 WAYS TO LEAVE YOUR LOVER *Paul Simon*
14 50 WAYS TO LEAVE YOUR LOVER *Paul Simon*
21 50 WAYS TO LEAVE YOUR LOVER *Paul Simon*
28 THEME FROM S.W.A.T. *Rhythm Heritage*

MARCH

6 LOVE MACHINE PT. 1 *Miracles*
13 DECEMBER, '63 (OH, WHAT A NIGHT) *Four Seasons*
20 DECEMBER, '63 (OH, WHAT A NIGHT) *Four Seasons*
27 DECEMBER, '63 (OH, WHAT A NIGHT) *Four Seasons*

APRIL

3 DISCO LADY *Johnny Taylor*
10 DISCO LADY *Johnny Taylor*
17 DISCO LADY *Johnny Taylor*
24 DISCO LADY *Johnny Taylor*

MAY

1 LET YOUR LOVE FLOW *Bellamy Brothers*
8 WELCOME BACK *John Sebastian*
15 BOOGIE FEVER *Sylvers*
22 SILLY LOVE SONGS *Wings*
29 LOVE HANGOVER *Diana Ross*

JUNE

5 LOVE HANGOVER *Diana Ross*
12 SILLY LOVE SONGS *Wings*
19 SILLY LOVE SONGS *Wings*
26 SILLY LOVE SONGS *Wings*

JULY

3 SILLY LOVE SONGS *Wings*
10 AFTERNOON DELIGHT *Starland Vocal Band*
17 AFTERNOON DELIGHT *Starland Vocal Band*
24 KISS AND SAY GOODBYE *Manhattans*
31 KISS AND SAY GOODBYE *Manhattans*

AUGUST

7 DON'T GO BREAKING MY HEART
Elton John and Kiki Dee
14 DON'T GO BREAKING MY HEART
Elton John and Kiki Dee
21 DON'T GO BREAKING MY HEART
Elton John and Kiki Dee
28 DON'T GO BREAKING MY HEART
Elton John and Kiki Dee

SEPTEMBER

4 YOU SHOULD BE DANCING *Bee Gees*
11 (SHAKE, SHAKE, SHAKE) SHAKE YOUR BOOTY
KC and the Sunshine Band
18 PLAY THAT FUNKY MUSIC *Wild Cherry*
25 PLAY THAT FUNKY MUSIC *Wild Cherry*

OCTOBER

2   PLAY THAT FUNKY MUSIC   *Wild Cherry*
9   A FIFTH OF BEETHOVEN
        Walter Murphy/The Big Apple Band
16   DISCO DUCK (PART 1)   *Rick Dees and His Cast of Idiots*
23   IF YOU LEAVE ME NOW   *Chicago*
30   IF YOU LEAVE ME NOW   *Chicago*

NOVEMBER

6   ROCK N' ME   *Steve Miller*
13   TONIGHT'S THE NIGHT (GONNA BE ALRIGHT)
        Rod Stewart
20   TONIGHT'S THE NIGHT (GONNA BE ALRIGHT)
        Rod Stewart
27   TONIGHT'S THE NIGHT (GONNA BE ALRIGHT)
        Rod Stewart

DECEMBER

4   TONIGHT'S THE NIGHT (GONNA BE ALRIGHT)
        Rod Stewart
11   TONIGHT'S THE NIGHT (GONNA BE ALRIGHT)
        Rod Stewart
18   TONIGHT'S THE NIGHT (GONNA BE ALRIGHT)
        Rod Stewart
25   TONIGHT'S THE NIGHT (GONNA BE ALRIGHT)
        Rod Stewart

1977

JANUARY

1   TONIGHT'S THE NIGHT (GONNA BE ALRIGHT)
        Rod Stewart
8   YOU DON'T HAVE TO BE A STAR
        Marilyn McCoo/Billy Davis Jr
15   YOU MAKE ME FEEL LIKE DANCING   *Leo Sayer*
22   I WISH   *Stevie Wonder*
29   CAR WASH   *Rose Royce*

FEBRUARY

5   TORN BETWEEN TWO LOVERS   *Mary MacGregor*
12   TORN BETWEEN TWO LOVERS   *Mary MacGregor*
19   BLINDED BY THE LIGHT   *Manfred Mann's Earth Band*
26   NEW KID IN TOWN   *Eagles*

MARCH

5   LOVE THEME FROM *A STAR IS BORN*   Barbra Streisand
12   LOVE THEME FROM *A STAR IS BORN*   Barbra Streisand
19   LOVE THEME FROM *A STAR IS BORN*   Barbra Streisand
26   RICH GIRL   *Darryl Hall and John Oates*

APRIL

2   RICH GIRL   *Darryl Hall and John Oates*
9   DANCING QUEEN   *Abba*
16   DON'T GIVE UP ON US   *David Soul*
23   DON'T LEAVE ME THIS WAY   *Thelma Houston*
30   SOUTHERN NIGHTS   *Glen Campbell*

MAY

7   HOTEL CALIFORNIA   *Eagles*
14   WHEN I NEED YOU   *Leo Sayer*
21   SIR DUKE   *Stevie Wonder*
28   SIR DUKE   *Stevie Wonder*

JUNE

4   SIR DUKE   *Stevie Wonder*
11   I'M YOUR BOOGIE MAN   *KC and the Sunshine Band*
18   DREAMS   *Fleetwood Mac*
25   GOT TO GIVE IT UP, PART 1   *Marvin Gaye*

JULY

2   GONNA FLY NOW (THEME FROM *ROCKY*)   *Bill Conti*
9   UNDERCOVER ANGEL   *Alan O'Day*
16   DA DOO RON RON   *Shaun Cassidy*
23   LOOKS LIKE WE MADE IT   *Barry Manilow*
30   I JUST WANT TO BE YOUR EVERYTHING   *Andy Gibb*

AUGUST

6   I JUST WANT TO BE YOUR EVERYTHING   *Andy Gibb*
13   I JUST WANT TO BE YOUR EVERYTHING   *Andy Gibb*
20   BEST OF MY LOVE   *Emotions*
27   BEST OF MY LOVE   *Emotions*

SEPTEMBER

3   BEST OF MY LOVE   *Emotions*
10   BEST OF MY LOVE   *Emotions*
17   I JUST WANT TO BE YOUR EVERYTHING   *Andy Gibb*
24   BEST OF MY LOVE   *Emotions*

OCTOBER

1   STAR WARS THEME/CANTINA BAND   *Meco*
8   STAR WARS THEME/CANTINA BAND   *Meco*
15   YOU LIGHT UP MY LIFE   *Debby Boone*
22   YOU LIGHT UP MY LIFE   *Debby Boone*
29   YOU LIGHT UP MY LIFE   *Debby Boone*

NOVEMBER

5   YOU LIGHT UP MY LIFE   *Debby Boone*
12   YOU LIGHT UP MY LIFE   *Debby Boone*
19   YOU LIGHT UP MY LIFE   *Debby Boone*
26   YOU LIGHT UP MY LIFE   *Debby Boone*

DECEMBER

3   YOU LIGHT UP MY LIFE   *Debby Boone*
10   YOU LIGHT UP MY LIFE   *Debby Boone*
17   YOU LIGHT UP MY LIFE   *Debby Boone*
24   HOW DEEP IS YOUR LOVE   *Bee Gees*
31   HOW DEEP IS YOUR LOVE   *Bee Gees*

1978

JANUARY

7 HOW DEEP IS YOUR LOVE   *Bee Gees*
14 BABY COME BACK   *Player*
21 BABY COME BACK   *Player*
28 BABY COME BACK   *Player*

FEBRUARY

4 STAYIN' ALIVE   *Bee Gees*
11 STAYIN' ALIVE   *Bee Gees*
18 STAYIN' ALIVE   *Bee Gees*
25 STAYIN' ALIVE   *Bee Gees*

MARCH

4 (LOVE IS) THICKER THAN WATER   *Andy Gibb*
11 (LOVE IS) THICKER THAN WATER   *Andy Gibb*
18 NIGHT FEVER   *Bee Gees*
25 NIGHT FEVER   *Bee Gees*

APRIL

1 NIGHT FEVER   *Bee Gees*
8 NIGHT FEVER   *Bee Gees*
15 NIGHT FEVER   *Bee Gees*
22 NIGHT FEVER   *Bee Gees*
29 NIGHT FEVER   *Bee Gees*

MAY

6 NIGHT FEVER   *Bee Gees*
13 IF I CAN'T HAVE YOU   *Yvonne Elliman*
20 WITH A LITTLE LUCK   *Wings*
27 WITH A LITTLE LUCK   *Wings*

JUNE

3 TOO MUCH, TOO LITTLE, TOO LATE
   Johnny Mathis/Deniece Williams
10 YOU'RE THE ONE THAT I WANT
   John Travolta/Olivia Newton-John
17 SHADOW DANCING   *Andy Gibb*
24 SHADOW DANCING   *Andy Gibb*

JULY

1 SHADOW DANCING   *Andy Gibb*
8 SHADOW DANCING   *Andy Gibb*
15 SHADOW DANCING   *Andy Gibb*
22 SHADOW DANCING   *Andy Gibb*

AUGUST

5 MISS YOU   *Rolling Stones*
12 THREE TIMES A LADY   *Commodores*
19 THREE TIMES A LADY   *Commodores*
26 GREASE   *Franki Valli*

SEPTEMBER

2 GREASE   *Franki Valli*
9 BOOGIE OOGIE OOGIE   *Taste of Honey*
16 BOOGIE OOGIE OOGIE   *Taste of Honey*

23 BOOGIE OOGIE OOGIE   *Taste of Honey*
30 KISS YOU ALL OVER   *Exile*

OCTOBER

7 KISS YOU ALL OVER   *Exile*
14 KISS YOU ALL OVER   *Exile*
21 KISS YOU ALL OVER   *Exile*
28 HOT CHILD IN THE CITY   *Nick Gilder*

NOVEMBER

4 YOU NEEDED ME   *Anne Murray*
11 MACARTHUR PARK   *Donna Summer*
18 MACARTHUR PARK   *Donna Summer*
25 MACARTHUR PARK   *Donna Summer*

DECEMBER

2 YOU DON'T BRING ME FLOWERS
   Barbra Streisand/Neil Diamond
9 LE FREAK   *Chic*
16 YOU DON'T BRING ME FLOWERS
   Barbra Streisand/Neil Diamond
23 LE FREAK   *Chic*
30 LE FREAK   *Chic*

1979

JANUARY

6 TOO MUCH HEAVEN   *Bee Gees*
13 TOO MUCH HEAVEN   *Bee Gees*
20 LE FREAK   *Chic*
27 LE FREAK   *Chic*

FEBRUARY

3 LE FREAK   *Chic*
10 DO YA THINK I'M SEXY?   *Rod Stewart*
17 DO YA THINK I'M SEXY?   *Rod Stewart*
24 DO YA THINK I'M SEXY?   *Rod Stewart*

MARCH

3 DO YA THINK I'M SEXY?   *Rod Stewart*
10 I WILL SURVIVE   *Gloria Gaynor*
17 I WILL SURVIVE   *Gloria Gaynor*
24 TRAGEDY   *Bee Gees*
31 TRAGEDY   *Bee Gees*

APRIL

7 I WILL SURVIVE   *Gloria Gaynor*
14 WHAT A FOOL BELIEVES   *Doobie Brothers*
21 KNOCK ON WOOD   *Amii Stewart*
28 HEART OF GLASS   *Blondie*

MAY

5 REUNITED   *Peaches and Herb*
12 REUNITED   *Peaches and Herb*
19 REUNITED   *Peaches and Herb*
26 REUNITED   *Peaches and Herb*

JUNE

2 HOT STUFF *Donna Summer*
9 LOVE YOU INSIDE OUT *Bee Gees*
16 HOT STUFF *Donna Summer*
23 HOT STUFF *Donna Summer*
30 RING MY BELL *Anita Ward*

JULY

7 RING MY BELL *Anita Ward*
14 BAD GIRLS *Donna Summer*
21 BAD GIRLS *Donna Summer*
28 BAD GIRLS *Donna Summer*

AUGUST

4 BAD GIRLS *Donna Summer*
11 BAD GIRLS *Donna Summer*
18 GOOD TIMES *Chic*
25 MY SHARONA *Knack*

SEPTEMBER

1 MY SHARONA *Knack*
8 MY SHARONA *Knack*
15 MY SHARONA *Knack*
22 MY SHARONA *Knack*
29 MY SHARONA *Knack*

OCTOBER

6 SAD EYES *Robert John*
13 DON'T STOP 'TIL YOU GET ENOUGH *Michael Jackson*
20 RISE *Herb Alpert*
27 RISE *Herb Alpert*

NOVEMBER

3 POP MUZIC *M*
10 HEARTACHE TONIGHT *Eagles*
17 STILL *Commodores*
24 NO MORE TEARS *Barbra Streisand/Donna Summer*

DECEMBER

1 NO MORE TEARS *Barbra Streisand/Donna Summer*
8 BABE *Styx*
15 BABE *Styx*
22 ESCAPE (THE PINA COLADA SONG) *Rupert Holmes*
29 ESCAPE (THE PINA COLADA SONG) *Rupert Holmes*

1980

JANUARY

5 PLEASE DON'T GO *KC and the Sunshine Band*
12 ESCAPE (THE PINA COLADA SONG) *Rupert Holmes*
19 ROCK WITH YOU *Michael Jackson*
26 ROCK WITH YOU *Michael Jackson*

FEBRUARY

2 ROCK WITH YOU *Michael Jackson*
9 ROCK WITH YOU *Michael Jackson*
16 DO THAT TO ME ONE MORE TIME *Captain and Tennille*
23 CRAZY LITTLE THING CALLED LOVE *Queen*

MARCH

1 CRAZY LITTLE THING CALLED LOVE *Queen*
8 CRAZY LITTLE THING CALLED LOVE *Queen*
15 CRAZY LITTLE THING CALLED LOVE *Queen*
22 ANOTHER BRICK IN THE WALL *Pink Floyd*
29 ANOTHER BRICK IN THE WALL *Pink Floyd*

APRIL

5 ANOTHER BRICK IN THE WALL *Pink Floyd*
12 ANOTHER BRICK IN THE WALL *Pink Floyd*
19 CALL ME *Blondie*
26 CALL ME *Blondie*

MAY

3 CALL ME *Blondie*
10 CALL ME *Blondie*
17 CALL ME *Blondie*
24 CALL ME *Blondie*
31 FUNKYTOWN *Lipps Inc*

JUNE

7 FUNKYTOWN *Lipps Inc*
14 FUNKYTOWN *Lipps Inc*
21 FUNKYTOWN *Lipps Inc*
28 COMING UP *Paul McCartney*

JULY

5 COMING UP *Paul McCartney*
12 COMING UP *Paul McCartney*
19 IT'S STILL ROCK AND ROLL TO ME *Billy Joel*
26 IT'S STILL ROCK AND ROLL TO ME *Billy Joel*

AUGUST

2 MAGIC *Olivia Newton-John*
9 MAGIC *Olivia Newton-John*
16 MAGIC *Olivia Newton-John*
23 MAGIC *Olivia Newton-John*
30 SAILING *Christopher Cross*

SEPTEMBER

6 UPSIDE DOWN *Diana Ross*
13 UPSIDE DOWN *Diana Ross*
20 UPSIDE DOWN *Diana Ross*
27 UPSIDE DOWN *Diana Ross*

OCTOBER

4 ANOTHER ONE BITES THE DUST *Queen*
11 ANOTHER ONE BITES THE DUST *Queen*
18 ANOTHER ONE BITES THE DUST *Queen*
25 WOMAN IN LOVE *Barbra Streisand*

NOVEMBER

1 WOMAN IN LOVE *Barbra Streisand*
8 WOMAN IN LOVE *Barbra Streisand*
15 LADY *Kenny Rogers*
22 LADY *Kenny Rogers*
29 LADY *Kenny Rogers*

DECEMBER

6 LADY *Kenny Rogers*
13 LADY *Kenny Rogers*
20 LADY *Kenny Rogers*
27 (JUST LIKE) STARTING OVER *John Lennon*

1981

JANUARY

3 (JUST LIKE) STARTING OVER *John Lennon*
10 (JUST LIKE) STARTING OVER *John Lennon*
17 (JUST LIKE) STARTING OVER *John Lennon*
24 (JUST LIKE) STARTING OVER *John Lennon*
31 THE TIDE IS HIGH *Blondie*

FEBRUARY

7 CELEBRATION *Kool and the Gang*
14 CELEBRATION *Kool and the Gang*
21 9 TO 5 *Dolly Parton*
28 I LOVE A RAINY NIGHT *Eddie Rabbit*

MARCH

7 I LOVE A RAINY NIGHT *Eddie Rabbit*
14 9 TO 5 *Dolly Parton*
21 KEEP ON LOVING YOU *REO Speedwagon*
28 RAPTURE *Blondie*

APRIL

4 RAPTURE *Blondie*
11 KISS ON MY LIST *Daryl Hall and John Oates*
18 KISS ON MY LIST *Daryl Hall and John Oates*
25 KISS ON MY LIST *Daryl Hall and John Oates*

MAY

2 MORNING TRAIN (NINE TO FIVE) *Sheena Easton*
9 MORNING TRAIN (NINE TO FIVE) *Sheena Easton*
16 BETTE DAVIS EYES *Kim Carnes*
23 BETTE DAVIS EYES *Kim Carnes*
30 BETTE DAVIS EYES *Kim Carnes*

JUNE

6 BETTE DAVIS EYES *Kim Carnes*
13 BETTE DAVIS EYES *Kim Carnes*
20 STARS ON 45 *Stars on 45*
27 BETTE DAVIS EYES *Kim Carnes*

JULY

4 BETTE DAVIS EYES *Kim Carnes*
11 BETTE DAVIS EYES *Kim Carnes*
18 BETTE DAVIS EYES *Kim Carnes*
25 THE ONE THAT YOU LOVE *Air Supply*

AUGUST

1 JESSIE'S GIRL *Rick Springfield*
8 JESSIE'S GIRL *Rick Springfield*
15 ENDLESS LOVE *Diana Ross and Lionel Richie*
22 ENDLESS LOVE *Diana Ross and Lionel Richie*
29 ENDLESS LOVE *Diana Ross and Lionel Richie*

SEPTEMBER

5 ENDLESS LOVE *Diana Ross and Lionel Richie*
12 ENDLESS LOVE *Diana Ross and Lionel Richie*
19 ENDLESS LOVE *Diana Ross and Lionel Richie*
26 ENDLESS LOVE *Diana Ross and Lionel Richie*

OCTOBER

3 ENDLESS LOVE *Diana Ross and Lionel Richie*
10 ENDLESS LOVE *Diana Ross and Lionel Richie*
17 ARTHUR'S THEME (BEST THAT YOU CAN DO)
    Christopher Cross
24 ARTHUR'S THEME (BEST THAT YOU CAN DO)
    Christopher Cross
31 ARTHUR'S THEME (BEST THAT YOU CAN DO)
    Christopher Cross

NOVEMBER

7 PRIVATE EYES *Daryl Hall and John Oates*
14 PRIVATE EYES *Daryl Hall and John Oates*
21 PHYSICAL *Olivia Newton-John*
28 PHYSICAL *Olivia Newton-John*

DECEMBER

5 PHYSICAL *Olivia Newton-John*
12 PHYSICAL *Olivia Newton-John*
19 PHYSICAL *Olivia Newton-John*
26 PHYSICAL *Olivia Newton-John*

1982

JANUARY

2 PHYSICAL *Olivia Newton-John*
9 PHYSICAL *Olivia Newton-John*
16 PHYSICAL *Olivia Newton-John*
23 PHYSICAL *Olivia Newton-John*
30 I CAN'T GO FOR THAT (NO CAN DO)
    Daryl Hall and John Oates

FEBRUARY

6 CENTERFOLD *J. Geils Band*
13 CENTERFOLD *J. Geils Band*
20 CENTERFOLD *J. Geils Band*
27 CENTERFOLD *J. Geils Band*

MARCH

6	CENTERFOLD	*J. Geils Band*
13	CENTERFOLD	*J. Geils Band*
20	I LOVE ROCK 'N' ROLL	*Joan Jett and the Blackhearts*
27	I LOVE ROCK 'N' ROLL	*Joan Jett and the Blackhearts*

APRIL

3	I LOVE ROCK 'N' ROLL	*Joan Jett and the Blackhearts*
10	I LOVE ROCK 'N' ROLL	*Joan Jett and the Blackhearts*
17	I LOVE ROCK 'N' ROLL	*Joan Jett and the Blackhearts*
24	I LOVE ROCK 'N' ROLL	*Joan Jett and the Blackhearts*

MAY

1	I LOVE ROCK 'N' ROLL	*Joan Jett and the Blackhearts*
8	CHARIOTS OF FIRE	*Vangelis*
15	EBONY AND IVORY	*Paul McCartney and Stevie Wonder*
22	EBONY AND IVORY	*Paul McCartney and Stevie Wonder*
29	EBONY AND IVORY	*Paul McCartney and Stevie Wonder*

JUNE

5	EBONY AND IVORY	*Paul McCartney and Stevie Wonder*
12	EBONY AND IVORY	*Paul McCartney and Stevie Wonder*
19	EBONY AND IVORY	*Paul McCartney and Stevie Wonder*
26	EBONY AND IVORY	*Paul McCartney and Stevie Wonder*

JULY

3	DON'T YOU WANT ME	*Human League*
10	DON'T YOU WANT ME	*Human League*
17	DON'T YOU WANT ME	*Human League*
24	EYE OF THE TIGER	*Survivor*
31	EYE OF THE TIGER	*Survivor*

AUGUST

7	EYE OF THE TIGER	*Survivor*
14	EYE OF THE TIGER	*Survivor*
21	EYE OF THE TIGER	*Survivor*
28	EYE OF THE TIGER	*Survivor*

SEPTEMBER

4	ABRACADABRA	*Steve Miller Band*
11	HARD TO SAY I'M SORRY	*Chicago*
18	HARD TO SAY I'M SORRY	*Chicago*
25	ABRACADABRA	*Steve Miller Band*

OCTOBER

2	JACK AND DIANE	*John Cougar*
9	JACK AND DIANE	*John Cougar*
16	JACK AND DIANE	*John Cougar*
23	JACK AND DIANE	*John Cougar*
30	WHO CAN IT BE NOW	*Men At Work*

NOVEMBER

6	UP WHERE WE BELONG	*Joe Cocker and Jennifer Warnes*
13	UP WHERE WE BELONG	*Joe Cocker and Jennifer Warnes*
20	UP WHERE WE BELONG	*Joe Cocker and Jennifer Warnes*
27	TRULY	*Lionel Richie*

DECEMBER

4	TRULY	*Lionel Richie*
11	MICKEY	*Toni Basil*
18	MANEATER	*Daryl Hall and John Oates*
25	MANEATER	*Daryl Hall and John Oates*

1983

JANUARY

1	MANEATER	*Daryl Hall and John Oates*
8	MANEATER	*Daryl Hall and John Oates*
15	DOWN UNDER	*Men At Work*
22	DOWN UNDER	*Men At Work*
29	DOWN UNDER	*Men At Work*

FEBRUARY

5	AFRICA	*Toto*
12	DOWN UNDER	*Men At Work*
19	BABY, COME TO ME	*Patti Austin and James Ingram*
26	BABY, COME TO ME	*Patti Austin and James Ingram*

MARCH

5	BILLIE JEAN	*Michael Jackson*
12	BILLIE JEAN	*Michael Jackson*
19	BILLIE JEAN	*Michael Jackson*
26	BILLIE JEAN	*Michael Jackson*

APRIL

2	BILLIE JEAN	*Michael Jackson*
9	BILLIE JEAN	*Michael Jackson*
16	BILLIE JEAN	*Michael Jackson*
23	COME ON EILEEN	*Dexy's Midnight Runners*
30	BEAT IT	*Michael Jackson*

MAY

7	BEAT IT	*Michael Jackson*
14	BEAT IT	*Michael Jackson*
21	LET'S DANCE	*David Bowie*
28	FLASHDANCE . . . WHAT A FEELING	*Irene Cara*

JUNE

4	FLASHDANCE . . . WHAT A FEELING	*Irene Cara*
11	FLASHDANCE . . . WHAT A FEELING	*Irene Cara*
18	FLASHDANCE . . . WHAT A FEELING	*Irene Cara*
25	FLASHDANCE . . . WHAT A FEELING	*Irene Cara*

JULY

2	FLASHDANCE . . . WHAT A FEELING	*Irene Cara*
9	EVERY BREATH YOU TAKE	*Police*
16	EVERY BREATH YOU TAKE	*Police*
23	EVERY BREATH YOU TAKE	*Police*
30	EVERY BREATH YOU TAKE	*Police*

AUGUST

6 EVERY BREATH YOU TAKE *Police*
13 EVERY BREATH YOU TAKE *Police*
20 EVERY BREATH YOU TAKE *Police*
27 EVERY BREATH YOU TAKE *Police*

SEPTEMBER

3 SWEET DREAMS (ARE MADE OF THIS) *Eurythmics*
10 MANIAC *Michael Sembello*
17 MANIAC *Michael Sembello*
24 TELL HER ABOUT IT *Billy Joel*

OCTOBER

1 TOTAL ECLIPSE OF THE HEART *Bonnie Tyler*
8 TOTAL ECLIPSE OF THE HEART *Bonnie Tyler*
15 TOTAL ECLIPSE OF THE HEART *Bonnie Tyler*
22 TOTAL ECLIPSE OF THE HEART *Bonnie Tyler*
29 ISLANDS IN THE STREAM
   Kenny Rogers and Dolly Parton

NOVEMBER

5 ISLANDS IN THE STREAM
   Kenny Rogers and Dolly Parton
12 ALL NIGHT LONG (ALL NIGHT) *Lionel Richie*
19 ALL NIGHT LONG (ALL NIGHT) *Lionel Richie*
26 ALL NIGHT LONG (ALL NIGHT) *Lionel Richie*

DECEMBER

3 ALL NIGHT LONG (ALL NIGHT) *Lionel Richie*
10 SAY, SAY, SAY *Paul McCartney and Michael Jackson*
17 SAY, SAY, SAY *Paul McCartney and Michael Jackson*
24 SAY, SAY, SAY *Paul McCartney and Michael Jackson*
31 SAY, SAY, SAY *Paul McCartney and Michael Jackson*

1984

JANUARY

7 SAY, SAY, SAY *Paul McCartney and Michael Jackson*
14 SAY, SAY, SAY *Paul McCartney and Michael Jackson*
21 OWNER OF A LONELY HEART *Yes*
28 OWNER OF A LONELY HEART *Yes*

FEBRUARY

4 KARMA CHAMELEON *Culture Club*
11 KARMA CHAMELEON *Culture Club*
18 KARMA CHAMELEON *Culture Club*
25 JUMP *Van Halen*

MARCH

3 JUMP *Van Halen*
10 JUMP *Van Halen*
17 JUMP *Van Halen*
24 JUMP *Van Halen*
31 FOOTLOOSE *Kenny Loggins*

APRIL

7 FOOTLOOSE *Kenny Loggins*
14 FOOTLOOSE *Kenny Loggins*
21 AGAINST ALL ODDS (TAKE A LOOK AT ME NOW)
   Phil Collins
28 AGAINST ALL ODDS (TAKE A LOOK AT ME NOW)
   Phil Collins

MAY

5 AGAINST ALL ODDS (TAKE A LOOK AT ME NOW)
   Phil Collins
12 HELLO *Lionel Richie*
19 HELLO *Lionel Richie*
26 LET'S HEAR IT FOR THE BOY *Deniece Williams*

JUNE

2 LET'S HEAR IT FOR THE BOY *Deniece Williams*
9 TIME AFTER TIME *Cyndi Lauper*
16 TIME AFTER TIME *Cyndi Lauper*
23 THE REFLEX *Duran Duran*
30 THE REFLEX *Duran Duran*

JULY

7 WHEN DOVES CRY *Prince*
14 WHEN DOVES CRY *Prince*
21 WHEN DOVES CRY *Prince*
28 WHEN DOVES CRY *Prince*

AUGUST

4 WHEN DOVES CRY *Prince*
11 GHOSTBUSTERS *Ray Parker Jr*
18 GHOSTBUSTERS *Ray Parker Jr*
25 GHOSTBUSTERS *Ray Parker Jr*

SEPTEMBER

1 WHAT'S LOVE GOT TO DO WITH IT *Tina Turner*
8 WHAT'S LOVE GOT TO DO WITH IT *Tina Turner*
15 WHAT'S LOVE GOT TO DO WITH IT *Tina Turner*
22 MISSING YOU *John Waite*
29 LET'S GO CRAZY *Prince*

OCTOBER

6 LET'S GO CRAZY *Prince*
13 I JUST CALLED TO SAY I LOVE YOU *Stevie Wonder*
20 I JUST CALLED TO SAY I LOVE YOU *Stevie Wonder*
27 I JUST CALLED TO SAY I LOVE YOU *Stevie Wonder*

NOVEMBER

3 CARIBBEAN QUEEN (NO MORE LOVE ON THE RUN)
   Billy Ocean
10 CARIBBEAN QUEEN (NO MORE LOVE ON THE RUN)
   Billy Ocean
17 WAKE ME UP BEFORE YOU GO GO *Wham!*
24 WAKE ME UP BEFORE YOU GO GO *Wham!*

DECEMBER

1	WAKE ME UP BEFORE YOU GO GO	*Wham!*
8	OUT OF TOUCH	*Daryl Hall and John Oates*
15	OUT OF TOUCH	*Daryl Hall and John Oates*
22	LIKE A VIRGIN	*Madonna*
29	LIKE A VIRGIN	*Madonna*

1985

JANUARY

5	LIKE A VIRGIN	*Madonna*
12	LIKE A VIRGIN	*Madonna*
19	LIKE A VIRGIN	*Madonna*
26	LIKE A VIRGIN	*Madonna*

FEBRUARY

2	I WANT TO KNOW WHAT LOVE IS	*Foreigner*
9	I WANT TO KNOW WHAT LOVE IS	*Foreigner*
16	CARELESS WHISPER	*George Michael*
23	CARELESS WHISPER	*George Michael*

MARCH

2	CARELESS WHISPER	*George Michael*
9	CAN'T FIGHT THIS FEELING	*REO Speedwagon*
16	CAN'T FIGHT THIS FEELING	*REO Speedwagon*
23	CAN'T FIGHT THIS FEELING	*REO Speedwagon*
30	ONE MORE NIGHT	*Phil Collins*

APRIL

6	ONE MORE NIGHT	*Phil Collins*
13	WE ARE THE WORLD	*USA for Africa*
20	WE ARE THE WORLD	*USA for Africa*
27	WE ARE THE WORLD	*USA for Africa*

MAY

4	WE ARE THE WORLD	*USA for Africa*
11	CRAZY FOR YOU	*Madonna*
18	DON'T YOU (FORGET ABOUT ME)	*Simple Minds*
25	EVERYTHING SHE WANTS	*Wham!*

JUNE

1	EVERYTHING SHE WANTS	*Wham!*
8	EVERYBODY WANTS TO RULE THE WORLD	
	Tears for Fears	
15	EVERYBODY WANTS TO RULE THE WORLD	
	Tears for Fears	
22	HEAVEN	*Bryan Adams*
29	HEAVEN	*Bryan Adams*

JULY

6	SUSSUDIO	*Phil Collins*
13	A VIEW TO KILL	*Duran Duran*
20	A VIEW TO KILL	*Duran Duran*
27	EVERY TIME YOU GO AWAY	*Paul Young*

AUGUST

3	SHOUT	*Tears for Fears*
10	SHOUT	*Tears for Fears*
17	SHOUT	*Tears for Fears*
24	POWER OF LOVE	*Huey Lewis and the News*
31	POWER OF LOVE	*Huey Lewis and the News*

SEPTEMBER

7	ST. ELMO'S FIRE (MAN IN MOTION)	*John Parr*
14	ST. ELMO'S FIRE (MAN IN MOTION)	*John Parr*
21	MONEY FOR NOTHING	*Dire Straits*
28	MONEY FOR NOTHING	*Dire Straits*

OCTOBER

5	MONEY FOR NOTHING	*Dire Straits*
12	OH SHEILA	*Ready for the World*
19	TAKE ON ME	*A-Ha*
26	SAVING ALL MY LOVE FOR YOU	*Whitney Houston*

NOVEMBER

2	PART-TIME LOVER	*Stevie Wonder*
9	MIAMI VICE THEME	*Jan Hammer*
16	WE BUILT THIS CITY	*Starship*
23	WE BUILT THIS CITY	*Starship*
30	SEPARATE LIVES	*Phil Collins and Marilyn Martin*

DECEMBER

7	BROKEN WINGS	*Mr Mister*
14	BROKEN WINGS	*Mr Mister*
21	SAY YOU, SAY ME	*Lionel Richie*
28	SAY YOU, SAY ME	*Lionel Richie*

1986

JANUARY

4	SAY YOU, SAY ME	*Lionel Richie*
11	SAY YOU, SAY ME	*Lionel Richie*
18	THAT'S WHAT FRIENDS ARE FOR	
	Dionne Warwick and Friends	
25	THAT'S WHAT FRIENDS ARE FOR	
	Dionne Warwick and Friends	

FEBRUARY

1	THAT'S WHAT FRIENDS ARE FOR	
	Dionne Warwick and Friends	
8	THAT'S WHAT FRIENDS ARE FOR	
	Dionne Warwick and Friends	
15	HOW WILL I KNOW	*Whitney Houston*
22	HOW WILL I KNOW	*Whitney Houston*

MARCH

1	KYRIE	*Mr Mister*
8	KYRIE	*Mr Mister*
15	SARA	*Starship*
22	THESE DREAMS	*Heart*
29	ROCK ME AMADEUS	*Falco*

APRIL

5 ROCK ME AMADEUS *Falco*
12 ROCK ME AMADEUS *Falco*
19 KISS *Prince*
26 KISS *Prince*

MAY

3 ADDICTED TO LOVE *Robert Palmer*
10 WEST END GIRLS *Pet Shop Boys*
17 THE GREATEST LOVE OF ALL *Whitney Houston*
24 THE GREATEST LOVE OF ALL *Whitney Houston*
31 THE GREATEST LOVE OF ALL *Whitney Houston*

JUNE

7 LIVE TO TELL *Madonna*
14 ON MY OWN *Patti LaBelle and Michael McDonald*
21 ON MY OWN *Patti LaBelle and Michael McDonald*
28 ON MY OWN *Patti LaBelle and Michael McDonald*

JULY

5 THERE'LL BE SAD SONGS *Billy Ocean*
12 HOLDING BACK THE YEARS *Simply Red*
19 INVISIBLE TOUCH *Genesis*
26 SLEDGEHAMMER *Peter Gabriel*

AUGUST

2 GLORY OF LOVE *Peter Cetera*
9 GLORY OF LOVE *Peter Cetera*
16 PAPA DON'T PREACH *Madonna*
23 PAPA DON'T PREACH *Madonna*
30 HIGHER LOVE *Steve Winwood*

SEPTEMBER

6 VENUS *Bananarama*
13 TAKE MY BREATH AWAY *Berlin*
20 STUCK WITH YOU *Huey Lewis and the News*
27 STUCK WITH YOU *Huey Lewis and the News*

OCTOBER

4 STUCK WITH YOU *Huey Lewis and the News*
11 WHEN I THINK OF YOU *Janet Jackson*
18 WHEN I THINK OF YOU *Janet Jackson*
25 TRUE COLOURS *Cyndi Lauper*

NOVEMBER

1 TRUE COLOURS *Cyndi Lauper*
8 AMANDA *Boston*
15 AMANDA *Boston*
22 HUMAN *Human League*
29 YOU GIVE LOVE A BAD NAME *Bon Jovi*

DECEMBER

6 THE NEXT TIME I FALL *Peter Cetera and Amy Grant*
13 THE WAY IT IS *Bruce Hornsby and the Range*
20 WALK LIKE AN EGYPTIAN *Bangles*
27 WALK LIKE AN EGYPTIAN *Bangles*

1987

JANUARY

3 WALK LIKE AN EGYPTIAN *Bangles*
10 WALK LIKE AN EGYPTIAN *Bangles*
17 SHAKE YOU DOWN *Gregory Abbott*
24 AT THIS MOMENT *Billy Vera & The Beaters*
31 AT THIS MOMENT *Billy Vera & The Beaters*

FEBRUARY

7 OPEN YOUR HEART *Madonna*
14 LIVIN' ON A PRAYER *Bon Jovi*
21 LIVIN' ON A PRAYER *Bon Jovi*
28 LIVIN' ON A PRAYER *Bon Jovi*

MARCH

7 LIVIN' ON A PRAYER *Bon Jovi*
14 JACOB'S LADDER *Huey Lewis and The News*
21 LEAN ON ME *Club Nouveau*
28 LEAN ON ME *Club Nouveau*

APRIL

4 NOTHING'S GONNA STOP US NOW *Starship*
11 NOTHING'S GONNA STOP US NOW *Starship*
18 I KNEW YOU WERE WAITING
   Aretha Franklin/George Michael
25 I KNEW YOU WERE WAITING
   Aretha Franklin/George Michael

MAY

2 (I JUST) DIED IN YOUR ARMS *Cutting Crew*
9 (I JUST) DIED IN YOUR ARMS *Cutting Crew*
16 WITH·OR WITHOUT YOU *U2*
23 WITH OR WITHOUT YOU *U2*
30 WITH OR WITHOUT YOU *U2*

JUNE

6 YOU KEEP ME HANGIN' ON *Kim Wilde*
13 ALWAYS *Atlantic Starr*
20 HEAD TO TOE *Lisa Lisa/Cult Jam*
27 I WANNA DANCE WITH SOMEBODY *Whitney Houston*

JULY

6 I WANNA DANCE WITH SOMEBODY *Whitney Houston*
11 ALONE *Heart*
18 ALONE *Heart*
25 ALONE *Heart*

AUGUST

1 SHAKEDOWN *Bob Seger*
8 I STILL HAVEN'T FOUND WHAT I'M LOOKING FOR *U2*
15 I STILL HAVEN'T FOUND WHAT I'M LOOKING FOR *U2*
22 WHO'S THAT GIRL *Madonna*
29 LA BAMBA *Los Lobos*

SEPTEMBER

5	LA BAMBA	*Los Lobos*
12	LA BAMBA	*Los Lobos*
19	I JUST CAN'T STOP LOVING YOU	*Michael Jackson*
26	DIDN'T WE ALMOST HAVE IT ALL	*Whitney Houston*

OCTOBER

3	DIDN'T WE ALMOST HAVE IT ALL	*Whitney Houston*
10	HERE I GO AGAIN	*Whitesnake*
17	LOST IN EMOTION	*Lisa Lisa/Cult Jam*
24	BAD	*Michael Jackson*
31	BAD	*Michael Jackson*

NOVEMBER

7	I THINK WE'RE ALONE NOW	*Tiffany*
14	I THINK WE'RE ALONE NOW	*Tiffany*
21	MONY MONY	*Billy Idol*
28	(I'VE HAD) THE TIME OF MY LIFE	
	Bill Medley/Jennifer Warnes	

DECEMBER

5	HEAVEN IS A PLACE ON EARTH	*Belinda Carlisle*
12	FAITH	*George Michael*
19	FAITH	*George Michael*
26	FAITH	*George Michael*

1988

JANUARY

2	FAITH	*George Michael*
9	SO EMOTIONAL	*Whitney Houston*
16	GOT MY MIND SET ON YOU	*George Harrison*
23	THE WAY YOU MAKE ME FEEL	*Michael Jackson*
30	NEED YOU TONIGHT	*Inxs*

FEBRUARY

6	COULD'VE BEEN	*Tiffany*
13	COULD'VE BEEN	*Tiffany*
20	SEASONS CHANGE	*Expose*
27	FATHER FIGURE	*George Michael*

MARCH

5	FATHER FIGURE	*George Michael*
12	NEVER GONNA GIVE YOU UP	*Rick Astley*
19	NEVER GONNA GIVE YOU UP	*Rick Astley*
26	MAN IN THE MIRROR	*Michael Jackson*

APRIL

2	MAN IN THE MIRROR	*Michael Jackson*
9	GET OUTTA MY DREAMS, GET INTO MY CAR	
	Billy Ocean	
16	GET OUTTA MY DREAMS, GET INTO MY CAR	
	Billy Ocean	
23	WHERE DO BROKEN HEARTS GO	*Whitney Houston*
30	WHERE DO BROKEN HEARTS GO	*Whitney Houston*

MAY

7	WISHING WELL	*Terence Trent d'Arby*
14	ANYTHING FOR YOU	
	Gloria Estefan/Miami Sound Machine	
21	ANYTHING FOR YOU	
	Gloria Estefan/Miami Sound Machine	
28	ONE MORE TRY	*George Michael*

JUNE

4	ONE MORE TRY	*George Michael*
11	ONE MORE TRY	*George Michael*
18	TOGETHER FOREVER	*Rick Astley*
25	FOOLISH BEAT	*Debbie Gibson*

JULY

2	DIRTY DIANA	*Michael Jackson*
9	THE FLAME	*Cheap Trick*
16	THE FLAME	*Cheap Trick*
23	HOLD ON TO THE NIGHTS	*Richard Marx*
30	ROLL WITH IT	*Steve Winwood*

AUGUST

6	ROLL WITH IT	*Steve Winwood*
13	ROLL WITH IT	*Steve Winwood*
20	ROLL WITH IT	*Steve Winwood*
27	MONKEY	*George Michael*

SEPTEMBER

3	MONKEY	*George Michael*
10	SWEET CHILD O' MINE	*Guns'n'Roses*
17	SWEET CHILD O' MINE	*Guns'n'Roses*
24	DON'T WORRY, BE HAPPY	*Bobby McFerrin*

OCTOBER

1	DON'T WORRY, BE HAPPY	*Bobby McFerrin*
8	LOVE BITES	*Def Leppard*
15	RED RED WINE	*UB40*
22	GROOVY KIND OF LOVE	*Phil Collins*
29	GROOVY KIND OF LOVE	*Phil Collins*

NOVEMBER

5	KOKOMO	*The Beach Boys*
12	WILD WILD WEST	*Escape Club*
19	BAD MEDICINE	*Bon Jovi*
26	BAD MEDICINE	*Bon Jovi*

DECEMBER

3	BABY I LOVE YOUR WAY	*Will To Power*
10	LOOK AWAY	*Chicago*
17	LOOK AWAY	*Chicago*
24	EVERY ROSE HAS ITS THORN	*Poison*
31	EVERY ROSE HAS ITS THORN	*Poison*

1989

JANUARY

7   EVERY ROSE HAS ITS THORN   *Poison*
14 MY PREROGATIVE   *Bobby Brown*
21 TWO HEARTS   *Phil Collins*
28 TWO HEARTS   *Phil Collins*

FEBRUARY

4   WHEN I'M WITH YOU   *Sheriff*
11 STRAIGHT UP   *Paula Abdul*
18 STRAIGHT UP   *Paula Abdul*
25 STRAIGHT UP   *Paula Abdul*

MARCH

4   LOST IN YOUR EYES   *Debbie Gibson*
11 LOST IN YOUR EYES   *Debbie Gibson*
18 LOST IN YOUR EYES   *Debbie Gibson*
25 THE LIVING YEARS   *Mike and the Mechanics*

APRIL

1   ETERNAL FLAME   *The Bangles*
8   THE LOOK   *Roxette*
15 SHE DRIVES ME CRAZY   *Fine Young Cannibals*
22 LIKE A PRAYER   *Madonna*
29 LIKE A PRAYER   *Madonna*

MAY

6   LIKE A PRAYER   *Madonna*
13 I'LL BE THERE FOR YOU   *Bon Jovi*
20 FOREVER YOUR GIRL   *Paula Abdul*
27 FOREVER YOUR GIRL   *Paula Abdul*

JUNE

3   ROCK ON   *Michael Damian*
10 WIND BENEATH MY WINGS   *Bette Midler*
17 I'LL BE LOVING YOU (FOREVER)
       New Kids On The Block
24 SATISFIED   *Richard Marx*

JULY

1   BABY DON'T FORGET MY NUMBER   *Milli Vanilli*
8   GOOD THING   *Fine Young Cannibals*
15 IF YOU DON'T KNOW ME BY NOW   *Simply Red*
22 TOY SOLDIERS   *Martika*
29 TOY SOLDIERS   *Martika*

AUGUST

5   BATDANCE   *Prince*
12 RIGHT HERE WAITING   *Richard Marx*
19 RIGHT HERE WAITING   *Richard Marx*
26 RIGHT HERE WAITING   *Richard Marx*

SEPTEMBER

2   COLD HEARTED   *Paula Abdul*
9   HANGIN' TOUGH   *New Kids On The Block*
16 HANGIN' TOUGH   *New Kids On The Block*
23 GIRL YOU KNOW IT'S TRUE   *Milli Vanilli*
30 GIRL YOU KNOW IT'S TRUE   *Milli Vanilli*

OCTOBER

7   FOREVER YOUR GIRL   *Paula Abdul*
14 DR FEELGOOD   *Motley Crue*
21 MISS YOU MUCH   *Janet Jackson*
28 MISS YOU MUCH   *Janet Jackson*

NOVEMBER

4   LISTEN TO YOUR HEART   *Roxette*
11 WHEN I SEE YOU SMILE   *Bad English*
18 WHEN I SEE YOU SMILE   *Bad English*
25 BLAME IT ON THE RAIN   *Milli Vanilli*

DECEMBER

2   BLAME IT ON THE RAIN   *Milli Vanilli*
9   BLAME IT ON THE RAIN   *Milli Vanilli*
16 WE DIDN'T START THE FIRE   *Billy Joel*
23 ANOTHER DAY IN PARADISE   *Phil Collins*

U.K. HIT SINGLES

1955

JANUARY

1 LET'S HAVE ANOTHER PARTY   *Winifred Atwell*
8 FINGER OF SUSPICION   *Dickie Valentine*
15 MAMBO ITALIANO   *Rosemary Clooney*
22 FINGER OF SUSPICION   *Dickie Valentine*
29 FINGER OF SUSPICION   *Dickie Valentine*

FEBRUARY

5 MAMBO ITALIANO   *Rosemary Clooney*
12 MAMBO ITALIANO   *Rosemary Clooney*
19 SOFTLY SOFTLY   *Ruby Murray*
26 SOFTLY SOFTLY   *Ruby Murray*

MARCH

5 SOFTLY SOFTLY   *Ruby Murray*
12 GIVE ME YOUR WORD   *Tennessee Ernie Ford*
19 GIVE ME YOUR WORD   *Tennessee Ernie Ford*
26 GIVE ME YOUR WORD   *Tennessee Ernie Ford*

APRIL

2 GIVE ME YOUR WORD   *Tennessee Ernie Ford*
9 GIVE ME YOUR WORD   *Tennessee Ernie Ford*
16 GIVE ME YOUR WORD   *Tennessee Ernie Ford*
23 GIVE ME YOUR WORD   *Tennessee Ernie Ford*
30 CHERRY PINK AND APPLE BLOSSOM WHITE
   Eddie Calvert

MAY

7 CHERRY PINK AND APPLE BLOSSOM WHITE
   Eddie Calvert
14 STRANGER IN PARADISE   *Tony Bennett*
21 STRANGER IN PARADISE   *Tony Bennett*
28 CHERRY PINK AND APPLE BLOSSOM WHITE
   Eddie Calvert

JUNE

4 CHERRY PINK AND APPLE BLOSSOM WHITE
   Eddie Calvert
11 CHERRY PINK AND APPLE BLOSSOM WHITE
   Eddie Calvert
18 CHERRY PINK AND APPLE BLOSSOM WHITE
   Eddie Calvert
25 UNCHAINED MELODY   *Jimmy Young*

JULY

2 UNCHAINED MELODY   *Jimmy Young*
9 UNCHAINED MELODY   *Jimmy Young*
16 DREAMBOAT   *Alma Cogan*
23 DREAMBOAT   *Alma Cogan*
30 ROSE MARIE   *Slim Whitman*

AUGUST

6 ROSE MARIE   *Slim Whitman*
13 ROSE MARIE   *Slim Whitman*
20 ROSE MARIE   *Slim Whitman*
27 ROSE MARIE   *Slim Whitman*

SEPTEMBER

3 ROSE MARIE   *Slim Whitman*
10 ROSE MARIE   *Slim Whitman*
17 ROSE MARIE   *Slim Whitman*
24 ROSE MARIE   *Slim Whitman*

OCTOBER

1 ROSE MARIE   *Slim Whitman*
8 ROSE MARIE   *Slim Whitman*
15 THE MAN FROM LARAMIE   *Jimmy Young*
22 THE MAN FROM LARAMIE   *Jimmy Young*
29 THE MAN FROM LARAMIE   *Jimmy Young*

NOVEMBER

5 THE MAN FROM LARAMIE   *Jimmy Young*
12 HERNANDO'S HIDEAWAY   *Johnston Brothers*
19 HERNANDO'S HIDEAWAY   *Johnston Brothers*
26 ROCK AROUND THE CLOCK
   Bill Haley and the Comets

DECEMBER

3 ROCK AROUND THE CLOCK
   Bill Haley and the Comets
10 ROCK AROUND THE CLOCK
   Bill Haley and the Comets
17 CHRISTMAS ALPHABET   *Dickie Valentine*
24 CHRISTMAS ALPHABET   *Dickie Valentine*
31 CHRISTMAS ALPHABET   *Dickie Valentine*

1956

JANUARY

7 ROCK AROUND THE CLOCK
  Bill Haley and the Comets
14 ROCK AROUND THE CLOCK
  Bill Haley and the Comets
21 SIXTEEN TONS *Tennessee Ernie Ford*
28 SIXTEEN TONS *Tennessee Ernie Ford*

FEBRUARY

4 SIXTEEN TONS *Tennessee Ernie Ford*
11 SIXTEEN TONS *Tennessee Ernie Ford*
18 MEMORIES ARE MADE OF THIS *Dean Martin*
25 MEMORIES ARE MADE OF THIS *Dean Martin*

MARCH

3 MEMORIES ARE MADE OF THIS *Dean Martin*
10 MEMORIES ARE MADE OF THIS *Dean Martin*
17 IT'S ALMOST TOMORROW *Dreamweavers*
24 IT'S ALMOST TOMORROW *Dreamweavers*
31 ROCK AND ROLL WALTZ *Kay Starr*

APRIL

7 IT'S ALMOST TOMORROW *Dreamweavers*
14 POOR PEOPLE OF PARIS *Winifred Atwell*
21 POOR PEOPLE OF PARIS *Winifred Atwell*
28 POOR PEOPLE OF PARIS *Winifred Atwell*

MAY

5 NO OTHER LOVE *Ronnie Hilton*
12 NO OTHER LOVE *Ronnie Hilton*
19 NO OTHER LOVE *Ronnie Hilton*
26 NO OTHER LOVE *Ronnie Hilton*

JUNE

2 NO OTHER LOVE *Ronnie Hilton*
9 NO OTHER LOVE *Ronnie Hilton*
16 I'LL BE HOME *Pat Boone*
23 I'LL BE HOME *Pat Boone*
30 I'LL BE HOME *Pat Boone*

JULY

7 I'LL BE HOME *Pat Boone*
14 I'LL BE HOME *Pat Boone*
21 WHY DO FOOLS FALL IN LOVE
  Teenagers Frankie Lymon
28 WHY DO FOOLS FALL IN LOVE
  Teenagers Frankie Lymon

AUGUST

4 WHY DO FOOLS FALL IN LOVE
  Teenagers Frankie Lymon
11 WHATEVER WILL BE WILL BE *Doris Day*
18 WHATEVER WILL BE WILL BE *Doris Day*
25 WHATEVER WILL BE WILL BE *Doris Day*

SEPTEMBER

1 WHATEVER WILL BE WILL BE *Doris Day*
8 WHATEVER WILL BE WILL BE *Doris Day*
15 WHATEVER WILL BE WILL BE *Doris Day*
22 LAY DOWN YOUR ARMS *Anne Shelton*
29 LAY DOWN YOUR ARMS *Anne Shelton*

OCTOBER

6 LAY DOWN YOUR ARMS *Anne Shelton*
13 LAY DOWN YOUR ARMS *Anne Shelton*
20 A WOMAN IN LOVE *Frankie Laine*
27 A WOMAN IN LOVE *Frankie Laine*

NOVEMBER

3 A WOMAN IN LOVE *Frankie Laine*
10 A WOMAN IN LOVE *Frankie Laine*
17 JUST WALKIN' IN THE RAIN *Johnnie Ray*
24 JUST WALKIN' IN THE RAIN *Johnnie Ray*

DECEMBER

1 JUST WALKIN' IN THE RAIN *Johnnie Ray*
8 JUST WALKIN' IN THE RAIN *Johnnie Ray*
15 JUST WALKIN' IN THE RAIN *Johnnie Ray*
22 JUST WALKIN' IN THE RAIN *Johnnie Ray*
29 JUST WALKIN' IN THE RAIN *Johnnie Ray*

1957

JANUARY

5 SINGING THE BLUES *Guy Mitchell*
12 SINGING THE BLUES *Tommy Steele*
19 SINGING THE BLUES *Guy Mitchell*
26 GARDEN OF EDEN *Frankie Vaughan*

FEBRUARY

2 GARDEN OF EDEN *Frankie Vaughan*
2 SINGING THE BLUES *Guy Mitchell*
9 GARDEN OF EDEN *Frankie Vaughan*
16 GARDEN OF EDEN *Frankie Vaughan*
23 YOUNG LOVE *Tab Hunter*

MARCH

2 YOUNG LOVE *Tab Hunter*
9 YOUNG LOVE *Tab Hunter*
16 YOUNG LOVE *Tab Hunter*
23 YOUNG LOVE *Tab Hunter*
30 YOUNG LOVE *Tab Hunter*

APRIL

6 YOUNG LOVE *Tab Hunter*
13 CUMBERLAND GAP *Lonnie Donegan*
20 CUMBERLAND GAP *Lonnie Donegan*
27 CUMBERLAND GAP *Lonnie Donegan*

MAY

4 CUMBERLAND GAP *Lonnie Donegan*
11 CUMBERLAND GAP *Lonnie Donegan*
18 ROCK-A-BILLY *Guy Mitchell*
25 BUTTERFLY *Andy Williams*

JUNE

1 BUTTERFLY *Andy Williams*
8 YES TONIGHT JOSEPHINE *Johnnie Ray*
15 YES TONIGHT JOSEPHINE *Johnnie Ray*
22 YES TONIGHT JOSEPHINE *Johnnie Ray*
29 GAMBLIN' MAN/PUTTING ON THE STYLE
   Lonnie Donegan

JULY

6 GAMBLIN' MAN/PUTTING ON THE STYLE
   Lonnie Donegan
13 ALL SHOOK UP *Elvis Presley*
20 ALL SHOOK UP *Elvis Presley*
27 ALL SHOOK UP *Elvis Presley*

AUGUST

3 ALL SHOOK UP *Elvis Presley*
10 ALL SHOOK UP *Elvis Presley*
17 ALL SHOOK UP *Elvis Presley*
24 ALL SHOOK UP *Elvis Presley*
31 DIANA *Paul Anka*

SEPTEMBER

7 DIANA *Paul Anka*
14 DIANA *Paul Anka*
21 DIANA *Paul Anka*
28 DIANA *Paul Anka*

OCTOBER

5 DIANA *Paul Anka*
12 DIANA *Paul Anka*
19 DIANA *Paul Anka*
26 DIANA *Paul Anka*

NOVEMBER

2 THAT'LL BE THE DAY *Crickets*
9 THAT'LL BE THE DAY *Crickets*
16 THAT'LL BE THE DAY *Crickets*
23 MARY'S BOY CHILD *Harry Belafonte*
30 MARY'S BOY CHILD *Harry Belafonte*

DECEMBER

7 MARY'S BOY CHILD *Harry Belafonte*
14 MARY'S BOY CHILD *Harry Belafonte*
21 MARY'S BOY CHILD *Harry Belafonte*
28 MARY'S BOY CHILD *Harry Belafonte*

1958

JANUARY

4 MARY'S BOY CHILD *Harry Belafonte*
11 GREAT BALLS OF FIRE *Jerry Lee Lewis*
18 GREAT BALLS OF FIRE *Jerry Lee Lewis*
25 JAILHOUSE ROCK *Elvis Presley*

FEBRUARY

1 JAILHOUSE ROCK *Elvis Presley*
8 JAILHOUSE ROCK *Elvis Presley*
15 THE STORY OF MY LIFE *Michael Holliday*
22 THE STORY OF MY LIFE *Michael Holliday*

MARCH

1 MAGIC MOMENTS *Perry Como*
8 MAGIC MOMENTS *Perry Como*
15 MAGIC MOMENTS *Perry Como*
22 MAGIC MOMENTS *Perry Como*
29 MAGIC MOMENTS *Perry Como*

APRIL

5 MAGIC MOMENTS *Perry Como*
12 MAGIC MOMENTS *Perry Como*
19 MAGIC MOMENTS *Perry Como*
26 WHOLE LOTTA WOMAN *Marvin Rainwater*

MAY

3 WHOLE LOTTA WOMAN *Marvin Rainwater*
10 WHOLE LOTTA WOMAN *Marvin Rainwater*
17 WHO'S SORRY NOW *Connie Francis*
24 WHO'S SORRY NOW *Connie Francis*
31 WHO'S SORRY NOW *Connie Francis*

JUNE

7 WHO'S SORRY NOW *Connie Francis*
14 WHO'S SORRY NOW *Connie Francis*
21 WHO'S SORRY NOW *Connie Francis*
28 ON THE STREET WHERE YOU LIVE *Vic Damone*

JULY

5 ON THE STREET WHERE YOU LIVE *Vic Damone*
5 ALL I HAVE TO DO IS DREAM/CLAUDETTE
   Everly Brothers
12 ALL I HAVE TO DO IS DREAM/CLAUDETTE
   Everly Brothers
19 ALL I HAVE TO DO IS DREAM/CLAUDETTE
   Everly Brothers
26 ALL I HAVE TO DO IS DREAM/CLAUDETTE
   Everly Brothers

AUGUST

2   ALL I HAVE TO DO IS DREAM/CLAUDETTE
    Everly Brothers
9   ALL I HAVE TO DO IS DREAM/CLAUDETTE
    Everly Brothers
16 ALL I HAVE TO DO IS DREAM/CLAUDETTE
    Everly Brothers
23 WHEN   *Kalin Twins*
30 WHEN   *Kalin Twins*

SEPTEMBER

6   WHEN   *Kalin Twins*
13 WHEN   *Kalin Twins*
20 WHEN   *Kalin Twins*
27 CAROLINA MOON/STUPID CUPID
    Connie Francis

OCTOBER

4   CAROLINA MOON/STUPID CUPID
    Connie Francis
11 CAROLINA MOON/STUPID CUPID
    Connie Francis
18 CAROLINA MOON/STUPID CUPID
    Connie Francis
25 CAROLINA MOON/STUPID CUPID
    Connie Francis

NOVEMBER

1   CAROLINA MOON/STUPID CUPID
    Connie Francis
8   IT'S ALL IN THE GAME   *Tommy Edwards*
15 IT'S ALL IN THE GAME   *Tommy Edwards*
22 IT'S ALL IN THE GAME   *Tommy Edwards*
29 HOOTS MON   *Lord Rockingham's XI*

DECEMBER

6   HOOTS MON   *Lord Rockingham's XI*
13 HOOTS MON   *Lord Rockingham's XI*
20 IT'S ONLY MAKE BELIEVE   *Conway Twitty*
27 IT'S ONLY MAKE BELIEVE   *Conway Twitty*

1959

JANUARY

3   IT'S ONLY MAKE BELIEVE   *Conway Twitty*
10 IT'S ONLY MAKE BELIEVE   *Conway Twitty*
17 IT'S ONLY MAKE BELIEVE   *Conway Twitty*
24 THE DAY THE RAINS CAME   *Jane Morgan*
31 ONE NIGHT/I GOT STUNG   *Elvis Presley*

FEBRUARY

7   ONE NIGHT/I GOT STUNG   *Elvis Presley*
14 ONE NIGHT/I GOT STUNG   *Elvis Presley*
21 AS I LOVE YOU   *Shirley Bassey*
28 AS I LOVE YOU   *Shirley Bassey*

MARCH

7   AS I LOVE YOU   *Shirley Bassey*
14 AS I LOVE YOU   *Shirley Bassey*
21 SMOKE GETS IN YOUR EYES   *Platters*
28 SIDE SADDLE   *Russ Conway*

APRIL

4   SIDE SADDLE   *Russ Conway*
11 SIDE SADDLE   *Russ Conway*
18 SIDE SADDLE   *Russ Conway*
25 IT DOESN'T MATTER ANYMORE   *Buddy Holly*

MAY

2   IT DOESN'T MATTER ANYMORE   *Buddy Holly*
9   IT DOESN'T MATTER ANYMORE   *Buddy Holly*
16 A FOOL SUCH AS I/I NEED YOUR LOVE TONIGHT
    Elvis Presley
23 A FOOL SUCH AS I/I NEED YOUR LOVE TONIGHT
    Elvis Presley
30 A FOOL SUCH AS I/I NEED YOUR LOVE TONIGHT
    Elvis Presley

JUNE

6   A FOOL SUCH AS I/I NEED YOUR LOVE TONIGHT
    Elvis Presley
13 A FOOL SUCH AS I/I NEED YOUR LOVE TONIGHT
    Elvis Presley
20 ROULETTE   *Russ Conway*
27 ROULETTE   *Russ Conway*

JULY

4   DREAM LOVER   *Bobby Darin*
11 DREAM LOVER   *Bobby Darin*
18 DREAM LOVER   *Bobby Darin*
25 DREAM LOVER   *Bobby Darin*

AUGUST

1   LIVING DOLL
    Cliff Richard and the Shadows
8   LIVING DOLL
    Cliff Richard and the Shadows
15 LIVING DOLL
    Cliff Richard and the Shadows
22 LIVING DOLL
    Cliff Richard and the Shadows
29 LIVING DOLL
    Cliff Richard and the Shadows

SEPTEMBER

5   LIVING DOLL
    Cliff Richard and the Shadows
12 ONLY SIXTEEN   *Craig Douglas*
19 ONLY SIXTEEN   *Craig Douglas*
26 ONLY SIXTEEN   *Craig Douglas*

OCTOBER

3 ONLY SIXTEEN *Craig Douglas*
10 HERE COMES SUMMER *Jerry Keller*
17 MACK THE KNIFE *Bobby Darin*
24 MACK THE KNIFE *Bobby Darin*
31 TRAVELLIN' LIGHT
    Cliff Richard and the Shadows

NOVEMBER

7 TRAVELLIN' LIGHT
    Cliff Richard and the Shadows
14 TRAVELLIN' LIGHT
    Cliff Richard and the Shadows
21 TRAVELLIN' LIGHT
    Cliff Richard and the Shadows
28 TRAVELLIN' LIGHT
    Cliff Richard and the Shadows

DECEMBER

5 WHAT DO YOU WANT *Adam Faith*
12 WHAT DO YOU WANT *Adam Faith*
19 WHAT DO YOU WANT *Adam Faith*
19 WHAT DO YOU WANT TO MAKE THOSE EYES
    AT ME FOR *Emil Ford/The Checkmates*
26 WHAT DO YOU WANT TO MAKE THOSE EYES
    AT ME FOR *Emil Ford/The Checkmates*

1960

JANUARY

2 WHAT DO YOU WANT TO MAKE THOSE EYES
    AT ME FOR *Emil Ford/The Checkmates*
9 WHAT DO YOU WANT TO MAKE THOSE EYES
    AT ME FOR *Emil Ford/The Checkmates*
16 WHAT DO YOU WANT TO MAKE THOSE EYES
    AT ME FOR *Emil Ford/The Checkmates*
23 WHAT DO YOU WANT TO MAKE THOSE EYES
    AT ME FOR *Emil Ford/The Checkmates*
30 STARRY EYED *Michael Holliday*

FEBRUARY

6 WHY *Anthony Newley*
13 WHY *Anthony Newley*
20 WHY *Anthony Newley*
27 WHY *Anthony Newley*

MARCH

5 POOR ME *Adam Faith*
12 POOR ME *Adam Faith*
19 RUNNING BEAR *Johnny Preston*
26 RUNNING BEAR *Johnny Preston*

APRIL

2 MY OLE MAN'S A DUSTMAN *Lonnie Donegan*
9 MY OLE MAN'S A DUSTMAN *Lonnie Donegan*
16 MY OLE MAN'S A DUSTMAN *Lonnie Donegan*
23 MY OLE MAN'S A DUSTMAN *Lonnie Donegan*
30 DO YOU MIND *Anthony Newley*

MAY

7 CATHY'S CLOWN *Everly Brothers*
14 CATHY'S CLOWN *Everly Brothers*
21 CATHY'S CLOWN *Everly Brothers*
28 CATHY'S CLOWN *Everly Brothers*

JUNE

4 CATHY'S CLOWN *Everly Brothers*
11 CATHY'S CLOWN *Everly Brothers*
18 CATHY'S CLOWN *Everly Brothers*
25 THREE STEPS TO HEAVEN *Eddie Cochran*

JULY

2 THREE STEPS TO HEAVEN *Eddie Cochran*
9 GOOD TIMIN' *Jimmy Jones*
16 GOOD TIMIN' *Jimmy Jones*
23 GOOD TIMIN' *Jimmy Jones*
30 PLEASE DON'T TEASE
    Cliff Richard and the Shadows

AUGUST

6 SHAKIN' ALL OVER
    Johnny Kidd and the Pirates
13 PLEASE DON'T TEASE
    Cliff Richard and the Shadows
20 PLEASE DON'T TEASE
    Cliff Richard and the Shadows
27 APACHE *Shadows*

SEPTEMBER

3 APACHE *Shadows*
10 APACHE *Shadows*
17 APACHE *Shadows*
24 APACHE *Shadows*

OCTOBER

1 TELL LAURA I LOVE HER *Ricky Valence*
8 TELL LAURA I LOVE HER *Ricky Valence*
15 TELL LAURA I LOVE HER *Ricky Valence*
22 ONLY THE LONELY *Roy Orbison*
29 ONLY THE LONELY *Roy Orbison*

NOVEMBER

5 IT'S NOW OR NEVER *Elvis Presley*
12 IT'S NOW OR NEVER *Elvis Presley*
19 IT'S NOW OR NEVER *Elvis Presley*
26 IT'S NOW OR NEVER *Elvis Presley*

DECEMBER

3   IT'S NOW OR NEVER   *Elvis Presley*
10   IT'S NOW OR NEVER   *Elvis Presley*
17   IT'S NOW OR NEVER   *Elvis Presley*
24   IT'S NOW OR NEVER   *Elvis Presley*
31   I LOVE YOU   *Cliff Richard and the Shadows*

1961

JANUARY

7   I LOVE YOU   *Cliff Richard and the Shadows*
14   POETRY IN MOTION   *Johnny Tillotson*
21   POETRY IN MOTION   *Johnny Tillotson*
28   ARE YOU LONESOME TONIGHT?   *Elvis Presley*

FEBRUARY

4   ARE YOU LONESOME TONIGHT?   *Elvis Presley*
11   ARE YOU LONESOME TONIGHT?   *Elvis Presley*
18   ARE YOU LONESOME TONIGHT?   *Elvis Presley*
25   SAILOR   *Petula Clark*

MARCH

4   WALK RIGHT BACK   *Everly Brothers*
11   WALK RIGHT BACK   *Everly Brothers*
18   WALK RIGHT BACK   *Everly Brothers*
25   WOODEN HEART   *Elvis Presley*

APRIL

1   WOODEN HEART   *Elvis Presley*
8   WOODEN HEART   *Elvis Presley*
15   WOODEN HEART   *Elvis Presley*
22   WOODEN HEART   *Elvis Presley*
29   WOODEN HEART   *Elvis Presley*

MAY

6   BLUE MOON   *Marcels*
13   BLUE MOON   *Marcels*
20   ON THE REBOUND   *Floyd Cramer*
27   YOU'RE DRIVING ME CRAZY   *Temperance Seven*

JUNE

3   SURRENDER   *Elvis Presley*
10   SURRENDER   *Elvis Presley*
17   SURRENDER   *Elvis Presley*
24   SURRENDER   *Elvis Presley*

JULY

1   RUNAWAY   *Del Shannon*
8   RUNAWAY   *Del Shannon*
15   RUNAWAY   *Del Shannon*
22   TEMPTATION   *Everly Brothers*
29   TEMPTATION   *Everly Brothers*

AUGUST

5   WELL I ASK YOU   *Eden Kane*
12   YOU DON'T KNOW   *Helen Shapiro*
19   YOU DON'T KNOW   *Helen Shapiro*
26   YOU DON'T KNOW   *Helen Shapiro*

SEPTEMBER

2   JOHNNY REMEMBER ME   *John Leyton*
9   JOHNNY REMEMBER ME   *John Leyton*
16   JOHNNY REMEMBER ME   *John Leyton*
23   REACH FOR THE STARS/CLIMB EV'RY MOUNTAIN   *Shirley Bassey*
30   JOHNNY REMEMBER ME   *John Leyton*

OCTOBER

7   KONTIKI   *Shadows*
14   HIGHWAYMAN   *Michael*
21   WALKIN' BACK TO HAPPINESS   *Helen Shapiro*
28   WALKIN' BACK TO HAPPINESS   *Helen Shapiro*

NOVEMBER

4   WALKIN' BACK TO HAPPINESS   *Helen Shapiro*
11   LITTLE SISTER/HIS LATEST FLAME   *Elvis Presley*
18   LITTLE SISTER/HIS LATEST FLAME   *Elvis Presley*
25   LITTLE SISTER/HIS LATEST FLAME   *Elvis Presley*

DECEMBER

2   LITTLE SISTER/HIS LATEST FLAME   *Elvis Presley*
9   TOWER OF STRENGTH   *Frankie Vaughan*
16   TOWER OF STRENGTH   *Frankie Vaughan*
23   TOWER OF STRENGTH   *Frankie Vaughan*
30   MOON RIVER   *Danny Williams*

1962

JANUARY

6   MOON RIVER   *Danny Williams*
13   THE YOUNG ONES   *Cliff Richard and the Shadows*
20   THE YOUNG ONES   *Cliff Richard and the Shadows*
27   THE YOUNG ONES   *Cliff Richard and the Shadows*

FEBRUARY

3   THE YOUNG ONES   *Cliff Richard and the Shadows*
10   THE YOUNG ONES   *Cliff Richard and the Shadows*
17   THE YOUNG ONES   *Cliff Richard and the Shadows*
24   ROCK-A-HULA BABY/CAN'T HELP FALLING IN LOVE   *Elvis Presley*

MARCH

3   ROCK-A-HULA BABY/CAN'T HELP FALLING IN LOVE   *Elvis Presley*
10   ROCK-A-HULA BABY/CAN'T HELP FALLING IN LOVE   *Elvis Presley*
17   ROCK-A-HULA BABY/CAN'T HELP FALLING IN LOVE   *Elvis Presley*
24   WONDERFUL LAND   *Shadows*
31   WONDERFUL LAND   *Shadows*

APRIL

7	WONDERFUL LAND	*Shadows*
14	WONDERFUL LAND	*Shadows*
21	WONDERFUL LAND	*Shadows*
28	WONDERFUL LAND	*Shadows*

MAY

5	WONDERFUL LAND	*Shadows*
12	WONDERFUL LAND	*Shadows*
19	NUT ROCKER	*B. Bumble and the Stingers*
26	GOOD LUCK CHARM	*Elvis Presley*

JUNE

2	GOOD LUCK CHARM	*Elvis Presley*
9	GOOD LUCK CHARM	*Elvis Presley*
16	GOOD LUCK CHARM	*Elvis Presley*
23	GOOD LUCK CHARM	*Elvis Presley*
30	COME OUTSIDE	*Mike Sarne*

JULY

7	COME OUTSIDE	*Mike Sarne*
14	I CAN'T STOP LOVING YOU	*Ray Charles*
21	I CAN'T STOP LOVING YOU	*Ray Charles*
28	I REMEMBER YOU	*Frank Ifield*

AUGUST

4	I REMEMBER YOU	*Frank Ifield*
11	I REMEMBER YOU	*Frank Ifield*
18	I REMEMBER YOU	*Frank Ifield*
25	I REMEMBER YOU	*Frank Ifield*

SEPTEMBER

1	I REMEMBER YOU	*Frank Ifield*
8	I REMEMBER YOU	*Frank Ifield*
15	SHE'S NOT YOU	*Elvis Presley*
22	SHE'S NOT YOU	*Elvis Presley*
29	SHE'S NOT YOU	*Elvis Presley*

OCTOBER

6	TELSTAR	*Tornadoes*
13	TELSTAR	*Tornadoes*
20	TELSTAR	*Tornadoes*
27	TELSTAR	*Tornadoes*

NOVEMBER

3	TELSTAR	*Tornadoes*
10	LOVESICK BLUES	*Frank Ifield*
17	LOVESICK BLUES	*Frank Ifield*
24	LOVESICK BLUES	*Frank Ifield*

DECEMBER

1	LOVESICK BLUES	*Frank Ifield*
8	LOVESICK BLUES	*Frank Ifield*
15	RETURN TO SENDER	*Elvis Presley*
22	RETURN TO SENDER	*Elvis Presley*
29	RETURN TO SENDER	*Elvis Presley*

1963

JANUARY

5	THE NEXT TIME/BACHELOR BOY *Cliff Richard and the Shadows*
12	THE NEXT TIME/BACHELOR BOY *Cliff Richard and the Shadows*
19	THE NEXT TIME/BACHELOR BOY *Cliff Richard and the Shadows*
26	DANCE ON *Shadows*

FEBRUARY

2	DIAMONDS	*Jet Harris and Tony Meehan*
9	DIAMONDS	*Jet Harris and Tony Meehan*
16	DIAMONDS	*Jet Harris and Tony Meehan*
23	WAYWARD WIND	*Frank Ifield*

MARCH

2	WAYWARD WIND	*Frank Ifield*
9	WAYWARD WIND	*Frank Ifield*
16	SUMMER HOLIDAY	*Cliff Richard and the Shadows*
23	SUMMER HOLIDAY	*Cliff Richard and the Shadows*
30	FOOT TAPPER	*Shadows*

APRIL

6	SUMMER HOLIDAY	*Cliff Richard and the Shadows*
13	HOW DO YOU DO IT?	*Gerry and the Pacemakers*
20	HOW DO YOU DO IT?	*Gerry and the Pacemakers*
27	HOW DO YOU DO IT?	*Gerry and the Pacemakers*

MAY

4	FROM ME TO YOU	*Beatles*
11	FROM ME TO YOU	*Beatles*
18	FROM ME TO YOU	*Beatles*
25	FROM ME TO YOU	*Beatles*

JUNE

1	FROM ME TO YOU	*Beatles*
8	FROM ME TO YOU	*Beatles*
15	FROM ME TO YOU	*Beatles*
22	I LIKE IT	*Gerry and the Pacemakers*
29	I LIKE IT	*Gerry and the Pacemakers*

JULY

6	I LIKE IT	*Gerry and the Pacemakers*
13	I LIKE IT	*Gerry and the Pacemakers*
20	CONFESSIN'	*Frank Ifield*
27	CONFESSIN'	*Frank Ifield*

AUGUST

3	(YOU'RE THE DEVIL) IN DISGUISE *Elvis Presley*
10	SWEET FOR MY SWEET *Searchers*
17	SWEET FOR MY SWEET *Searchers*
24	BAD TO ME *Billy J. Kramer and the Dakotas*
31	BAD TO ME *Billy J. Kramer and the Dakotas*

SEPTEMBER

7   BAD TO ME   *Billy J. Kramer and the Dakotas*
14 SHE LOVES YOU   *Beatles*
21 SHE LOVES YOU   *Beatles*
28 SHE LOVES YOU   *Beatles*

OCTOBER

5   SHE LOVES YOU   *Beatles*
12 DO YOU LOVE ME?   *Brian Poole and the Tremeloes*
19 DO YOU LOVE ME?   *Brian Poole and the Tremeloes*
26 DO YOU LOVE ME?   *Brian Poole and the Tremeloes*

NOVEMBER

2   YOU'LL NEVER WALK ALONE
   Gerry and the Pacemakers
9   YOU'LL NEVER WALK ALONE
   Gerry and the Pacemakers
16 YOU'LL NEVER WALK ALONE
   Gerry and the Pacemakers
23 YOU'LL NEVER WALK ALONE
   Gerry and the Pacemakers
30 SHE LOVES YOU   *Beatles*

DECEMBER

7   SHE LOVES YOU   *Beatles*
14 I WANT TO HOLD YOUR HAND   *Beatles*
21 I WANT TO HOLD YOUR HAND   *Beatles*
28 I WANT TO HOLD YOUR HAND   *Beatles*

1964

JANUARY

4   I WANT TO HOLD YOUR HAND   *Beatles*
11 I WANT TO HOLD YOUR HAND   *Beatles*
18 GLAD ALL OVER   *Dave Clark Five*
25 GLAD ALL OVER   *Dave Clark Five*

FEBRUARY

1   NEEDLES AND PINS   *Searchers*
8   NEEDLES AND PINS   *Searchers*
15 NEEDLES AND PINS   *Searchers*
22 DIANE   *Bachelors*
29 ANYONE WHO HAD A HEART   *Cilla Black*

MARCH

7   ANYONE WHO HAD A HEART   *Cilla Black*
14 ANYONE WHO HAD A HEART   *Cilla Black*
21 LITTLE CHILDREN
   Billy J. Kramer and the Dakotas
28 LITTLE CHILDREN
   Billy J. Kramer and the Dakotas

APRIL

4   CAN'T BUY ME LOVE   *Beatles*
11 CAN'T BUY ME LOVE   *Beatles*
18 CAN'T BUY ME LOVE   *Beatles*
25 WORLD WITHOUT LOVE   *Peter and Gordon*

MAY

2   WORLD WITHOUT LOVE   *Peter and Gordon*
9   DON'T THROW YOUR LOVE AWAY   *Searchers*
16 DON'T THROW YOUR LOVE AWAY   *Searchers*
23 JULIET   *Four Pennies*
30 YOU'RE MY WORLD   *Cilla Black*

JUNE

6   YOU'RE MY WORLD   *Cilla Black*
13 YOU'RE MY WORLD   *Cilla Black*
20 YOU'RE MY WORLD   *Cilla Black*
27 IT'S OVER   *Roy Orbison*

JULY

4   IT'S OVER   *Roy Orbison*
11 HOUSE OF THE RISING SUN   *Animals*
18 IT'S ALL OVER NOW   *Rolling Stones*
25 A HARD DAY'S NIGHT   *Beatles*

AUGUST

1   A HARD DAY'S NIGHT   *Beatles*
8   A HARD DAY'S NIGHT   *Beatles*
15 DO WAH DIDDY DIDDY   *Manfred Mann*
22 DO WAH DIDDY DIDDY   *Manfred Mann*
29 HAVE I THE RIGHT   *Honeycombs*

SEPTEMBER

5   HAVE I THE RIGHT   *Honeycombs*
12 YOU REALLY GOT ME   *Kinks*
19 YOU REALLY GOT ME   *Kinks*
26 I'M INTO SOMETHING GOOD   *Herman's Hermits*

OCTOBER

3   I'M INTO SOMETHING GOOD   *Herman's Hermits*
10 OH, PRETTY WOMAN   *Roy Orbison*
17 OH, PRETTY WOMAN   *Roy Orbison*
24 ALWAYS SOMETHING THERE TO REMIND ME
   Sandie Shaw
31 ALWAYS SOMETHING THERE TO REMIND ME
   Sandie Shaw

NOVEMBER

7   ALWAYS SOMETHING THERE TO REMIND ME
   Sandie Shaw
14 OH, PRETTY WOMAN   *Roy Orbison*
21 BABY LOVE   *Supremes*
28 BABY LOVE   *Supremes*

DECEMBER

5 LITTLE RED ROOSTER   *Rolling Stones*
12 I FEEL FINE   *Beatles*
19 I FEEL FINE   *Beatles*
26 I FEEL FINE   *Beatles*

1965

JANUARY

2 I FEEL FINE   *Beatles*
9 I FEEL FINE   *Beatles*
16 YEH YEH   *Georgie Fame*
23 YEH YEH   *Georgie Fame*
30 GO NOW   *Moody Blues*

FEBRUARY

6 YOU'VE LOST THAT LOVIN' FEELIN'
   Righteous Brothers
13 YOU'VE LOST THAT LOVIN' FEELIN'
   Righteous Brothers
20 TIRED OF WAITING FOR YOU   *Kinks*
27 I'LL NEVER FIND ANOTHER YOU
   Seekers

MARCH

6 I'LL NEVER FIND ANOTHER YOU
   Seekers
13 IT'S NOT UNUSUAL   *Tom Jones*
20 THE LAST TIME   *Rolling Stones*
27 THE LAST TIME   *Rolling Stones*

APRIL

3 THE LAST TIME   *Rolling Stones*
10 CONCRETE AND CLAY   *Unit 4+2*
17 THE MINUTE YOU'RE GONE
   Cliff Richard
24 TICKET TO RIDE   *Beatles*

MAY

1 TICKET TO RIDE   *Beatles*
8 TICKET TO RIDE   *Beatles*
15 KING OF THE ROAD   *Roger Miller*
22 WHERE ARE YOU NOW (MY LOVE)
   Jackie Trent
29 LONG LIVE LOVE   *Sandie Shaw*

JUNE

5 LONG LIVE LOVE   *Sandie Shaw*
12 LONG LIVE LOVE   *Sandie Shaw*
19 CRYING IN THE CHAPEL   *Elvis Presley*
26 I'M ALIVE   *Hollies*

JULY

3 CRYING IN THE CHAPEL   *Elvis Presley*
10 I'M ALIVE   *Hollies*
17 I'M ALIVE   *Hollies*
24 MR TAMBOURINE MAN   *Byrds*
31 MR TAMBOURINE MAN   *Byrds*

AUGUST

7 HELP   *Beatles*
14 HELP   *Beatles*
21 HELP   *Beatles*
28 I GOT YOU BABE   *Sonny and Cher*

SEPTEMBER

4 I GOT YOU BABE   *Sonny and Cher*
11 (I CAN'T GET NO) SATISFACTION
   Rolling Stones
18 (I CAN'T GET NO) SATISFACTION
   Rolling Stones
25 MAKE IT EASY ON YOURSELF
   Walker Brothers

OCTOBER

2 TEARS   *Ken Dodd*
9 TEARS   *Ken Dodd*
16 TEARS   *Ken Dodd*
23 TEARS   *Ken Dodd*
30 TEARS   *Ken Dodd*

NOVEMBER

6 GET OFF MY CLOUD   *Rolling Stones*
13 GET OFF MY CLOUD   *Rolling Stones*
20 GET OFF MY CLOUD   *Rolling Stones*
27 GET OFF MY CLOUD   *Rolling Stones*

DECEMBER

4 THE CARNIVAL IS OVER   *Seekers*
11 THE CARNIVAL IS OVER   *Seekers*
18 DAY/TRIPPER WE CAN WORK IT OUT
   Beatles
18 DAY TRIPPER/WE CAN WORK IT OUT
   Beatles
25 DAY TRIPPER/WE CAN WORK IT OUT
   Beatles

1966

JANUARY

1 DAY TRIPPER/WE CAN WORK IT OUT
   Beatles
8 DAY TRIPPER/WE CAN WORK IT OUT
   Beatles
15 DAY TRIPPER/WE CAN WORK IT OUT
   Beatles
22 KEEP ON RUNNING   *Spencer Davis Group*
29 MICHELLE   *Overlanders*

FEBRUARY

5 MICHELLE *Overlanders*
12 MICHELLE *Overlanders*
19 THESE BOOTS ARE MADE FOR WALKIN'
    Nancy Sinatra
26 THESE BOOTS ARE MADE FOR WALKIN'
    Nancy Sinatra

MARCH

5 THESE BOOTS ARE MADE FOR WALKIN'
    Nancy Sinatra
12 THESE BOOTS ARE MADE FOR WALKIN'
    Nancy Sinatra
19 THE SUN AIN'T GONNA SHINE ANYMORE
    Walker Brothers
26 THE SUN AIN'T GONNA SHINE ANYMORE
    Walker Brothers

APRIL

2 THE SUN AIN'T GONNA SHINE ANYMORE
    Walker Brothers
9 THE SUN AIN'T GONNA SHINE ANYMORE
    Walker Brothers
16 SOMEBODY HELP ME
    Spencer Davis Group
23 SOMEBODY HELP ME
    Spencer Davis Group
30 YOU DON'T HAVE TO SAY YOU LOVE ME
    Dusty Springfield

MAY

7 PRETTY FLAMINGO *Manfred Mann*
14 PRETTY FLAMINGO *Manfred Mann*
21 PRETTY FLAMINGO *Manfred Mann*
28 PAINT IT BLACK *Rolling Stones*

JUNE

4 STRANGERS IN THE NIGHT
    Frank Sinatra
11 STRANGERS IN THE NIGHT
    Frank Sinatra
18 STRANGERS IN THE NIGHT
    Frank Sinatra
25 PAPERBACK WRITER *Beatles*

JULY

2 PAPERBACK WRITER *Beatles*
9 SUNNY AFTERNOON *Kinks*
16 SUNNY AFTERNOON *Kinks*
23 GET AWAY *George Fame*
30 OUT OF TIME *Chris Farlowe*

AUGUST

6 WITH A GIRL LIKE YOU *Troggs*
13 WITH A GIRL LIKE YOU *Troggs*
20 YELLOW SUBMARINE/ELEANOR RIGBY
    Beatles
27 YELLOW SUBMARINE/ELEANOR RIGBY
    Beatles

SEPTEMBER

3 YELLOW SUBMARINE/ELEANOR RIGBY
    Beatles
10 YELLOW SUBMARINE/ELEANOR RIGBY
    Beatles
17 ALL OR NOTHING *Small Faces*
24 DISTANT DRUMS *Jim Reeves*

OCTOBER

1 DISTANT DRUMS *Jim Reeves*
8 DISTANT DRUMS *Jim Reeves*
15 DISTANT DRUMS *Jim Reeves*
22 DISTANT DRUMS *Jim Reeves*
29 REACH OUT I'LL BE THERE *Four Tops*

NOVEMBER

5 REACH OUT I'LL BE THERE *Four Tops*
12 REACH OUT I'LL BE THERE *Four Tops*
19 GOOD VIBRATIONS *Beach Boys*
26 GOOD VIBRATIONS *Beach Boys*

DECEMBER

3 GREEN GREEN GRASS OF HOME *Tom Jones*
10 GREEN GREEN GRASS OF HOME *Tom Jones*
17 GREEN GREEN GRASS OF HOME *Tom Jones*
24 GREEN GREEN GRASS OF HOME *Tom Jones*
31 GREEN GREEN GRASS OF HOME *Tom Jones*

1967

JANUARY

7 GREEN GREEN GRASS OF HOME *Tom Jones*
14 GREEN GREEN GRASS OF HOME *Tom Jones*
21 I'M A BELIEVER *Monkees*
28 I'M A BELIEVER *Monkees*

FEBRUARY

4 I'M A BELIEVER *Monkees*
11 I'M A BELIEVER *Monkees*
18 THIS IS MY SONG *Petula Clark*
25 THIS IS MY SONG *Petula Clark*

MARCH

4 RELEASE ME *Engelbert Humperdinck*
11 RELEASE ME *Engelbert Humperdinck*
18 RELEASE ME *Engelbert Humperdinck*
25 RELEASE ME *Engelbert Humperdinck*

APRIL

1 RELEASE ME *Engelbert Humperdinck*
8 RELEASE ME *Engelbert Humperdinck*
15 SOMETHIN' STUPID *Nancy and Frank Sinatra*
22 SOMETHIN' STUPID *Nancy and Frank Sinatra*
29 PUPPET ON A STRING *Sandie Shaw*

MAY

6	PUPPET ON A STRING	*Sandie Shaw*
13	PUPPET ON A STRING	*Sandie Shaw*
20	SILENCE IS GOLDEN	*Tremeloes*
27	SILENCE IS GOLDEN	*Tremeloes*

JUNE

3	SILENCE IS GOLDEN	*Tremeloes*
10	A WHITER SHADE OF PALE *Procol Harum*	
17	A WHITER SHADE OF PALE *Procol Harum*	
24	A WHITER SHADE OF PALE *Procol Harum*	

JULY

1	A WHITER SHADE OF PALE *Procol Harum*	
8	A WHITER SHADE OF PALE *Procol Harum*	
15	A WHITER SHADE OF PALE *Procol Harum*	
22	ALL YOU NEED IS LOVE	*Beatles*
29	ALL YOU NEED IS LOVE	*Beatles*

AUGUST

5	ALL YOU NEED IS LOVE	*Beatles*
19	SAN FRANCISCO	*Scott McKenzie*
26	SAN FRANCISCO	*Scott McKenzie*

SEPTEMBER

2	SAN FRANCISCO	*Scott McKenzie*
9	THE LAST WALTZ	*Engelbert Humperdinck*
16	THE LAST WALTZ	*Engelbert Humperdinck*
23	THE LAST WALTZ	*Engelbert Humperdinck*
30	THE LAST WALTZ	*Engelbert Humperdinck*

OCTOBER

7	THE LAST WALTZ	*Engelbert Humperdinck*
14	MASSACHUSETTS	*Bee Gees*
21	MASSACHUSETTS	*Bee Gees*
28	MASSACHUSETTS	*Bee Gees*

NOVEMBER

4	MASSACHUSETTS	*Bee Gees*
11	BABY NOW THAT I'VE FOUND YOU *Foundations*	
18	BABY NOW THAT I'VE FOUND YOU *Foundations*	
25	LET THE HEARTACHES BEGIN *Long John Baldry*	

DECEMBER

2	LET THE HEARTACHES BEGIN *Long John Baldry*	
9	HELLO GOODBYE	*Beatles*
16	HELLO GOODBYE	*Beatles*
23	HELLO GOODBYE	*Beatles*
30	HELLO GOODBYE	*Beatles*

1968

JANUARY

6	HELLO GOODBYE	*Beatles*
13	HELLO GOODBYE	*Beatles*
20	HELLO GOODBYE	*Beatles*
27	BALLAD OF BONNIE AND CLYDE *Georgie Fame*	

FEBRUARY

3	EVERLASTING LOVE	*Love Affair*
10	EVERLASTING LOVE	*Love Affair*
17	MIGHTY QUINN	*Manfred Mann*
24	MIGHTY QUINN	*Manfred Mann*

MARCH

2	CINDERELLA ROCKEFELLA *Esther and Abi Ofarim*	
9	CINDERELLA ROCKEFELLA *Esther and Abi Ofarim*	
16	CINDERELLA ROCKEFELLA *Esther and Abi Ofarim*	
23	THE LEGEND OF XANADU *Dave Dee, Dozy, Beaky, Mick and Tich*	
30	LADY MADONNA	*Beatles*

APRIL

6	LADY MADONNA	*Beatles*
13	CONGRATULATIONS	*Cliff Richard*
20	CONGRATULATIONS	*Cliff Richard*
27	WHAT A WONDERFUL WORLD	*Louis Armstrong*

MAY

4	WHAT A WONDERFUL WORLD *Louis Armstrong*	
11	WHAT A WONDERFUL WORLD *Louis Armstrong*	
18	WHAT A WONDERFUL WORLD *Louis Armstrong*	
25	YOUNG GIRL *Union Gap Featuring Gary Puckett*	

JUNE

1 YOUNG GIRL
Union Gap Featuring Gary Puckett
8 YOUNG GIRL
Union Gap Featuring Gary Puckett
15 YOUNG GIRL
Union Gap Featuring Gary Puckett
22 JUMPING JACK FLASH   *Rolling Stones*
29 JUMPING JACK FLASH   *Rolling Stones*

JULY

6 BABY COME BACK   *Equals*
13 BABY COME BACK   *Equals*
20 BABY COME BACK   *Equals*
27 I PRETEND   *Des O'Conner*

AUGUST

3 MONY MONY
Tommy James and the Shondells
10 MONY MONY
Tommy James and the Shondells
17 FIRE   *Crazy World of Arthur Brown*
24 MONY MONY
Tommy James and the Shondells
31 DO IT AGAIN   *Beach Boys*

SEPTEMBER

7 I'VE GOTTA GET A MESSAGE TO YOU
Bee Gees
14 HEY JUDE   *Beatles*
21 HEY JUDE   *Beatles*
28 THOSE WERE THE DAYS   *Mary Hopkin*

OCTOBER

5 THOSE WERE THE DAYS   *Mary Hopkin*
12 THOSE WERE THE DAYS   *Mary Hopkin*
19 THOSE WERE THE DAYS   *Mary Hopkin*
26 THOSE WERE THE DAYS   *Mary Hopkin*

NOVEMBER

2 THOSE WERE THE DAYS   *Mary Hopkin*
9 WITH A LITTLE HELP FROM MY FRIENDS
Joe Cocker
16 THE GOOD, THE BAD AND THE UGLY
Hugo Montenegro
23 THE GOOD, THE BAD AND THE UGLY
Hugo Montenegro
30 THE GOOD, THE BAD AND THE UGLY
Hugo Montenegro

DECEMBER

7 THE GOOD, THE BAD AND THE UGLY
Hugo Montenegro
14 LILY THE PINK   *Scaffold*
21 LILY THE PINK   *Scaffold*
28 LILY THE PINK   *Scaffold*

1969

JANUARY

4 OB-LA-DI OB-LA-DA   *Marmalade*
11 LILY THE PINK   *Scaffold*
18 OB-LA-DI OB-LA-DA   *Marmalade*
25 OB-LA-DI OB-LA-DA   *Marmalade*

FEBRUARY

1 ALBATROSS   *Fleetwood Mac*
8 BLACKBERRY WAY   *Move*
15 (IF PARADISE IS) HALF AS NICE
Amen Corner
22 (IF PARADISE IS) HALF AS NICE
Amen Corner

MARCH

1 WHERE DO YOU GO TO MY LOVELY
Peter Sarstedt
8 WHERE DO YOU GO TO MY LOVELY
Peter Sarstedt
15 WHERE DO YOU GO TO MY LOVELY
Peter Sarstedt
22 WHERE DO YOU GO TO MY LOVELY
Peter Sarstedt
29 I HEARD IT THROUGH THE GRAPEVINE
Marvin Gaye

APRIL

5 I HEARD IT THROUGH THE GRAPEVINE
Marvin Gaye
12 I HEARD IT THROUGH THE GRAPEVINE
Marvin Gaye
19 THE ISRAELITES
Desmond Dekker and the Aces
26 GET BACK   *Beatles with Billy Preston*

MAY

3 GET BACK   *Beatles with Billy Preston*
10 GET BACK   *Beatles with Billy Preston*
17 GET BACK   *Beatles with Billy Preston*
24 GET BACK   *Beatles with Billy Preston*
31 GET BACK   *Beatles with Billy Preston*

JUNE

7 DIZZY   *Tommy Roe*
14 THE BALLAD OF JOHN AND YOKO   *Beatles*
21 THE BALLAD OF JOHN AND YOKO   *Beatles*
28 THE BALLAD OF JOHN AND YOKO   *Beatles*

JULY

5 SOMETHING IN THE AIR
Thunderclap Newman
12 SOMETHING IN THE AIR
Thunderclap Newman
19 SOMETHING IN THE AIR
Thunderclap Newman
26 HONKY TONK WOMEN   *Rolling Stones*

AUGUST

2	HONKY TONK WOMEN	*Rolling Stones*
9	HONKY TONK WOMEN	*Rolling Stones*
16	HONKY TONK WOMEN	*Rolling Stones*
23	HONKY TONK WOMEN	*Rolling Stones*
30	IN THE YEAR 2525	*Zager and Evans*

SEPTEMBER

6	IN THE YEAR 2525	*Zager and Evans*
13	IN THE YEAR 2525	*Zager and Evans*
20	BAD MOON RISING	
	Credence Clearwater Revival	
27	BAD MOON RISING	
	Credence Clearwater Revival	

OCTOBER

4	BAD MOON RISING	
	Credence Clearwater Revival	
11	JE T'AIME MOI NON PLUS	
	Jane Birkin/Serge Gainsbourg	
18	I'LL NEVER FALL IN LOVE AGAIN	
	Bobby Gentry	
25	SUGAR SUGAR	*Archies*

NOVEMBER

1	SUGAR SUGAR	*Archies*
8	SUGAR SUGAR	*Archies*
15	SUGAR SUGAR	*Archies*
22	SUGAR SUGAR	*Archies*
29	SUGAR SUGAR	*Archies*

DECEMBER

6	SUGAR SUGAR	*Archies*
13	SUGAR SUGAR	*Archies*
20	TWO LITTLE BOYS	*Rolf Harris*
27	TWO LITTLE BOYS	*Rolf Harris*

1970

JANUARY

3	TWO LITTLE BOYS	*Rolf Harris*
10	TWO LITTLE BOYS	*Rolf Harris*
17	TWO LITTLE BOYS	*Rolf Harris*
24	TWO LITTLE BOYS	*Rolf Harris*
31	LOVE GROWS	*Edison Lighthouse*

FEBRUARY

7	LOVE GROWS	*Edison Lighthouse*
14	LOVE GROWS	*Edison Lighthouse*
21	LOVE GROWS	*Edison Lighthouse*
28	LOVE GROWS	*Edison Lighthouse*

MARCH

7	WAND'RIN STAR	*Lee Marvin*
14	WAND'RIN STAR	*Lee Marvin*
21	WAND'RIN STAR	*Lee Marvin*
28	BRIDGE OVER TROUBLED WATER	
	Simon and Garfunkel	

APRIL

4	BRIDGE OVER TROUBLED WATER	
	Simon and Garfunkel	
11	BRIDGE OVER TROUBLED WATER	
	Simon and Garfunkel	
18	ALL KINDS OF EVERYTHING	*Dana*
25	ALL KINDS OF EVERYTHING	*Dana*

MAY

2	SPIRIT IN THE SKY	*Norman Greenbaum*
9	SPIRIT IN THE SKY	*Norman Greenbaum*
16	BACK HOME	*England World Cup Squad*
23	BACK HOME	*England World Cup Squad*
30	BACK HOME	*England World Cup Squad*

JUNE

6	YELLOW RIVER	*Christie*
13	IN THE SUMMERTIME	*Mungo Gerry*
20	IN THE SUMMERTIME	*Mungo Gerry*
27	IN THE SUMMERTIME	*Mungo Gerry*

JULY

4	IN THE SUMMERTIME	*Mungo Gerry*
11	IN THE SUMMERTIME	*Mungo Gerry*
18	IN THE SUMMERTIME	*Mungo Gerry*
25	IN THE SUMMERTIME	*Mungo Gerry*

AUGUST

1	THE WONDER OF YOU	*Elvis Presley*
8	THE WONDER OF YOU	*Elvis Presley*
15	THE WONDER OF YOU	*Elvis Presley*
22	THE WONDER OF YOU	*Elvis Presley*
29	THE WONDER OF YOU	*Elvis Presley*

SEPTEMBER

5	THE WONDER OF YOU	*Elvis Presley*
12	TEARS OF A CLOWN	
	Smokey Robinson and the Miracles	
19	BAND OF GOLD	*Freda Payne*
26	BAND OF GOLD	*Freda Payne*

OCTOBER

3	BAND OF GOLD	*Freda Payne*
10	BAND OF GOLD	*Freda Payne*
17	BAND OF GOLD	*Freda Payne*
24	BAND OF GOLD	*Freda Payne*
31	WOODSTOCK	
	Matthew's Southern Comfort	

NOVEMBER

7	WOODSTOCK	
	Matthew's Southern Comfort	
14	WOODSTOCK	
	Matthew's Southern Comfort	
21	VOODOO CHILE	
	Jimi Hendrix Experience	
28	I HEAR YOU KNOCKIN'	*Dave Edmunds*

DECEMBER

5	I HEAR YOU KNOCKIN'	*Dave Edmunds*
12	I HEAR YOU KNOCKIN'	*Dave Edmunds*
19	I HEAR YOU KNOCKIN'	*Dave Edmunds*
26	I HEAR YOU KNOCKIN'	*Dave Edmunds*

1971

JANUARY

2	I HEAR YOU KNOCKIN'	*Dave Edmunds*
9	GRANDAD	*Clive Dunn*
16	GRANDAD	*Clive Dunn*
23	GRANDAD	*Clive Dunn*
30	MY SWEET LORD	*George Harrison*

FEBRUARY

6	MY SWEET LORD	*George Harrison*
13	MY SWEET LORD	*George Harrison*
20	MY SWEET LORD	*George Harrison*
27	MY SWEET LORD	*George Harrison*

MARCH

6	BABY JUMP	*Mungo Jerry*
13	BABY JUMP	*Mungo Jerry*
20	HOT LOVE	*T. Rex*
27	HOT LOVE	*T. Rex*

APRIL

3	HOT LOVE	*T. Rex*
10	HOT LOVE	*T. Rex*
17	HOT LOVE	*T. Rex*
24	HOT LOVE	*T. Rex*

MAY

1	DOUBLE BARREL	
	Dave and Ansil Collins	
8	DOUBLE BARREL	
	Dave and Ansil Collins	
15	KNOCK THREE TIMES	*Dawn*
22	KNOCK THREE TIMES	*Dawn*
29	KNOCK THREE TIMES	*Dawn*

JUNE

5	KNOCK THREE TIMES	*Dawn*
12	KNOCK THREE TIMES	*Dawn*
19	CHIRPY CHIRPY CHEEP CHEEP	
	Middle of the Road	
26	CHIRPY CHIRPY CHEEP CHEEP	
	Middle of the Road	

JULY

3	CHIRPY CHIRPY CHEEP CHEEP	
	Middle of the Road	
10	CHIRPY CHIRPY CHEEP CHEEP	
	Middle of the Road	
17	CHIRPY CHIRPY CHEEP CHEEP	
	Middle of the Road	
24	GET IT ON	*T. Rex*
31	GET IT ON	*T. Rex*

AUGUST

7	GET IT ON	*T. Rex*
14	GET IT ON	*T. Rex*
21	I'M STILL WAITING	*Diana Ross*
28	I'M STILL WAITING	*Diana Ross*

SEPTEMBER

4	I'M STILL WAITING	*Diana Ross*
11	I'M STILL WAITING	*Diana Ross*
18	HEY GIRL DON'T BOTHER ME	*Tams*
25	HEY GIRL DON'T BOTHER ME	*Tams*

OCTOBER

2	HEY GIRL DON'T BOTHER ME	*Tams*
9	MAGGIE MAY	*Rod Stewart*
16	MAGGIE MAY	*Rod Stewart*
23	MAGGIE MAY	*Rod Stewart*
30	MAGGIE MAY	*Rod Stewart*

NOVEMBER

6	MAGGIE MAY	*Rod Stewart*
13	COZ I LOVE YOU	*Slade*
20	COZ I LOVE YOU	*Slade*
27	COZ I LOVE YOU	*Slade*

DECEMBER

4	COZ I LOVE YOU	*Slade*
11	ERNIE (THE FASTEST MILKMAN IN THE WEST)	*Benny Hill*
18	ERNIE (THE FASTEST MILKMAN IN THE WEST	*Benny Hill*
25	ERNIE (THE FASTEST MILKMAN IN THE WEST	*Benny Hill*

1972

JANUARY

1 ERNIE (THE FASTEST MILKMAN IN THE
  WEST *Benny Hill*
8 I'D LIKE TO TEACH THE WORLD TO SING
  New Seekers
15 I'D LIKE TO TEACH THE WORLD TO SING
  New Seekers
22 I'D LIKE TO TEACH THE WORLD TO SING
  New Seekers

FEBRUARY

5 TELEGRAM SAM *T. Rex*
12 TELEGRAM SAM *T. Rex*
19 SON OF MY FATHER *Chicory Tip*
26 SON OF MY FATHER *Chicory Tip*

MARCH

4 SON OF MY FATHER *Chicory Tip*
11 WITHOUT YOU *Nilsson*
18 WITHOUT YOU *Nilsson*
25 WITHOUT YOU *Nilsson*

APRIL

1 WITHOUT YOU *Nilsson*
8 WITHOUT YOU *Nilsson*
15 AMAZING GRACE
  The Royal Scots Dragoon Guards
22 AMAZING GRACE
  The Royal Scots Dragoon Guards
29 AMAZING GRACE
  The Royal Scots Dragoon Guards

MAY

6 AMAZING GRACE
  The Royal Scots Dragoon Guards
13 AMAZING GRACE
  The Royal Scots Dragoon Guards
20 METAL GURU *T. Rex*
27 METAL GURU *T. Rex*

JUNE

3 METAL GURU *T. Rex*
10 METAL GURU *T. Rex*
17 VINCENT *Don McLean*
24 VINCENT *Don McLean*

JULY

1 TAKE ME BAK'OME *Slade*
8 PUPPY LOVE *Donny Osmond*
15 PUPPY LOVE *Donny Osmond*
22 PUPPY LOVE *Donny Osmond*
29 PUPPY LOVE *Donny Osmond*

AUGUST

5 PUPPY LOVE *Donny Osmond*
12 SCHOOL'S OUT *Alice Cooper*
19 SCHOOL'S OUT *Alice Cooper*
26 SCHOOL'S OUT *Alice Cooper*

SEPTEMBER

2 YOU WEAR IT WELL *Rod Stewart*
9 MAMA WEER ALL CRAZEE NOW *Slade*
16 MAMA WEER ALL CRAZEE NOW *Slade*
23 MAMA WEER ALL CRAZEE NOW *Slade*
30 HOW CAN I BE SURE? *David Cassidy*

OCTOBER

7 HOW CAN I BE SURE? *David Cassidy*
14 MOULDY OLD DOUGH *Lieutenant Pigeon*
28 MOULDY OLD DOUGH *Lieutenant Pigeon*

NOVEMBER

4 MOULDY OLD DOUGH *Lieutenant Pigeon*
11 CLAIR *Gilbert O'Sullivan*
18 CLAIR *Gilbert O'Sullivan*
25 MY DING-A-LING *Chuck Berry*

DECEMBER

2 MY DING-A-LING *Chuck Berry*
9 MY DING-A-LING *Chuck Berry*
16 MY DING-A-LING *Chuck Berry*
23 LONG HAIRED LOVER FROM LIVERPOOL
  Little Jimmy Osmond
30 LONG HAIRED LOVER FROM LIVERPOOL
  Little Jimmy Osmond

1973

JANUARY

6 LONG HAIRED LOVER FROM LIVERPOOL
  Little Jimmy Osmond
13 LONG HAIRED LOVER FROM LIVERPOOL
  Little Jimmy Osmond
20 LONG HAIRED LOVER FROM LIVERPOOL
  Little Jimmy Osmond
27 BLOCKBUSTER *Sweet*

FEBRUARY

3 BLOCKBUSTER *Sweet*
10 BLOCKBUSTER *Sweet*
17 BLOCKBUSTER *Sweet*
24 BLOCKBUSTER *Sweet*

MARCH

3	CUM ON FEEL THE NOIZE	*Slade*
10	CUM ON FEEL THE NOIZE	*Slade*
17	CUM ON FEEL THE NOIZE	*Slade*
24	CUM ON FEEL THE NOIZE	*Slade*
31	THE TWELFTH OF NEVER	*Donny Osmond*

APRIL

7	GET DOWN	*Gilbert O'Sullivan*
14	GET DOWN	*Gilbert O'Sullivan*
21	TIE A YELLOW RIBBON ROUND THE OLE OAK TREE	*Dawn*
28	TIE A YELLOW RIBBON ROUND THE OLE OAK TREE	*Dawn*

MAY

5	TIE A YELLOW RIBBON ROUND THE OLE OAK TREE	*Dawn*
12	TIE A YELLOW RIBBON ROUND THE OLE OAK TREE	*Dawn*
19	SEE MY BABY JIVE	*Wizzard*
26	SEE MY BABY JIVE	*Wizzard*

JUNE

2	SEE MY BABY JIVE	*Wizzard*
9	SEE MY BABY JIVE	*Wizzard*
16	CAN THE CAN	*Suzi Quatro*
23	RUBBER BULLETS	*10cc*
30	SQWEZE ME PLEEZE ME	*Slade*

JULY

7	SQWEZE ME PLEEZE ME	*Slade*
14	SQWEZE ME PLEEZE ME	*Slade*
21	WELCOME HOME	*Peters and Lee*
28	I'M LEADER OF THE GANG (I AM)	*Gary Glitter*

AUGUST

4	I'M LEADER OF THE GANG (I AM)	*Gary Glitter*
11	I'M LEADER OF THE GANG (I AM)	*Gary Glitter*
18	I'M LEADER OF THE GANG (I AM)	*Gary Glitter*
25	YOUNG LOVE	*Donny Osmond*

SEPTEMBER

1	YOUNG LOVE	*Donny Osmond*
8	YOUNG LOVE	*Donny Osmond*
15	YOUNG LOVE	*Donny Osmond*
22	ANGEL FINGERS	*Wizzard*
29	EYE LEVEL	*Simon Park Orchestra*

OCTOBER

6	EYE LEVEL	*Simon Park Orchestra*
13	EYE LEVEL	*Simon Park Orchestra*
20	EYE LEVEL	*Simon Park Orchestra*
27	DAYDREAMER/THE PUPPY SONG	*David Cassidy*

NOVEMBER

3	DAYDREAMER/THE PUPPY SONG	*David Cassidy*
10	DAYDREAMER/THE PUPPY SONG	*David Cassidy*
17	I LOVE YOU LOVE ME LOVE	*Gary Glitter*
24	I LOVE YOU LOVE ME LOVE	*Gary Glitter*

DECEMBER

1	I LOVE YOU LOVE ME LOVE	*Gary Glitter*
8	I LOVE YOU LOVE ME LOVE	*Gary Glitter*
15	MERRY XMAS EVERYBODY	*Slade*
22	MERRY XMAS EVERYBODY	*Slade*
29	MERRY XMAS EVERYBODY	*Slade*

1974

JANUARY

5	MERRY XMAS EVERYBODY	*Slade*
12	MERRY XMAS EVERYBODY	*Slade*
19	YOU WON'T FIND ANOTHER FOOL LIKE ME	*New Seekers*
26	TIGER FEET	*Mud*

FEBRUARY

2	TIGER FEET	*Mud*
9	TIGER FEET	*Mud*
16	TIGER FEET	*Mud*
23	DEVIL GATE DRIVE	*Suzi Quatro*

MARCH

2	DEVIL GATE DRIVE	*Suzi Quatro*
9	JEALOUS FRIEND	*Alvin Stardust*
16	BILLY DON'T BE A HERO	*Paper Lace*
23	BILLY DON'T BE A HERO	*Paper Lace*
30	BILLY DON'T BE A HERO	*Paper Lace*

APRIL

6	SEASONS IN THE SUN	*Terry Jacks*
13	SEASONS IN THE SUN	*Terry Jacks*
20	SEASONS IN THE SUN	*Terry Jacks*
27	SEASONS IN THE SUN	*Terry Jacks*

MAY

4 WATERLOO *Abba*
11 WATERLOO *Abba*
18 SUGAR BABY LOVE *Rubettes*
25 SUGAR BABY LOVE *Rubettes*

JUNE

1 SUGAR BABY LOVE *Rubettes*
8 SUGAR BABY LOVE *Rubettes*
15 THE STREAK *Ray Stevens*
22 ALWAYS YOURS *Gary Glitter*
29 SHE *Charles Aznavour*

JULY

6 SHE *Charles Aznavour*
13 SHE *Charles Aznavour*
20 SHE *Charles Aznavour*
27 ROCK YOUR BABY *George McCrae*

AUGUST

3 ROCK YOUR BABY *George McCrae*
10 ROCK YOUR BABY *George McCrae*
17 WHEN WILL I SEE YOU AGAIN
   Three Degrees
24 WHEN WILL I SEE YOU AGAIN
   Three Degrees
31 LOVE ME FOR A REASON *Osmonds*

SEPTEMBER

7 LOVE ME FOR A REASON *Osmonds*
14 LOVE ME FOR A REASON *Osmonds*
21 KUNG FU FIGHTING *Carl Douglas*
28 KUNG FU FIGHTING *Carl Douglas*

OCTOBER

5 KUNG FU FIGHTING *Carl Douglas*
12 ANNIE'S SONG *John Denver*
19 SAD SWEET DREAMER *Sweet Sensation*
26 EVERYTHING I OWN *Ken Boothe*

NOVEMBER

2 EVERYTHING I OWN *Ken Boothe*
9 EVERYTHING I OWN *Ken Boothe*
16 GONNA MAKE YOU A STAR *David Essex*
23 GONNA MAKE YOU A STAR *David Essex*
30 GONNA MAKE YOU A STAR *David Essex*

DECEMBER

7 YOU'RE THE FIRST THE LAST MY
   EVERYTHING *Barry White*
14 YOU'RE THE FIRST THE LAST MY
   EVERYTHING *Barry White*
21 LONELY THIS CHRISTMAS *Mud*
28 LONELY THIS CHRISTMAS *Mud*

1975

JANUARY

4 LONELY THIS CHRISTMAS *Mud*
11 LONELY THIS CHRISTMAS *Mud*
18 DOWN DOWN *Status Quo*
25 MS GRACE *Tymes*

FEBRUARY

1 JANUARY *Pilot*
8 JANUARY *Pilot*
15 JANUARY *Pilot*
22 MAKE ME SMILE *Steve Harley/Cockney Rebel*

MARCH

1 MAKE ME SMILE *Steve Harley/Cockney Rebel*
8 IF *Telly Savalas*
15 IF *Telly Savalas*
22 BYE BYE BABY *Bay City Rollers*
29 BYE BYE BABY *Bay City Rollers*

APRIL

5 BYE BYE BABY *Bay City Rollers*
12 BYE BYE BABY *Bay City Rollers*
19 BYE BYE BABY *Bay City Rollers*
26 BYE BYE BABY *Bay City Rollers*

MAY

3 OH BOY *Mud*
10 OH BOY *Mud*
17 STAND BY YOUR MAN *Tammy Wynette*
24 STAND BY YOUR MAN *Tammy Wynette*
31 STAND BY YOUR MAN *Tammy Wynette*

JUNE

7 WHISPERING GRASS
   Windsor Davies and Don Estelle
14 WHISPERING GRASS
   Windsor Davies and Don Estelle
21 WHISPERING GRASS
   Windsor Davies and Don Estelle
28 I'M NOT IN LOVE *10cc*

JULY

5 I'M NOT IN LOVE *10cc*
12 TEARS ON MY PILLOW *Johnny Cash*
19 GIVE A LITTLE LOVE *Bay City Rollers*
26 GIVE A LITTLE LOVE *Bay City Rollers*

AUGUST

2 GIVE A LITTLE LOVE *Bay City Rollers*
9 BARBADOS *Typically Tropical*
16 I CAN'T GIVE YOU ANYTHING (BUT MY LOVE)
   Stylistics
23 I CAN'T GIVE YOU ANYTHING (BUT MY LOVE)
   Stylistics

30   I CAN'T GIVE YOU ANYTHING (BUT MY LOVE)
     Stylistics

SEPTEMBER

6   SAILING   *Rod Stewart*
13   SAILING   *Rod Stewart*
20   SAILING   *Rod Stewart*
27   SAILING   *Rod Stewart*

OCTOBER

4   HOLD ME CLOSE   *David Essex*
11   HOLD ME CLOSE   *David Essex*
18   HOLD ME CLOSE   *David Essex*
25   I ONLY HAVE EYES FOR YOU   *Art Garfunkel*

NOVEMBER

1   I ONLY HAVE EYES FOR YOU   *Art Garfunkel*
8   SPACE ODDITY   *David Bowie*
15   SPACE ODDITY   *David Bowie*
22   D.I.V.O.R.C.E.   *Billy Connolly*
29   BOHEMIAN RHAPSODY   *Queen*

DECEMBER

6   BOHEMIAN RHAPSODY   *Queen*
13   BOHEMIAN RHAPSODY   *Queen*
20   BOHEMIAN RHAPSODY   *Queen*
27   BOHEMIAN RHAPSODY   *Queen*

1976

JANUARY

3   BOHEMIAN RHAPSODY   *Queen*
10   BOHEMIAN RHAPSODY   *Queen*
17   BOHEMIAN RHAPSODY   *Queen*
24   BOHEMIAN RHAPSODY   *Queen*
31   MAMMA MIA   *Abba*

FEBRUARY

7   MAMMA MIA   *Abba*
14   FOREVER AND EVER   *Silk*
21   DECEMBER, '63 (OH, WHAT A NIGHT)
     Four Seasons
28   DECEMBER, '63 (OH, WHAT A NIGHT)
     Four Seasons

MARCH

6   I LOVE TO LOVE   *Tina Charles*
13   I LOVE TO LOVE   *Tina Charles*
20   I LOVE TO LOVE   *Tina Charles*
27   SAVE YOUR KISSES FOR ME
     Brotherhood of Man

APRIL

3   SAVE YOUR KISSES FOR ME
     Brotherhood of Man
10   SAVE YOUR KISSES FOR ME
     Brotherhood of Man
17   SAVE YOUR KISSES FOR ME
     Brotherhood of Man
24   SAVE YOUR KISSES FOR ME
     Brotherhood of Man

MAY

1   SAVE YOUR KISSES FOR ME
     Brotherhood of Man
8   FERNANDO   *Abba*
15   FERNANDO   *Abba*
22   FERNANDO   *Abba*
29   FERNANDO   *Abba*

JUNE

5   NO CHARGE   *JJ Barrie*
12   COMBINE HARVESTER   *Wurzels*
19   COMBINE HARVESTER   *Wurzels*
26   YOU TO ME ARE E''ERYTHING   *Real Thing*

JULY

3   YOU TO ME ARE EVERYTHING   *Real Thing*
10   YOU TO ME ARE EVERYTHING   *Real Thing*
17   THE ROUSSOS PHENOMENON (EP)
     Demis Roussos
24   DON'T GO BREAKING MY HEART
     Elton John and Kiki Dee
31   DON'T GO BREAKING MY HEART
     Elton John and Kiki Dee

AUGUST

7   DON'T GO BREAKING MY HEART
     Elton John and Kiki Dee
14   DON'T GO BREAKING MY HEART
     Elton John and Kiki Dee
21   DON'T GO BREAKING MY HEART
     Elton John and Kiki Dee
28   DON'T GO BREAKING MY HEART
     Elton John and Kiki Dee

SEPTEMBER

4   DANCING QUEEN   *Abba*
11   DANCING QUEEN   *Abba*
18   DANCING QUEEN   *Abba*
25   DANCING QUEEN   *Abba*

OCTOBER

2   DANCING QUEEN   *Abba*
9   DANCING QUEEN   *Abba*
16   MISSISSIPPI   *Pussycat*
23   MISSISSIPPI   *Pussycat*
30   MISSISSIPPI   *Pussycat*

NOVEMBER

6	MISSISSIPPI	*Pussycat*
13	IF YOU LEAVE ME NOW	*Chicago*
20	IF YOU LEAVE ME NOW	*Chicago*
27	IF YOU LEAVE ME NOW	*Chicago*

DECEMBER

4	UNDER THE MOON OF LOVE	
	Showaddywaddy	
11	UNDER THE MOON OF LOVE	
	Showaddywaddy	
18	UNDER THE MOON OF LOVE	
	Showaddywaddy	
25	WHEN A CHILD IS BORN	*Johnny Mathis*

1977

JANUARY

1	WHEN A CHILD IS BORN	*Johnny Mathis*
8	WHEN A CHILD IS BORN	*Johnny Mathis*
15	DON'T GIVE UP ON US	*David Soul*
22	DON'T GIVE UP ON US	*David Soul*
29	DON'T GIVE UP ON US	*David Soul*

FEBRUARY

5	DON'T GIVE UP ON US	*David Soul*
12	DON'T CRY FOR ME ARGENTINA	
	Julie Covington	
19	WHEN I NEED YOU	*Leo Sayer*
26	WHEN I NEED YOU	*Leo Sayer*

MARCH

5	WHEN I NEED YOU	*Leo Sayer*
12	CHANSON D'AMOUR	*Manhattan Transfer*
19	CHANSON D'AMOUR	*Manhattan Transfer*
26	CHANSON D'AMOUR	*Manhattan Transfer*

APRIL

2	KNOWING ME KNOWING YOU	*Abba*
9	KNOWING ME KNOWING YOU	*Abba*
16	KNOWING ME KNOWING YOU	*Abba*
23	KNOWING ME KNOWING YOU	*Abba*
30	KNOWING ME KNOWING YOU	*Abba*

MAY

7	FREE *Deniece Williams*	
14	FREE *Deniece Williams*	
21	I DON'T WANT TO TALK ABOUT IT/	
	FIRST CUT IS THE DEEPEST	*Rod Stewart*
28	I DON'T WANT TO TALK ABOUT IT/	
	FIRST CUT IS THE DEEPEST	*Rod Stewart*

JUNE

4	I DON'T WANT TO TALK ABOUT IT/	
	FIRST CUT IS THE DEEPEST	*Rod Stewart*
11	I DON'T WANT TO TALK ABOUT IT/	
	FIRST CUT IS THE DEEPEST	*Rod Stewart*
18	LUCILLE	*Kenny Rogers*
25	SHOW YOU THE WAY TO GO	*Jacksons*

JULY

2	SO YOU WIN AGAIN	*Hot Chocolate*
9	SO YOU WIN AGAIN	*Hot Chocolate*
16	SO YOU WIN AGAIN	*Hot Chocolate*
23	I FEEL LOVE	*Donna Summer*
30	I FEEL LOVE	*Donna Summer*

VOLUME 14

AUGUST

6	I FEEL LOVE	*Donna Summer*
13	I FEEL LOVE	*Donna Summer*
20	ANGELO	*Brotherhood of Man*
27	FLOAT ON	*Floaters*

SEPTEMBER

3	WAY DOWN	*Elvis Presley*
10	WAY DOWN	*Elvis Presley*
17	WAY DOWN	*Elvis Presley*
24	WAY DOWN	*Elvis Presley*

OCTOBER

1	WAY DOWN	*Elvis Presley*
8	SILVER LADY	*David Soul*
15	SILVER LADY	*David Soul*
22	SILVER LADY	*David Soul*
29	YES SIR I CAN BOOGIE	*Baccara*

NOVEMBER

5	NAME OF THE GAME	*Abba*
12	NAME OF THE GAME	*Abba*
19	NAME OF THE GAME	*Abba*
26	NAME OF THE GAME	*Abba*

DECEMBER

3	MULL OF KINTYRE	*Wings*
10	MULL OF KINTYRE	*Wings*
17	MULL OF KINTYRE	*Wings*
24	MULL OF KINTYRE	*Wings*
31	MULL OF KINTYRE	*Wings*

1978

JANUARY

7	MULL OF KINTYRE	*Wings*
14	MULL OF KINTYRE	*Wings*
21	MULL OF KINTYRE	*Wings*
28	MULL OF KINTYRE	*Wings*

FEBRUARY

4	UPTOWN TOP RANKING	*Althia and Donna*
11	FIGARO	*Brotherhood of Man*
18	TAKE A CHANCE ON ME	*Abba*
25	TAKE A CHANCE ON ME	*Abba*

MARCH

4	TAKE A CHANCE ON ME	*Abba*
11	WUTHERING HEIGHTS	*Kate Bush*
18	WUTHERING HEIGHTS	*Kate Bush*
25	WUTHERING HEIGHTS	*Kate Bush*

APRIL

1 WUTHERING HEIGHTS *Kate Bush*
8 MATCHSTALK MEN AND MATCHSTALK CATS
AND DOGS *Brian/Michael*
15 MATCHSTALK MEN AND MATCHSTALK CATS
AND DOGS *Brian/Michael*
22 MATCHSTALK MEN AND MATCHSTALK CATS
AND DOGS *Brian/Michael*
29 NIGHT FEVER *Bee Gees*

MAY

6	NIGHT FEVER	*Bee Gees*
13	RIVERS OF BABYLON	*Boney M*
20	RIVERS OF BABYLON	*Boney M*
27	RIVERS OF BABYLON	*Boney M*

JUNE

3 RIVERS OF BABYLON *Boney M*
10 RIVERS OF BABYLON *Boney M*
17 YOU'RE THE ONE THAT I WANT
John Travolta/Olivia Newton-John
24 YOU'RE THE ONE THAT I WANT
John Travolta/Olivia Newton-John

JULY

1 YOU'RE THE ONE THAT I WANT
John Travolta/Olivia Newton-John
8 YOU'RE THE ONE THAT I WANT
John Travolta/Olivia Newton-John
15 YOU'RE THE ONE THAT I WANT
John Travolta/Olivia Newton-John
22 YOU'RE THE ONE THAT I WANT
John Travolta/Olivia Newton-John
29 YOU'RE THE ONE THAT I WANT
John Travolta/Olivia Newton-John

AUGUST

5 YOU'RE THE ONE THAT I WANT
John Travolta/Olivia Newton-John
12 YOU'RE THE ONE THAT I WANT
John Travolta/Olivia Newton-John
19 THREE TIMES A LADY *Commodores*
26 THREE TIMES A LADY *Commodores*

SEPTEMBER

2 THREE TIMES A LADY *Commodores*
9 THREE TIMES A LADY *Commodores*
16 THREE TIMES A LADY *Commodores*
23 DREADLOCK HOLIDAY *10cc*
30 SUMMER NIGHTS
John Travolta/Olivia Newton-John

OCTOBER

7 SUMMER NIGHTS
John Travolta/Olivia Newton-John
14 SUMMER NIGHTS
John Travolta/Olivia Newton-John
21 SUMMER NIGHTS
John Travolta/Olivia Newton-John
28 SUMMER NIGHTS
John Travolta/Olivia Newton-John

NOVEMBER

4 SUMMER NIGHTS
John Travolta/Olivia Newton-John
11 SUMMER NIGHTS
John Travolta/Olivia Newton-John
18 RAT TRAP *Boomtown Rats*
25 RAT TRAP *Boomtown Rats*

DECEMBER

2 DO YA THINK I'M SEXY *Rod Stewart*
9 MARY'S BOY CHILD—OH MY LORD
Boney M
16 MARY'S BOY CHILD—OH MY LORD
Boney M
23 MARY'S BOY CHILD—OH MY LORD
Boney M
30 MARY'S BOY CHILD—OH MY LORD
Boney M

1979

JANUARY

6 Y.M.C.A. *Village People*
13 Y.M.C.A. *Village People*
20 Y.M.C.A. *Village People*
27 HIT ME WITH YOUR RHYTHM STICK
Ian Dury/The Blockheads

FEBRUARY

3	HEART OF GLASS	*Blondie*
10	HEART OF GLASS	*Blondie*
17	HEART OF GLASS	*Blondie*
24	HEART OF GLASS	*Blondie*

MARCH

3	TRAGEDY	*Bee Gees*
10	TRAGEDY	*Bee Gees*
17	I WILL SURVIVE	*Gloria Gaynor*
24	I WILL SURVIVE	*Gloria Gaynor*
31	I WILL SURVIVE	*Gloria Gaynor*

APRIL

7	I WILL SURVIVE	*Gloria Gaynor*
14	BRIGHT EYES	*Art Garfunkel*
21	BRIGHT EYES	*Art Garfunkel*
28	BRIGHT EYES	*Art Garfunkel*

MAY

5	BRIGHT EYES	*Art Garfunkel*
12	BRIGHT EYES	*Art Garfunkel*
19	BRIGHT EYES	*Art Garfunkel*
26	SUNDAY GIRL	*Blondie*

JUNE

2	SUNDAY GIRL	*Blondie*
9	SUNDAY GIRL	*Blondie*
16	RING MY BELL	*Anita Ward*
23	RING MY BELL	*Anita Ward*
30	ARE "FRIENDS" ELECTRIC?	*Tubeway Army*

JULY

7	ARE "FRIENDS" ELECTRIC?	*Tubeway Army*
14	ARE "FRIENDS" ELECTRIC?	*Tubeway Army*
21	ARE "FRIENDS" ELECTRIC?	*Tubeway Army*
28	I DON'T LIKE MONDAYS	*Boomtown Rats*

AUGUST

4	I DON'T LIKE MONDAYS	*Boomtown Rats*
11	I DON'T LIKE MONDAYS	*Boomtown Rats*
18	I DON'T LIKE MONDAYS	*Boomtown Rats*
25	WE DON'T TALK ANYMORE	*Cliff Richard*

SEPTEMBER

1	WE DON'T TALK ANYMORE	*Cliff Richard*
8	WE DON'T TALK ANYMORE	*Cliff Richard*
15	WE DON'T TALK ANYMORE	*Cliff Richard*
22	CARS	*Gary Numan*
29	MESSAGE IN A BOTTLE	*Police*

OCTOBER

6	MESSAGE IN A BOTTLE	*Police*
13	MESSAGE IN A BOTTLE	*Police*
20	VIDEO KILLED THE RADIO STAR	*Buggles*
27	ONE DAY AT A TIME	*Lena Martell*

NOVEMBER

3	ONE DAY AT A TIME	*Lena Martell*
10	ONE DAY AT A TIME	*Lena Martell*
17	WHEN YOU'RE IN LOVE WITH A BEAUTIFUL WOMAN	*Dr Hook*
24	WHEN YOU'RE IN LOVE WITH A BEAUTIFUL WOMAN	*Dr Hook*

DECEMBER

1	WHEN YOU'RE IN LOVE WITH A BEAUTIFUL WOMAN	*Dr Hook*
8	WALKING ON THE MOON	*Police*
15	ANOTHER BRICK IN THE WALL	*Pink Floyd*
22	ANOTHER BRICK IN THE WALL	*Pink Floyd*
29	ANOTHER BRICK IN THE WALL	*Pink Floyd*

1980

5	ANOTHER BRICK IN THE WALL	*Pink Floyd*
12	ANOTHER BRICK IN THE WALL	*Pink Floyd*
19	BRASS IN POCKET	*Pretenders*
26	BRASS IN POCKET	*Pretenders*

FEBRUARY

2	THE SPECIAL AKA LIVE (EP)	*Specials*
9	THE SPECIAL AKA LIVE (EP)	*Specials*
16	COWARD OF THE COUNTRY	*Kenny Rogers*
23	COWARD OF THE COUNTRY	*Kenny Rogers*

MARCH

1	ATOMIC	*Blondie*
8	ATOMIC	*Blondie*
15	TOGETHER WE ARE BEAUTIFUL	*Fern Kinney*
22	GOING UNDERGROUND	*Jam*
29	GOING UNDERGROUND	*Jam*

APRIL

5	GOING UNDERGROUND	*Jam*
12	WORKING MY WAY BACK TO YOU	*Detroit Spinners*
19	WORKING MY WAY BACK TO YOU	*Detroit Spinners*
26	CALL ME	*Blondie*

MAY

3	GENO	*Dexy's Midnight Runners*
10	GENO	*Dexy's Midnight Runners*
17	WHAT'S ANOTHER YEAR	*Johnny Logan*
24	WHAT'S ANOTHER YEAR	*Johnny Logan*
31	THEME FROM M*A*S*H (SUICIDE IS PAINLESS)	*Mash*

JUNE

7	THEME FROM M*A*S*H (SUICIDE IS PAINLESS)	*Mash*
14	THEME FROM M*A*S*H (SUICIDE IS PAINLESS)	*Mash*
21	CRYING	*Don McLean*
28	CRYING	*Don McLean*

JULY

5 CRYING   *Don McLean*
12 XANADU   *Olivia Newton-John and E.L.O.*
19 XANADU   *Olivia Newton-John and E.L.O.*
26 USE IT UP AND WEAR IT OUT   *Odyssey*

AUGUST

2 USE IT UP AND WEAR IT OUT   *Odyssey*
9 THE WINNER TAKES IT ALL   *Abba*
16 THE WINNER TAKES IT ALL   *Abba*
23 ASHES TO ASHES   *David Bowie*
30 ASHES TO ASHES   *David Bowie*

SEPTEMBER

6 START   *Jam*
13 FEELS LIKE I'M IN LOVE   *Kelly Marie*
20 FEELS LIKE I'M IN LOVE   *Kelly Marie*
27 DON'T STAND SO CLOSE TO ME   *Police*

OCTOBER

4 DON'T STAND SO CLOSE TO ME   *Police*
11 DON'T STAND SO CLOSE TO ME   *Police*
18 DON'T STAND SO CLOSE TO ME   *Police*
25 WOMAN IN LOVE   *Barbra Streisand*

NOVEMBER

1 WOMAN IN LOVE   *Barbra Streisand*
8 WOMAN IN LOVE   *Barbra Streisand*
15 THE TIDE IS HIGH   *Blondie*
22 THE TIDE IS HIGH   *Blondie*
29 SUPER TROUPER   *Abba*

DECEMBER

6 SUPER TROUPER   *Abba*
13 SUPER TROUPER   *Abba*
20 (JUST LIKE) STARTING OVER   *John Lennon*
27 THERE'S NO ONE QUITE LIKE GRANDMA
   St Winfred's Choir

1981

JANUARY

3 THERE'S NO ONE QUITE LIKE GRANDMA
   St Winfred's Choir
10 IMAGINE   *John Lennon*
17 IMAGINE   *John Lennon*
24 IMAGINE   *John Lennon*
31 IMAGINE   *John Lennon*

FEBRUARY

7 WOMAN   *John Lennon*
14 WOMAN   *John Lennon*
21 SHADDUP YOU FACE   *Joe Dolce*
28 SHADDUP YOU FACE   *Joe Dolce*

MARCH

7 SHADDUP YOU FACE   *Joe Dolce*
14 JEALOUS GUY   *Roxy Music*
21 JEALOUS GUY   *Roxy Music*
28 THIS OLE HOUSE   *Shakin' Stevens*

APRIL

4 THIS OLE HOUSE   *Shakin' Stevens*
11 THIS OLE HOUSE   *Shakin' Stevens*
18 MAKING YOUR MIND UP   *Bucks Fizz*
25 MAKING YOUR MIND UP   *Bucks Fizz*

MAY

2 MAKING YOUR MIND UP   *Bucks Fizz*
9 STAND AND DELIVER   *Adam and the Ants*
16 STAND AND DELIVER   *Adam and the Ants*
23 STAND AND DELIVER   *Adam and the Ants*
30 STAND AND DELIVER   *Adam and the Ants*

JUNE

6 STAND AND DELIVER   *Adam and the Ants*
13 BEING WITH YOU   *Smokey Robinson*
20 BEING WITH YOU   *Smokey Robinson*
27 ONE DAY IN YOUR LIFE   *Michael Jackson*

JULY

4 ONE DAY IN YOUR LIFE   *Michael Jackson*
11 GHOST TOWN   *Specials*
18 GHOST TOWN   *Specials*
25 GHOST TOWN   *Specials*

AUGUST

1 GREEN DOOR   *Shakin' Stevens*
8 GREEN DOOR   *Shakin' Stevens*
15 GREEN DOOR   *Shakin' Stevens*
22 GREEN DOOR   *Shakin' Stevens*
29 JAPANESE BOY   *Aneka*

SEPTEMBER

5 TAINTED LOVE   *Soft Cell*
12 TAINTED LOVE   *Soft Cell*
19 PRINCE CHARMING   *Adam and the Ants*
26 PRINCE CHARMING   *Adam and the Ants*

OCTOBER

3 PRINCE CHARMING   *Adam and the Ants*
10 PRINCE CHARMING   *Adam and the Ants*
17 IT'S MY PARTY   *Dave Stewart with Barbara Gaskin*
24 IT'S MY PARTY   *Dave Stewart with Barbara Gaskin*
31 IT'S MY PARTY   *Dave Stewart with Barbara Gaskin*

NOVEMBER

7 IT'S MY PARTY   *Dave Stewart with Barbara Gaskin*
14 EVERY LITTLE THING SHE DOES IS MAGIC   *Police*
21 UNDER PRESSURE   *Queen and David Bowie*
28 UNDER PRESSURE   *Queen and David Bowie*

DECEMBER

5	BEGIN THE BEGUINE	*Julio Iglesias*
12	DON'T YOU WANT ME	*Human League*
19	DON'T YOU WANT ME	*Human League*
26	DON'T YOU WANT ME	*Human League*

1982

JANUARY

2	DON'T YOU WANT ME	*Human League*
9	DON'T YOU WANT ME	*Human League*
16	THE LAND OF MAKE BELIEVE	*Bucks Fizz*
23	THE LAND OF MAKE BELIEVE	*Bucks Fizz*
30	OH JULIE	*Shakin' Stevens*

FEBRUARY

6	THE MODEL/COMPUTER LOVE	*Kraftwerk*
13	A TOWN CALLED MALICE/PRECIOUS	*Jam*
20	A TOWN CALLED MALICE/PRECIOUS	*Jam*
27	A TOWN CALLED MALICE/PRECIOUS	*Jam*

MARCH

6	THE LION SLEEPS TONIGHT	*Tight Fit*
13	THE LION SLEEPS TONIGHT	*Tight Fit*
20	THE LION SLEEPS TONIGHT	*Tight Fit*
27	SEVEN TEARS	*Goombay Dance Band*

APRIL

3	SEVEN TEARS	*Goombay Dance Band*
10	SEVEN TEARS	*Goombay Dance Band*
17	MY CAMERA NEVER LIES	*Bucks Fizz*
24	EBONY AND IVORY	*Paul McCartney and Stevie Wonder*

MAY

1	EBONY AND IVORY	*Paul McCartney and Stevie Wonder*
8	EBONY AND IVORY	*Paul McCartney and Stevie Wonder*
15	A LITTLE PEACE	*Nicole*
22	A LITTLE PEACE	*Nicole*
29	HOUSE OF FUN	*Madness*

JUNE

5	HOUSE OF FUN	*Madness*
12	GOODY TWO SHOES	*Adam Ant*
19	GOODY TWO SHOES	*Adam Ant*
26	I'VE NEVER BEEN TO ME	*Charlene*

JULY

3	HAPPY TALK	*Captain Sensible*
10	HAPPY TALK	*Captain Sensible*
17	FAME	*Irene Cara*
24	FAME	*Irene Cara*
31	FAME	*Irene Cara*

AUGUST

7	COME ON EILEEN	*Dexy's Midnight Runners*
14	COME ON EILEEN	*Dexy's Midnight Runners*
21	COME ON EILEEN	*Dexy's Midnight Runners*
28	COME ON EILEEN	*Dexy's Midnight Runners*

SEPTEMBER

4	EYE OF THE TIGER	*Survivor*
11	EYE OF THE TIGER	*Survivor*
18	EYE OF THE TIGER	*Survivor*
25	EYE OF THE TIGER	*Survivor*

OCTOBER

2	PASS THE DUTCHIE	*Musical Youth*
9	PASS THE DUTCHIE	*Musical Youth*
16	PASS THE DUTCHIE	*Musical Youth*
23	DO YOU REALLY WANT TO HURT ME	*Culture Club*
30	DO YOU REALLY WANT TO HURT ME	*Culture Club*

NOVEMBER

6	DO YOU REALLY WANT TO HURT ME	*Culture Club*
13	I DON'T WANNA DANCE	*Eddy Grant*
20	I DON'T WANNA DANCE	*Eddy Grant*
27	I DON'T WANNA DANCE	*Eddy Grant*

DECEMBER

4	BEAT SURRENDER	*Jam*
11	BEAT SURRENDER	*Jam*
18	SAVE YOUR LOVE	*Renee and Renato*
25	SAVE YOUR LOVE	*Renee and Renato*

1983

JANUARY

1	SAVE YOUR LOVE	*Renee and Renato*
8	SAVE YOUR LOVE	*Renee and Renato*
15	YOU CAN'T HURRY LOVE	*Phil Collins*
22	YOU CAN'T HURRY LOVE	*Phil Collins*
29	DOWN UNDER	*Men At Work*

FEBRUARY

5	DOWN UNDER	*Men At Work*
12	DOWN UNDER	*Men At Work*
19	TOO SHY	*Kajagoogoo*
26	TOO SHY	*Kajagoogoo*

MARCH

5	BILLIE JEAN	*Michael Jackson*
12	TOTAL ECLIPSE OF THE HEART	*Bonnie Tyler*
19	TOTAL ECLIPSE OF THE HEART	*Bonnie Tyler*
26	IS THERE SOMETHING I SHOULD KNOW	*Duran Duran*

APRIL

2	IS THERE SOMETHING I SHOULD KNOW	*Duran Duran*
9	LET'S DANCE	*David Bowie*
16	LET'S DANCE	*David Bowie*
23	LET'S DANCE	*David Bowie*
30	TRUE	*Spandau Ballet*

MAY

7	TRUE	*Spandau Ballet*
14	TRUE	*Spandau Ballet*
21	TRUE	*Spandau Ballet*
28	CANDY GIRL	*New Edition*

JUNE

4	EVERY BREATH YOU TAKE	*Police*
11	EVERY BREATH YOU TAKE	*Police*
18	EVERY BREATH YOU TAKE	*Police*
25	EVERY BREATH YOU TAKE	*Police*

JULY

2	BABY JANE	*Rod Stewart*
9	BABY JANE	*Rod Stewart*
16	BABY JANE	*Rod Stewart*
23	WHEREVER I LAY MY HAT (THAT'S MY HOME) *Paul Young*	
30	WHEREVER I LAY MY HAT (THAT'S MY HOME) *Paul Young*	

AUGUST

6	WHEREVER I LAY MY HAT (THAT'S MY HOME) *Paul Young*	
13	GIVE IT UP	*KC and the Sunshine Band*
20	GIVE IT UP	*KC and the Sunshine Band*
27	GIVE IT UP	*KC and the Sunshine Band*

SEPTEMBER

3	RED RED WINE	*UB40*
10	RED RED WINE	*UB40*
17	RED RED WINE	*UB40*
24	KARMA CHAMELEON	*Culture Club*

OCTOBER

1	KARMA CHAMELEON	*Culture Club*
8	KARMA CHAMELEON	*Culture Club*
15	KARMA CHAMELEON	*Culture Club*
22	KARMA CHAMELEON	*Culture Club*
29	KARMA CHAMELEON	*Culture Club*

NOVEMBER

5	UPTOWN GIRL	*Billy Joel*
12	UPTOWN GIRL	*Billy Joel*
19	UPTOWN GIRL	*Billy Joel*
26	UPTOWN GIRL	*Billy Joel*

DECEMBER

3	UPTOWN GIRL	*Billy Joel*
10	ONLY YOU	*Flying Pickets*
17	ONLY YOU	*Flying Pickets*
24	ONLY YOU	*Flying Pickets*
31	ONLY YOU	*Flying Pickets*

1984

JANUARY

7	ONLY YOU	*Flying Pickets*
14	PIPES OF PEACE	*Paul McCartney*
21	PIPES OF PEACE	*Paul McCartney*
28	RELAX	*Frankie Goes to Hollywood*

FEBRUARY

4	RELAX	*Frankie Goes to Hollywood*
11	RELAX	*Frankie Goes to Hollywood*
18	RELAX	*Frankie Goes to Hollywood*
25	RELAX	*Frankie Goes to Hollywood*

MARCH

3	99 RED BALLOONS	*Nena*
10	99 RED BALLOONS	*Nena*
17	99 RED BALLOONS	*Nena*
24	HELLO	*Lionel Richie*
31	HELLO	*Lionel Richie*

APRIL

7	HELLO	*Lionel Richie*
14	HELLO	*Lionel Richie*
21	HELLO	*Lionel Richie*
28	HELLO	*Lionel Richie*

MAY

5	THE REFLEX	*Duran Duran*
12	THE REFLEX	*Duran Duran*
19	THE REFLEX	*Duran Duran*
26	THE REFLEX	*Duran Duran*

JUNE

2	WAKE ME UP BEFORE YOU GO GO	*Wham!*
9	WAKE ME UP BEFORE YOU GO GO	*Wham!*
19	TWO TRIBES	*Frankie Goes to Hollywood*
23	TWO TRIBES	*Frankie Goes to Hollywood*
30	TWO TRIBES	*Frankie Goes to Hollywood*

JULY

7	TWO TRIBES	*Frankie Goes to Hollywood*
14	TWO TRIBES	*Frankie Goes to Hollywood*
21	TWO TRIBES	*Frankie Goes to Hollywood*
28	TWO TRIBES	*Frankie Goes to Hollywood*

AUGUST

4	TWO TRIBES	*Frankie Goes to Hollywood*
11	TWO TRIBES	*Frankie Goes to Hollywood*
18	CARELESS WHISPER	*George Michael*
25	CARELESS WHISPER	*George Michael*

SEPTEMBER

1	CARELESS WHISPER	*George Michael*
8	I JUST CALLED TO SAY I LOVE YOU	*Stevie Wonder*
15	I JUST CALLED TO SAY I LOVE YOU	*Stevie Wonder*
22	I JUST CALLED TO SAY I LOVE YOU	*Stevie Wonder*
29	I JUST CALLED TO SAY I LOVE YOU	*Stevie Wonder*

OCTOBER

6	I JUST CALLED TO SAY I LOVE YOU	*Stevie Wonder*
13	I JUST CALLED TO SAY I LOVE YOU	*Stevie Wonder*
20	FREEDOM	*Wham!*
27	FREEDOM	*Wham!*

NOVEMBER

3	FREEDOM	*Wham!*
10	I FEEL FOR YOU	*Chaka Khan*
17	I FEEL FOR YOU	*Chaka Khan*
24	I FEEL FOR YOU	*Chaka Khan*

DECEMBER

1	I SHOULD HAVE KNOWN BETTER	*Jim Diamond*
8	THE POWER OF LOVE	*Frankie Goes to Hollywood*
15	DO THEY KNOW IT'S CHRISTMAS	*Band Aid*
22	DO THEY KNOW IT'S CHRISTMAS	*Band Aid*
29	DO THEY KNOW IT'S CHRISTMAS	*Band Aid*

1985

JANUARY

5	DO THEY KNOW IT'S CHRISTMAS	*Band Aid*
12	DO THEY KNOW IT'S CHRISTMAS	*Band Aid*
19	I WANT TO KNOW WHAT LOVE IS	*Foreigner*
26	I WANT TO KNOW WHAT LOVE IS	*Foreigner*

FEBRUARY

2	I KNOW HIM SO WELL	*Elaine Paige and Barbara Dickson*
9	I KNOW HIM SO WELL	*Elaine Paige and Barbara Dickson*
16	I KNOW HIM SO WELL	*Elaine Paige and Barbara Dickson*
23	I KNOW HIM SO WELL	*Elaine Paige and Barbara Dickson*

MARCH

2	I KNOW HIM SO WELL	*Elaine Paige and Barbara Dickson*
9	YOU SPIN ME ROUND (LIKE A RECORD) *Dead or Alive*	
16	YOU SPIN ME ROUND (LIKE A RECORD) *Dead or Alive*	
23	EASY LOVER	*Philip Bailey and Phil Collins*
30	EASY LOVER	*Philip Bailey and Phil Collins*

APRIL

6	EASY LOVER	*Philip Bailey and Phil Collins*
13	EASY LOVER	*Philip Bailey and Phil Collins*
20	WE ARE THE WORLD	*USA for Africa*
27	WE ARE THE WORLD	*USA for Africa*

MAY

4	MOVE CLOSER	*Phyllis Nelson*
11	19	*Paul Hardcastle*
18	19	*Paul Hardcastle*
25	19	*Paul Hardcastle*

JUNE

1	19	*Paul Hardcastle*
8	19	*Paul Hardcastle*
15	YOU'LL NEVER WALK ALONE	*The Crowd*
22	YOU'LL NEVER WALK ALONE	*The Crowd*
29	FRANKIE	*Sister Sledge*

JULY

6	FRANKIE	*Sister Sledge*
13	FRANKIE	*Sister Sledge*
20	FRANKIE	*Sister Sledge*
27	THERE MUST BE AN ANGEL (PLAYING WITH MY HEART)	*Eurythmics*

AUGUST

3	INTO THE GROOVE	*Madonna*
10	INTO THE GROOVE	*Madonna*
17	INTO THE GROOVE	*Madonna*
24	INTO THE GROOVE	*Madonna*
31	I GOT YOU BABE	*UB40 and Chrissie Hynde*

SEPTEMBER

7	DANCING IN THE STREET	*David Bowie and Mick Jagger*
14	DANCING IN THE STREET	*David Bowie and Mick Jagger*
21	DANCING IN THE STREET	*David Bowie and Mick Jagger*
28	DANCING IN THE STREET	*David Bowie and Mick Jagger*

OCTOBER

5	IF I WAS	*Midge Ure*
12	THE POWER OF LOVE	*Jennifer Rush*
19	THE POWER OF LOVE	*Jennifer Rush*
26	THE POWER OF LOVE	*Jennifer Rush*

NOVEMBER

2	THE POWER OF LOVE	*Jennifer Rush*
9	THE POWER OF LOVE	*Jennifer Rush*
16	A GOOD HEART	*Feargal Sharkey*
23	A GOOD HEART	*Feargal Sharkey*
30	I'M YOUR MAN	*Wham!*

DECEMBER

7	I'M YOUR MAN	*Wham!*
14	SAVING ALL MY LOVE FOR YOU	*Whitney Houston*
21	SAVING ALL MY LOVE FOR YOU	*Whitney Houston*
28	MERRY CHRISTMAS EVERYONE	*Shakin' Stevens*

1986

JANUARY

4   MERRY CHRISTMAS EVERYONE   *Shakin' Stevens*
11 WEST END GIRLS   *Pet Shop Boys*
18 WEST END GIRLS   *Pet Shop Boys*
25 THE SUN ALWAYS SHINES ON TV   *A-Ha*

FEBRUARY

1   THE SUN ALWAYS SHINES ON TV   *A-Ha*
8   WHEN THE GOING GETS TOUGH, THE TOUGH GET GOING   *Billy Ocean*
15 WHEN THE GOING GETS TOUGH, THE TOUGH GET GOING   *Billy Ocean*
22 WHEN THE GOING GETS TOUGH, THE TOUGH GET GOING   *Billy Ocean*

MARCH

1   WHEN THE GOING GETS TOUGH, THE TOUGH GET GOING   *Billy Ocean*
8   CHAIN REACTION   *Diana Ross*
15 CHAIN REACTION   *Diana Ross*
22 CHAIN REACTION   *Diana Ross*
29 LIVING DOLL   *Cliff Richard and the Young Ones*

APRIL

5   LIVING DOLL   *Cliff Richard and the Young Ones*
12 LIVING DOLL   *Cliff Richard and the Young Ones*
19 A DIFFERENT CORNER   *George Michael*
26 A DIFFERENT CORNER   *George Michael*

MAY

3   A DIFFERENT CORNER   *George Michael*
10 ROCK ME AMADEUS   *Falco*
17 THE CHICKEN SONG   *Spitting Image*
24 THE CHICKEN SONG   *Spitting Image*
31 THE CHICKEN SONG   *Spitting Image*

JUNE

7   SPIRIT IN THE SKY   *Doctor and the Medics*
14 SPIRIT IN THE SKY   *Doctor and the Medics*
21 SPIRIT IN THE SKY   *Doctor and the Medics*
28 THE EDGE OF HEAVEN   *Wham!*

JULY

5   THE EDGE OF HEAVEN   *Wham!*
12 PAPA DON'T PREACH   *Madonna*
19 PAPA DON'T PREACH   *Madonna*
26 PAPA DON'T PREACH   *Madonna*

AUGUST

2   THE LADY IN RED   *Chris de Burgh*
9   THE LADY IN RED   *Chris de Burgh*
16 THE LADY IN RED   *Chris de Burgh*
23 I WANT TO WAKE UP WITH YOU   *Boris Gardiner*
30 I WANT TO WAKE UP WITH YOU   *Boris Gardiner*

SEPTEMBER

6   I WANT TO WAKE UP WITH YOU   *Boris Gardiner*
13 DON'T LEAVE ME THIS WAY   *Communards*
20 DON'T LEAVE ME THIS WAY   *Communards*
27 DON'T LEAVE ME THIS WAY   *Communards*

OCTOBER

4   DON'T LEAVE ME THIS WAY   *Communards*
11 TRUE BLUE   *Madonna*
18 EVERY LOSER WINS   *Nick Berry*
25 EVERY LOSER WINS   *Nick Berry*

NOVEMBER

1   EVERY LOSER WINS   *Nick Berry*
8   TAKE MY BREATH AWAY   *Berlin*
15 TAKE MY BREATH AWAY   *Berlin*
22 TAKE MY BREATH AWAY   *Berlin*
29 TAKE MY BREATH AWAY   *Berlin*

DECEMBER

6   THE FINAL COUNTDOWN   *Europe*
13 THE FINAL COUNTDOWN   *Europe*
20 CARAVAN OF LOVE   *Housemartins*
27 REET PETITE   *Jackie Wilson*

1987

JANUARY

3   REET PETITE   *Jackie Wilson*
10 REET PETITE   *Jackie Wilson*
17 REET PETITE   *Jackie Wilson*
24 JACK YOUR BODY   *Steve 'Silk' Hurley*
31 JACK YOUR BODY   *Steve 'Silk' Hurley*

FEBRUARY

7   I KNEW YOU WERE WAITING   *Aretha Franklin & George Michael*
14 I KNEW YOU WERE WAITING   *Aretha Franklin & George Michael*
21 STAND BY ME   *Ben E King*
28 STAND BY ME   *Ben E King*

MARCH

7   STAND BY ME   *Ben E King*
14 EVERYTHING I OWN   *Boy George*
21 EVERYTHING I OWN   *Boy George*
28 RESPECTABLE   *Mel & Kim*

APRIL

4   LET IT BE   *Ferry Aid*
11 LET IT BE   *Ferry Aid*
18 LET IT BE   *Ferry Aid*
25 LA ISLA BONITA   *Madonna*

MAY

2   LA ISLA BONITA   *Madonna*
9   NOTHING'S GONNA STOP US NOW   *Starship*
16   NOTHING'S GONNA STOP US NOW   *Starship*
23   NOTHING'S GONNA STOP US NOW   *Starship*
30   NOTHING'S GONNA STOP US NOW   *Starship*

JUNE

6   I WANNA DANCE WITH SOMEBODY   *Whitney Houston*
13   I WANNA DANCE WITH SOMEBODY   *Whitney Houston*
20   STAR TREKKIN'   *The Firm*
27   STAR TREKKIN'   *The Firm*

JULY

4   IT'S A SIN   *Pet Shop Boys*
11   IT'S A SIN   *Pet Shop Boys*
18   IT'S A SIN   *Pet Shop Boys*
25   WHO'S THAT GIRL   *Madonna*

AUGUST

1   LA BAMBA   *Los Lobos*
8   LA BAMBA   *Los Lobos*
15   I JUST CAN'T STOP LOVING YOU
     Michael Jackson/Siedah Garrett
22   I JUST CAN'T STOP LOVING YOU
     Michael Jackson/Siedah Garrett
29   NEVER GONNA GIVE YOU UP   *Rick Astley*

SEPTEMBER

5   NEVER GONNA GIVE YOU UP   *Rick Astley*
12   NEVER GONNA GIVE YOU UP   *Rick Astley*
19   NEVER GONNA GIVE YOU UP   *Rick Astley*
26   NEVER GONNA GIVE YOU UP   *Rick Astley*

OCTOBER

3   PUMP UP THE VOLUME   *M/A/R/R/S*
10   PUMP UP THE VOLUME   *M/A/R/R/S*
17   YOU WIN AGAIN   *Bee Gees*
24   YOU WIN AGAIN   *Bee Gees*
31   YOU WIN AGAIN   *Bee Gees*

NOVEMBER

7   YOU WIN AGAIN   *Bee Gees*
14   CHINA IN YOUR HAND   *T'Pau*
21   CHINA IN YOUR HAND   *T'Pau*
28   CHINA IN YOUR HAND   *T'Pau*

DECEMBER

5   CHINA IN YOUR HAND   *T'Pau*
12   CHINA IN YOUR HAND   *T'Pau*
19   ALWAYS ON MY MIND   *Pet Shop Boys*
26   ALWAYS ON MY MIND   *Pet Shop Boys*

1988

JANUARY

2   ALWAYS ON MY MIND   *Pet Shop Boys*
9   ALWAYS ON MY MIND   *Pet Shop Boys*
16   HEAVEN IS A PLACE ON EARTH   *Belinda Carlisle*
23   HEAVEN IS A PLACE ON EARTH   *Belinda Carlisle*
30   I THINK WE'RE ALONE NOW   *Tiffany*

FEBRUARY

6   I THINK WE'RE ALONE NOW   *Tiffany*
13   I THINK WE'RE ALONE NOW   *Tiffany*
20   I SHOULD BE SO LUCKY   *Kylie Minogue*
27   I SHOULD BE SO LUCKY   *Kylie Minogue*

MARCH

5   I SHOULD BE SO LUCKY   *Kylie Minogue*
12   I SHOULD BE SO LUCKY   *Kylie Minogue*
19   I SHOULD BE SO LUCKY   *Kylie Minogue*
26   DON'T TURN AROUND   *Aswad*

APRIL

2   DON'T TURN AROUND   *Aswad*
9   HEART   *Pet Shop Boys*
16   HEART   *Pet Shop Boys*
23   HEART   *Pet Shop Boys*
30   THEME FROM S'XPRESS   *S'Express*

MAY

7   THEME FROM S'XPRESS   *S'Express*
14   PERFECT   *Fairground Attraction*
21   WITH A LITTLE . . .   *Wet Wet Wet*
     SHE'S LEAVING HOME   *Billy Bragg*
28   WITH A LITTLE . . .   *Wet Wet Wet*
     SHE'S LEAVING HOME   *Billy Bragg*

JUNE

4   WITH A LITTLE . . .   *Wet Wet Wet*
     SHE'S LEAVING HOME   *Billy Bragg*
11   WITH A LITTLE . . .   *Wet Wet Wet*
     SHE'S LEAVING HOME   *Billy Bragg*
18   DOCTORIN' THE TARDIS   *The Timelords*
25   I OWE YOU NOTHING   *Bros*

JULY

2   I OWE YOU NOTHING   *Bros*
9   NOTHING'S GONNA CHANGE MY LOVE FOR YOU
     Glen Medeiros
16   NOTHING'S GONNA CHANGE MY LOVE FOR YOU
     Glen Medeiros
23   NOTHING'S GONNA CHANGE MY LOVE FOR YOU
     Glen Medeiros
30   NOTHING'S GONNA CHANGE MY LOVE FOR YOU
     Glen Medeiros

AUGUST

6	THE ONLY WAY IS UP	*Yazz and the Plastic Population*
13	THE ONLY WAY IS UP	*Yazz and the Plastic Population*
20	THE ONLY WAY IS UP	*Yazz and the Plastic Population*
27	THE ONLY WAY IS UP	*Yazz and the Plastic Population*

SEPTEMBER

3	THE ONLY WAY IS UP	*Yazz and the Plastic Population*
10	A GROOVY KIND OF LOVE	*Phil Collins*
17	A GROOVY KIND OF LOVE	*Phil Collins*
24	HE AIN'T HEAVY, HE'S MY BROTHER	*The Hollies*

OCTOBER

1	DESIRE	*U2*
8	DESIRE	*U2*
15	ONE MOMENT IN TIME	*Whitney Houston*
22	ONE MOMENT IN TIME	*Whitney Houston*
29	ORINOCO FLOW	*Enya*

NOVEMBER

5	ORINOCO FLOW	*Enya*
12	ORINOCO FLOW	*Enya*
19	FIRST TIME	*Robin Beck*
26	FIRST TIME	*Robin Beck*

DECEMBER

3	FIRST TIME	*Robin Beck*
10	MISTLETOE AND WINE	*Cliff Richard*
17	MISTLETOE AND WINE	*Cliff Richard*
24	MISTLETOE AND WINE	*Cliff Richard*
31	MISTLETOE AND WINE	*Cliff Richard*

1989

JANUARY

7	ESPECIALLY FOR YOU	
	Kylie Minogue and Jason Donovan	
14	ESPECIALLY FOR YOU	
	Kylie Minogue and Jason Donovan	
21	ESPECIALLY FOR YOU	
	Kylie Minogue and Jason Donovan	
28	SOMETHING'S GOTTEN HOLD OF MY HEART	
	Marc Almond featuring Gene Pitney	

FEBRUARY

4	SOMETHING'S GOTTEN HOLD OF MY HEART	
	Marc Almond featuring Gene Pitney	
11	SOMETHING'S GOTTEN HOLD OF MY HEART	
	Marc Almond featuring Gene Pitney	
18	SOMETHING'S GOTTEN HOLD OF MY HEART	
	Marc Almond featuring Gene Pitney	
25	BELFAST CHILD	*Simple Minds*

MARCH

4	BELFAST CHILD	*Simple Minds*
11	TOO MANY BROKEN HEARTS	*Jason Donovan*
18	TOO MANY BROKEN HEARTS	*Jason Donovan*
25	LIKE A PRAYER	*Madonna*

APRIL

1	LIKE A PRAYER	*Madonna*
8	LIKE A PRAYER	*Madonna*
15	ETERNAL FLAME	*The Bangles*
22	ETERNAL FLAME	*The Bangles*
29	ETERNAL FLAME	*The Bangles*

MAY

6	ETERNAL FLAME	*The Bangles*
13	HAND ON YOUR HEART	*Kylie Minogue*
20	FERRY CROSS THE MERSEY	*Various*
27	FERRY CROSS THE MERSEY	*Various*

JUNE

3	FERRY CROSS THE MERSEY	*Various*
10	SEALED WITH A KISS	*Jason Donovan*
17	SEALED WITH A KISS	*Jason Donovan*
24	BACK TO LIFE	*Soul II Soul featuring Caron Wheeler*

JULY

1	BACK TO LIFE	*Soul II Soul featuring Caron Wheeler*
8	BACK TO LIFE	*Soul II Soul featuring Caron Wheeler*
15	BACK TO LIFE	*Soul II Soul featuring Caron Wheeler*
22	YOU'LL NEVER STOP ME LOVING YOU	*Sonia*
29	YOU'LL NEVER STOP ME LOVING YOU	*Sonia*

AUGUST

5	SWING THE MOOD	*Jive Bunny and the Mastermixers*
12	SWING THE MOOD	*Jive Bunny and the Mastermixers*
19	SWING THE MOOD	*Jive Bunny and the Mastermixers*
26	SWING THE MOOD	*Jive Bunny and the Mastermixers*

SEPTEMBER

2	SWING THE MOOD	*Jive Bunny and the Mastermixers*
9	RIDE ON TIME	*Black Box*
16	RIDE ON TIME	*Black Box*
23	RIDE ON TIME	*Black Box*
30	RIDE ON TIME	*Black Box*

OCTOBER

7	RIDE ON TIME	*Black Box*
14	RIDE ON TIME	*Black Box*
21	THAT'S WHAT I LIKE	*Jive Bunny and the Mastermixers*
28	THAT'S WHAT I LIKE	*Jive Bunny and the Mastermixers*

NOVEMBER

4	THAT'S WHAT I LIKE	*Jive Bunny and the Mastermixers*
11	ALL AROUND THE WORLD	*Lisa Stansfield*
18	ALL AROUND THE WORLD	*Lisa Stansfield*
25	YOU'VE GOT IT	*New Kids On The Block*

DECEMBER

2 YOU'VE GOT IT *New Kids On The Block*
9 YOU'VE GOT IT *New Kids On The Block*
16 LET'S PARTY
    Jive Bunny and the Mastermixers
23 DO THEY KNOW IT'S CHRISTMAS? *Band Aid II*

INDEX

Bold numbers refer to volume number.
Numbers in *italics* refer to illustrations.
Entries in *italics* refer to film titles.

A

A & M Records **5:** 503, *503,* 515, 517
ABC Records **3:** 307, 309, *324,* 328, **20:** *2342,* 2396
AC/DC **6:** 697, **9:** 1020, **11:** *1285,* **17:** 1983, **19:** 2223, *2226,* 2227-9, 2237, **20:** 2362, 2370, 2371
Abba **6:** 700, **9:** 983, **10:** 1140, **14:** *1678,* 1680, **16:** 1901, **17:** *1941,* 1942, 1943-7, 1956-7, **18:** 2103, 2120, **20:** 2292, 2362, 2367, 2395-6
Abbott, Drew **16:** 1856
Abner, Ewart, Jr **5:** 595, **9:** 1058
Abrahams, Mick **14:** 1570-1
Abrahamson, Herb **1:** 43, *59,* **3:** 272, *273,* 274, 345, **7:** 727
Abyssinian Baptist Choir **3:** 321
Abyssinians **16:** 1887, *1887*
AC and the Silvertones *see* Guess Who
Ace **3:** *261,* 264, *264,* **17:** 1922, 1924
Ace, Johnny **3:** 339, **5:** 574, **7:** 799
Ace, Richard **9:** 976
Aces **9:** *972, 973*
Ackerman, Paul **8:** 935
Ackland, Joss **20:** *2337*
Action **7:** 759, 802, 818-19, *818*
Acuff, Roy **1:** 39, 91
Acuff-Rose Publishing Co. **2:** 225, 227, 230, 231, 232, **4:** 414, 415
Adam and the Ants **18:** 2050, 2054, *2055,* 2058, 2060, **20:** *2323, 2324,* 2323-5, 2360
Adams, Arthur **19:** 2173
Adams, Billy **19:** 2220
Adams, Johnny **3:** 337
Adamson, Barry **18:** 2075
Adamson, Billy **5:** *530*
Adamson, Stuart **19:** 2275, *2275*
Aday, Marvin Lee 'Meatloaf' **18:** 2122-4, *2123*
Adderley, Cannonball **13:** 1532
Ade, King Sunny **9:** 964, 966-7, **14:** 1657, **20:** 2362, 2378, 2379, 2380, *2380*
Alder, Danny **10:** 1107
Adler, Larry **6:** 654
Adler, Lou **3:** 266, **5:** 503, **6:** 675-6, **7:** 766-7, 839, **9:** 982, **10:** 1081-2, 1094, *1094,* 1098-9, **11:** 1252, **14:** 1614, **15:** 1715
Ad Libs **1:** 63

'Adventures of Ozzie and Harriet, The' **3:** 302, *302*
Advert, Gaye **18:** 2071
Adverts **18:** 2061, *2061,* 2063, 2071
Aerosmith **14:** 1601, **16:** *1841,* 1848-9, 2121
African Beats **20:** 2380
African Brothers **16:** 1897
Afrika Bambaataa **19:** *2168,* 2168-9, 2177
Afrikan Beat Band **14:** 1657
Agnew, Pete **17:** *1988,* 1989
Ahern, Brian **17:** 2025
Aiken, Ben **10:** 1162
Airdales **6:** 699
Airforce **9:** 1031, **10:** 1189
Airey, Don **17:** 1986
Air Supply **20:** 2371, *2371*
Aitken, Jonathan **12:** 1322
Aitken, Laurel **2:** 147, **9:** 962, 976, *977,* **19:** 2216
Akkerman, Jan **20:** 2367
Akuna, Sherwood **9:** 1017
Aladdin **3:** 262, 264, 271, 340, **5:** 502
Alaimo, Steve **8:** 937
Alan Brown Set **7:** 820, *820*
Alan Price Combo **6:** 657
Alarm **20:** 2381, 2420
Albemarle Jazz Band **4:** 439
Albert, Ron and Howie **15:** 1737
Albert, Ted **6:** 697
Albertine, Bruce **18:** 2149
Albertine, Viv **18:** 2062
Alberts **4:** 439, *439,* **14:** 1578
Albin, Peter **10:** 1097, 1170
Albion Band **10:** 1125, **13:** 1462, 1464
Aldo, Steve **5:** 523 *523*
Aldon Music **4:** 441-4, 447, *448,* 450-2, 459, **5:** 502
Aldred, Michael **8:** 849
Aldridge, Alan **12:** 1379
Alexander, Dave **13:** 1498
Alexander, George **19:** 2227
Alexander, J. W. **3:** 333, 334, 335
Alexander, Michael **8:** 849
Alexander, Willie **17:** 2004
Alexandra, Chris **19:** 2242
Alexandra Palace, London **11:** *1303,* 1305, *1305,* 1308
Alice, Cooper **16:** *1862,* 1864-7, **20:** 2339
Alice Doesn't Live Here Anymore **14:** 1652
Alice's Restaurant **8:** 849
Allah and the Knife-Wielding Punks **18:** 2114
Allan, Davie, and the Arrows **4:** 392
Allan, Elkan **8:** 849
Allan, Johnnie **13:** 1455, *1455*
Allbitten, Dub **3:** *319*

All Coppers Are **13:** 1508
Alldis, Barry **17:** 1958
Alldred, Dave **2:** 192, 193
Allen, Chad **14:** 1616-17
Allen, Colin **10:** 1114, *1114-15*
Allen, Daevid **11:** 1305, **14:** *1579,* 1579-80, **20:** 2368
Allen, Frank **5:** *529, 530*
Allen, Gary **20:** 2376
Allen, 'Hos' **1:** 57-68
Allen, Lee **2:** 149, 151, 154, **4:** 389, **13:** 1451
Allen, Les **4:** 389
Allen, Mike **17:** *1960*
Allen, Rick **10:** 1174, **19:** 2236-7, *2237*
Allen, Steve **19:** 2278
Allen, Verden **16:** 1818, 1819, *1820*
Allison, Jerry **2:** *183,* 185, *185, 186,* 188, *189,* 193, 227, **4:** 457
Allisons **17:** 1955
Allison, Luther **10:** 1102
Allison, Mose **5:** 596, 597
Allman, Duane **8:** 940, **9:** 1035, 1036, **10:** 1176, **14:** 1601, *1603,* 1604, 1605, **16:** 1843
Allman, Gregg **7:** 837, **14:** 1603-5, *1605*
Allman Brothers Band **11:** 1254, **13:** 1443, *1443,* **14:** 1601-5, **16:** 1841, 1843
Allman Joys *see* Allman Brothers Band
'All My Loving' **8:** 851
Allred, Byron **9:** 979, **11:** 1227
All Stars **6:** 708-9, *709,* 719, **7:** 758, **15:** 1724
All-Stars *see* Cyril Davies' All Stars
Almanac Singers **6:** 662, *663,* 667
Almendros, Nestor **11:** 1316
Almond, Johnny **10:** 1115
Almond, Marc **16:** *1862,* **20:** 2405
Alomar, Carlos **14:** 1628, 1633
Alpert, Herb **5:** 503, *503,* 580, **7:** 740, 766, **14:** 1654, **17:** 1942, *1942,* 1949
Alphonso, Roland **9:** 976
Alston, Barbara **5:** 514
Alston, Shirley **5:** 566-7
Altamont concert **8:** 893, 894, 895, 915, **10:** 1091, **11:** 1242-3, 1254, 1258-60
Altered Images **16:** 1902, **20:** 2329, 2395, *2396*
Alway, Michael **18:** 2157
Amao, Loughty **9:** 969
Amarfio, Sol **9:** 969
Amazones de Guinée, Les **20:** *2380*
Ambassadeurs, Les **20:** 2379
Ambler, Mark **18:** 2146, 2147
Amboy Dukes **14:** 1601
Ambrose, Dave **18:** 2130
Ambrose Slade *see* Slade

Amen Corner 8: 952-3
America 10: 1125, 15: 1776-7, 17: 2037
'American Bandstand' 1: 106, 2: 202, 219, 220, 3: 263, 308, 309, 341, 342, 343, 344, 348, 350, 352, 353, 355, 356, 357-60, 5: 483, 484-5, *484*, 496, 497, 499, 571, 8: 843, 9: 981, 13: 1502
American Blues 16: 1855
American Graffiti 20: 2327
Ames, Roy C. 11: 1234
Ames Brothers 2: 235
Amey, Ian (DDBM&T) 8: 950
Ammons, Albert 2: 179, *180*
Ammons, Gene 2: 173, 4: 464
Amon Duul 20: 2367
Amy and the Angels 18: 2072
Anarchy Tour 19: 2261
Andantes 6: 716
Anderle, David 13: 1449
Anders, Pete 5: 509, 514
Andersen, Eric 6: 664, 677
Anderson, Al 16: 1893
Anderson, Alfa 18: 2114
Anderson, Cat 4: *462*
Anderson, Ian 14: 1570-3, 15: 1742
Anderson, John 8: 865, 9: 1015
Anderson, Jon 14: 1565, 15: *1690*, 1692, 1693, 1694, *1695*, 1742
Anderson, Katherine (Marvelettes) 6: 719
Anderson, Kim 17: 2032
Anderson, Laurie 20: 2339, *2340*
Anderson, Lynn 17: 2021
Anderson, Miller 12: 1440
Anderson, Richard 16: 1873, *1873*
Anderson, Rita 16: 1890
Anderson, Robin 17: 2032
Anderson, Signe Toly 8: *909*, 909-10, 10: 1170
Anderson, Stikken 'Stig' 17: 1944, *1945*, 1946
Andersson, Benny 6: 700, 13: *1443*, 1444, 17: 1945, 1946, 1947
Andes, Mark 14: 1614, *1615*
Andress, Ursula 2: *212*
Andrew, Sam 10: 1170, 1172
Andrews, Bernie 4: 377, *377*
Andrews, Bob 17: 1936
Andrews, Chris 4: 372, 6: 622, 626, *627*, 628, 10: 1087, 17: 1953
Andrews, Eddie 'Punch' 16: 1830, 1856
Andrews, Lee and the Hearts 1: 62
Andrews, Nancy 17: 1976
Andy Fraser Band 17: 1740
'Andy Williams Show, The' 13: 1504
Angel, David 9: 1017
Angelic Upstarts 18: 2145, 2152, *2153*, 2154, 2157
Angels 5: 567
Angels From Hell 8: 848
Anglo-Amalgamated 4: 430
Animals 1: 67, 4: 447, 448, 5: 537, 575, 588, 595, *598*, 599, 600, 6: 624, *625*, 642-3, 656-60, 677, 681, 693, 7: 741, 757, 8: 941, 9: 1022, 1065, 10: *1085*,

1087, 1099, 1159, 11: 1205, 1218, 15: 1795, 1832, 1834
Anita Kerr Singers 2: 234, *234*, 4: 406
Anja 18: *2156*
Anka, Paul 1: 18, 2: *238*, 239, 3: 243, *243*, 251, *254*, 256, 259, 260, 284, 301, 306-9, 5: 501, 7: 739-40, 17: 1941
Ann Arbor Jazz and Blues Festival 11: 1243, *1253*
Ann-Margaret 2: *213*
Anslinger, Harry 9: 1019
Ant, Adam 18: 2054-5, *2055*, 20: 2321, 2322-5, 2328, 2343, 2360, *2402*, 2405 see also Adam and the Ants
Anthony, Dee 13: 1445, 17: 2027, 2039, 2040
Anthony, John 16: 1814
Anthony, Michael 18: 2130
Anthony, Richard 3: 243, *243*, 250
Anti-Nowhere League 19: 2186
Antoni, Robert 'Stewkey' 16: 1903
Antonioni, Michelangelo 6: 652, 8: 843, 847-8, 11: 1273-4, 1304, 1316
Apollo 3: 262
Apollo Theatre, Harlem 4: *462*
Appel, Mike 18: 2089
Appell, Dave 3: 342, 350, 355
Appice, Carmine 9: 1070-1, *1070*, 11: *1230*, 1231-2, 1240, 14: 1601, *1618*
Appice, Vinnie 12: 1370, 1371
Apple (Beatles) 5: 542, 555, 557, 10: 1143, 1150-1, 1156-60, 14: 1679, 16: 1826, 17: 1968, 1979
Applejacks 3: 342, 6: 602, *602*, 603, 7: 752, 10: 1181, 12: *1343*
Aquarium 20: *2377*
Arcade Funk 19: 2169
Arcadia 20: 2391, 2418
Archer, Al 19: *2218*, 2218-20
Archibald (Leon T. Gross) 2: 145, 154, 157
Archies 4: 444, 9: 981-2, 983, *998*, 999-1000, *1000*, 13: 1502, 18: 2098
Arden Don 1: 107, 7: 806-7, 817, *817*, 8: 952, 12: 1370, 15: 1747
Area Code 6: 615, 17: 2023
Areas, José 'Chepito' 13: 1535, *1536*
Argent, Rod 6: 688-9, *690*, 691, *691*
Arias, Olivia 17: 1968
Aristocrat 4: 464
Armageddon 6: 653
Armatrading, Joan 18: 2072, 19: 2196-7, *2196-7*
Armstrong, Dan 9: 1079
Armoury Show 19: 2275
Arms and Legs 19: 2254
Armstrong, Louis 12: *1424*
Armstrong, Ralph 13: 1525
Arnell, Ginny 7: 727
Arnesen, Pete 6: 608
Arnold, Billy Boy 5: 590
Arnold, Eddy 1: 30, 91 2: 230, 232
Arnold, Jerome 11: 1239
Arnold, Jerry 4: 392
Arnold, Malcolm 12: 1397, 15: *1682*, 1683
Arnold, P. P. 1: 11, 12: 1354, 15: 1685

Arnold, Paul 6: 688
Arnold, Peter 6: 694-5
Arnold, Vance see Cocker, Joe
'Around the Beatles' 7: 734
Aronowitz, Al 12: 1330
Arri Up 18: 2062, *2063*
Arrows 16: *1822*
Art Quatro Trio 16: 1830
Artwoods 12: 1377
Asbury Jukes 3: 332, 5: 515, *515*
ASCAP (American Society of Composers, Authors and Publishers) 4: 438, 460, 5: 580
Ash, Leslie 12: *1393*
Ashburn, Benny 19: 2217
Asher, Jane 10: *1148* 15: 1707
Asher, Peter 6: 693-4, 8: 852, 10: 1125, 1158, 14: 1679, 15: 1707, 1771 see also Peter and Gordon
Asher, Tony 7: 775, 779
Asheton, Ron 13: 1498
Asheton, Scott 13: 1498
Ashford, Jack 9: 1057
Ashford, Nickolas 6: 704, 9: 1042, 1043, 14: 1587, 1590, 1591, 1592, 1593
Ashford, Roseline 6: 717
Ashman, Tony 12: 1380
Ashton, Tony 10: 1200
Asia 15: 1688, 1695, 1729
Aspel, Michael 17: *1960*
Aspinall, Neil 5: 556-7, *556-7*
Aspinall, Vicki 18: 2072
Assault 13: 1508
Associates 19: *2272*, 2273, 2275
Association 2: 182, 7: 819, 10: 1082, 1099
Association of Country Entertainers 14: 1658-9
Astaire, Fred 15: 1713
Astley, Virginia 18: 2151
Astors 8: 929
Astro 19: 2214, *2214-5*
Astronauts 4: 392, 7: 765
Aswad 16: 1894, 19: 2216, *2217*
Asylum Records 15: 1762-3
Atkins, Chet 1: 94, 2: 222, *222*, 225, 228, 230, 231, 233-4, *233*, 4: 402, 414-15, 14: 1654, 1655, 1658
Atkins, John 14: 1598
Atkinson, Paul 6: 688, *689*, 691
Atlanta Pop Festival 11: 1243
Atlanta Rhythm Section 13: 1443
Atlantic Blues 15: 1697
Atlantic Records 1: 43, *43*, *59*, 74-5, 3: 261, 262, 271-5, 280, 282, 288, 289, 290-3, 295, 297, 325, 327, 328, 345, *345*, 346, 5: 578-9, 7: 732-3, 782, 785, 797, 8: 875-7, 922, *922*, 925, 928-33, 935, *935*, 937, 938-40
Atlantics 4: 393
Atomic Enchilada 9: 993
Atomic Rooster 7: 815, 15: 1687, 1697
Attractions 5: 574, 17: 1925, 19: 2193, *2194*, 2195, see also Costello, Elvis
Atwell, Winifred 2: 179
Atwood, Bill 7: 835, 14: 1563

Aucoin, Bill **16:** 1869
Audiomasters: **18:** 2139-40
Auger, Brian **6:** 651, **7:** 816, *817,* **9:** 990, **13:** 1523, 1524, **15:** 1699, 1724
Au Go Go Singers **7:** 825
Ausin, Gene **1:** 91
Austin, Leon **7:** 788
Automatic Man **13:** 1537
Autry, Gene **18:** 2084
Avalon, Frankie **2:** 204, 209, 239, **3:** 242, 256, 260, *260,* 284, 311, 341, *341,* 342, 343, 344, 348-9, 350, 351, 352, 359, **8:** 845, *878,* **11:** 1297
Avalon Ballroom, San Francisco **8:** 914, 917, *919,* 920, **10:** 1170
Avengers **10:** 1167, 1193
Average White Band **1:** 68, **15:** 1763, **20:** 2393
Avons **4:** 363
Avory, Mick : 750, *750*
Axton, Estelle **8:** 928-9, *928*
Ayers, Kevin **11:** 1305, 1318, **13:** 1478, **14:** 1579-80, *1579,* 1639, **16:** 1916
Aynsley Dunbar Retaliation **10:** 1102, 1107, 1114
Ayout, Diana **3:** 307
Azimuth Co-ordinator **11:** 1309, 1310
Azoff, Irving **15:** 1763, 1774, **16:** 1920
Aztec Camera **18:** 2157, **19:** 2273, *2275*

B

B. Boys **19:** 2168-9
B. Bumble and the Stingers **4:** 382, 389, 395
BB (Burt and Blanchard) **18:** 2147
BBC radio **8:** 841-2
BBC Radio One **7:** 746
B-52s **17:** 2004, **20:** 2286-7, *2286*
B-Sides **20:** 2323
Babbington, Roy **14:** 1580
Babyemi, Timi Tupe Yomi Abeyomi **19:** 2214
Bach, Barbara **17:** *1976,* 1977
Bacharach, Burt **3:** 292, **5:** 562, *562,* 577, 578-80, **8:** 859, **9:** 963, 1017, **10:** 1175
Bachelors **7:** 757-8, **10:** 1138-9, *1138*
Bachman, Randy **7:** 772, **14:** 1616, *1616,* 1617
Bachman-Turner Overdrive **14:** 1617
Back Door **17:** 1984
Badanjek, Johnny 'Bee' **10:** 1178
Bad Company **12:** 1366, **15:** 1740, **16:** 1819
Badfinger **14:** 1679, **16:** 1903
Badger **15:** 1692
Bad Manners **19:** *2203*
Badowski, Henry **18:** 2080
Bad Timing **10:** 1131

Baez, Joan **1:** 16, 18, **6:***624,* 662, 664, *665,* 670, 680, **10:** 1138,1139, **11:** 1201, *1204,* 1205, *1208,* 1211, *1212,* 1251 **12:** 1349, 1351, *1360,* **14:** 1659, **15:** 1780
Bagby, Doc **3:** 343
Bagdasarian, Ross **3:** 269
Bailey, Bill **2:** 125
Bailey, David **11:** 1289, **20:** 2321
Bailey, Derek **14:** 1569
Bailey, Philip **19:** 2163, 2165
Bailey, Robert **9:** 969
Bain, Jimmy **17:** 1985-6
Bainbridge, Harvey **17:** 1997
Baion **5:** 579, **9:** 963
Baird, Roy **11:** 1275
Baker, Arthur **19:** 2168, 2169, 2177, **20:** 2303, 3392
Baker, Ginger **1:** *9,* 16, **5:** *584,* 586, **6:** *642,* **9:** 1021-2, *1021, 1024,* 1026-31, *1027,* 1034-5, **10:** 1113, 1189, **17:** 1981
Baker, Keith **15:** 1728
Baker, LaVern **3:** 274, *274,* 311, *311,* 360, **4:** 452
Baker, Mickey **2:** 174, **3:** 273, 274, 337, **4:** 389, **19:** 2177
Baker, Roy Thomas **7:** 733, **16:** 1814, 1817, **18:** 2133
Bakerband **9:** 1031
Baker-Gurvitz Army **9:** 1031, *1030-1*
Bakerloo Blues Line **10:** 1102
Baldry, Long John **5:** 587, *587,* 600, **11:** *1243,* **14:** 1665, **15:** 1724
Baldwin, James **1:** 83
Balfe, David **19:** 2276-9
Balgobin, Rupert **7:** 812
Balin, Marty **8:** 909-13, *911*
Balk, Harry **3:** 337, **4:** 396, 397, 417, 419, *419*
Ball, Dave **10:** 1089
Ball, Kenny **3:** 267, **4:** 439, 440, *440,* 454, **5:** 586
Ballard, Florence **4:** 478, **9:** 1045, *1045,* 1046, 1048
Ballard, Hank, and the Midnighters **1:** 75, **2:** 221, **3:** 269, 330, 337, **5:** *482,* 483, 484-5, 494-5, 500
Ballard, J. G. **11:** 1297
Ballard, Russ **4:** 372, **17:** 1986
Ballen, Ivin **3:** 354
Ballrooms, British **6:** 618-20
Baltimore Jazz Festival **11:** 1253
Bananarama **17:** 2207, 2260
Banco **20:** 2367
Bancroft, Anne **8:** *846*
Band **1:** 18, **3:** 251, **10:** 1125, 1132, 1155, **11:** *1206-7,* 1209-10, 1220, *1220,* 1253-4, **13:** 1443, 1541, 1542, *1542,* 1543, 1546-9
'Band Aid' **9:** 1017, **19:** 2248, 2271, **20:** 2401, 2403, 2409
Band of Gypsies **9:** 1063, 1068
Bangladesh benefit concert (1971) **13:** 1445
Bangs, Lester **12:** 1330, *1331,* 1339, **13:** 1482, 1483

Banks, Jeff **6:** 628
Banks, Pete **15:** 1691
Banks, Tony **15:** *1750,* 1752, 1753, 1754, 1755
Bannerman, Kari **9:** 969
Banshees **16:** 1806, **18:** 2046
Barbarians **6:** 681, *683,* **8:** 872
Barbarosa **14:** 1647
Barbata, John **8:** 912, **9:** 993, **15:** 1765
Barbe, Dave **20:** 2323
Barber, Adrian **5:** 540
Barber, Chris **2:** 123, 124, 125, 128, **3:** 267, *267,* **4:** 439, 440, **5:** 584, *584,* 585-6, 588, **10:** 1101, **11:** 1245
Barber, Jack **7:** 834-5
Barbieri, Richard **20:** 2355, 2356, *2357*
Barclay, Bob **4:** 439
Barclay James Harvest **15:** *1743*
Barclay, Michael **6:** 632
Bare, Bobby **14:** 1654
Barefoot **15:** 1748
Barefoot Jerry **17:** 2023
Barge, Gene 'Daddy G' **4:** 389, **5:** 492
Bar-Kays **4:** 390, **12:** 1409
Barkdull, Wiley **2:** 231
Barlow, Barriemore **14:** *1570*
Barlow, John **8:** 905-6
Barnacle, Pete **17:** 1984
Barnes, Johnny **3:** 300
Barnes, Ken **12:** 1339
Barnett, Angela **14:** 1625, 1629
Barnstorm **14:** 1613, **15:** 1775
Barnum, H. B. **2:** 149, 151
Barre, Martin **14:** *1570,* 1571, 1573
Barreda, Antonio de la **10:** 1117
Barrère, Paul **16:** 1858, *1859,* 1860
Barrett, Aston 'Family Man' **16:** 1890, 1892, 1893
Barrett, Carlton **16:** 1890, 1892, 1893
Barrett, Pat **2:** 235
Barrett, Richard **1:** 76, **14:** 1597
Barrett, Richie **5:** 566
Barrett, Syd **1:** 8, *8,* 9, **9:** 1063, **11:** 1297, 1301-2, *1301,* 1307-10, *1307,* 1311, 1312, 1318-20, **14:** 1622, 1639
Barri, Steve **3:** 266, **7:** 800
Barrie, Amanda **4:** 427
Barron, Ronnie **13:** 1452
Barron, Steve **13:** 1502, **14:** 1585, **20:** 2359-60, *2360*
Barron Knights **5:** 534, **6:** 603
Barrow, Tony **5:** *556,* 557
Barry, Jeff **1:** 13, **3:** 292, **4:** 403, 441, 444, *444,* 449, **5:** 509, 514, 515, 562, 567, 569, **9:** 982-3, 988, 1000 *see also* Greenwich, Ellie
Barry, Joe **13:** 1455
Barry, John **4:** 362, 371, 372, *373,* 392, *421,* 422, 423
Barry, Lee *see* White, Barry
Barry, Len **10:** 1162
Barry, Sandra **7:** 818
Barson, Mike **15:** 1700, **19:** *2210,* 2210-11, 2213
Bart, Ben **4:** 463, **7:** 789

Bart, Lionel **4:** 368, 421-2, *423,* 430, **8:** 859
Barthol, Bruce **10:** 1097
Bartholomew, Dave **2:** 142, *144,* 145, 146, 154, 156, **3:** 273, **4:** 463, **9:** 975
Bartholomew, Peter **6:** 694-5
Barton, Cliff **5:** 586
Bartos, Karl **20:** 2312
Basie, Count **9:** 975
Bass, Fontella **9:** 1059
Bass, Ralph **1:** 74, **5:** 494-5, **7:** 789
Batcave Club **20:** 2382, *2382*
Bateman, Robert **4:** 473
Bates, Deacon L. J. *see* Jefferson, Blind Lemon
Bates Motel **13:** 1520
Bates, Simon **17:** *1959*
Bath City Pop Festival **11:** 1243
Bath Festival of Blues and Progressive Music **11:** 1255-7
Batt, Mike **13:** 1473, 1509
Battersea Festival (1978) **15:** 1757
Battin, Skip **7:** 830
Battiste, Harold **2:** 155, **5:** 519, **6:** 676, **7:** 836-7, **13:** 1452
Baughn, David **3:** 290
Bauhaus **14:** 1623, **16:** 1863, **18:** 2141
Bautista, Roland **19:** 2163
Bavistock, Jim **12:** 1427
Baxter, Art **2:** 122, 129
Baxter, Jeff 'Skunk' **16:** *1850 1852,* 1919-20, **17:** 1989
Bay City Rollers **6:** 687, **8:** 960, **12:** 1433, **13:** 1506, 1510-13
Bayer, Carole **9:** 988
Bayer-Sager, Carloe **5:** 580
Bazooka Joe **20:** 2323, *2323*
Beach Boys **1:** 13, 18, 63, **3:** 261, **4:** 391, **5:** 503, 564, *564,* **7:** 761-3, 764, 765, 767, 768- 9, 770-3, *774,* 775-7, 778-90, **8:** 845, *845,* 879-80, 902, **9:** 981, 987, 1039, **10:** 1082, 1092, *1092,* 1099, 1155, **11:** 1298, **15:** 1741, 1761, 1766, 1772, 1777
Beach Party **8:** 879
Beadle, Buddy **7:** *810,* 811
Beale, Michael **19:** 2163
Beale Streeters **3:** 339, **7:** 799
Beard, Frank **16:** 1854, 1855
Beat **10:** 1181, **18:** 2158, *2160,* **19:** 2203, 2208-9, *2208-9,* 2214
Beat Boys **2:** 139
'Beat Girl' **4:** 372, 431, *431*
Beat Generation **12:** 1351, 1357
'Beat Room, The' **8:** 849
Beatlemania **5:** 550, 557, 558-60, **17:** 1978-80
Beatles **1:** 2, 3, 4 *4,* 5, *5,* 7, 8, *18, 19,* 67, 103, 110, 118, **2:** 149, 150, 179, 180, **3:** 243, 249-50, 266, 309, 343, *359,* 360, **4:** 363, 372, 375, 377, *377, 398,* 409, *414,* 416, 418, 431, 433, 437, 439, **5:** 483, 504, 512, 517, 522, 523, 524, 525, 527, 532, 533-4, 535, 536-7, 538, *539,* 541-60, 571, 582, 583, **6:** 601, 602, 615, 624, *624,* 629, 630, 637, 639-40, *639,* 681-2, 685, 686, *692,* 693, 706, **7:** 724, 727, 734, 741-2, 749, 757, 802, 821-2, 825, 828, **8:** 843, 844, 847, 850, 851, 854-7, 879-80, 881, 941-2, 959, **9:** 963, 984, 987, 989, *1001,* 1007, 1019, 1021, 1027, 1035, 1039, 1045, 1054, 1074, *1075,* 1077, **10:** *1081,* 1085, 1086, 1092, *1098,* 1099, 1141-60, 1167, **11:** 1205, 1218, 1281, *1282, 1288-9,* 1289, 1291-2, 1297, **12:** 1322, 1325, *1334,* 1335, 1381, 1384, *1385,* 1387, 1393, 1395, 1397, *1397,* 1398, 1434, **13:** 1445, 1449, 1477, 1493, 1502, 1503, 1514, **14:** 1562, 1609, 1620, 1661, 1662, 1665, 1679, **15:** 1681, 1702, 1707, 1741, 1748, 1767, 1768, 1772, 1778, 1797, **16:** 1803, 1845, 1862, 1901, 1908-9, 1912, **17:** 1941, 1961-80, **18:** *2138,* **19:** 2241, 2242, 2243, 2253, **20:** 2288-9, 2327, 2376
'Beatles at Shea Stadium, The' **8:** 851
'Beatles Christmas Show, The' **10:** 1146
Beatles Monthly **5:** 559, *560*
Beatty, Leon **7:** 834-5
Beau Brummels **8:** 872, 914, *915,* **12:** 1406
Beau, Ritchie **17:** 2011
Beaulieu, Priscilla **3:** 256
Beaulieu Jazz Festivals **11:** 1244, 1245, *1245,* 1248
Beaumont, Jimmy **2:** 237
Becaud, Gilbert **2:** 227
Beck, Bogart and Appice **9:** 1071, **11:** *1230,* 1232
Beck, Jeff **4:** 383, *383,* **5:** 582, **6:** 642, 651-3, *651, 652,* **9:** 1021-2, *1023,* 1063, 1065, 1071, 1079, **10:** 1114, 1135, **11:** 1221, 1228-32, 1253, 1274, **14:** 1663, 1673, **15:** 1721, 1725, **16:** 1822, 1830, 1834, 1841, 1851, **17:** 1982
Beck, Jim **2:** 190
Becker, Steve **18:** 2093
Becker, Walter **16:** 1841, 1851, 1919
Beckett, Barry **10:** 1179
Beckett, Barry **15:** 1793, **16:** 1843, **18:** 2093, **19:** 2199
Beckett, Larry **13:** 1554, 1555
Beckford, Theo **9:** 976
Beckley, Gerry **15:** 1776, *1777*
Bedford, David **13:** 1479, **16:** 1916, 1917
Bedford, Mark 'Bedders' **19:** 2210, *2211*
Beecham, John **7:** 756
Beefeaters **7:** 828
Bee Gees **1:** 6, 8, **5:** 482, **6:** *639,* **9:** 1033, *1084,* **10:** 1085, **17:** 1942, 1733, 1942, 2021, 2026, 2028, **18:** 2103, 2104-7, 2109, **20:** 2327-8, 2370
Bees Make Honey **15:** 1758, **17:** 1921, *1922,* 1924
Beggs, Nick **20:** *2381*
Belafonte, Harry **3:** *268,* 269, **11:** 1204
Belew, Adrian **14:** *1567,* 1597, **20:** 2284-5
Belgrave, Marcus **3:** 327
Bell, Al **8:** *921-2,* 932-3, **15:** 1793
Bell, Chris **10:** 1175
Bell, Eric **17:** *1990,* 1991, 1992
Bell, Kevin **18:** 2109
Bell, Maggie **8:** 947, **12:** 1366, **15:** 1726
Bell, Marc **17:** 2011, *2012*
Bell, Richard **10:** 1172
Bell, Robert 'Kool' **18:** *2108,* 2109
Bell, Ronald **18:** 2109
Bell, Rrussel (sic) **20:** 2314, 2315
Bell, Thom **3:** 343, **5:** *563,* 577, **9:** 1052, **14:** 1594, 1596, *1596,* 1598, 1600, 1668
Bell, William **8:** *922,* 929, 932-3
Bellcats **2:** 122
Belle Stars **17:** 1940, *1940,* **18:** 2070, **19:** 2203, 2260, **20:** 2396
Belli, Remo **4:** 400
Bellotte, Pete **14:** 1668, **18:** 2110-1, 2119
Bell Records **3:** 293, **4:** 459
Belmont, Martin **17:** 1936, *1937*
Belmonts *see* Dion and the Belmonts
Ben, Mohammed Malcolm **20:** 2378, *2379*
Benatar, Pat **18:** 2121, 2134-6, *2134-6*
Benberg, Bob C. **15:** 1758, *1758*
Bender, Ariel **16:** 1819, 1820, *1820*
Benham, Bo **19:** 2242
Benitez, John 'Jellybean' **19:** 2169
Benjamin, Benny **4:** 477, **16:** 716, **9:** 1057
Benjamin, Nigel **16:** 1820
Bennett, Al **5:** 502
Bennett, Brian **2:** 139, **4:** *386,* 387, *387,* 388, *399,* 400
Bennett, Cliff **5:** 534, **10:** 1149
Bennett, Duster **10:** 1109
Bennett, Jeannie **3:** 298, 299, 300
Bennett, Pete **17:** *1967*
Bennett, Ronnie **3:** *270*
Bennett, Roy **4:** 363, 422
Bennett, Tony **1:** 37
Bennett, Veronica and Estelle **5:** 514-15 *see also* Spector, Ronnie
Bennett, Wayne **7:** 800
Benno, Marc **13:** 1444
Benson, Al **1:** 56, *56*
Benson, George **19:** 2166-7, *2166-7*
Benson, Renaldo 'Obie' **6:** 710-13
Bentley, Jack **9:** 989
Bentley, John **19:** 2257, *2257*
Benton, Brook **17:** 1941
Berberich, Bob **16:** 1846
Berger, Alan **18:** 2092
Berkeley Barb **13:** 1489
Berlin, Colin **10:** 1194-5
Berliner, Emile **12:** 1392
Berman, Bess **8:** 935
Bernard, Rod **13:** 1455
Bernhag, Bengt **17:** 1944-5
Berns, Bert **3:** *265,* 266, 281, 282, 292, 293, **4:** 403, 444, *444,* 449, **5:** 562, **8:** 939, **13:** 1551
Bernstein, Leonard **15:** 1686
Bernstein, Sid **8:** 863, 875
Berrow, Michael **20:** 2389
Berry, Bruce **9:** 1020, **15:** 1770
Berry, Chuck **1:** 2, 12, 22, 32, 35, 61, *61,* 64-8, 110, 113, 118, **2:** 149, 197, 204, 205, 209, 210, 217, 229, **3:** 242, *252-3,* 254, 269, 284, **4:** *464,* 465, 467, **5:** 591,

7: 739, 761, 765, 775, 802-3, 816, **8:** 886, *887,* 891, **9:** 961, *963,* 1021, 1026, **10:** 1089, **11:** 1221, 1223, 1225, 1239, 1252-3, *1284,* **12:** *1356,* 1357, *1357,* **12:** 1419, 1435, **15:** 1681
Berry, Dave **7:** 752, 758
Berry, Emmett **3:** 274
Berry, Jan *see* Jan and Dean
Berry, John **5:** 485
Berry, Mike, and the Outlaws **4:** 437
Best, Mona **5:** 547
Best, Pete **5:** *544,* 547-50, 555, 556-7, **6:** 639
Betrock, Alan **12:** 1331, 1339
Bettis, John **17:** 1949
Betts, Dickie **14:** 1601, 1603, 1604-5, *1604*
Bevan, Bev **10:** 1183, 1185, *1185,* **15:** 1746, 1747, 1748, 1749, *1749*
Beverley **10:** 1099
Beverley Hills Cop **20:** 2420
Beyond the Valley of the Dolls **16:** 1879
Bhaktivedanta, A. C. **12:** 1400
Bicknell, Alf **5:** *556*
Bidell, Lou **5:** 506-7
Big Apple Band **18:** 2114
'Big Beat Show' **2:** 217
Big Bopper **2:** 163, 176-7, 181, *182,* 183, 188, 194, *194, 195,* 197, **3:** 254
Big Brother and the Holding Company **1:** 15, **8:** 903, 905, 915, **10:** 1083, 1092, 1099-1100, 1170-2, *1173,* **11:** 1223
Big Country **19:** 2271, 2275, **20:** 2303, 2381
Biggs, Howard **3:** 273, 274
Big in Japan **19:** 2268, 2279, 2280
Big Roll Band **5:** 588, *588-9, 598,* **19:** *2184*
Bigsby, Paul **1:** 79
Big Star **10:** 1175, **15:** 1721, *1721,* **20:** 2288
Big Thing *see* Chicago
Big Three **5:** *523,* 534, *535,* 537, **6:** 601, 630
Big Three Trio **3:** 339
Big Time Sarah **4:** *464*
Big Town **3:** 340
Big Youth **16:** *1884*
Bihari Brothers **10:** 1108
Bikel, Theo **11:** 1205
Bikini Beach **3:** 317, **14:** 1672
Bilk, Acker **3:** 267, *267,* **4:** *438,* 439, 440, 454
Bill Black's Combo **4:** 392
Billboard **1:** 59, *60,* **12:** 1321, 1329
Billingham, Micky **19:** 2220
Billings, Vic **7:** 732, **12:** 1430
Billingsley, Jo **16:** 1844
Bill Smith Combo **4:** 390
Billy and Lillie **3:** 342
Billy Joe and the Checkmates **4:** 382
Billy's Club **20:** 2351
Bingstrom, Billy **4:** 457
Binks, Les **17:** 2000
Binnick, Bernie **3:** 342, 343
Biondo, George **9:** 1072
Birch, Martin **18:** 2127
Birch, Will **17:** 1928, **19:** 2243
Bird, Brian **12:** 1322

Birds **7:** 819-20
Birdsong, Cynthis (Cindy) **9:** *1046,* 1048-9, **12:** 1415, 1416
Birkin, Jane **6:** 699
Birrell, Pete **6:** *612-13,* 614, *614*
Bishop, Elvin **11:** 1221, 1239
Bishop, Jimmy **14:** 1596-7
Bittan, Roy **16:** 1857, **18:** 2089, *2100,* **19:** 2199-2200
Black, Bill **1:** 46, 52, *52,* 53, 80, *87,* 94, 95, *95,* **2:** 211, **4:** 390, *392, 392*
Black, Cilla **5:** 523, 527, 532, *532,* 534, 535, 537, 551, 555, **6:** 621-2, *623,* 626, 629-31, 639, *639,* 640, **7:** 729, **8:** 880
Black, Jet **19:** 2188, *2188*
Black, Jimmy Carl **13:** 1490, 1493, **16:** 1858
Black, Johnny **1:** 114-15
Black and White **3:** 340
Blackberries **11:** 1312
Blackberry Booze Band **18:** 2092
Blackboard Jungle, The **1:** 21, 23, 26-7, **2:** 201, 207, *207,* **12:** 1385
Blackburn, Tony **1:** 7, **7:** 745, *745,* **8:** 842, *842,* **17:** *1958,* 1960
Blackbushe Airfield Festival **11:** 1243, *1243,* 1248, 1260, *1260*
Black Cat Bones **15:** 1738
Blackhill Enterprises **11:** 1308-9, **12:** 1438
Black Micado, The **20:** 2339
Blackmore, Ritchie **4:** 363, 393, 437, **5:** 531, **12:** *1361,* 1377, *1377,* 1379-80, *1380,* **15:** 1737, **17:** 1984-7, *1986*
Black Oak Arkansas **14:** 1601
Blackouts **13:** 1484, 1490
Black Roots **19:** 2216
Black Sabbath **12:** 1341, 1361, 1369-71, 1373, **14:** 1607, **17:** 1982-4, **18:** 2126, 2127, 2130, **19:** 2223
Black Sheep **18:** 2133
Black Slate **19:** 2216
Blacks Unlimited **20:** 2378
Black Uhuru **9:** 979, **20:** *2373,* 2374-5
Blackwell, Charles **4:** 437, **11:** 1237
Blackwell, Chris **1:** 18, **7:** *758,* 759, 788, 802, 815, 816, **9:** 961-2, *963,* 971, 978-9, **10:** 1187, 1189, **15:** 1739, **16:** 1892, 1893, **18:** 2133, **20:** 2300
Blackwell, Otis **3:** 355, **4:** 445, *455,* **5:** 570
Blackwell Portraits **2:** 149
Blackwell, Robert A. ('Bumps') **2:** 149, 150, 151, 156
Blackwell, Rory **2:** *121,* 122, 129, 134
Black Widow **12:** *1372,* 1373, **17:** 1983
Blaikley, Alan **8:** 859, 949, 950, *951,* 954-5, **10:** 1085
Blaine, Hal **1:** 95, **4:** 400, **5:** 510, 514, *518,* 519, 520, **6:** 675, **7:** 829
Blair, Lionel **4:** *363,* **5:** *487*
Blair, Ron **18:** *2085,* 2086
Blake, Peter **1:** 4, 5, **11:** 1291, 1297, *1297,* 1300
Blake, Tim **17:** 1997, **20:** 2368
Blakely, Alan **6:** 615-16, *616,* **9:** 1151

Blakley, Ronee **11:** 1211, *1212*
Blanchard, Stevie **18:** 2147
Blancmange **20:** 2301, 2302
Bland, Bobby 'Blue' **1:** 44, **3:** 339, **7:** 797, 798-800, **10:** *1102,* 1109, 1110, **11:** 1293, *1293,* **15:** 1781
Blane, Marsie **3:** 312
Blauner, Steve **3:** 345
Blesh, Rudi **2:** 125
Bley, Carla **9:** 1033
Bleyer, Archie **2:** 225, 227, 228, **4:** 390, 406, **5:** 508, **7:** 739
Blind Boy Fuller **6:** 680
Blind Boys of Mississippi **3:** 333
Blind Faith **9:** 1031, *1034,* 1035, **10:** 1189, *1189,* 1199
Blind Lemon Jefferson **6:** *678,* 679
Blind Faith **11:** 1247, **13:** 1449
Blitz Club **16:** *1802,* **20:** 2351
Block, Martin **1:** 55, *55,* **2:** *219,* 220, **3:** *341*
Block Busters **3:** 300
Blocker, Joe **9:** 1017
Blockhead, Dave **19:** 2209
Blockheads **17:** *1921, 1930,* 1932, 1933
Blodwyn Pig **14:** 1571
Blondel **20:** 2337
Blondie **9:** 1002, **15:** 1763, **16:** 1823, 1863, **17:** 2001, 2003, 2004, 2005, 2007, 2008, 2011, 2012, **18:** 2072, 2115, 2119, 2123, 2135, **20:** 2281, 2290-3, 2329, 2386
Blood Sweat and Tears **3:** 251, **5:** 596, **9:** 1074, **10:** *1094,* **11:** 1240, 1253, **13:** 1527, 1538-40
Bloodvessel, Buster **19:** *2202,* 2219
Bloom, Bobby **15:** *1744*
Bloom, Eric **18:** 2125-6, *2125-6*
Bloom, Howard **9:** 1054
Bloom, James and Bobby **9:** 995
Bloomfield, Mike **10:** 1110, 1116, **11:** 1207, *1207,* 1221, 1223, 1238-40, **13:** 1535, 1539
Blossoms **13:** *1445*
Blow Up **6:** 652, **8:** 843, *846,* 847, **11:** 1274
Bluebells *see* LaBelle
Blue, Barry **12:** 1423
Blue Boys **8:** 889
Blue Caps **1:** 80, *105,* 106, **2:** 199, *199,* 200 *see also* Vincent, Gene
Blue Cats **1:** 120
Blue Cheer **14:** 1601
Blue Collar **13:** 1560
Blue Flames **2:** 139, **5:** 583, 588, 596-7, *596,* 599, **7:** 759, 806, 817, 818, **9:** 975
Blue Grass Boys **1:** *39,* 52, **2:** 225
Blue Hawaii **2:** 214
Blue Horizon **10:** 1102-3, *1102,* 1118-19
Blue Jays **10:** 1196, *1196*
Blue Notes **1:** 62, **9:** 966, **14:** 1597-8, *1598,* 1600
Blue Oyster Cult **12:** *1373,* **16:** 1869, **17:** 2019, **18:** *2121,* 2125-7, *2126-7*
Blues Band **6:** 647, *648,* 655, **10:** 1103, 1116, 1124
Blues Blasters **9:** 976

Bluesbreakers **4:** 454, **9:** 1022, 1027, **10:** 1102, 1103, 1112-14, *1113*, 1118, **11:** 1253, **15:** 1721, **20:** 2364
Blues Brothers **8:** 937, **15:** 1791
Blues By Six **5:** 588
Blues Consolidated **7:** 799-800
Blues Incorporated **2:** 128, **4:** 454, **5:** 583-4, *583*, 586-8, *586*, 600, **8:** 889-90, **9:** 1024, 1027, **13:** 1476
Blues Magoos **8:** *862*, 864
Bluesology **14:** 1664-5, **15:** 1773
Blues Project **8:** 864, **10:** 1100, **11:** 1223, *1223*, 1240, **13:** 1539
Blues Syndicate **6:** 657
Blues Unlimited **12:** 1338, *1338*
Blue Velvets *see* Creedence Clearwater Revival
Bluesville **6:** 695
Blunstone, Colin **6:** 688-9, 691, *691*
Blunt, Johnny **5:** 531
Blythe, Jeff 'J. B.' **19:** 2218, 2220
BMI (Broadcast Music Incorporated) **4:** 460
BMI-ASCAP dispute **2:** 220
Bo, Eddie **2:** 145
Bob B. Sox and the Blue Jeans **5:** 509
Bobby Soxers **3:** 307
Bob Cort Skiffle Group **2:** 134
Bodacious **8:** 912
Bodnar, Andrew **17:** 1936, *1937*, **19:** 2193
Bodysnatchers **19:** *2202*, 2203, 2205, 2212
Bofill, Angela **18:** *2102*, 2103
Bogan, Ann **4:** 473, **6:** 719
Bogart, Neil **9:** 981, 983, *983*, 997, *999*, 1070, **16:** 1869
Bogen, Joel **20:** 2335
Bogert, Tim **9:** 1070-1, **11:** 1231-2, *1230*, **14:** 1601
Boggs, Tom **10:** 1174
Bogle, Bob **4:** 391
Bolan, Marc **1:** 6, **7:** 760, *760, 818*, 820, **9:** *1079*, **10:** 1085, **11:** 1248, *1287*, 1318, **12:** *1421*, 1422, 1433, 1436-40, **13:** 1503, 1513, **14:** 1613, 1622, 1625, 1633, *1633*, 1667, **16:** 1863, **17:** 1976, **18:** 2060, *2064, 2076*, 2077, 2079, **20:** 2327, 2399
Bolder, Trevor **15:** 1729, 1737
Bolin, Tommy **12:** *1378*, 1380, **14:** 1613
Bomp! **12:** 1329, 1339, *1339*
Bond, Angelo **9:** 1052
Bond, Graham **6:** *642*, **9:** 1027, **10:** 1189, **13:** 1523, 1524 *see also* Graham Bond Association
Bond, Ronnie **8:** 944
Bonds, Gary US **3:** 337, **4:** 446, *455*, **5:** 490-3
Boney M **18:** 2103, *2119*, 2120, **20:** 2362
Bongi-Bongi **20:** 2365
Bongiovi, Tony **18:** 2102
Bongo Man **9:** 979
Bonham, John **6:** *642*, 653, **12:** 1364, 1366, 1368, *1368*, 1373, **14:** 1620, **17:** 1981
Bonner, Gary **8:** *862*, 864, **9:** 993
Bonner, Juke Boy **12:** 1338

Bonnet, Graham **17:** 1986
Bono, Sonny *see* Sonny and Cher
Bono Vox **19:** 2270, *2270*, 2271, *2271*
Bonzo Dog Doo-Dah Band **8:** 848, **10:** 1103
Booker, James **2:** 145
Booker T. **7:** 782, 784-5, **8:** 921, 925, 929-30, 932, **10:** 1099
Booker T and the MGs **4:** 390, 392, **7:** 782, *784-5*, **8:** 921, 929, 930, 932, **10:** 1099, 1178, **12:** *1402-3*
Boomtown Rats **17:** 1929, **19:** 2242, 2249-51, *2250*, **20:** 2403
Boone, Debbie **16:** 1942
Boone, Pat **2:** 204, *204*, 217, 239, **3:** 262, *263*, 284, 301, *301*, 313-15, *355*, **4:** 401, 413
Boone, Steve **8:** *866*, 867-8, *869*
Boorman, John **8:** 845
Booth, Henry **5:** 494
Boothe, Ken **9:** 977, *977*
Bootsy's Rubber Band **19:** 2172
Border, The **13:** 1560
Born, Georgie **14:** 1569
Born to Boogie **12:** 1440, **15:** 1667, **20:** 2327
Boskent, Bill **2:** 156
Bossa Nova **5:** 504, *505*, **9:** 963
Bostock, Harry **5:** 522
Boston **14:** 1679, **17:** *1927*
Bothy, Pauline **11:** 1297
Botnick, Bruce **9:** 1013
Botts, Mike **5:** 519
Bouchard, Albert **18:** 2125-6, *2126*
Bouchard, Joe **18:** 2125-6, *2126*
Bouens, George **6:** 699
Bound for Glory **19:** 2249
Bovell, Dennis **19:** 2216
Bovens, George **18:** 2118
Bowden, Ron **4:** 439
Bowen, Jeffery **9:** 1052
Bowen, Jimmy **2:** 190, 192, 193, 200
Bower, Joey **5:** 534
Bowie, David **1:** 2, 6, 7, **5:** 500, **6:** 636, **8:** 848, 942, **9:** 1008, **10:** 1085, **11:** 1220, 1318, **12:** 1336, 1360, *1402*, 1422-3, 1440, **13:** 1498-9, 1503, **14:** 1567, 1622-31, 1632, 1633, 1634, 1638, 1640, **15:** 1697, 1721, 1737, *1742*, **16:** 1802, 1803, 1806, 1807, 1817, 1819, 1863, **17:** *1960*, **18:** 2099, 2103, 2115, 2158, 2159, **19:** *2264*, **20:** 2284, 2285, 2298, 2301, 2311, 2313, *2326*, 2327, 2339, 2343, 2351, 2352, 2353, *2359*, 2360, 2399, 2403, *2417*, 2419
Bowman, Derek **13:** 1508
Bown, Andy **8:** 954-5, *955*, **15:** 1735, **17:** 2038, *2038*, 2040
Bow Wow **20:** *2363*, 2365
Bow Wow Wow **9:** *983*, **13:** 1503, **17:** *1983*, **18:** 2050, 2055, **19:** 2264, *2264*, **20:** 2323, 2399
Box, Mick **15:** 1728, 1729, *1729*
Box Tops **10:** 1174-5
'Boy Called Donovan, A' **8:** 851
Boyce, Don **18:** 2109

Boyce, Tommy **3:** 265, **9:** 981, 982-3, *982*, 987, 988, 990, *990*
Boyd, Eddie **4:** 465
Boyd, Eva **4:** 447
Boyd, Franklyn **4:** 366, 368
Boyd, Idalia **5:** 489
Boyd, Joe **10:** 1188, **11:** 1304, 1308, **13:** 1465
Boyd, Pattie **6:** 683
Boyer, Elisa **3:** 335, *335*
Boyers, Jacqueline **17:** *1955*
Boy George **16:** *1803*, **20:** 2344, 2345, *2345*, 2351, 2356, 2381, 2386, 2398-2400, *2398-2400*, 2408
Boylan, John **15:** 1772, 1773
'Boy Meets Girls' **1:** 107, **4:** *379*, 380
Boysie, Count **9:** 978
Boz (Burrell) **14:** 1565, *1565-6*
Boz People **7:** 806
Brabanec, Vratislav **20:** 2376
Bracelin, Jack **11:** 1306
Bracken, Jimmy **5:** 595, *595*
Bracken, Vivian and James **9:** 1058
Brackman, Jacob **15:** 1710
Bradbury, John 'Brad' **19:** 2203, 2204, 2207
Bradford, Geoff **8:** 889
Bradford, Janie **4:** 473
Bradley, Harold **4:** 407
Bradley, Jerry **14:** 1655
Bradley, Owen **2:** 199, *199*, 200, 234, **3:** 319, *319*, **14:** 1658
Bradshaw, Sonny **9:** 975
Bradshaw, Tiny **1:** 30
Bragg, Billy **20:** 2405, *2406-7*
Bragg, Johnny **1:** *45*
Brain Records **20:** 2367
Braithwaite, Junior **16:** 1885, 1889
Brambell, Wilfred **8:** *854*
Bramlett, Delaney and Bonnie *see* Delaney and Bonnie
Brand, Oscar **10:** 1124
Brando, Marlon **2:** 206, *207*, **12:** 1385, **16:** *1825*
Brandon, Tony **7:** 745, **17:** 1958, 1960
Brandt, Jerry **15:** 1709
Brand X **15:** 1755
Brann, Erik **9:** 1071
Brann, Michael **12:** 1322
Branson, Richard **16:** 1916, **17:** *2026*, 2027
Brantley, Clint **7:** 789
Beas, Dan Ar **13:** 1467
Braun, Michael **12:** 1322
Brave Belt **14:** 1617
Bravos, Los **6:** 699, *699*
Bread **5:** *518*, 519, **10:** *1124*, 1125
Brecker, Randy **13:** 1539, *1539*
Bredin, Patricia **17:** 1955
Breen, Bobby, **2:** 129
Bremner, Billy **17:** 1935, **19:** 2253
Brennan, Steve **19:** 2220
Brenston, Jackie **1:** 44
Brethren *see* Lindisfarne
Brett, Steve **12:** 1427
Brewer, Don **14:** *1609*, 1610, 1611, *1611*

Brian Auger Trio **7**: 816, 817
Brico, Dr. Antonio **12**: 1349
Brides of Funkenstein **19**: 2172
Bridges, Russell *see* Russell, Leon
Brigati, Eddie **8**: 874-7, *875*
Briggs, David **16**: 1846, 1847
Briggs, Mick **15**: 1724
Briggs, Vic **6**: 660
Bright, Bette **19**: 2278
Bright, Guilly **9**: 979
Brilleaux, Lee **6**: 655, **17**: 1928-9, *1929,*
   1939
Brim, John **4**: 465
Brinco, Los **6**: 683
Brinsley Schwarz **17**: 1924-5, 1935, 1939
Brinston, Johnny **4**: 473, **6**: 708-9, 713,
   719, *720,* **9**: 1043
Briquette, Pete **19**: 2249, *2250,* 2251
British Lions *see* Mott the Hoople
Britten, Terry **17**: 1953
Britton, Chris **8**: 944, 946
Britz, Chuck **7**: 776
Broadside **11**: 1204, **12**: 1349
Brock, Dave **17**: 1996, *1997*
Brockie, Doug **9**: 1031
Bron, Gerry **15**: 1728, 1729
Bronski Beat **20**: *2419*
Brookemeyer, Bob **13**: 1521
Brooker, Gary **9**: 1036, 1086-9, *1089*
Brookes, Steve **19**: 2244
Brooks, Billy **2**: 217
Brooks, Elkie **12**: *1328*
Brooks, Ernie **17**: 2016
Brooks, Hadda **1**: 30
Brooks, Harvey **11**: 1239-40
Brooks, Lala **5**: 514
Brooks, Richard and Arthur **7**: 793, 795
Broonzy, Big Bill **2**: 125, **3**: *322,* 327, **5**:
   584-5, *585,* 593, **10**: 1102, 1104
Brotherhood of Man **17**: *1926, 1956*
Brothers Four **6**: 669
Brothers Johnson **9**: 1039
Broudie, Ian 'Kingbird' **16**: 1902
Broven, John **12**: 1324, 1338
Browder, Stony **20**: 2295, 2297
Brown, Archie **19**: 2219
Brown, Arthur **11**: 1297, 1305, **12**: *1343,*
   1372, 1373
Brown, Billie Jean **6**: 718
Brown, Charles **1**: 30, **3**: 286, 324, 330,
   339, 340, **4**: 462, **9**: 975, **10**: 1108
Brown, David **12**: 1358, 1402, 1419, **13**:
   1535
Brown, Dennis **16**: 1894-5, 1897, **20**:
   2374-5
Brown, Eddie Bongo **6**: 717, **9**: 1057
Brown, Errol **16**: 1826, *1827, 1828,* 1830
Brown, 'Funky' George **18**: 2109
Brown, Gerald **19**: 2178
Brown, James **1**: 10, 33, 35, **2**: 150, 153,
   160, 327, 337, **5**: 495, 562, **7**: 781, *783,*
   786-92, 796-7, **8**: 845, 923-4, 926, 939,
   9: 1003, **10**: 1162, *1162,* 1163, **11**: 1253,
   12: 1358, 1402, 1419
Brown, Jim **19**: 2214, *2214*

Brown, Joe **4**: 426, 465
Brown, Joe and his Bruvvers **2**: 139, *140,*
   4: 379, 380, 418, 423, 431, **8**: 844, 859
Brown, Joel and Toni **11**: 1308
Brown, Laurie **7**: 756
Brown, Lawrence **14**: 1598
Brown, Pete **1**: 16, **9**: *1028,* 1029, 1032-3
Brown, Peter **5**: 557, **11**: 1303
Brown, Ray **6**: 682
Brown, Roy **1**: 30, 35, 113, **2**: 142, 153,
   154, *154,* **3**: 262, 332, 338, **4**: 462, 463,
   463
Brown, Ruth **1**: 31, 74, **3**: 272, *272, 273,*
   274, 311
Brown, Shirley **15**: 1782
Brown, Texas Johnny **3**: 272
Brown, Tommy **14**: 1586
Browne, Jackson **10**: 1124, **11**: 1220, **12**:
   1346, **15**: 1702, 1718, *1761,* 1763, 1772,
   1773, 1778-80, **18**: 2089, **20**: 2329
Browne, Ken **5**: 547-8
Browns **5**: 574
Brown Sugar **15**: 1738
Brubeck, Dave **3**: *268,* **4**: 454, *455,* **12**:
   1387, **14**: 1563
Bruce, Jack **1**: 8, *9,* 16, **5**: *583-4,* 586, **6**:
   642, 647, **9**: 1021-2, *1021, 1024-5,* 1026-
   9, 1031, 1032-3, 1034, 1039, **10**: 1113,
   1188, **11**: 1247, **13**: 1523, **14**: 1607,
   1608, **17**: 1973
Bruce, Michael **16**: 1865
Bruce and Terry **7**: 778
Bruford, Bill **13**: 1479, **14**: *1564,* 1566,
   1567, 1620, **15**: 1691, *1691,* 1692, 1754
Brumley, Tom **3**: 304, *305*
Brunning, Bob **10**: 1118
Brunson, Frankie **14**: 1600
Brunswick Records **3**: 331-2
Bryan Morrison Agency **7**: 817
Bryant, Boudleaux and Felice **2**: 163,
   222, 223, *223,* 225, 228, 230-1, **4**: *414*
Bryant, Eldridge **9**: 1050
Brydon, Beryl **2**: 124
Bryon, Dennis **8**: 952-3
Bryson, Peabo **15**: 1800
Bryson, Wally **8**: *876*
Brzezicki, Mark **11**: 1280
Buchanan, Peter **2**: 127
Buckaroos **3**: 304
Buckingham, Lindsay **10**: 1120
Buckingham, Steve **5**: 577
Buckinghams **8**: 872
Buckler, Rick **19**: 2244, *2245, 2247,*
   2247-8
Buckley, Tim **10**: 1125, 1293, **13**: 1541,
   1542, 1543, 1544-5, **15**: 1778
Buckmaster, Paul **14**: 1632, 1667
Buck Ram Platters **3**: 300, *300*
Bucks Fizz **10**: 1140, **13**: 1502, **17**: *1956,*
   1957, **20**: *2304, 2395, 2396*
Buckwheat **13**: 1486
Buddah Records **9**: 981, 983, 997, 999, *999*
Buddy, Bob and Larry **14**: 1654
Buddy Miles Express **9**: 990
Buddys *see* Mott the Hoople

Budgie **4**: 372, *372,* **17**: *1982,* 1983, **18**:
   2150, *2151*
Budinger, Vic **10**: *1165*
Buffalo, Norton **11**: 1227
Buffalo Bearcats **3**: 338
Buffalo Springfield **1**: 12, 16, **7**: 821, 824-
   6, **8**: 902-3, **10**: 1099-1100, 1123, **12**:
   1324, **15**: 1761, *1764,* 1768, 1770, 1773,
   16: 1846
Buggles **15**: *1692,* 1695, **20**: 2396
Bugs **6**: 682
Bullock, Mitchell **9**: 1059
Bulsara, Fred *see* Mercury, Freddie
Bumblies, **8**: 959
Bumps Blackwell Orchestra **3**: 334
Bumpus, Cornelius **16**: 1852
Bundrick, John 'Rabbit' **11**: 1269, **15**:
   1740, **16**: 1891, **19**: 2196
Bunker, Clive **14**: 1570
Bunn, Allen *see* Tarheel Slim
Bunnell, Dewey **15**: 1776-7, *1777*
Bunny Lake is Missing **8**: 847
Burchill, Charlie **19**: 2274
Burden, Ian **20**: 2308, *2308*
Burdon, Eric **1**: 15, **5**: 582, **6**: 643, 656-60,
   7: 760, **8**: 880, **9**: 1022, 1065, **10**: 1085,
   1099, 1102, **11**: 1205, *1218,* **12**: *1424*
Bureau **19**: 2219, 2248
Burgess, John **6**: 640, 644, **7**: 759
Burgess, Paul **16**: 1914-15, *1914*
Burgess, Sonny **1**: 46
Bürgi, Chuck **17**: 1987
Burke, Clem **20**: 2292-3, 2386
Burke, Solomon **7**: 782, 796-7, **8**: 923, 926,
   934-5, 939, **9**: 1065, **10**: 1162, 1176, **12**:
   1409, **15**: 1782, **16**: 1881
Burley, Dan **2**: 124, 125
Burlison, Paul **1**: 114, *115,* **9**: 1021, **10**:
   1114-15, *1115 see also* Rock 'n' Roll Trio
Burman, Maurice **4**: 433
Burnel, Jean-Jacques **19**: 2188-90, *2188-*
   91
Burnett, Paul **17**: *1959*
Burnette, Billy **1**: 115
Burnette Brothers **1**: 102, 103, 113, 114-
   15, 118, **2**: 195, **3**: 303 *see also* Rock 'n'
   Roll Trio
Burnette, Dorsey **3**: *253*
Burnette, Johnny **2**: 194, **5**: *491,* 492, 502,
   9: 1021
Burnette, Rocky **1**: 115
Burney, Mike **10**: 1185
Burning Spear **11**: *1288,* **16**: *1882, 1885,*
   1886, **20**: 2374
Burns, Bob **16**: 1843, 1844
Burns, Eddie 'Guitar' **11**: 1320
Burns, Hugh **9**: 1033
Burns, Mike **10**: 1185
Burns, Pete **19**: *2262*
Burns, Ray *see* Captain Sensible
Burns, Tito **4**: *362, 368,* **6**: 689, **8**: 897
Burr, Clive **19**: 2231-2
Burrell, 'Boz' **14**: 1565, *1566*
Burrell, Kenny **11**: *1290,* 1291, 1320 **15**:
   1740, **17**: 2038

Burris, Eddie 11: 1291, 14: 1648
Burritos *see* Flying Burrito Brothers
Burroughs, William 18: 2095
Burt, Jo 18: 2147
Burton, Gary 13: 1521
Burton, James 1: 95, 3: 303, 5: 519, 520, 9: 1021, 13: 1557, 17: 2022
Burton, Trevor 10: 1183, 1185
Busey, Gary 20: *2329*
Bush, Kate 18: 2072, 2158, 20: 2321, 2330-3, *2331, 2333,* 2405
Bushell, Garry 18: 2141
Bushy, Ron 9: 1071
Buster, Prince 1: 10, 9: 962, 970-1, 976-7, *977*
Butch Cassidy and the Sundance Kid 5: 580
Butler, Billy 9: 1060, 11: 1221
Butler, Geezer 12: *1369-70,* 1371
Butler, Jerry 3: 266, 5: 562, 7: 793, 795, *795,* 8: 926, 9: 1043, 1059-60, *1060,* 14: 1600
Butler, Joe 8: 867-8, *866, 868-9*
Butler, Tony 11: 1280, 19: 2253
Butterfield 16: 1903
Butterfield Blues Band 11: *1238,* 1239
Butterfield, Paul 8: 917, 10: 1103, 1116, 1124, 1163, 11: 1221, *1238-9, 1240*
Buttrey, Kenny 11: 1209, 17: 2023
Butts Band 9: 1013
Buxton, Glen 16: 1865
Buzzcocks 18: *2043,* 2058, 2060, 2061, 2073-5, 2156
Bye Bye Birdie 3: 351, 5: 498, 8: 859
Byers, Roddy 'Radiation' 19: 2204, 2207
Byrd, Bobby 7: *788,* 788-9
Byrd, Donald 13: 1523
Byrd, Ron *see,* Professor Longhair
Byrd, Steve 17: 1984
Byrds 1: 16, 18, 5: 543, 6: 675-6, 677, 682, 7: 821-2, *821,* 824, 825-6, 827-31, 837, 8: 880, 902-3, 914, 941, 9: 987, 992, 1016, 1017, 1070, 1077, 10: 1082, 1092, 1100, 1121, 1123, 1125, 1155, 1168, 11: 1218, 1223, 1257, 1306, 12: 1340, 13: 1443, 1556, 14: 1657, 15: 1702, 1761, *1764,* 1765, 1766, 1768, 16: 1810, 17: 2022
Byrne, David 14:1640, 20: *2281, 2283, 2284,* 2283-5, 2287
Byrne, Fran 17: 1925
Byrne, John Patrick 18: 2028
Byrnes, Ed 5: 502
Byrom, Larry 9: 1072
Byron, David 15: 1728, *1729*

C

Cabaret 16: *1802,* 1803
Caberet Voltaire 19: 2261, 2268

Cactus 14: 1601
Cactus Jack 1: 56
Caddy, Alan 4: 434
Cadence Records 2: 225, 227, *228,* 231, 4: 406, 407, 5: 508
Cadillac Records 3: 354
Cafe Au-Go-Go 8: 862, 864
Cafe La Mama Troupe 8: 860
Café Society 18: 2146
Cahill, Thaddeus 20: 2318
Cahill, Tony 6: 697
Cain, Mark 'Doidie' 18: *2144,* 2145
Cake, Pat T. 8: 924
Cakewalk 5: *481,* 482, 483
Caldwell, Bobby 11: 1235
Cale, John 1: 20, *20* 5: 562, 8: *864,* 865, 9: 1004-7, 1035-6, 13: 1444, 1446, 1449, 1498, 14: 1638, 1639, 17: 2016, 2019, 19: 2182, 2256
Caledonian Soul Orchestra 13: 1553
Calhoun, Charles 3: 272
California, Randy 9: 1062, 14: 1614-15, *1615*
California Ballroom, Dunstable 6: 619-20, *619-20*
California Jam 12: 1379
Callahan, Andre 18: 2117
Callender, Peter 6: 616
Callis, Jo 20: 2307, *2308,* 2309, 2395
Calloway, Cab 1: 30
Calvert, Bernie 6: 606, *606*
Calvert, Bob 17: 1996, *1997*
Calvert, Reg 7: 744, 745
Calypso 3: 267, 269
Cambridge Folk Festival 11: 1248, 13: 1473, 1477
Camden Place 20: *2343,* 2350-51
Camel 10: 1118, 15: *1743,* 17: 2040
Camelot 5: 498
Cameo-Parkway Records 3: 260, 5: 484, 485, 487
Cameo Records 3: 341-2, *342,* 343, *343,* 349, 350-1, 355, 358, 9: 997
Camillo, Tony 14: 1587
Campaign for Nuclear Disarmament 12: *1387,* 1387
Campbell, Alexis 5: 585
Campbell, Ali 19: 2214, *2214-5*
Campbell, Brad 10: 1172
Campbell, Chris 16: 1856
Campbell, Glen 3: 246, 5: *518,* 519, 520 7: 740, 778, 821-2, 17: 1942, 2021, 2024
Campbell, Ian 13: 1465-6
Campbell, Jo Ann 3: 312
Campbell, Junior 8: 947-9, 15: 1682
Campbell, Michael *see* Mikey Dread
Campbell, Mike 9: *1079,* 18: 2085-6, *2086*
Campbell, Robin 19: 2214, *2214-5*
Campbell, Stan 19: 2207
Campi, Ray 1: 120, *120*
Can 11: 1316, 20: 2362, 2367, *2367,* 2368, *2368*
Canadaires *see* Crewcuts
Canadian pop music 6: 682

Cann, Warren 20: *2352-3,* 2352-4
Canned Heat 10: 1099, 1103, 1115, 1116-17, 11: 1251, 12: *1414*
Cannon, Dyann 14: *1647*
Cannon, Freddy 3: 342, 343, 360, 4: 380, 5: 496-7
Cannon, Gus 6: 678
Cantrall, Bobby 4: 397
Cantrelli, Tjay 9: 1017
Capaldi, Jim 9: 1036, 10: 1188-89, *1190,* 1192
Capehart, Jerry 3: 245-6, *245,* 247, 248
Capital Radio 17: 1959, *1960*
Capitol Records 1: *104,* 105, 3: 262, 266, 5: 501, 503
Capitol Tower, Hollywood 2: *198-9,* 199-200
Capitols 5: 483
Capris 1: 63
Captain Beefheart 1: 19, 7: 816, 11: 1306, 12: 1435, 13: 1481, 1482, *1483,* 1484-7, 1490, 1492, 1495, 1559, 18: 2077
Captain Groovy and his Bubblegum Army 9: 983, 998
Carabello, Mike 13: 1535
Caravan 8: *852,* 14: 1580
Caravans 15: 1783
Caravelles 6: 629
Cardinals 1: 31, 3: 273
Carelli, Justine 3: 360
Carey, Bill 5: 583, 588
Carey, Tony 17: 1985-6
Carillo, Frank 17: 2040
Carlo, Tyran 3: 331
Carlos, Walter 20: 2319
Carlton, Larry 19: 2173-5
Carlton, Joe 5: 469
Carlton and the Shoes 16: 1887
Carmen, Eric 20: 2288
Carmichael, Hoagy 15: 1718
Carmichael, James 18: 2117
Carmichael, Stokely 7: 783
Carn, Jean 14: 1600
Carnaby Street, London 6: 683, 7: *741,* 742-3, 748-9, 801, 806
Carnal Knowledge 10: 1131
Carnes, Kim 4: 479
Carney, Pete 7: *810*
Carny 14: 1680
Caro, Nick de 5: 520
Carousel Club, Nashville 2: 233, *233*
Carpenter, Karen 17: *1948-9,* 1949
Carpenter, Richard 17: *1948,* 1949
Carpenters 15: 1763, 17: 1942, 1948-9
Carpetbaggers, The 5: 498, *499*
Carr, Eric 16: 1869, *1869*
Carr, John 10: 1135
Carr, Michael 4: 423
Carr, Paul 3: 316
Carr, Pearl 17: 1955
Carr, Tony: 10: 1135
Carrack, Paul 19: 2257
Carroll, Earl 2: 217
Carroll, Ronnie 17: 1955
Carroll, Ted 19: 2239

Carruthers, Brother Genie **2**: *160*
Cars **17**: 2016, 2027
Carson, Fiddlin' John **1**: 39
Carter, Calvin **5**: 595, **9**: 1058
Carter, Carlene **17**: 1935
Carter, Hal **2**: 138, *138,* 139, 140
Carter, Johnny **9**: 1059, 1085
Carter, Vivian **5**: 595, *595*
Carter Family **1**: 39, **14**: 1649
Carter, Jane **14**: *1644,* 1645
Carter, Nina **15**: *1697*
Carter, President Jimmy **13**: 1443
Carter, Ron **13**: 1530
Carthy, Martin **13**: 1465, 1472
Cartwright, Alan **10**: 1089, *1089*
Casablanca **16**: 1807
Casady, Jack **1**: 14, **8**: 909-12, *909-12,* **9**: 1039
Casale, Jerry and Bob **17**: 2014
Casey, Al **4**: 394, 395, **7**: 765
Casie, Howie **3**: 249
Casey Jones and the Engineers **6**: 645
Cash, Alvin **9**: *1058,* 1060
Cash, Dave **7**: 745, **17**: 1958
Cash, Fred **7**: 793, *793-4,* 795
Cash, Johnny **1**: 42, 44, *46-7,* 47, *54,* 103, 110-11, *110,* 118, **2**: 160, 232, *232,* 234, **3**: 254, 303, **14**: 1641, 1642-5, 1650, 1652, 1659
Cashbox **1**: 59, *59,* **12**: 1321
Casio electronic instruments **20**: 2302
Cass and the Casanovas **3**: 249
Cassidy, David **3**: 309, **8**: *843,* **12**: 1386, **13**: 1501, *1501,* 1502-3, 1507, 1514, 1516-7
Cassidy, Ed **14**: 1614, *1615*
Castaways **8**: 872
Castelles **1**: 62
Castle, Vernon and Irene **5**: 482
Caston, Leonard Jr. **9**: 1059
Cat **3**: *265*
Catch My Soul **7**: 735, *735,* **19**: *2238,* **20**: 2339
Catch-22 **10**: *1128,* 1129
Catch Us If You Can **6**: 611, **8**: 845, *845*
Catherall, Joanne **20**: 2308, *2308*
Catroni, Joe **8**: 959
'Cats' **6**: 699, **20**: 2337
Cattini, Clem **2**: 139, **4**: 434, 437
Catwoman, Sue **18**: *2053*
Cavaliere, Felix **8**: 862-3, 874-7
Cavern Club, Liverpool **5**: *521,* 522, 532, *536,* 537, 540, *547,* 549, *549,* 554
Cavern Club, London **6**: *604*
Cecil, Malcolm **14**: 1673
Cedarwood **2**: 232
Celebration at Big Sur **8**: *869,* **20**: 2326
Celentano, Adriano **3**: 251
Cellar Club, London **5**: *600*
Celtic Rock **10**: 1135
Central Line **20**: 2393
Cetera, Pete **13**: 1526-7, *1528*
Chad and Jeremy **6**: 693, 694, *694,* 695
Chad Mitchell Trio **6**: 662
Chadwick, Les **5**: 524-7, 540

Chaman, Clive **11**: 1232
Chambers, Paddy **5**: 534
Chambers, Martin **19**: 2253, *2253*
Chambre, Tim **12**: 1325
Champs **2**: 196, **4**: 382, *389,* 390
Chance, Floyd 'Lightnin' ' **2**: 225
Chancellor Records **3**: 260, 341, *341,* 342, 343, 348-9, 350, 352-3, 358
Chandler Bryan 'Chas' **6**: 657, *657, 659,* 660, **9**: 1063, 1065-6, 1068, **11**: *1243,* **12**: 1422, 1427-8
Chandler, Gene **3**: 266, **5**: 487, **9**: 1059-60, *1060*
Chantays **7**: *764,* 765
Chantels **5**: 513, 566, *569,* **9**: 1045
Chants **5**: 523
Chapel, Jean **3**: 311
Chapin, Harry **10**: 1125
Chaplin, Blondie **7**: 772, 780
Chapman, Mark **17**: 1973
Chapman, Mike **16**: 1821-3, 1831, 1834, 1835, 1836, 1902, **17**: 1947, **18**: 2099, **20**: 2281, 2293
Chapman, Roger **10**: 1198-1200, *1198-1200*
Chapman, Tony **8**: 889-90
Chaquico, Craig **8**: 913
Charlatans **8**: 905, 914, 920, **12**: *1389*
Charles, Bobby **1**: 27, **13**: 1455
Charles, Charley **17**: 1931, *1933*
Charles, Nick **8**: 929
Charles, Ray **1**: 35, **2**: 145, 149, 153, 155, 158, 160, **3**: 273-4, 322, 324-9, *323,* 346, **4**: *454-5,* 462, **7**: 781, **9**: 971, 1060, **10**: 1162, 1167, **12**: 1409, **14**: 1672, **15**: 1790, 1797
Charles, Sonny **5**: 509
Charlesworth, Dick **11**: 1245
Charlie Girl **5**: *526,* 527, **8**: 859
Charlie Is My Darling **8**: 845
Charlie Musslewhite Band **11**: 1221
Charlton, Manuel **17**: *1988,* 1989
Charmers, Lloyd **9**: 977, **16**: 1887
Charmetts **5**: 567
Charro **2**: 212
Charters, Samuel B. **6**: 678
Chas and Dave **13**: 1455
Chas McDevitt Skiffle Group **4**: 430
Chastity **7**: 837
Cheap Trick **6**: 640
Checker, Chubby **2**: 210, *210,* **3**: 269, *270, 342,* 343, *343,* 351, 359, *359,* 360, **4**: 404, **5**: 482, *482-3,* 483, 484-7, 489, 494, 495, 498, 500, 504, **12**: 1419, **18**: 2105
Cheeks, Julius **15**: 1781
Cheetah **20**: *2372*
Cheetah, New York **8**: 863, *863*
Chelsea **17**: 1929
Chelsea Girls, The **16**: 1863
Chen, Philip **7**: 812
Cher **14**: 1605, **18**: 2124 *see also* Sonny and Cher
Cherry, John **17**: 1933
Cherry Red Records **18**: 2156-7
Chess **9**: 1058, 1059

Chess, Leonard **1**: 65, 66, **5**: 590, **14**: 1596
Chess, Leonard and Phil **4**: 464-7, **6**: 702
Chess, Marshall **4**: 467
Chess Records **1**: 65, *66,* 68, **3**: 262, 264, 271, **4**: 461, 463, 464-7, 475, 478, **8**:. 891, **9**: 1058-9, 1060, **18**: 2102
Chessmen **5**: 588
Chester, Peter **4**: 385, **16**: 1832
Chevlons **8**: 947
Chic **14**: 1593, 1631, *1632,* **15**: 1791, **18**: 2103, 2113-5, *2114-15,* 2161, 2177, 2179
Chicago **7**: 780, *780,* **10**: 1093, *1094-5,* 1125, **13**: 1523, 1526-8, **17**: 2021, **20**: 2364
Chicago Transit Authority *see* Chicago
Chicken Shack **10**: *1101,* 1102, 1107, 1119
Chicory Tip **12**: *1422,* 1423
Chieftains **13**: 1477
Chiffons **5**: 566, 567, *568*
Child, June **12**: 1438, 1440
Childs, Andy **12**: 1340
Chi-Lites **9**: 1060
Chilli Willi and the Red Hot Peppers **17**: 1922, 1924, 1925, 1928, 1939, **18**: 2042
Chilton, Alex **10**: 1174-5, *1175,* **20**: 2288
Chimes, Terry **18**: 2066-7, *2097,* 2069
Chin, Nicky **16**: 1821-3, 1835, 1836, **18**: 2099
Chipetz, Harry **3**: 360
Chipmunks **3**: 269, 284
Chirowsky, Josef **16**: 1866
Chi-Sound **9**: 1060
Chiswick Records **18**: 2156
Chocolate Watch Band **6**: 682, **8**: 847, 872, *873*
Choir **8**: *871,* 872
'Chorus Girls' **20**: 2340
Chosen Few **13**: 1475, 1498
Chris Barker Band **5**: 585-6, *584-5*
Christgue, Robert **12**: 1323, 1325, 1330, 1331
Christian, Charlie **1**: 78, *79,* **10**: 1107, **19**: 2166, 2167
Christian, Roger **7**: 778
Chron Gen **18**: 2141
Chrysalis Records **20**: 2293
Chudd, Lew **2**: 142, 145, 147, 155, 156 **3**: 303, **5**: 507
Churchill, Chick **12**: 1374-5
Ciccione, Don **5**: *570,* 573
Cimarons **19**: 2216, *2217*
Cinquetti, Gigliola **17**: 1957
Circus **12**: 1330-1
Circus Maximus **10**: 1085
Cisco Pike **14**: 1652
City **15**: 1715
City Ramblers **2**: *123*
Clancy **17**: 1922, 1924
Clancy Brothers **11**: 1204
Clanton, Jimmy **4**: 452, **5**: *561*
Clapton, Eric **1**: *9,* 16, **4**: 383, **5**: 582, *582,* 588, *589,* **6**: 642-3, 645, 650-1, 652-3, *652,* **9**: 1020, 1021-2, *1021,* 1025, 1026-9, *1027,* 1030-1, 1034-7, 1063, 1065,

1074-5, 1079, *1080*, **10**: 1102, 1110, 1113, 1115, 1188-9, 1199, **11**: *1232*, **12**: 1397, **13**: 1443, 1445, *1446*, *1449*, 1452, 1560, **14**: 1562, 1603, **15**: 1692, **16**: 1892, **17**: 1968, 1972, 2025, **18**: 2158
Clarence, Henry **2**: 145
Clarendonians **9**: 977
Clark, Alan **19**: *2199*, 2200
Clark, Allan **16**: 605-8, *606*
Clark, Chris **10**: 1163
Clark, Dave **6**: 609-11, *693*, **8**: 845, *845*
Clark, Dee **9**: 1058
Clark, Dick **1**: 106, **2**: 202, 209, *219*, 220, 236, **3**: 263, 341, 342, 343, *343*, 344, 348, 349, 352, 353, 356-60, **5**: 485, 495, 496, 499, 500, 571, *571*, **7**: 833, **9**: 981, 990, 1046, **13**: 1502
Clark, Gene **6**: 662, **7**: 821, *827-8*, 828-30, *830-1*, 831
Clark, Harvey **1**: 83
Clark, Joe **4**: 439, *439*
Clark, Louis **15**: 1748-9
Clark, Nobby **13**: 1511
Clark, Petula **5**: 483, **6**: 621-2, *622*, 626, 632-3
Clark, Roy **2**: 231
Clark, Sam **5**: 501
Clark, Sanford **1**: 102, **4**: *412*
Clark, Steve **19**: 2236, *2237*
Clarke, Allan **6**: 605, *606*, 608
Clarke, Eddie **19**: 2239, *2240*
Clarke, Iain **15**: 1728
Clarke, Mark **17**: 1986
Clarke, Michael **7**: 828, 830
Clarke, Stanley **9**: 1039, **13**: *1523*
Clarke, Tony **6**: 713, **10**: 1195
Clarke, Vince **20**: 2320, *2320*
Clash **8**: 883, **11**: 1281, 1283, *1291*, **12**: 1357, **17**: 1925, 1929, **18**: *2042*, 2043, 2046, 2048, 2053, 2058, 2061-3, 2066-9, 2072, 2073, 2074, 2075, 2080, 2141, *2142*, 2148, 2158-9, **19**: 2188, 2203, 2204, 2216, 2244, 2251, 2254, 2260, 2261, 2279, **20**: 2329, 2352, 2373
Class **5**: 502
Classix Nouveaux **11**: *1283*
Claudine **14**: 1587
Clavell, James **6**: 636
Clay, Judy **8**: 932
Clay, Otis **9**: *1058*, 1060
Clay, Tom **2**: 220
Clayton, Adam **19**: 2270-1, *2271*
Clayton, Bob **2**: 220
Clayton, Merry **3**: *325*
Clayton, Sam **16**: 1858, *1858*
Clayton-Thomas, David **3**: 251, **13**: *1539*, 1540
Cleaves, Jessica **19**: 2163
Clement, Jack **2**: 168
Clements, Rod **13**: *1475*
Clements, Terry **10**: 1172
Cleminson, Zal **17**: 1989, *1994*, 1995
Clemons, Clarence **15**: 1688, **18**: *2087*, 2089, *2089*
Clempson, Dave 'Clem' **9**: 1033, **10**: 1102

Cleopatra **5**: 498, *499*
Cleveland, Al **4**: 479
Cleveland, James **15**: 1790, *1799*
Cliff, Jimmy **9**: *961*, 963, 966, 971, 973, 978-80, **12**: 1355, **18**: 2109, **20**: 2327
Clifford, Doug **7**: 835, **13**: 1456, *1456*, 1457, 1458, *1458*
Cline, Patsy **2**: 194, 232, 234, **14**: 1647
Clinton, George **12**: 1402, **19**: 2169, *2171*, 2171-2
Clique **7**: 760
Clive's Incredible String Band *see* Incredible String Band
Clooney, Rosemary **3**: 310
Close, Bob **11**: 1307
Clover **17**: 1925
Clovers **1**: 31, *70*, 72, 73, *73*, **3**: *271*, 273, 286, **4**: 414
Clowes, Sue **20**: 2400
Clue, J. **9**: 976
Clyde, Jeremy **6**: 694
Clyde Valley Stompers **4**: 439
Coal Miner's Daughter **14**: 1660
Coasters **1**: 71, *71*, **2**: 200, **3**: 247, 269, 274, 275, 281-3, *282*, 284, 287-8, *287*, 289, 294-7, **4**: 376, **5**: 507, 533, **9**: 990, **12**: 1393
Coati Mundi **20**: 2295, 2297
Cobb, Arnett **2**: 173
Cobb, Ed **6**: 682, **8**: 872
Cobham, Billy **9**: 1033, **13**: 1523, 1524, 1525, 1531, **14**: 1620, *1620*
Cobham, Michael **9**: 1033
Coburn, Roy **9**: 975
Cochran, Bobby **9**: 1072
Cochran, Eddie **1**: 107, **2**: 138, 140, *140*, 194, 197, 205, 208, 209, 239, **3**: *242*, 243, 244-8, 259, 297, *325*, **4**: *375*, 380, *404*, **9**: 1021, **13**: 1442
Cochran, Hank **3**: 245, *245*, **14**: 1647, *1647*
Cochran, Wayne **10**: 1162, *1162*
Cochran Brothers **3**: 245
Cocker, Joe **10**: 1088, 1166-9, **11**: *1250*, 1253, **13**: 1443, 1445, **15**: 1763, **17**: 2025, **20**: 2329, 2337
Cockney Rebel **16**: 1802, 1838-40
Cockney Rejects **18**: 2152, 2153, 2154
Coconuts **19**: 2271, *2279*
Cocteau Twins **18**: *2157*, **20**: 2381
Cody, Phil **4**: 453
Coe, Charles **7**: 833
Coffey, Dan **1**: 118
Cogan, Alma **3**: 310, *311*
Cogbill, Tommy **10**: 1174
Coghlan, John **15**: *1730*, 1731, *1732*, 1735
Cohen, David **10**: 1097
Cohen, Herb **13**: 1493, 1554
Cohen, Leonard **1**: 18, **12**: *1341*, 1349, 1350-2, 1359, *1360*
Cohen, Paul **2**: 185
Cohn, Nik **7**: 771, **11**: 1298-9, **12**: 1324
Cold Turkey **15**: 1719
Cole, Cozy **3**: 268-9
Cole, Marylin **16**: 1810

Cole, Natalie **15**: 1791
Cole, Nat King **1**: 30, 31, **3**: 324, 325
Coleman, Cornelius **2**: 146, 154
Coleman, Jaz **12**: 1371
Coleman, Ornette **13**: 1521, 1529, **14**: 1563
Coleman, Peter **18**: 2135
Coletta, John **12**: 1377
Colgems Records **9**: 987, 989-90
Collen, Phil **19**: 2237, *2237*
Colley, Simon **20**: 2389
Collier, Mike **7**: 760
Collier, Mitty **9**: 1059
Collins, Albert **4**: 390
Collins, Allen **16**: *1842*, 1843, 1844, *1844*
Collins, Bernard **16**: 1887
Collins, Betty **3**: 300
Collins, Bootsy *see* Collins, William 'Bootsy'
Collins, Charles 'Chuck' **12**: 1349
Collins, Edwyn **19**: 2273, *2273*
Collins, Frances **5**: 514
Collins, Gail **14**: 1607-8
Collins, Jackie **16**: *1822*
Collins, Judy **1**: 18, **6**: 662, 680, **10**: 1124, *1124*, **12**: 1341, 1348-9
Collins, Lorrie **1**: 113
Collins, Mel **14**: 1564-5, *1566*, **19**: 2196
Collins, Peter **20**: 2396
Collins, Phelps **7**: 791
Collins, Phil **15**: *1751*, 1752, 1754, **16**: 1917, **17**: 1947, **20**: 2325, *2404*, 2405
Collins, Ray **13**: *1491*, 1492, 1493
Collins, Shirley **13**: 1461-2, 1465
Collins, Tom **14**: 1658
Collins, William 'Bootsy' **7**: *790*, 791, **19**: 2171, *2172*
Colomby, Bobby **9**: 1074, **13**: *1538*, 1539
Colonel Abrams **20**: 2420
Colosseum **7**: 815, **10**: 1112, 1114, **11**: 1257
Colour Field **19**: 2207
'Colour Me Pop' **8**: 853, *853*
Colpix **5**: 501-2, 503, 514
Colt, Steve **10**: 1162
Colter, Jessi **14**: 1655, 1660
Coltrane, John **3**: 321, **13**: 1521, *1521*, 1530, 1537, **14**: 1563
Colts **3**: 300
Columbia Records **3**: 262, *280* **4**: 432, 433, **6**: 685-6, 694, 699, **11**: 1204-5, 1210
Colyer, Ken **2**: 121, *121*, 123, 124-5, *125* 128, 133, **4**: *438*, 439, **13**: 1461
Comets **1**: 22, 25, 26, 27, 28, 35, **2**: *201*, 205, 207, **3**: 341, **9**: 969
Commodores **9**: 1043, **14**: 1581, 1583, **18**: 2103, *2116*, 2116-17
Como, Perry **5**: 578, **15**: 1713, **19** *2258*, 2260
Compton, Tom **12**: 1375
Comsat Angels **19**: 2262, **20**: 2403
Concert for Bangladesh **20**: 2403
Concord Quartet **15**: 1697
Condition Green **20**: 2364
Confederates **4**: *440*

Conka, Don **9:** 1016-17
Conklin, Jim **5:** 501
Conley, Arthur **1:** 10, **8:** 926
Connolly, Billy **17:** 2028
Connolly, Brian **16:** 1835, *1835,* 1837
Connolly, Ray **20:** 2327
Connor, Tony **16:** 1826
Conny and the Bell Hops **4:** 391
Conrad, Jess **2:** 139, *140,* **4:** 374, 380
Constanten, Tom 'T. C.' **8:** 906
Constellation **3:** 266, **9:** 1058-9
Continental Kids *see* Flash Cadillac and
    the Continental Kids
Contours **4:** 477, **5:** 483, **9:** 1052 **11:** *1283*
Conway Records **7:** 757
Conway, Russ **2:** 179
Cooder, Ry **5:** 520, *520,* **8:** 882, **10:** 1125,
    11: 1237, **12:** 1340, **13:** 1484, 1541,
    1542, 1543, 1558-60, **15:** 1703, 1719,
    1763, **20:** 2326
Cook, Frank **10:** 1116
Cook, Little Joe **7:** 815
Cook, Paul **11:** 1280, **18:** 2045, *2047,* 2048,
    2145
Cook, Roger **3:** 290, 293, **6:** 695, *695,* **16:**
    1821
Cook, Stu **7:** 835, **13:** 1456, *1456,* 1457,
    1458, *1458*
Cook, Tommy **9:** 976
Cooke, Barbara **3:** 335, *335*
Cooke, James 'Curley' **11:** 1225
Cooke, L. C. **3:** 334
Cooke, Ray **11:** 1230
Cooke, Ron **10:** 1178
Cooke, Sam **2:** 160, *164,* 196, **3:** 266, 322,
    322, 327, 333-5, **4:** *405,* **5:** 483, 489, 502,
    561, **6:** *693,* **7:** 781, 797, **8:** 923, 930,
    935, **9:** 963, 971, 978, 1051, 1065, **10:**
    1159, **12:** 1355, **15:** 1725, 1726, 1793,
    1797
Cookie and the Cupcakes **13:** 1445
Cookies **3:** 312, **5:** 489, 567
Cooksey, Rob **12:** 1380
'Cool For Cats' **4:** 378, **8:** 842
Coolidge, Rita **10:** 1169, **13:** 1443, 1444,
    1445, 1449, **14:** *1651,* 1652
Coombes, Peet **20:** 2386, *2386*
Coombes, Rod **11:** 1230
Coon, Caroline **18:** 2068
Cooper, Alice **12:** 1336, **13:** 1483, *1545,* **16:**
    1862, *1862,* 1864-7, **20:** 2339
Cooper, Dolly **3:** 299
Cooper, Jackie **9:** 987, 989
Cooper, Lindsay **14:** 1569
Cooper, Martin **20:** 2317
Cooper, Ray **4:** 1668
Cooper-Clarke, John **2:** 224, **19:** 2269, **20:**
    2339
Copas, Cowboy **2:** 194
Cope, Julian **8:** 957, **19:** 2276, 2279-80,
    2279, 2280
Copeland, Greg **15:** 1780
Copeland, Ian **20:** 2281
Copeland, Miles **15:** 1737, **18:** 2145, **19:**
    2181-2, *2182,* 2184-5, 2256, 2257

Copeland, Stewart **14:** 1576, **19:** 2184-5,
    2186, 2256, 2257
Copping, Chris **10:** 1086, *1088,* 1089
Cordell, Denny **10:** 1088, 1167-8, *1182,*
    13: 1445, 1446, **15:** 1779
Cordell, Ritchie **9:** 994-5, 998, **17:** 2011
Cordet, Louise **6:** 629
Corea, Chick **13:** 1523, *1523,* 1531
Corman, Glenn **14:** 1570-1
Corman, Roger **8:** 847-8, *848*
Cornelius, Hugh **19:** *2188,* 2188-90, *2191*
Cornish, Gene **8:** 874-7
Correro, Joe **7:** 833
Cort, Bob **2:** 134
Cortese, Dom **11:** 1211
Cortez, Dave 'Baby' **4:** 389, **9:** 1055
Corvettes *see* Bluesology
Coryell, Larry **9:** 1032
Cosby, Hank **4:** 479, **6:** 716, 719, **14:** 1672
Cosines **15:** 1714
Costa, Don **3:** 307, 309
Costa, Sam **4:** 376
Costello, Elvis **2:** *181,* 183, 187, **5:** 574, *574*
    9: *1077,* **11:** 1220, *1290,* **12:** 1360, **17:**
    1921, 1922, 1925, 1931, 1935, 1939,
    1966, **18:** 2063, *2065,* 2158, **19:** *2181,*
    2181-2, *2192,* 2192-5, *2193, 2194,* 2205,
    2257
Coster, Tom **13:** 1537
Cott, Gerry **19:** 2249, *2250,* 2251
Cotten, Michael **16:** 1873
Cotton, James **11:** 1235
Cotton, Jeff **13:** 1484
Coulter, Phil **13:** 1511, **16:** 1821
Count Five **8:** *870, 872*
Count Machouki **19:** 2177
Country for Bangladesh **20:** 2327
Country Joe and the Fish **1:** 15, **8:** 903,
    905, 914-15, **9:** 1015, 1075, **10:** 1090,
    1091, 1092, 1096-7, 1100, *1122,* 1123,
    1134, 1170, **11:** 1223, 1250, **12:** 1390
Country Music Association **14:** 1658
Country Music Stars Museum and Mall
    14: *1641*
County, Wayne/Jayne **16:** *1825, 1862,*
    1863, *1863,* 1879
Coupe de Ville *see* Premiers
Cousin Joe **2:** 154
Cousins, Dave **14:** 1679
Cousins, Tony **9:** 973
Covay, Don **4:** 385, **5:** 483. **6:** 702, **14:** 1600
Coverdale, David **12:** 1376, *1377,* 1379-
    80, **17:** 1985, 1986, 1987, *1987*
Covington, Bogus Ben **6:** 680
Covington, Joey **8:** 912-13
Covington, Julie **20:** 2337
Cow, Henry **14:** 1568-9
Cowart, Juanita **6:** 719
Cowe, Simon **13:** 1475, *1475*
Cowley, Elizabeth **8:** 852
Cox, Andy **19:** 2208-9, *2209*
Cox, Billy **9:** 1068
Cox, Michael **4:** 362, 423, 437
Cox, Terry **13:** 1476
Coxhill, Lol **14:** 1569, **18:** 2079-80

Crabtree, Lee **8:** 865, **9:** 1015
Craddock, Kenny **13:** 1475
Cradle **16:** 1830
Craft, Morty **5:** 562
Craig, Andy **15:** 1747
Craig, Mikey **20:** 2399, *2399*
Crain, Roy **3:** 333
Cramer, Floyd **1:** 94, *94,* 95, **2:** 225, 233,
    233
Cramps **1:** 120, *120*
Crandall, Eddie **2:** 185
Crane, Vincent **15:** 1697
Crane, River Band **2:** 125, **4:** *438,* 439
Crass **17:** 2141, **18:** 2160
Crawdaddy **12:** 1388
Crawdaddy **12:** 1329-30, 1339, *1339*
Crawdaddy Club, Richmond **5:** 599-600,
    599, **7:** 803, 816, **8:** 890-1, 896
Crawford, Dave **8:** 937, 940
Crawford, Hank **10:** 1109
Crawford, Johnny **4:** 452
Crawford, Randy **17:** 2021, **18:** 2103,
    2175, *2175*
Crawlers **9:** *1058,* 1060
Crayton, Pee Wee **1:** 30
Crazy Cadillacs **1:** *70*
Crazy Cavan **1:** 118, *119,* 120
Crazy Elephant **9:** 983, 998
Crazy Horse **5:** 519, **15:** 1765, 1768, *1770,*
    16: 1845, 1846
Crazy World of Arthur Brown **9:** 1017, **11:**
    1297
Creach, Papa John **8:** 912-13
Cream **1:** 2, *9,* 16, 18, **6:** 643, 647, **7:** 804,
    804, **8:** 848, **9:** *1021,* 1021-2, 1024-9,
    1030, 1031, 1032, 1033, 1034-5, 1039,
    1066, 1070, 1071, **10:** 1099, 1102,
    1112-13, **11:** 1245, 1290, 1292, **12:**
    1361, 1391, 1403, **13:** 1449, 1488,
    1523, **14:** 1601, 1606-7, **15:** 1633, 1662,
    1686, 1691, 1739, 1762, **16:** 1830, **17:**
    1981, **19:** 2221, 2234
Creamcheese, Suzy **9:** 1074
Cream's Last Concert **9:** 848
Creation **7:** 758-9, 819-20, *819,* **14:** 1608
Creations **15:** 1785
Creatures **18:** 2151
Creed, Linda **5:** *563,* **14:** 1594
Creedence Clearwater Revival **1:** 103, **10:**
    1155, **11:** 1251, 1253, **13:** *1442,* 1443,
    1449, 1456-60
Creem **12:** 1330, *1330-1*
Cregan, Jim **10:** 1200, *1200* **16:** 1839, 1840
Creme, Lol **6:** 602, **14:** *1678,* 1680, **16:**
    1913-15, *1913, 1914,* **20:** 2360
Crescendos **2:** 236
Crescent City Street Band **2:** *153*
Crespo, Jim **16:** 1849
Crest Records **3:** 245-6, 247
Crests **2:** 236, *236,* 237
Crew Cuts **1:** 71, **2:** *223,* 235, 236, *236-7,* **3:**
    251, 262, *262*
Crewe, Bob **2:** 240, **3:** *264,* 266, 342, **5:** 496,
    497, 562, *563,* 571, *571* 572, **10:** 1178,
    12: 1416 *see also* Slay and Crew

Crewe Folk Festival **11:** 1248
Crewsdon, Roy **6:** *612-13,* 613-14, *614*
Cribbins, Bernard **3:** 269
Crickets **1:** *80,* **2:** 163, 165, *181,* 182, *183,* 185, *185,* 186, 187, 188, *189,* 190, 191, 193, 200, 227, 240, **3:** *259*
Criss, Peter **16:** 1869, *1871*
Critters **10:** 1123
Croce, Jim **13:** 1556
Crocker, Jean-Paul **16:** 1839, *1839*
Crockett, G. L. **1:** 113
Crombie, Tony **2:** 122, *122,* **4:** 366, *398*
Crompton, Bill **4:** 423
Cromwellian Club **7:** *742*
Crook, Max **4:** 417
Cropper, Steve **7:** 784-5, *784,* **8:** 921-2, 925, *927,* 929, 931-2, 937, 939, **10:** 1178, **11:** 1292, **12:** 1401, **15:** 1793, **17:** 1976
Crosby, Bing **14:** 1633
Crosby, David **7:** 821, 826, 828, 830-1, **8:** 909, 911-12, **10:** 1123, **11:** *1250, 1252,* **12:** 1345, **15:** 1702, 1703, *1764,* 1765, 1766, *1767*
Crosby, Stills, Nash and Young **6:** 607, **7:** 825, 826, **9:** 1019, **10:** 1123, 1164, **11:** 1253, 1259, **12:** 1345, **15:** 1702, 1703, 1742, 1761, 1764-7, 1770, 1776, 1777, 1780, **16:** 1841, **17:** 2022
Cross, Chris **20:** 2352, *2352-3,* 2353
Cross, David **14:** *1564,* 1565-6
Cross, Sylvester **3:** 246, 247
Crossover Records **3:** 328
Crow, Alvin **7:** 835
Crow, Dr Joseph **20:** 2376
Crowe, Simon **19:** 2249, 2251
Crowell, Rodney **17:** 2025
Crowns **1:** 72, **3:** 283, 291, *291 see also* Drifters
Crucial Three **19:** 2276, 2279
Crudup, Arthur 'Big Boy' **1:** 53, 88
Cruise **20:** 2376, *2376*
Crusaders **10:** 1110, **13:** 1513, 1523, **19:** 2173-5, *2174-5*
Crutchfield, Jerry **4:** 407
Cryan, Shames **8:** *870,* 872
Crystal Mesh **16:** 1845
Crystal Palace Garden Party **11:** 1312, **16:** 1839
Crystals **1:** 12, **2:** 240, **5:** 508-9, *509,* 511, 513-15, *513, 515,* 566, 567, 569, **7:** 728, **8:** 879, **12:** 1381, **15:** 1682
CS-80 synthesiser **20:** 2319
Cuckoo Patrol **6:** 614, **8:** 845
Cues **3:** 300
Culley, Frank **3:** 273
Cult **20:** 2420
Culture **18:** 2061, **20:** 2372
Culture Club **18:** 2115, 2161, **19:** 2258, **20:** 2325, 2344, 2345, 2349, *2381,* 2383, 2394, 2397, 2398-2400, *2398-2400,* 2418
Cummings, Burton **14:** *1616,* 1617
Cummings, Jerry **14:** 1598
Cunningham, Bill **10:** 1174-5

Cunningham, Blair **20:** 2384
Curb, Mike **8:** 935, **10:** 1093, *1093*
Curbishley, Bill **7:** 817, **11:** 1275, *1277*
Cure **18:** 2141, 2150, *2151*
Currie, Billy **20:** 2351, *2352-3,* 2352-4
Currie, Kevin **15:** 1758
Currie, Steve **12:** 1439-40
Curry, Tim **16:** 1876, *1877*
Curtis, Alan **20:** 2389
Curtis, Chris **5:** 528-31, **12:** 1377
Curtis, Ian **19:** *2266,* 2266-8, *2267,* 2269
Curtis, King **3:** 265, 282, 288, 296, *297,* **4:** 389, **8:** 937, 940, **15:** 1790, 1799
Curtis, Mac **1:** 103, 112-13, 116, *116,* **2:** 217
Curtis, Sonny **2:** 185, 188, *189,* 227, 228 **4:** 457
Curulewski, John **18:** 2128
Curved Air **14:** 1562, 1563, 1565-7, **18:** *2076,* **19:** 2184
Cuthell, Dick **19:** 2205, **20:** 2387
Cutler, Adge **10:** 1139
Cutler, Chris **14:** 1569, 1620
Cutler, Ivor **18:** *2076*
Cutler, Sam **11:** 1259
Cybernetics **11:** 1279
Cyril Davies' All-Stars **5:** 583, 586, 587, *587,* 588
Cyrus Erie **8:** *870-1,* 872
Czezowski, Andy **18:** 2058, 2059, *2060*
Czukay, Holger **20:** 2367, 2386

D

d'Abo, Mike **6:** 647-9, *647*
Dacus, Donnie **13:** 1528
Daddy *see* Supertramp
Daddy G and the Church Street Five **5:** 492
Dae, Sonny **1:** 26
Dagger, Steve **20:** 2347
Daily, Pappy **2:** 176, 177
Daily Express **12:** 1334, 1336
Daily Mirror **12:** 1335-6
Dairo, I. K. **9:** *966*
Daisley, Bob **15:** 1729, **17:** 1986
Dakar, Rhoda **19:** 2203, 2205, 2207
Dakotas **5:** 533-4, 537, **6:** 639
D'Albuquerque, Michael **15:** 1747, 1748
Dale, Dick **4:** 383, 391, **7:** 760, 764-5, *765,* 767, **8:** 901
Dale, Jim **4:** 430
Dalek I Love You **19:** 2278, 2280, *2280*
D'Aleo, Angelo **4:** 409
Daley, Lloyd **16:** 1898, 1900
Dali, Salvador **16:** 1866, *1867*
Dallas, Boys **2:** 138
Dalton, John **7:** 754, *755*
Daltrey, Roger **1:** 7, **4:** 372, *373,* **11:** 1261-77, 1280, **20:** 2327, *2402 see also* Who

Daly, Brian **15:** 1724
Daly, Steven **19:** 2273
D'Ambrosia, Joey **1:** 26
Dameron, Douna **2:** 177
Dammers, Jerry **19:** 2201, *2201,* 2203, 2204, 2205, 2207, 2211, 2212
Damned, The **17:** 1925, 1939, 2008, **18:** 2046, 2054, 2056, *2059,* 2060, 2061, 2074, 2077, 2078-80, 2156, **19:** 2188, 2261
Dana **12:** *1342,* **17:** 1957
Dandy, Jim **14:** 1601
Danelli, Dino **8:** 874-7, *875, 876*
Daniels, Jeffrey **19:** 2178, 2180, **20:** 2394
Danko, Rick **11:** 1209, *1220,* **13:** *1547,* 1549
Dankworth, Johnny **4:** *429,* **11:** 1245
Danniels, Ray **19:** 2233
Danny and the Juniors **1:** 100, **2:** 165, *165,* 179, 236, 240, **3:** 241, **5:** 502
Danse Society **19:** 2262, *2263*
Dantalion's Chariot **19:** 2184
Dante, Ron **9:** *999,* 1000
Darin, Bobby **2:** 193, 239, **3:** 242, 274, 275, *275,* 341, 344-7, **4:** 404, *405,* 441, *441,* 442, **7:** *738,* 739-40, 827, **10:** *1127,* 1159, **11:** 1297, **17:** 1941
Darlow, Simon **20:** 2335
Darnell, August **18:** 2103, **20:** 2292, *2295,* 2295-7, *2297*
Darnell, Larry **2:** 153
Darren, James **5:** 502, 509
Darts **1:** 63, **12:** *1356, 1357*
Dash, Sarah **12:** *1415-16,* 1416
Datebook **12:** *1329*
Dateline Diamonds **8:** 845
Daugherty, Jay Dee **17:** 2019
Davani, Dave **5:** 588
Dave Brubeck Quartet **3:** 268, *268*
Dave Clark Five **3:** 266, **5:** 537, **6:** 603, 609-11, *618,* 693, *693,* **8:** 845, **9:** 997, 1074, **10:** 1159
Dave Dee Dozy Beaky Mick and Tich (DDDBM&T) **1:** *7,* **8:** 943, 950-1, 954, **10:** 1085
David, Anne-Marie **17:** 1957
David, Hal **5:** 562, 577, 578-80, *579*
'David Essex Showcase, The' **13:** 1509
David and Jonathan **6:** 695, *695*
Davies, Alun **10:** 1187
Davies, Cyril **5:** 583, 584, 585-7, *587,* 588, 598, **6:** 655, **7:** 758, **15:** 1724
Davies, Dave **7:** 750, *750, 752,* 753, 754, 756
Davies, Hunter **12:** 1322
Davies, John R. T. **4:** *438,* 439
Davies, Mandy Rice **7:** 737
Davies, Noel **19:** 2204
Davies, Pete **18:** *2154*
Davies, Ray **7:** 750-6, *750-1, 755,* **9:** 993, **12:** 1359, *1359,* 1434, **15:** 1719, **19:** 2244, 2245, 2253, **20:** 2340
Davies, Rick **15:** 1758, *1758,* 1759, 1760, *1760*
Davies, Trevor **8:** 950

Davis, Betty **12:** 1403
Davis, Bill 'Sheriff Tex' **1:** 105
Davis, Billie **6:** 635
Davis, Billy **3:** *292,* 293, **4:** 471, 472, **6:** 710, **9:** 1059
Davis, Bo **3:** 245, 246
Davis, Carl **3:** 332, **9:** 1059-60
Davis, Clifford **10:** 1120
Davis, Clive **10:** 1093-4, *1095,* 1129
Davis, Denny **14:** 1633
Davis, Don **8:** 930, **9:** 1059
Davis, Hal **6:** 719, **9:** 1046
Davis, J. C. **7:** 789
Davis, Jesse Ed **11:** 1227, 1237, *1237*
Davis, Link **2:** 176
Davis, Mark **12:** 1407
Davis, Michael **13:** 1488-9
Davis, Mike **9:** 1031
Davis, Miles **1:** 2, 16, **3:** 321, *321,* **9:** 966, 1032, **13:** *1521,* 1523-4, 1529-31, 1532, **17:** 1981, **18:** 2095, 2103
Davis, Reverend Gary **13:** 1559
Davis, Robert Hartford **12:** 1430
Davis Jr., Sammy **17:** 1942
Davis, Spencer **8:** 847, **10:** 1186-7, *1186-7,* 1188
Davis, Tim **11:** *1225,* 1225-7
Davis, Tyrone **9:** 1060
Davis, Wild Bill **1:** 34
Davison, Brian 'Blinky' **15:** 1685, 1687, *1687*
Davison, Harold **7:** 807
Davison, Lenny **6:** 609-11, *610*
Dawkins, Jimmy **10:** 1102
Dawn **4:** 459, *459,* **15:** *1705 see also* Orlando, Tony
Dawson, John **8:** 905
Day, Bobby **5:** 502
Day, Doris **3:** 310, 311, **7:** 766
Day, Frankie **3:** 350
Day, James Cayton **2:** 225
Daye, Johnny **10:** 1163
Deacon, John **16:** 1812, *1812,* 1814, *1816,* 1817
Dead End Kids **18:** *2064*
Dead Kennedys **1:** 19
Dead or Alive **19:** 2263, **20:** 2385
Deaf School **19:** 2278, 2279, *2280*
Dean, Elton **14:** 1580, 1665
Dean, Eric **9:** 975
Dean, James **1:** 22, *83,* 90, **2:** *195,* 207, *207,* 211, **11:** *1219,* **12:** 1385
Dean, Rob **20:** 2355-6, *2357*
Dean, Roger **10:** 1112-13, **11:** 1295, **15:** 1692, 1693, 1694
DeAngelis, Peter **3:** 342, 348, 352, 358
Death Cult **18:** 2055
Decca record company **3:** 262, 266, 319, 320, 331, **4:** 425, 426, *426,* **6:** 688-90, *689,* 699, **7:** 757-8, 759, **8:** 896-7, *943,* 949, 952, 959-60, *960,* **17:** 2026
Dechert, Gregg **15:** 1729
DeCoteaux, Bert **18:** 2103
Dee, Dave **1:** *7,* 8: 943, 950-1, *951*
Dee, Joey **5:** 483, **8:** 874-5, *875*

Dee, Kiki **14:** 1667, *1668*
Dee, Simon **6:** 628, **7:** 744, 745, *745*
Dee, Tommy **5:** 574, **17:** 1958
Dee Gee Records **3:** 330
Deejays **6:** 682
Deep Purple **7:** 760, **10:** 1176, **12:** 1361, 1369, 1376-80, **15:** 1682, 1683, 1687, 1691, 1697, 1728, 1737, **17:** 1982, 1983, 1984-7, 1989, **19:** *2138-9,* 2223
Dees, Bill **4:** 415
Def Leppard **19:** 2223, 2231, 2236-7, *2237*
De Fries, Tony **13:** 1498-9, **14:** 1625, 1628, 1629, **16:** 1818
DeFreitas, Pete **19:** *2276,* 2277, *2277*
Deheen, Pat **14:** 1576
Dekker, Desmond **1:** 10, **9:** 962, 971, 972-3, 978, 979, **16:** 1882, 1889
Delaney and Bonnie **9:** 1035, *1035,* **10:** 1163, 1169, **13:** *1443,* 1444, 1445, 1448-9, **15:** 1763, **19:** 2195
Delbridge, Jimmy **4:** 394
Del-fi **5:** 502
Delfonics **14:** 1594, 1595
Dells **9:** 1059
Delmore Brothers **1:** 32, 40, *40*
DeLoach, Darryl **9:** 1071
Del-Rios **8:** 929
Del-Satins **4:** 409
Delta 5 **9:** 1071
Deltones **7:** 764, 767
Del-Vikings **2:** 236
Delmelza **10:** 1182
Demoiselles **5:** 523
Dempsey, Michael **19:** 2275
Dene, Terry **2:** 122, 135-6, *135,* 137, **3:** 249, **4:** 430
Denis, Jackie **2:** 134
Dennisons **7:** 758
Dennon, Jerry **6:** 695
Denny, Jim **2:** 185
Denny, Sandy **13:** 1462, *1465,* 1465-7, *1467*
Densmore, John **9:** 1009-10, 1012, 1013
Denver, John **1:** 18, **6:** 662, **12:** 1342, **14:** 1658, **17:** 1942, 2024, 2034-5, *2034*
Denver, Karl **10:** 1138-9, *1139*
Denver, Pop Festival **11:** 1253
Deodato, Eumir **18:** 2109
deOliveira, Laudir **13:** 1528
Depeche Mode **18:** 2070, 2157, **20:** 2302-3, *2303,* 2343, 2397
Deptford Fun City **18:** 2156
Deramic Super Sound **10:** 1195
Derek and the Dominos **9:** 1035, *1035*
Derelicts **18:** 2071
Derrick, Diz **10:** 1086
Derringer, Rick **11:** 1235, *1235*
Derry and the Seniors **5:** 538
DeSanto, Sugar Pie **8:** 934
DeShannon, Jackie **3:** 248, **5:** 502, *502,* 530, *566,* 569, **7:** 758, **13:** 1559, **15:** 1718
Desperate Bicycles **18:** 2156
Desperately Seeking Susan **20:** 2411, *2411,* 2412
Destri, Jimmy **20:** 2293

Detergents **5:** 575
Detours **11:** 1264, 1276 *see alo* Who
Detroit Spinners **14:** 1673
Detroit Wheels **10:** 1178
Deuces of Rhythm **2:** 149
Deutsche Amerikanisches Freundschaft **20:** 2368, *2368*
Deverson, Jane **12:** 1322
Deville, Mink **4:** 446
Devine, John **13:** 1511
Devito, Karla **18:** *2124*
DeVito, Nick **5:** 570, 571, *571*
DeVito, Tommy **5:** 570, 572
Devo **17:** 2004, 2014-15, **19:** 2252, **20:** *2320*
Devotions **1:** 63
Devoto, Howard **18:** *2073,* 2073-4, **20:** 2301
Dew-Drop Inn **2:** *153,* 155, *155*
Dewhurst, Keith **13:** 1473
Dexys Midnight Runners **1:** 11, **10:** 1181, **13:** 1463, 1553, **16:** 1902, **19:** 2214, 2218-20, *2219-20,* 2248
De Young, Dennis **18:** *2128,* 2128-9
Dharma, Buck **18:** 2125-6, *2126-7*
Dial Records **7:** 796-7
Diamond, Billy **2:** 145, 154
Diamond, Dinky **13:** 1519
Diamond, Neil **1:** 13, **3:** 265, 293, **4:** 444, 449, 453, **5:** 562, **9:** 981-2, 987, 988, **15:** 1702, *1702,* **17:** 1942, 2034
Diamonde, Dick **6:** 697
Diamonds **2:** 235-6, *235,* 240, **3:** 251
Di'anno, Paul **19:** 2230, *2231,* 2232
Dias, Denny **16:** 1919-20, *1919*
Dibango, Manu **9:** 963-4, *965,* 966, **20:** 2380
'Dick Clark Saturday Night Show, The' **3:** 360
Dickey, David **15:** 1777
Dickey Doo and the Don'ts **2:** 193, **3:** 342
Dickin, Bernard **19:** 2266, *2266,* 2267, 2268, *2269*
Dickinson, Angie **5:** *580*
Dickinson, Bruce **19:** *2231-2,* 2232
Dickinson, Jim **7:** 828
Dickson, Barbara **20:** *2337*
Diddley, Bo **1:** 35, **3:** 269, **4:** 464, 465, 467, *467,* **5:** 582, 590-1, **8:** *886,* 887, 891, **9:** 1046, 1058, 1059, **11:** 1221, **13:** 1547
Dietrich, Marlene **5:** 578, *580*
Difford, Chris **19:** 2256-7, *2256-7,* **20:** 2340
Digeroos **2:** 139
Diggle, Steve **18:** 2073, 2074-5
Dillard and Clarke **15:** 1773
Dillinger **16:** *1884*
Di Martino, Andy **13:** 1486
Dimention **3:** 266, *266,* **5:** 489, 567
Dimension Records **4:** 444, 447
Dimensions **15:** 1724
Dines, Dino **12:** 1440
Ding Dongs *see* Darin, Bobby
Dinwiddie Colored Quartet **2:** 159
Dio, Ronnie James **12:** 1370, *1371,* **17:** 1984-5
Dion and the Belmonts **1:** 63, **2:** *187,* 194,

197, *197,* 235, 237, 239, 240, **3:** 254, 260, *260,* 307, **4:** 401, *402,* 403, 408-9, 418, 446, *455,* 457, **5:** 487

Diplomats **10:** 1183, 1193

Dire Straits **17:** 1935, **19:** 2182, 2199-2200, *2199, 2200,* **20:** 2391, 2420

Disc **4:** 366, 368, **12:** 1327-8, *1327*

Disc Jockey Jamboree **2:** 204, 209, 210, **3:** 355

Discharge **18:** 2141

Discipline **14:** 1567

'Disco 2' **8:** 853

Disley, Diz **2:** 126

Dixie Cups **3:** 282, *283,* 289, **5:** 567, *568,* 569

Dixie Hummingbirds **2:** *159,* 160, **3:** 322

Dixielanders **4:** 438, 439, *439,* **15:** 1783

Dixon, Doc **16:** 1914, 1915

Dixon, Floyd **1:** 30, **3:** 339

Dixon, Luther **5:** 579

Dixon, Willie **3:** 339, **5:** 595, **12:** 1372

D-Men **5:** 588

Dobson, Lyn **6:** 647

Doc Thomas Group *see* Mott the Hoople

Dodd, Clement 'Sir Coxsone' **9:** 961, 970-1, 973, 975-7, **16:** *1882,* 1883, 1885, 1886, 1887, 1889, 1890, 1894, 1897, 1900, **19:** 2177

Dodd, Rory **18:** 2124

Doggelt, Bill **1:** 34, **4:** 395, **11:** 1221

Doherty, Denny **7:** 822, 838-40, *838, 840,* **8:** 867

Dolby, Thomas **18:** 2133, 2168 **20:** 2360

Dolce, Joe **20:** *2305*

Dolenz, Micky **9:** 983, 987-91

Dollar **20:** *2396,* 2397

Dolphins *see* Paul Dowell and the Dolphins

Domino, Fats **1:** 2, *22,* 30, 32, 35, 81, **2:** 141-2, *143,* 144-7, 149, 151, 153-5, 156, 163, 164, 174, 179-80, 184, 200, 204, 205, 208, 209, 217, **3:** 262, *263,* 273, 284, 302, 303, 307, 311, 338, 339, **4:** 462, 463, **5:** 502, **9:** 975, 978, 990, **10:** 1176, **13:** 1442, 1451, 1455

Dominoes **1:** 31, 32, 74, **2:** 160, 215, **3:** 281, 322, 330-1, *331,* **5:** 522, 538

Donahue, Jerry **13:** 1466, *1466,* **19:** 2196

Donahue, Tom **12:** 1406, **13:** 1543, **17:** *2036,* 2037

Don and Dewey **5:** 516, 517

Don Harrison Band **13:** 1458

'Don Kirshner's Rock Concert' **4:** 441

Doncaster, Patrick **4:** 366

Donce, Bob **7:** 816

Donegan, Lonnie **2:** 123, 124-8, 134, 205, **3:** 267, **4:** 430, 436, 439, 440, **5:** 551, 585, **6:** 601, 613, **13:** 1461, 1515

Donellan, Jay **9:** 1017

Donis, Carnaby Street **7:** 738, *749*

Donovan **1:** 8, *9,* 18, **6:** 622, 635, 636, *674,* 676, 677, **7:** 724, 757, 821, **8:** 848, 851, **10:** *1084,* 1085, 1121, 1124, 1134-7, 1138, 1159, **11:** 1231, 1245, 1247, 1256, *1257,* **12:** 1358, 1359

Don't Knock The Twist **5:** 487

Don't Look Back **11:** 1207

Doobie Brothers **16:** *1825,* 1841, 1850-3, 1920

Doomed **18:** 2080

Doors **1:** 19, **8:** 848, 902, **9:** *984,* 1002, *1002,* 1009-13, **10:** 1090, 1099, 1124, **11:** 1306, **12:** 1357, **15:** 1691, 1700, 1761, **16:** 1862

Doran, Terry **5:** 557, **10:** 1158

Dore Records **5:** 503, 507, **7:** 766

Dorman, Lee **9:** 1071

Dorn, Joel **15:** 1799

Dorsey, Lee **5:** 483, **18:** 2093

Dorsey, Thomas **3:** 333

Dorsey, Thomas A. **2:** 159

Dot **3:** 262, 313-14

Doubleday, Marcus **10:** 1172

Double Trouble **6:** 683

Doucette, Salvador **2:** 145

Doug DeMont Band **4:** 417

Douglas, Carl **7:** 820

Douglas, Chip **9:** 983, 989

Douglas, Craig **4:** 361, 363, 374-5, 427, 440

Douglas, Jack **16:** 1849, **17:** 2020

Douglas, Josephine **4:** 378, *378,* 429

Dovells **5:** 487

Dovey, Gary **19:** 2210

Dowd, Tom **2:** 200, **3:** 273, *273,* 274, **7:** 773, **8:** 876-7, **13:** 1528, **15:** 1726, 1737, **16:** 1844, **18:** 2124

Dowle, David 'Duck' **17:** 1984

Downes, Geoff **15:** 1688, *1692,* 1695, **20:** 2320, *2397*

Downey, Brian **17:** 1990, *1991,* 1992

Downey, Tyrone **16:** 1893

Downing, Big Al **1:** 113

Downing, K. Kenny **17:** *1998,* 1999

Downtown Faction *see* Lindisfarne

Dozier, Gene **19:** 2179

Dozier, Lamont **18:** 2102, 2107, *see also* Holland, Dozier and Holland

Dr Hook and the Medicine Show **12:** 1333

Dr Buzzards Original Savannah Band **20:** 2295, 2297

Dr Feelgood **4:** 435, **17:** *1923,* 1924-5, 1928-9, 1933, 1935, 1939, **18:** 2042, **19:** 2258

Dr J. Jones and the Interns *see* Aerosmith

Dr John **11:** 1220, 1240, 1257, **12:** 1372, **13:** 1443, 1450-3, 1455

Dr John and the Night Tripper **12:** 1372, 1373, **13:** 1443, 1450-3, 1455

Dracula **16:** 1863

Dragon, Darryl **7:** *776*

Dragonaires **9:** 962, 971, 978

Drake, Bill **8:** 841, **17:** 2036, *2037*

Drake, Jay **4:** 397

Drake, Pete **11:** 1209, **14:** 1657

Dramatics **8:** 933

Dramatis **20:** 2314-15

Dranes, Arizona **2:** 159

Dread, Mikey **18:** 2068, **20:** 2373, *2374*

Dreamers **6:** 602-3, 612-14

Dreja, Chris **6:** 650, *650,* 652-3

Drifters **1:** 72, *72,* 74, 75, **2:** 134, 160, 240, **3:** 242, *253,* 254, 275, *275,* 281-3, *282,* 288, 290-3, 322, **4:** 365-6, 368, 385-6, 401, 446, 447, 459, **5:** 507, 577, 579, **6:** 714, **7:** 759

Drifting Cowboys **1:** 37

Driscoll, Gary **17:** 1985

Driscoll, Julie **7:** 816, *817,* **9:** 990, **15:** 1724, 1699, 1724

Drits and Dravy *see* Dr John

Drive 'Em Down **2:** 154

Druce, Bob **11:** 1276

Drucker, Lee 'Rocker' **19:** 2260

'Drumbeat' **2:** 137, **4:** 371, 380

Drumbo **13:** 1484

Drummond, Bill **19:** 2276, 2277, 2279

Drummond, Don **9:** 976, **16:** 1890

Drummond, Pete **7:** 745, **8:** 853, **17:** 1958

Drummond, Tim **15:** *1767*

Dryden, Spencer **8:** 910-12, *911*

Ducek, Les **11:** *1226,* 1227

Duchess, The **5:** *591*

Ducks Deluxe **17:** 1922, *1922,* 1924, 1936

Duconge, Wendell **2:** 154

Dudgeon, Gus **14:** 1632, 1667, **16:** *1912*

Dufay, Rick, **16:** 1849

Duffy, Raymond **8:** 947

Duffy, Steve **20:** 2389

Duffy, Tommy **13:** 1475

Duke, George **13:** 1495

Duke Wore Jeans, The **4:** 430

'Dukes of Hazard' **14:** 1641

Dummer, John **19:** 2257

Dunaway, Dennis **16:** 1865

Dunaway, Shelton **13:** 1445

Dunbar, Ainsley **8:** 913, **10:** 1102, 1113-14, **11:** 1230, **13:** 1495, **14:** 1576, 1620, **16:** 1847, **17:** 1981, **18:** 2121

Dunbar, Sly **16:** 1884, 1887, 1894, **17:** 1933, **20:** 2300, 2374, *2375*

Duncan, Billy **7:** 799

Duncan, Cleveland **1:** 71

Duncan, 'Hi-pockets' **2:** 185

Duncan, Johnny **2:** 125

Duncan, Lesley **7:** 817

Duncan, Molly **20:** 2387

Dunhill **6:** 675

Dunkley, Errol **16:** 1896

Dunn, Bob **14:** 1656

Dunn, Clive **12:** *1424*

Dunn, Donald 'Duck' **7:** *784,* 785, **8:** 926, 929, *929,* 937, **9:** 1039, **11:** 1220, **12:** 1401

Dunn, James **14:** 1594-5, *1595*

Dunn, Larry **19:** 2163-5

Dunne, Phil **16:** *1912*

Dupree, Champion Jack **2:** 145, 154, **3:** 338, **10:** 1102

Duran Duran **16:** 1803, 1806, **19:** 2258, **20:** 2325, 2348, 2360, 2381, 2388-91, *2388, 2390, 2391,* 2397, 2401, 2418

Durham, Judith **10:** 1140

Durutti Column **19:** 2262, 2268

Dury, Ian **11:** 1295, **12:** *1358,* 1360, **17:** 1922, 1925, *1925,* 1930-3, *1938,* 1940,

18: 2042
Dwyer, Bernie **6:** 613
Dyble, Judy **13:** *1464,* 1465
Dye, Graham **19:** 2243
Dylan, Bob **1:** 8, *12,* 13, 18, **2:** 151, 195, **3:**
283, **5:** 542, 543, 551, 552, **6:** 654, *655,*
661, 662, 664, *672,* 673, *675,* 677, 680,
7: *821,* 822, 828, 831, 835, 836, **8:** 902,
941, **9:** 978, 992, 1007, 1017, 1036,
1066, **10:** 1121, 1123, 1124, 1125,
1127, 1128, 1129, 1134, 1138, 1153,
1176, **11:** 1201-20, *1239,* 1240, *1243,*
1248, 1253, 1259, 1260, *1286,* 1293,
1300, **12:** 1341, 1349, 1351, *1357,* 1358,
1359, 1382, 1387, 1400, **13:** 1442,
1443, 1445, 1542, 1547, *1549,* 1644,
1645, *1651,* 1652, 1659, **14:** 1667, **15:**
1686, 1699, 1702, 1703, 1707, 1709,
1766, 1778, 1799, **16:** 1803, 1808,
1818, 1843, 1862, **17:** 1968, 2019, **18:**
2089, 2098, 2100
Dylan, Sara **11:** 1201, 1208-9, *1208,* 1210-
11
Dynamics **15:** 1772
Dymond, John **8:** 950
Dynasty **19:** 2178, 2179, *2180*
Dzidzorhu, Kwasi **11:** 1237

E

Eager, Vince **2:** 122, *136,* 137, 138, 139,
139, 140, **4:** 361, 380, *426,* 427
Eagles **4:** 363, 383, **10:** 1125, **14:** 1613,
1679, **15:** 1720, *1761, 1763,* 1772-5,
1777, 1779, **16:** *1822,* 1823, **17:** 2026,
2027, **18:** 2085, *2099,* 2100
Earls **1:** 63
Earth Band **6:** *649*
Earth, Wind and Fire **9:** *1038,* 1039, **13:**
1528, **15:** 1783, **16:** 1817, 1883, **17:** 2013
19: 2161, 2162-7, *2162-5*
Earthworks **20:** 2378
Eastman, John **10:** 1159-60
Easton, Eric **7:** 816, **8:** 896-7, *897*
Easton, Sheena **13:** 1502, **17:** 2025, **18:**
2072
Eastwood, Clint **20:** 2373, 2374
'Easy Beat' **4:** 377
Easybeats **6:** 682, 696-7, **7:** 759, **14:** 1616
Easy Come Easy Go **7:** 767
Easy Rider **7:** 830, **8:** 843, *843,* 848, *848,* **9:**
1072, **13:** 1443, **15:** 1715
Eater **18:** *2155,* 2156
Eaton, Cleveland **19:** 2162
Ebo, David **14:** 1598
Ebonys **14:** 1598
Eccles, Clancy **16:** 1893
Echo and the Bunnymen **16:** 1902, **18:**
2060, 2141, 2151, 2157, **19:** 2262, 2266,
2270, *2276,* 2276-7, *2277,* 2279-80, **20:**
2346

Echols, John **9:** 1016
Eckhorn, Peter **5:** 538
Eckstine, Billy **1:** 31, **5:** 501, **6:** 710
Economedies, John **12:** 1436
Eddie and the Hot Rods **17:** 1925, **18:** 2077
Eddie the Head **19:** *2232*
Eddy, Duane **2:** 198, *199,* **3:** 269, 319, *342,*
343, *359,* 360, **4:** 381, *382,* 390, 391,
394-5, **7:** 764, 765, **9:** 1021, **10:** 1177, **17:**
1942
Edelman, Randy **17:** 1942
Edenton, Ray **2:** 225, 228
Edgar Broughton Band **11:** 1247, **17:**
1983
Edge, Graeme **10:** 1193-4, *1195,* 1196
Edge, The (David Evans) **19:** 2270-1,
2270-1
Edison, Thomas **3:** 276, *276,* **12:** 1392
Edmonds, Noel **17:** 1959
Edmonton, Jerry **9:** 1072
Edmunds, Dave **1:** *110,* 120, **4:** 419, **15:**
1749, **17:** *1921,* 1928, 1934-5, **19:** 2193,
20: 2327, 2329
Edmunds, Robert **18:** 2079
'Ed Sullivan Show' **2:** *193,* **3:** *242,* **6:** 610,
610
Edward Bear **19:** 2254
Edwards, Bernard **14:** 1593, **15:** 1791, **18:**
2113. 2114-15
Edwards, Dennis **9:** 1052, 1057
Edwards, Greg **20:** 2394
Edwards, Jackie **9:** 962
Edwards, King **9:** 975
Edwards, Mark **14:** 1576
Edwards, Mike **15:** 1747, 1748
Edwards, Percy **22:** 2333
Edwards, Tom **7:** 745
Edwards, Tommy **3:** 342, **12:** 1393
Edwards, Tony **12:** 1377
Eek A Mouse *see* Hilton, Ripton
Egan, Joe **17:** 2028, *2028*
Egan, Rusty **19:** *2241,* **20:** 2350-1, *2351*
Eger, Joseph **15:** *1683,* 1686
Eggs over Easy **17:** 1921-2, *1922*
Eisen, Jonathan **12:** 1323
Ekland, Britt **10:** *1094,* **15:** 1726, *1726*
Ekseption **20:** 2367
Elbow Bones and the Racketeers **20:** 2297
El Dorados **5:** 495
Electric Flag **1:** 16, **9:** 1068, **10:** 1099, **11:**
1239-40
Electric Horseman, The **14:** 1647
Electric Light Orchestra **10:** 1181, 1185,
15: 1683, 1720, 1742, 1746-9, 1800
Electric Prunes **1:** 13, **8:** 872
Elegants **2:** 237
Elephant Man, The **14:** 1629-30
'Elephant Man, The' **19:** *2264*
Elf **17:** 1985
Elias and his Zig-Zag Jive Flutes **3:** 270
Elliman, Yvonne **9:** 1036
Ellington, Duke **5:** 581, *582,* 588,
12: *1419*
Ellington, Ray **1:** 35
Elliot, Cass **7:** 740, 822, 838-40, *838, 840*

Elliott, Bobby **6:** *604,* 605, 606, **13:** 1514
Elliott, Dennis **18:** *2132,* 2133
Elliott, Earl **10:** 1178
Elliott, Joe **19:** 2236, *2237*
Elliott, Ramblin' Jack **11:** 1204, *1212,* **14:**
1644, 1652
Elliott, Stuart **16:** 1839, *1839*
Ellis, Alfred 'Pee Wee' **7:** 791, **13:** *1552*
Ellis, Alton **9:** 977, *977,* **16:** 1881
Ellis, Billy Par **4:** 414
Ellis, Geoffrey **5:** 557
Ellis, Terry **12:** 1375, **18:** 2135
Ellison, Andy **7:** 820
El Riot and the Rebels **10:** 1193
'Elvis' **20:** *2338,* 2340
Elvis Monthly **1:** *96-7*
Elvis On Tour **2:** 214
Elvis—That's The Way It Is **2:** 214, *214*
Ely, Brother Claude **10:** 1162
Emanon **6:** 648-9
Embee Productions **4:** 417, 418, 419
Emerald Express **19:** 2220
Emerson, Billy 'The Kid' **1:** 45
Emerson, Eric **17:** 2001
Emerson, Hunt **19:** 2208
Emerson, Keith **1:** 11, **9:** 1033, **15:** *1684,*
1685, *1685,* 1686, 1687, *1687,* 1688,
1697, 1699, 1700, 1741, **16:** 1802
Emerson, Vic **16:** 1915
Emerson, Lake and Palmer **15:** 1683,
1684-9, 1697, 1728, 1742, **16:** 1901, **17:**
1921, 1922, 1981
EMI Records **5:** 524, 536-7, 550, 555, **6:**
638, 640, **17:** 2026
Emmons, Buddy **14:** 1656-7, *1657*
Emotions **8:** 922, *931,* 933, **19:** 2163, 2164
Emperor Rosko **7:** 745, **8:** *842*
Empires **3:** 300
End Records **4:** 475, 478
Energetics *see* Planet Patrol
Energy Crisis **10:** 1097
Engel, Scott **8:** 956-7, *957*
English, Joe **17:** 1964, *1964*
English, Michael **7:** 816, **12:** 1391
Eno, Brian **14:** *1566,* 1567, 1629, 1633,
1638-40, **15:** 1754, **16:** 1802, 1803, *1803,*
1804, 1807, 1808, 1810, **17:** 2007, 2014,
20: 2283-5, *2284,* 2301, *2303,* 2312,
2343, 2351
Entwhistle, John **1:** 6, **9:** 1022, **11:** 1261-7,
see also Who
Epics **18:** 2084
Episode Six **12:** 1379
Epps, Preston **4:** 389
Epstein, Brian **1:** 8, *18,* **5:** 523, 524-5, 527,
528, 532-5, 537, *537,* 549-50, 554-5,
556-7, 560, **6:** 629, 630, 631, 639-40,
682, *692,* 710, **7:** 734, 749, **8:** 854-6, **10:**
1147, *1147,* 1149, 1156, 1158, 1194, **11:**
1281, **12:** 1322, 1325, **13:** 1503, 1513,
17: 1978-9
Epstein, Clive **5:** 532, 537, 557
Epstein, Howie **18:** 2086
Equals **10:** *1133*
Era Records **5:** 506-7

Eric's Club **19:** 2278-9, *2279*

Erikson, Roky **13:** 1458, **17:** 1972, 1977

Errico, Greg **12:** *1405,* 1406, 1407

Ertegun, Ahmet **1:** *43, 59,* 74, 75, **3:** 262, 271-2, 273, *273,* 274, *275,* 282, *282,* 290, 291, 345, *345,* **5:** 500, **8:** 875, 897, *922*

Ertegun, Nesuhi **3:** 272, 274, *274,* 288, 328

Escorts **5:** *522*

Escott, Colin **12:** 1324

Escovedo, Coke **13:** 1535

Esquerita **2:** 145, *163,* 179

Essex, David **13:** *1502,* 1507-9, **20:** 2327, 2336, 2337, 2338

Essex Records **3:** 341, *341*

Estes, Sleepy John **6:** 680, **11:** 1238, **13:** 1559

Estrada, Roy **13:** *1490,* 1493, **16:** 1858

E Street Band **5:** 492, 515, **18:** 2089-90, *2090*

Eternals **16:** 1887

Ethridge, Chris **13:** 1556

Europe, Jim **5:** 482

Eurorock **20:** 2367-9

Eurovision Song Contest **6:** 626, 636, **13:** 1502, **17:** 1954-7

Eurythmics **14:** *1622,* **20:** 2301, 2303, 2309, *2359,* 2360, 2381, 2366-7, *2387,* 2394

Eutemey, Loring **11:** 1293

Evans, Bill **15:** 1698

Evans, David *see* The Edge

Evans, Gil **13:** 1530

Evans, John **10:** 1174-5, **14:** *1570,* 1571

Evans, Mal **5:** 556-7, *556-7*

Evans, Mark **19:** *2226,* 2227

Evans, Mike **7:** 818-19

Evans, Paul **5:** 574

Evans, Rod **12:** 1377, *1377,* 1379, **17:** 1984

Evans, Sam **1:** 56

Eve, Mick **5:** 596

Even Dozen Jug Band **12:** 1123

Everett, Betty **7:** 795, **9:** 1059, *1060*

Everett, Kenny **7:** 745, *746,* 845, **17:** 1960, *1960*

Everly Brothers **1:** 28, **2:** 163, 165, *165,* 221-2, *221,* 223, 224-9, 231, 232, 239, **3:** 259, *259,* 265, *358,* **4:** 401, 402, 414, 415, 452, *455,* **5:** 502, **10:** 1126, 1131, **17:** 1953, **20:** 2401

Everons **13:** 1508

Ever Ready Gospel Singers **3:** 330

Every Day's A Holiday **6:** 614, **8:** 844

Every Which Way **15:** 1687

Every Which Way But Loose **14:** 1660

Evita **13:** 1509, **20:** 2321, 2337

Exciters **5:** *567*

Exile **16:** 1823

Expelaires **19:** 2262

Exploding Plastic Inevitable **9:** 1006

Exploited **18:** 2141

Expresso Bongo **4:** 430, *431*

Eyden, Billy **10:** 1087

Eyeless in Gaza **18:** 2157

Eyes **7:** *819,* 820

Eyre, Ian **14:** 1576, *1577*

Ezrin, Bob **14:** 1635, **16:** 1847, 1865, 1869

F

Fabares, Shelley **3:** 312, **5:** 502, 503

Fabian **2:** 239, *240,* **3:** 242, 260, 284, 311, 319, 341, *341,* 342, 343, 344, 349, 352-3, 359, **4:** 401, 404, **11:** 1297

Fabulous Continentals **4:** 392

Fabulous Corsayers **15:** 1707

Fabulous Music Ltd **11:** 1266

Fabulous Thunderbirds **10:** 1163

Face **12:** *1327*

Faces **11:** 1248, **15:** 1721, 1723, 1724, 1725-7, **16:** 1879, **18:** *2076,* 2077

Factory Records **19:** 2262, 2268, 2279

Fagen, Donald **16:** 1841, 1851, 1919-20, **20:** 2360

Fahey, John **6:** 680, *680*

Fair, Yvonne **9:** 1052, 1057, **14:** 1587

Fair Deal Production **7:** 789

Fairfax, Reuben **15:** 1786

Fairies **7:** 817

Fairlie, Pat **8:** 947, *947,* 949

Fairport Convention **1:** 8, **10:** *1124,* 1125, 1140, **11:** 1256, **12:** 1340, **13:** *1461, 1462,* 1463, 1464-7, 1471, 1477

Fair Weather **8:** 953

Faith, Adam **2:** 134, 239, **4:** 361, 362, 363, *363,* 367, *370,* 371-3, 380, *404,* 422, 427, 431, *431,* 433, **5:** 504, *504,* **6:** 626, 627, **7:** 721, 737, **12:** *1393,* **13:** 1508, 1573, **20:** 2327

Faith, Russ **3:** 342

Faithfull, Marianne **6:** 622, *623,* 626, 635, **7:** 723, **8:** 847, 880, *892,* 893, **9:** 1003, **11:** 1304, **14:** 1633

Fakir, Abdul 'Duke' **6:** 710-13, **7:** 783

Falcon, Joe **13:** 1455

Falconer, Earl **19:** 2214, *2214*

Fall, The **18:** 2060, 2144, *2155,* 2157, **19:** 2262

Fallen Angels **17:** 2022

Fallon, B. P. **12:** 1436

Fallon, Jack (and the Sons of the Saddle) **2:** 130

Fallon, Larry **13:** 1552

Falsia, Joe **13:** 1555

Faltermeyer, Harold **20:** 2420

Faltskog, Agnetha **17:** *1943,* 1944, 1945-7

Fame **16:** 1877

'Fame' **13:** 1502, *1502*

Fame, Georgie **2:** 139, **5:** 582, 588, 596-7, *598,* 599, 600, **6:** 660, **7:** 744, 759, 806, 817, 818, **19:** 2196

Family **9:** 1031, **10:** 1198-1200

Family Dog **8:** 917, 920, **12:** 1389

Family Way, The **8:** 847

Famous Flames **7:** 789

Fanny **18:** 2071

Fantasticks, The **13:** 1508

Fantoni, Barry **8:** 852, *853,* **11:** 1297

Farian, Frank **18:** 2103, *2119,* 2119-20, **20:** 2362

Farinas **10:** 1198

Farley, Frank **4:** 435, *435*

Farlowe, Chris **5:** 588, **6:** 642, **7:** 760, *805,* 814-15, 817, **8:** 897, **15:** 1687

Farndon, Pete **19:** 2253, *2253*

Farner, Mark **14:** *1609,* 1610, 1611

Farnham, John **20:** 2371

Farr, Gary **11:** *1243*

Farr, Rikki **16:** 1873

Farrar, John **4:** 388, **20:** 2371

Farrell, Frank **15:** 1758

Farrell, Wes **13:** 1517

Fast, Larry **15:** 1757, **20:** 2320

Fast Product Records **19:** 2262

Fataar, Ricky **7:** 772, 780

Fat Angel **12:** 1340

Fatback Band **19:** 2177

Faulkner, Eric **13:** *1510,* 1511-12

Faure, Duncan **13:** 1513

Faust **6:** 700

Fayad, Frank **9:** 1017

Fearless Four **19:** 2177

Feathers, Charlie **1:** 102-3, 115

Federaci, Danny **18:** 2089

Federal **3:** 299

Feinstem, Harley **13:** 1519

Feiten, Buzzy **8:** 877, **9:** 1017

Feld, Irvin **3:** 253, 307, 308-9

Felder, Don **15:** *1773,* 1774, 1775, **18:** 2085

Felder, Wilton **19:** *2173,* 2173-5, *2174*

Feldman, Eric Drew **13:** 1486

Feldman, Victor **18:** 2097

Felix, Julie **16:** *1822*

Feller, Sid **2:** 147

Felt **18:** 2157

Feltham, Mark **6:** 655

Fender, Freddy **2:** 182, 196, **13:** 1455

Fender, Leo **1:** 78-80, **9:** 1038, 1040, 1078

Fenn, Rick **16:** *1914,* 1915

Fenton, P. T. **18:** 2149

Fenton, Shane **2:** 139 *see also* Stardust, Alvin

Fentones **4:** 392, **13:** 1514

Fenwick, Ray **10:** 1187, **17:** 1984

Ferguson, Jay **14:** 1614-15, *1615*

Ferguson, Larry **16:** 1826

Ferguson, 'Major' Jim **1:** 25

Ferguson, Michael **12:** 1388, *1389*

Ferguson, Sheila **14:** 1597, 1600

Ferlinghetti, Lawrence **8:** 919

Ferrio, Martin **7:** 835

Ferry, Brian **1:** 6, **14:** 1638, **16:** 1801, *1801,* 1802, 1803, 1805-10, **20:** 2389, *2404,* 2405, 2419-20

Ferry Cross The Mersey **5:** 526-7, 527, **6:** 631, **8:** 844, *844*

Ficca, Billy **17:** *2006,* 2007-8, 2012

Fickle Pickle **11:** 1223

Fiddler, John **16**: 1820
Fiddler's Dram **19**: *2225*
Fidelitones **4**: 473
Field, Tim **7**: 730
Fielder, Jim **7**: 826, **13**: *1538,* 1539, 1554
Fielding, Harold **2**: 131
Fields, Danny **10**: 1093
Fifth Dimension **1**: 13, **7**: 740
Fillmore **20**: 2327
Fillmore Auditoriums, San Francisco **8**: *916,* 917, 920, *927*
Finan, Joe **2**: 219, 220
Finch, Barry **10**: 1158
Findlay, Bruce **19**: 2273
Findley, Chuck **18**: 2097
Fine Young Cannibals **19**: 2209
Fingerling, Winged Eel **13**: 1486
Fingers, Johnny **19**: 2249, 2250, 2251
Finian's Rainbow **6**; 633
Finn, Mickey **12**: 1438, *1439,* 1440
Finnie, Lance **8**: 939
Fireballs **2**: 191, **4**: 390
Fire Engines **19**: 2274
First National Band **8**: *990-1*
Fischer, Wild Man **13**: 1495
Fisher, Jerry **13**: *1538*
Fisher, Matthew **10**: 1087-9
Fisher, Morgan **16**: 1819, *1819,* 1820
Fisher, Sonny **1**: 102-3, 120, *120*
Fisk Jubilee Singers **2**: 159
Fitzcarraldo **11**: 1316
Fitzgerald, Ella **6**: 640
Fitzsimmons, Dale **3**: 246
Five Americans **8**: *870,* 872
Five Blind Boys **14**: 1600
Five Duotones **9**: 1060
Five Keys **1**: *62*
Five Royales **5**: 495
Five Stairsteps **7**: 795, **9**: 1059-60, *1059*
Five Willows **12**: *1418*
Five Wings **5**: 574
Flack, Roberta **15**: 1713, 1798-1800
Flairs **3**: 300
Flames **16**: 1832
Flamingo Club, London **5**: 588, 596-7, *596,* 598-9, *598,* **7**: 802, 811, 815, 817
Flamingos **4**: 465
Flamin' Grooves **15**: 1721, **20**: *2288,* 2288-9
Flaming Star **2**: 212
Flaming Youth **15**: 1752
Flanagan, Paul **20**: 2323
Flash **15**: 1691
Flash Cadillac and the Continental Kids **1**: 63
Flash Gordon **16**: 1817
Flee-Rekkers **4**: 363, 393, **5**: 492
Fleet, Gordon 'Snowy' **6**: 697
Fleetwood, Mick **17**: 2031-2
Fleetwood Mac **6**: 642, **10**: 1102-3, 1112, 1113, 1118-20, 1132, *1133,* **11**: 1245, **15**: 1679, 1685, 1721, 1739, **17**: 2021, 2026, 2030-2, **18**: 2086
Fleetwoods **2**: 236, 237, *237*
Fleming, Gabriel **2**: 145

Fleming, George **11**: 1192
Fleming, Teagle **3**: 325
Flemmons, Wade **19**: 2163
Fletcher, Colin **8**: 946, *946*
Flett, Dave **17**: 1993
Fleur de Lys **7**: 820
Flies **7**: 820
Flint, Hughie **5**: 586, **6**: 648, **10**: 1112-13
Flip **12**: *1329*
Flo and Eddie **9**: 993, *992-3,* **13**: 1495
Flock **11**: 1257
Floribunda Rose **10**: 1085
Florida Playboys **3**: 324
Flowerpot Men **1**: 15, **8**: *959,* **10**: *1084,* 1085, 1090
Flowers, Herbie **12**: 1440, **14**: 1633
Flower Travelin' Band **20**: 2364-5
Floyd, Eddie **8**: 922, 930, 931, 932, 939
Flur, Woldgang **20**: 2311, 2312
Flying Burrito Brothers **7**: 830, **13**: *1542,* 1543, 1556, **14**: 1657, **15**: 1773, 1774, **17**: 2022
Flying Elephant Productions Ltd **9**: 969
Flying Machine **8**: 864, **15**: 1702, 1707
Flying Padovanis **19**: 2184
Flying Saucers **1**: 120
Flynn, Roy **15**: 1691
Focus **20**: *2361,* 2367
Fogerty, John **13**: *1456,* 1457, 1458
Fogerty, Tom **13**: *1456, 1458,* 1458
Foghat **14**: 1601, **15**: 1735
Foley, Ellen **18**: 2124, 2127
Foley, Red **3**: 319
Foley, Shirley **3**: 313
Folk music **6**: 661-80, **7**: 724, **10**: 1121-40, **11**: 1201, 1203-7
Follow That Dream **2**: 214
Follow The Boys **3**: 317
Fonda, Peter **8**: *843, 846,* 847-8, *848*
Fonfara, Michael **14**: 1637
Fontana, D. J. **1**: *53,* 54, 94, *95*
Fontana, Wayne **6**: 603, 695
Fontane Sisters **3**: 310
Furious Five **19**: 2177
Fury, Billy **2**: 137, 138, *138,* 139, *139,* 140, *140,* 239, **4**: 361, *361,* 362, 363, 380, 421, 423, 424-8, **5**: 504, *504,* 536, 596, **8**: 844, *859,* **20**: *2382*
Fusion **12**: *1330*
Fyfield, Bill (Legend) **12**: 1439-40
'Fool, The' **10**: *1156,* 1158
Forbert, Steve **11**: 1220
Forbes, Derek **19**: 2274
Ford, Dean **8**: 947, *947,* 949
Ford, Ernie **1**: 40
Ford, George **16**: 1839
Ford, Glen **2**: *207*
Ford, Mary **1**: *80*
Ford, Tennessee Ernie **1**: 40, 118
Forde, Brinsley **19**: 2216
Fordyce, Keith **4**: 380, **6**: 657
Foreigner **18**: 2121, 2128, 2132-3, **20**: 2419
Foreman, Chris **19**: 2210-11, *2211*
Formula, Dave **20**: 2301, 2351

Forrest, Earl **7**: 799
Forssi, Ken **9**: 1016
Forsyth, Bill **19**: 2200
Fortunes **7**: 758
Foster, Malcolm **19**: 2253
Foster, Winston **20**: 2374
Foster, Baby Face Leroy **4**: 464
Foster, Fred **4**: 415, 416
Fotheringay **13**: 1464, 1466-7
Fotomaker **8**: *876,* 877
Foundations **1**: 11
Four Aces **2**: 235
Four Aces of Western Swing **1**: 24, *25*
Four Dates **3**: 352
4AD Records **18**: 2157
Four Gents **4**: 458
Four Knights **1**: 31
Four Lovers **2**: 236, **5**: 570, *571*
Fourmost **5**: 527, 534, *535,* 551, **8**: 844, 845
Four Pennies **5**: 567, **6**: 603, *603*
Four Preps **2**: 236, **8**: 878, 879
Four Seasons **2**: 236, 240, **5**: 504, 562, 570-3, **6**: 718, **7**: 761, 767, **11**: *1292,* 1293
Four Skins **18**: *2141*
Four Star **3**: 340
Four Steps of Rhythm **7**: 788
'14 Hour Technicolor Dream' **11**: 1297, 1301, 1305, *1305,* 1308, **14**: 1580
Four Tops **1**: 10, 62, **5**: 494, **6**: 710-13, 715-16, 718, **9**: 1042-3, 1055, **14**: 1581
Four Tunes **1**: 31
Fowler, T. J. **4**: 397
Fowley, Kim **5**: 503, *503,* **10**: 1198, **12**: 1427, **17**: 2016, **18**: 2071
Fox, Charles **15**: 1713
Fox, Jimmy **14**: *1612,* 1613
Fox, Lucas **19**: 2238-9
Fox, Mark **20**: 2384-5
Foxton, Bruce **19**: 2244, *2245, 2247,* 2248
Foxtrot **5**: 482
Foxx, John **20**: 2352-4
Fradley, Kenny **19**: 2271
Frame, Pete **12**: 1340, *1340*
Frame, Roddy **19**: 2273
Frampton, Peter **8**: 954-5, *955,* **15**: 1721, **16**: 1817, **17**: 2021, 2026, *2027,* 2038-40, **19**: 2106, *2107,* 2133, **20**: 2327
Frampton's Camel **2**: 210, **8**: 955, **17**: 2040
Francis, Connie **2**: 204, 210, 240, *240,* **3**: 259, 284, *284,* 301, 311-12, 316-17, **4**: 442, *442,* 452, **5**: 501, **8**: 879
Francis, Panama **2**: 174, **3**: 337
Franco **20**: 2378, *2378*
François, Claude **3**: 250, 309
Frank, Eduard **2**: 145
Frank, Robert **8**: 893-4, **9**: 1074
Franke, Christopher **20**: *2369*
Frankenstein (1931) **16**: 1863, 1877
Frankie Goes to Hollywood **12**: 1397, **20**: 2408, 2409, 2414-15, 2418
Franklin, Aretha **1**: 10, **2**: 160, **3**: 274, 327, *328,* **6**: 706, 713, 782-3, **10**: 1198, **12**: 1401, **15**: 1781, 1788-91, 1792, 1797, **18**: 2103, 2105, 2111, 2115, **19**:

2167, **20:** 2387, 2405, 2413
Franklin, Bertha **3:** 335, *335*
Franklin, Jim **12:** 1390
Franklin Melvin **1:** 62, **9:** 1050, *1050,* 1052
Franklin, Reverend C. L. **7:** 800
Frante, Christoph **20:** 2369
Frantic Five **2:** 134
Frantz, Chris **20:** *2283,* 2283-5
Franz, Johnny **7:** 730
Fraser, Andy **10:** 1114, **15:** 1738, 1739, *1739,* 1740
Fratto, Russ **1:** 66
Frazers **6:** 700
Frazier, Tom **13:** 1535
Freddie and the Dreamers **6:** 602-3, 612-14, **7:** 741, **8:** 845, 880
Freddie and the Midnighters **5:** 538-9
Freddys, Los **6:** 683
Fredericks, Bill **3:** 290
Frederika **7:** 744, *744*
Free **10:** 1103, 1114, **11:** 1247, **15:** 1721, 1738-40
Free At Last **5:** 586
Freed, Alan **1:** 7, 22, 31, 35, 43, *43,* 57, 58, *58,* 60, 66, 73, **2:** *162,* 173-4, 192, 197, 202, *203,* 204, 206, 209, 215-7, *218,* 219, *219,* 220, **3:** 242, *242,* 252-3, 263, 299, 360, **4:** 377, **8:** 841, **12:** 1334, **13:** 1503, **17:** 2036
Freedman, Max C. **1:** 26
'Freedom Road' **14:** 1652
Freedom Singers **11:** *1204*
Freeman, Alan **16:** *1822,* **17:** 1959, *1959*
Freeman, Alan A. **6:** 622, 632-3
Freeman, Alan 'Fluff' **8:** 849
Freeman, Robert **11:** 1289
Freeman, Bobby **4:** 363
Freeman, Ernie **3:** 299, **4:** 389
Freeman, Ray **6:** 708
Freeman, Whitney **7:** 835
Freez **20:** 2392-3
Frehley, Ace **16:** 1869, *1869, 1871*
Freiberg, David **8:** 912-13
French Connection, The **14:** 1597
Frey, Glenn **15:** 1772, 1773, *1773,* 1774, 1775, 1778, **16:** 1857
Fricke, Florian **11:** 1316
Fried, Bob **12:** 1390, *1391*
Friedkin, William **8:** 847
Friedman, Michael **16:** 1903
Friends **15:** 1763
Fripp, Robert **14:** *1561,* 1563, 1564-7, 1630, 1633, 1638, 1639, **15:** 1757, **19:** 2185-6, *2187*
Frith, Fred **14:** 1569, *1569*
Frizzell, David **14:** 1641
Frizzell, Lefty **2:** 234
Froese, Edgar **20:** 2369, *2369*
Frogman **4:** 391
Frontier Booking International **20:** 2281
Frost, Craig **14:** 1611, *1611,* **16:** 1857
Fruit Jar Drinkers **1:** 39
Fry, Glenn **20:** 2420
Fry, Martin **20:** 2397

Fugitives **16:** 1830
Fugs **1:** 19, **8:** *864,* **9:** 1014-15
Fuller, Blind Boy **2:** 159, **6:** 680
Fuller, Jerry **3:** 303
Fuller, Jesse **6:** *678,* 679-80
Full Tilt Boogie Band **10:** 1172-3
Fulson, Lowell **3:** 325, 340, **10:** 1108-9
Fun Boy Three **18:** 2055, 2070, *2072,* **19:** *2207-8,* 2207
Funicello, Annette **3:** 309, *310,* 312, 317, 349, **8:** 844-5, *845,* 847, *878,* 879, 901
Fun In Acapulco **2:** *213*
Funkadelic **12:** 1402, 1407, **18:** 2103, 2172
Funkapolitan **20:** 2295
Funny Girl **8:** 859
Fuqua, Charles **1:** 69
Fuqua, Harvey **1:** 73, *73,* **4:** 473, **6:** 702, 708, 719, **9:** 1046, 1059
Furay, Richie **7:** 821, 825-6, *826,* **15:** 1768
Furie, Sydney J. **4:** 431

G

Gabler, Milt **1:** 26, 27, 35, **16:** 1901, *1901*
Gabriel, Peter **9:** 966, **15:** 1742, *1750,* 1752, *1752-3,* 1753, 1754, 1755, 1756-7, **18:** 2098
Gadd, Steve **13:** 1523, **18:** 2097
Gage, Pete **7:** *810,* 811
Gagliardi, Ed **18:** 2132, 2133
Gaillard, Slim **3:** 340, *340*
Gaines, Cassie **16:** 1843, 1844
Gaines, Steve **16:** 1843, 1844, *1844*
Gale, Melvyn **15:** 1748, 1749
Galfas, Steven **18:** 2123
Galkin, Joe **8:** 925
Gallagher and Lyle **16:** 1826
Gallagher, Mickey **17:** 1931, *1933,* 2040, **20:** 2387
Gallagher, Rory **15:** 1721
Galley, Mel **17:** 1984
Gallucci, Don **13:** 1498
Gallup, Cliff **1:** 80, 105, *105,* **9:** 1021, 1077
Galuten, Albhy **18:** 2106, 2107
Gambaccini, Paul **12:** *1325*
Gamble, Kenny **3:** 266, 343, **7:** 795, **8:** 940, **9:** 1043, **14:** 1594, 1596-1600, **18:** 2102
Gang of Four **18:** 2158-9, **19:** 2261-2, *2262*
Ganjou, George **4:** 366
Ganser, Mary Ann and Margie **5:** 569
Gant, Cecil **1:** 30 **3:** 339
Gantry, Elmer **10:** 1120
Garcia, Jerry **1:** *14,* **8:** 905-8, 910, 919-20, **12:** 1397
Gardener, Kris **9:** *998*
Gardiner, Paul **20:** 2314
Gardner, Buck **13:** *1491,* 1493
Gardner, Carl **3:** *294,* 295, *295*
Gardner, Kim **7:** 819

Garfunkel, Art **7:** *822*
Garland, Hank **1:** 94, 112, **2:** 228, 233
Garner, Bob **7:** 819
Garratt, Nicky **18:** 2152-3, *2154*
Garred, Wilt **3:** 324
Garrett, Lee **14:** 1673
Garrett, Malcolm **11:** *1294*
Garrett, Tommy 'Snuff' **3:** 248, **4:** 457, **5:** 502, 562, *563,* **13:** 1444
Garson, Mike **14:** 1633
Garth, Gene **3:** 303
Garvey, Nick **17:** *1922,* **19:** 2242
Garvey, Steve **18:** *2073,* 2074-5
'Gastank' **15:** 1697
Gates, Bill **18:** 2105
Gates, David **5:** 502, *518,* 519, **9:** 988, **13:** 1444
Gates, Rev. J. M. **2:** 159
Gaudio, Bob **2:** 240, **5:** 571-3, *573*
Gayden, Mac **17:** 2023
Gaye, Angus **19:** 2216
Gaye, Barbie **2:** 217
Gaye, Marvin **1:** 10, **4:** *463, 471,* 473, 478, **6:** 702-5, 706, 713, 714-5, 717-18, 719, **7:** 781-2, 783, **9:** 1006, 1042-3, *1042,* 1046, 1057, **12:** 1403, 1413-14, *1419,* 1420, **13:** *1445,* **14:** 1583, 1587, 1589, 1592, 1672, 1673, **15:** 1763, 1785, 1786, **20:** 2360, *2416*
Gaylads **9:** 977
Gayle, Crystal **14:** 1659, *1659,* **17:** 2021, 2024, 2095
Gaylords **8:** 947
Gaynor, Gloria **18:** *2101,* 2102, 2118
Gayton, Paul **1:** 30, **2:** 142, 145, 153-4, 155, **4:** *462*
Gee, Rosko **10:** 1189
Geffen, David **10:** 1094, **15:** *1761,* 1762-3, 1773, 1774, 1779, **16:** 1841
Geggus, Micky **18:** *2153,* 2154
Geils, J. **8:** 872, **10:** 1163
Geldof, Bob **11:** *1316,* 1317, **19:** 2249, *2249-50,* 2251, **20:** *2401, 2402,* 2403
General Public **19:** 2209
Generation X **18:** *2059,* 2060, 2061, *2063*
Genesis **8:** *960,* **15:** 1741, 1742, 1750-5, 1756, 1757, **16:** 1802, **18:** 2098, *2140,* **20:** 2354
Gentle, Johnny **2:** 122, *136,* 137, 138, 140, **4:** 427, **5:** 547
Gentry, Bo **9:** 994-5
Gentry, Bobby **1:** 18, **5:** 575, *575*
Geordie **12:** 1423
George, Barbara **3:** 266
George Baker Selection **6:** 699, **18:** 2118, **20:** 2361, 2362
George, Lowell **16:** 1858, *1858,* 1859, *1859,* 1860, **18:** 2097, **19:** 2224
Geraldo, Neil **18:** 2135, *2136*
Gerry and the Pacemakers **3:** 266, **4:** *414,* **5:** 523, 524-7, 532, 537, 538, 564, *564,* **6:** 639, *692,* 693, **7:** 729, **8:** 844, 850, 880
Gers, Janick **17:** 1984
Gestures **8:** 872
Get Yourself A College Girl **6:** 659

Gets, Dave **10:** 1097, 1170
Gibb, Andy **17:** *1941,* **18:** 2104, 2106, 2107
Gibb, Barry **6:** *639*
Gibb, Maurice **6:** 636, *636,* **18:** 2104, 2105, 2106
Gibb, Robin **6:** *639,* **18:** 2104, *2105*
Gibbons, Billy **16:** 1854-5, *1854*
Gibbons, Steve **11:** *1277*
Gibbs, Georgia **1:** 32, **3:** 310
Gibbs, Joe **9:** *975,* **16:** 1882, 1883, 1894, 1896, *1898,* 1900
Gibbs, Mike **13:** 1525
GI Blues **2:** 212, **3:** 250, *255*
Gibson, Brian **18:** 2129
Gibson, Don **2:** 234, **4:** 415, 416
Gibson, Gillian **7:** 839
Gibson, Henry **12:** 1413
Gibson, Wilf **15:** 1747
Gilbert, Gillian **19:** *2268,* 2269
Gilbert, John **10:** 1199
Gilbert, Michael **18:** 2117
Gilbert, Ronnie **6:** 667
Gilder, Nick **16:** 1823
Giles, Giles and Fripp **13:** 1465, **14:** 1564
Giles, Mike **14:** 1564
Giles, Peter **14:** 1564, *1565*
Gill, Pete **19:** 2239
Gill, Peter **20:** 2415
Gillan **17:** 1982, 1984, 1987
Gillan, Ian **12:** 1361, 1377, *1377,* 1379, **17:** 1982, 1984, *1985,* 1987
Gillespie, Dizzy **3:** 265, 321, 322, 330, 336-7
Gillett, Charlie **12:** *1324,* **17:** 1925, 1930, 1936, 1960
Gilliland, Henry **1:** 39
Gilmer, Jimmy **2:** 191, **4:** 390
Gilmour, Dave **11:** 1307, 1309, *1311,* 1312, 1319-20, **20:** 2330
Gimbel, Norman **15:** 1713
Gimme Shelter **8:** 893, **20:** 2326
Ginger Baker's Nutters **9:** 1031
Ginsberg, Allen **1:** 15, **8:** *918,* 919-20, **11:** 1216, 1303, **18:** 2095
Ginsburg, Arnie **7:** 766
Giordano, Charlie **18:** 2135
Girl Can't Help It, The **1:** *105,* 106, **2:** 146, 151, 208, 209, **3:** 247, *247,* 248, 312
Girlfriends **5:** 567
Girl On A Motorcycle **8:** 847
Girls At Our Best **19:** 2261-2
Girls On The Beach **7:** *770-1*
Girlschool **19:** 2239, *2240*
Girls! Girls! Girls! **2:** *213-13,* 214
Giscombe, Junior **20:** 2393, *2394*
Gitton, James **6:** 717
Giuffre, Jimmy **13:** 1521
Give My Regards To Broad Street **14:** 1680
Gladiators **16:** *1885* 1886
Glan, Whitey **16:** 1866
Glascock, John **14:** *1572*
Glaser, Tompall **14:** 1655, *1660*
Glastonbury Fayre **11:** 1243, 1248
Gleason, Bob **11:** 1204
Gleason, Jackie **1:** 87, 91

Gleason, Ralph **8:** 915, **10:** 1129, **12:** 1322, 1323, 1330, 1332, *1332,* 1333, **13:** 1456
Glen, Chris **17:** 1995
Gleneagles **6:** 635
Glenn, Lloyd **1:** 30
Glitter Band **12:** 1432
Glitter, Gary **12:** 1422-3, *1423,* 1430-3, *1435,* **13:** 1503, 1507, 1515, **14:** *1668,* 1680, **16:** 1802, 1803, 1863
Glossup, Mick **16:** 1902, **20:** 2397
Glotker, Nigel **20:** 2335
Glove **18:** 2151
Glover, Henry **3:** 337
Glover, Roger **12:** 1377, *1377,* 1379, **17:** 1984, 1989, 1999
Glover, Tony **6:** 662
Go-Go **20:** 2281
Go Johnny Go! **2:** 197, 209, 216, 217, 248, **12:** 1419
Goalby, Pete **15:** 1729
Goble, Graham **20:** 2371
Godard, Jean-Luc **8:** 848, **11:** 1316
Godard, Vic **18:** 2062
Godchaux, Keith and Donna **8:** 906, 908
Goddard, Geoff **4:** 362, 437
Godfrey, Arthur **1:** 55, **2:** 202
Godley, Kevin **6:** 602, **14:** *1678,* 1680, **16:** 1913-15, *1913, 1914,* **20:** 2360
'Godspell' **13:** 1507, 1508, 1509, **16:** 1876, **20:** 2338, *2339*
Godz **9:** 1015
Goffin, Gerry **3:** 265, *266,* 288, 292, 312, **4:** 441, 443, 444, 447, 449, 452, 457, 458, 459, **5:** 509, 513, 567, **9:** 981, 982, 988, 990, **10:** 1153, **14:** 1593, **15:** 1714, 1715, 1789
Gogan, Barbara **18:** 2071
Goins, Herbie **7:** 818
Goldberg, Barry **4:** 447, **10:** 1163, **11:** 1221, 1225, 1239-40
Goldberg-Miller Blues Band **11:** 1221, *1223*
'Golden Boy' **8:** 859
Golden Chords **11:** 1203
Golden Crusaders **8:** 947
'Golden Disc, The' **2:** 135
Golden Disc, The **4:** 430
Golden Earring **6:** 700, *700*
Golden Gate Quarter **1:** 70, **2:** 160
Golding, Lynval **19:** 2201, 2203, 2204, *2206,* 2207
Golding, Wilber **8:** 939
Goldman, Albert **12:** 1321, 1325
Goldmark, Peter **12:** 1392, *1392*
Goldner, George **1:** 76, 77, **3:** 266, 289, **5:** 508, **9:** 1053
Gold Star Studios, Hollywood **3:** 247, *247,* 248, **5:** 509-10, 514, 520, 562, *563*
Goldstein, Jerry **5:** 562
Goldstein, Richard **12:** 1323, 1330
Gomelsky, Giorgio **5:** 599-600, *599,* **6:** 650-1, **7:** 759, *759,* 816, *817,* **8:** 896, **11:** 1228
Gong **14:** 1580, **20:** 2368, *2368*
Gonks **6:** 682

Good, Jack **1:** 107, *108,* **2:** 134, 137, **4:** 362, 366-8, 371, 378-80, *378, 379,* 385, 423, 429, 435, **5:** 517, **7:** 734-5, **8:** 842, 849, **11:** 1281, **13:** 1515, **15:** 1797
Goode, Bill **18:** 2105
Gooden, Sam **7:** 793, *793-4,* 795
'Good Evening' **8:** *959,* 960
Goodman, Jerry **13:** 1524-5
Goodman, Steve **3:** 309, **11:** 1220
Good Times **7:** 837, **8:** 847
Goodwin, Gus **4:** 377
Goodwin, Laurel **2:** *212*
Gorden, Helmut **7:** 816, **11:** 1276, *1276*
Gordon, Alan **8:** *862,* 864, **9:** 993
Gordon, Bob **16:** 1846
Gordon, Dexter **3:** 245
Gordon, Henry 'Raleigh' **9:** 970-1
Gordon, Jim **9:** 1035, **10:** 1189, **15:** 1710, 1715, 1719
Gordon, Marc **6:** 719, **9:** 1046
Gordon, Robert **1:** 114, **4:** 390
Gordon, Rosco **1:** 30, 44, **3:** 339, **7:** 799
Gordon, Shep **16:** 1865, **20:** 2293
Gordy, Anna **4:** *471,* 473, **6:** 702, 704, 705
Gordy, Berry **3:** *265,* 266, 280, 331, **4:** 401, 461, 470-3, 475, 476, 477-8, 479, **5:** 494, 562, 572, **6:** 701, *701,* 702, 704, 706-7, 710, 714, 176-20, **7:** 740, 782, **9:** 981, 1041-3, *1043,* 1045-9, 1050, 1054, 1057, **12:** 1420, **14:** 1581, 1583, 1584, 1590, 1592, 1593, 1672, 1673, *1675,* **19:** 2180
Gordy, Gwendolyn **4:** 471, *471,* 473, **6:** 702, 708
Gordy, Raymona **6:** 714
Gore, Lesley **5:** *566,* 569
Gorham, Scott **17:** 1990, 1992, *1993*
Gorl, Robert **20:** 2386
Gorman, Lee **20:** 2323
Gorme, Eydie **5:** 489
Gornley, Peter **4:** 368
Gosling, John **7:** *755,* 756
Gospel Starlighters **7:** 788-9
Gottehrer, Richard **5:** 562, **17:** 1929
Gottschalk, Louis Moreau **2:** 178
Goude, Jean-Paul **20:** *2300*
Gould, Jack **1:** 89
Goulding, Steve **17:** 1936, *1937,* **19:** 2193
Gouldman, Graham **1:** 6, **6:** 602, 606, 607, 643, 651-2, **11:** 1230, **16:** 1913-15, *1913*
Grabham, Mick **10:** *1088,* 1089
Gracie, Charlie **3:** 341-2, 343, 354-5
Gracie, Joan **3:** *355*
Grade, Leslie **4:** 369
Grade, Lew **4:** 369
Gradney, Kenny **16:** 1858
Graduate, The **8:** *846,* 847, **10:** 1129
Graham, Bill **1:** 15 **8:** 900, 917, *917,* 920, **10:** 1091, 1094, **11:** 1223, **12:** 1375, 1389, **13:** 1535, 1548, 1553, **16:** *1825,* 1841
Graham, Bobby **7:** 758, **15:** 1724
Graham, Chick **5:** 533
Graham, Davy **13:** 1461-2, *1463,* 1465, 1476

Graham, Johnny **19**: 2163

Graham, Larry **1**: 62, **9**: 1039, **12**: *1405,* 1406, 1407

Graham Bond Organization **5**: 588, **6**: 642, 647, **7**: 816-17, **9**: *1024,* 1027, 1032, **11**: 1276, **13**: 1524

Graham Central Station **12**: 1407

Grainge, Nigel **17**: 1936

Grainger, Percy **13**: 1471

Gramm, Lou **18**: *2132,* 2132-3

Gramolini, Loel **18**: 2093

Granberg, Per 'Elvis' **3**: 243, 251, *251*

Grande, Johnny **1**: 26

Grand Funk Railroad **12**: 1341, **14**: 1601, 1607, 1609-11, **15**: 1721, **16**: 1905, **18**: 2121, **20**: 2364

Grand Ole Opry **1**: 39, *39-40,* 54, 57, **2**: 232, **14**: 1660

Grand Wisard Theodor **19**: 2177

Grandmaster Flash **18**: 2103, *2176,* 2177, **20**: 2303

Grant, David **15**: 1783, **20**: 2392, 2393

Grant, Eddy **12**: 1372

Grant, Gogi **3**: 310

Grant, Marshall **14**: 1643, 1645

Grant, Peter **12**: *1363,* 1364-6, 1368

Grant 'Tarzan' Steve **13**: *1503*

Grass **16**: 1845

Grass Roots **9**: 1016

Grateful Dead **1**: 15, *15,* 16, 19, **6**: 680, **8**: 903, *903,* 904-8, 914, 915, 917, 919, *927,* **9**: 1019, 1020, 1029, **10**: 1090, 1097, 1099, 1100, 1123, 1170, **11**: 1223, *1242,* 1251, 1254, 1259, *1289,* 1292, 1301, **12**: 1383, 1387, 1390, 1397, 1403, **15**: 1761, **16**: 1860, **18**: 2077

Gravatt, Eric **13**: 1532

Gravenites, Nick **11**: *1238,* 1238-9, 1240

Graves, Jimmy **6**: 708

Gray, Dobie **13**: 1521

Gray, Douglas **4**: 439, *439*

Gray, Eddie **9**: 994-5

Gray, Les **16**: 1822, 1823

Gray, Nigel **16**: 1902, **19**: 2182

Gray, Owen **9**: 962, 976-7, *977*

Gray, Paul **18**: 2080

Gray, Tony **4**: 439

Grayden, Ivey **9**: 975

Graydon, Jay **19**: 2167

Grease **20**: 2327, *2328*

Grease Band **10**: *1166,* 1168

Great Rock 'n' Roll Swindle, The **13**: 1503, **20**: 2329

Great Society **8**: 909, 914, **10**: 1170

Great Southern **14**: 1605

Great Stampede **7**: 820

Greaves, John **14**: 1569

Grech, Rick **9**: 1031, 1035-6, **10**: 1189, 1198-9, *1198,* **11**: 1240, **13**: 1557

Green, Al **3**: 272, 274, 331, 337, **12**: 1410, **15**: 1782, *1782,* 1784-7

Green, Charlie **7**: 825

Green, Colin **5**: 596

Green Doc **3**: 291

Green, Jerome **5**: *591*

Green, Karl **6**: 685

Green, Lloyd **14**: *1656,* 1657

Green, Mick **4**: 435, *435,* **9**: 1021, **17**: 1928

Green, Peter **4**: 383, **6**: 642, **9**: 1022, **10**: 1102, 1113, 1115, 1118-19, *1118,* 1120, *1120,* **12**: *1342,* **17**: 2031

Green, Susaye **9**: 1049, *1049*

Green, Willie Jr. **13**: 1560

Greenaway, Roger **3**: 290, 293, **6**: 695, *695,* **16**: 1821

Greene, Lorna **5**: 575

Greene Brothers **15**: 1785

Greene, Ed **13**: 1555

Greenfield, Dave **19**: *2188,* 2189-90

Greenfield, Howie **3**: 265, **4**: 441, *442, 443, 443,* 448, 450, 452-3

Greenfield, Robert **8**: 894

Greenidge, Robert **11**: 1237, **19**: 2165

Greenslade, Dave **7**: 814, 815

Greenwich, Ellie **3**: 265, 292, **5**: 508, 509, *511,* 512, 514, 515, *563,* 567, 569, **9**: 982, 1000

Greenwood, Al **18**: *2132,* 2133

Gregg, Brian **4**: 434, *434,* 435

Gregory, Glenn **20**: *2309,* 2360

Grennan, Winston **14**: 1620

Gretton, Rob **19**: 2269

Grey, Carole **4**: 431

Grey, Owen **2**: 147

Griffey, Dick **19**: *2178,* 2178-80

Griffin, Bill **4**: 478

Griffin, Dale 'Buffin' **16**: 1818, *1819,* 1820

Griffin, Herman **6**: 706-7

Griffin, James **5**: *518,* 519, 520

Griffin, Rick **12**: 1389-90, *1391*

Griffin Brothers **1**: 30

Griffiths, Brian **5**: 534, 540

Griffiths, Carl **7**: 812

Griffiths, Donald **19**: 2216

Griffiths, Eric **5**: 547

Griffiths, Marcia **16**: 1892, *1893*

Grima, Charlie **10**: 1185

Grimes, Hamish **5**: 599-600

Grimes, Tiny **2**: 173-4

Grimes, Ty **3**: *305*

Grimshaw, Gary **12**: 1390

Grin **16**: 1846, 1847

Grogan, Clare **16**: 1902

Grossman, Albert **1**: 15, **6**: 664, 669, **10**: 1094, 1170, **11**: 1205, 1207, **15**: 1709, **16**: 1903

Grosvenor, Luther **17**: 2028, **18**: 2133, *see also* Bender, Ariel

Groucutt, Michael 'Kelly' **15**: 1748, 1749, *1749*

Group Image **8**: 864

Growcott, Andy 'Stoker' **19**: 2219

Gruber, Craig **17**: 1985

Grundy, Bill **18**: 2043, 2046

Grundy, Hugh **6**: 688, 691

Grunt Records **8**: 912-13

Grupo **1**: 15, **6**: 683

Guard, Dave **6**: 662, *668-9,* 669

Guercio, James William **7**: 772, 780, *780,*

10: 1094, **13**: 1527, 1528, 1540

Guerin, John **13**: 1495

Guess, Don **2**: 185

Guess Who **11**: 1293, *1295,* **14**: 1601, 1616-17

Guest, Rod **15**: 1724

Guida, Frank **5**: 491-2

Gunfight, The **14**: *1643*

Gunnell, John and Rik **5**: 596-7, *598,* 599, **7**: 811, 817

Gunning, Sarah Ogan **6**: 679

Gunter, Cornelius **3**: *294, 295,* 296

Gunther, Shirley **3**: 299

Guralnick, Peter **12**: 1325

Gurley, James **10**: 1170

Gurvitz, Adrian and Paul **9**: 1031, **10**: 1196

Gustafson, Johnny **5**: 534, **17**: 1984

Guthrie, Arlo **11**: *1212,* **16**: 1851

Guthrie, Jack **1**: 40

Guthrie, Woody **6**: 661-2, *661, 663,* 667, *674,* 675, 679, **10**: 1097, 1134, 1138, 1170, **11**: 1201, 1203-4, *1203, 1207,* 1209, 1218, **12**: 1349, 1358

Guy, Athol **10**: 1140

Guy, Billy **3**: *294,* 295, *295,* 297

Guy, Buddy **3**: 322, **4**: *466,* 467, **9**: 1026, **10**: 1102, *1102,* 1114, **11**: 1221, 1225, 1227, 1228, 1238

Guyden Records **3**: 343

Guzman, Eddie **16**: 1851

Gyngell, Denise **13**: *1503*

Gzelenschikov, Bob **20**: *2376*

H

Hackett, Steve **15**: *1751,* 1752, 1753, 1754, 1755

Hadley, Tony **16**: *1801,* **20**: 2347, *2348-9,* 2356

Hagans, Buddy **2**: 154

Hagen, Nina **20**: *2377*

Haggard, Merle **13**: 1556, 1557, **14**: 1648-9

Hague, Ian **15**: 1685

Haig, Paul **19**: 2273

Haines, Denis **20**: 2314

'Hair' **8**: *841,* 843, *858,* 859-60, *860,* **14**: 1576, **16**: 1876, **20**: 2328, 2338

Haircut **20**: 2325, *2384,* 2384-5

Hajime Tachibana **20**: 2365

Halcos, Pat **4**: 439

Hale, Keith **9**: 1031

Halee, Roy **10**: 1128, 1129

Haley, Bill **1**: 21, *21,* 22, 23, 24-28, 32, 35, 39, 60, *84,* 85, 118, **2**: 122, 124, 129, 161, 164, 201, *201,* 205, 206, 207, *209,* 221, **3**: 314, 354, **4**: *376,* 429, **8**: 843, **12**: 1334, 1385, **14**: 1619, 1657, **20**: *2304*

Halford, Rob **17**: 1999, *2000*

Hall and Oates **17:** 2021
Hall, Bobbye **17:** 2071
Hall, Daryl **10:** *1162,* 1163, **20:** 2344
Hall, Jerry **8:** *893,* **16:** *1807,* 1810
Hall, Rene **2:** 197, **3:** 334, **4:** 389
Hall, Rick **8:** 940
Hall, Roy **1:** 40
Hall, Terry **18:** 2055, **19:** 2203, 2204, *2206,* 2207
Hall, Tony **8:** 959
Halliday, Johnny **18:** 2133
Halligan, Dick **13:** 1539, *1539*
Hallman, Marc **15:** 1715
Hallucinations **8:** 872
Hallyday, Johnny **3:** *241,* 243, 250, *251,* **6:** 698
Ham, Bill **16:** 1855
Ham, Greg **20:** 2372
Hamblett, Charles **12:** 1322
Hamburg clubs **5:** 523, 528, 538-40, *548,* 548-9, 550
Hamill, Claire **15:** 1737
Hamilton, Richard **11:** 1291, 1297
Hamilton, Roy **4:** 452
Hamilton, Tom **16:** 1848
Hamman Jr., Clarence **19:** 2177
Hammer, Jan **13:** 1524-5, *1525*
Hammond, John Jr. **10:** 1163, **11:** 1221, 1223, 1240, **15:** 1788, **18:** 2089
Hammond, John Sr. **11:** 1204. 1238
Hammond, Laurens **15:** 1699
Hammond-Hammond, Jeffery **14:** *1570,* 1519
Hampton, Ian **14:** 1519
Hampton, Riley **9:** 1059
Hanan, Mark **14:** 1576
Hancock, Butch **10:** 1097
Hancock, Herbie **13:** *1522-3,* 1523, 1530, 1531, **15:** 1699, **18:** 2103, **20:** 2302, *2303*

Hancock, Hunter **1:** 56, **2:** 202, **3:** 245, 263, 299
Handley, Jerry **13:** 1484
Handy, W. C. **4:** 438
Hannett, Martin **18:** 2074, **19:** 2268, 2269, 2270
Hansen, Jack **2:** 200
Hanson, Colin **5:** 547
Harcourt, Charlie **13:** 1475
Hardaway, Lula **14:** 1672-3, *1675*
Hard Day's Night, A **4:** 431, 483, **5:** 543, 555, **7:** 825, **8:** 843-4, 848, 854-5, *854-5*
Harder They Come, The **9:** 979, **20:** 2326, 2327, *2327*
Hardesty, Herb **2:** 154
Hardin, Eddie **10:** 1187
Hardin, Glen D. **14:** 1557, **17:** 2022
Hardin, Tim **3:** 346, **6:** 665, 677, **10:** 1123-4
Hardman, Blair **10:** 1096
Hardy, François **6:** 698-9
Hardy, Phil **12:** 1325
Hardy, Russell **17:** 1930, 1931, *1933*
Hare, David **20:** 2340
Hargrove, Wesley **5:** 495

Harley, Steve **16:** 1802, 1838-40
Harlots **17:** 2001
Harman, Murray 'Buddy' **2:** 225, 233
Harold Melvin and the Blue Notes **14:** 1597, 1598, 1600
Harper, Charlie **18:** 2152-4, *2154*
Harper, Roy **11:** 1247, **12:** 1396, **13:** 1461, 1462, 1478-80
Harper's Bizarre **8:** 902, **13:** 1444
Harpo, Slim **3:** *338,* 339
Harris, Betty **5:** 483
Harris, Bob **17:** 1959-60
Harris, Damon Otis **9:** 1052
Harris, Don 'Sugarcane' **10:** *1114,* 1115, **13:** 1495
Harris, Emmylou **11:** 1211, **13:** 1557, **16:** *1859,* **17:** 2023, *2023,* 2025
Harris, Jet **2:** 127, **4:** 362, 368, *384,* 385, 386, 387, 388, 423, **9:** 1039, **11:** 1228, 1230, **16:** 1832
Harris, Jo **2:** 154
Harris, Julie **13:** *1503*
Harris, Oren **2:** *202,* 219
Harris, R. H. **3:** 322, 333
Harris, Rolf **2:** 139, **3:** *268,* 269, **6:** 681, **10:** 1138-9, *1165,* **20:** 2333
Harris, Steve **19:** 2230, *2231,* 2232
Harris, Wee Willie **2:** 122 **4:** 361
Harris, Wynonie **1:** 30, 35, **2:** 174
Harris Sisters **3:** 299
Harrison, Bobby **10:** 1087, 1089
Harrison, George **1:** 110, **4:** 458, **5:** 512, 515, 541-60, **8:** 854-7, **9:** 963, 1021, 1029, 1035, 1077-8, **10:** 1141-60, **11:** 1210, **12:** *1397,* 1400, *1424,* **13:** 1443, 1445, 1449, *1449,* **14:** 1679, **15:** 1703, 1797, **17:** 1961, 1966, 1967-9, 1972, 1976, 1980, 2039 **20:** 2327
Harrison, Jerry **17:** 2016, **20:** 2283, *2283,* 2285
Harrison, John **17:** 1996
Harrison, Nigel **20:** *2290, 2291,* 2293
Harrison, Noel **10:** 1139
Harrison, Patti **10:** 1149, *1149,* **17:** 1968
Harrison, Philip **4:** 439
Harry, Bill **5:** 537, 547, 549, **6:** 601
Harry, Debbie **5:** 500, **9:** *1075,* **16:** 1863, **17:** 2001, *2005,* 2012, **18:** 2072, 2114, 2115, 2123, *2124,* 2135, **20:** *2290,* 2292-3, *2292-3*
Hart, Bobby **3:** 265, **9:** 981, 982-3, *982,* 988, 990, *990*
Hart, Charlie **17:** 1925
Hart, Mickey **8:** *905,* 906, 908
Hart, Roger **7:** 832
Hart, Tim **13:** 1462, *1471,* 1472-3
Hartley, Keef **10:** 1102, 1113-14, 1115
Hartman, John **16:** *1825,* 1851, *1851,* 1852, *1853*
Harvey, Alex **17:** 1994-5
Harvey, Bob **8:** 909
Harvey, Paul **18:** 2154
Harwood, Barry **16:** 1844
Haskell, Gordon **14:** 1564-5
Haskell, Jimmie **10:** 1125

Haslam, Michael **5:** 534
Haslev, John **19:** 2210
Hassan, Norman **19:** 2214, *2214*
Hassles **8:** 863
Hasted, Dr John **2:** *126*
Hatch, Tony **3:** 351, **5:** 528-9, **6:** 622, 633, *633,* 694
Hatcher, George **17:** 1929
Hathaway, Donny **15:** 1799, 1800
Havens, Ritchie, **11:** 1251
Havoc, Steve **18:** 2148
Hawker, Mike **4:** 422
Hawkes, Chip **6:** 616, *617*
Hawkins, Dale **1:** 102, *102*
Hawkins, Hawkshaw **2:** 194
Hawkins, Hoyt **1:** 94
Hawkins, Leslie **16:** 1844
Hawkins, Martin **12:** 1324
Hawkins, Roger **10:** 1189
Hawkins, Ronnie **1:** 112, **3:** *250,* 251, **5:** 591, **10:** 1162, **13:** 1444, 1547, 1548
Hawkins, Screamin' Jay **1:** 56, **2:** 163, 173-5, **12:** 1373, **18:** 2095
Hawks **3:** 251, **11:** 1209, **13:** 1444, 1547
Hawkwind **16:** 1824, **17:** 1997-8, **19:** 2238
Hay, Colin **20:** 2372
Hay, Roy **20:** 2399, *2399*
Haydock, Eric **6:** 605-6
Hayes, Ernie **3:** 273
Hayes, Isaac **1:** 10, **7:** 785, **8:** 922, *928,* 930, 932, *933,* 936-7, **9:** 1043, **12:** 1403, 1408-11, 1414, 1420, **14:** 1588-9, **15:** 1742, **18:** 2100, 2102
Hayes, Linda **3:** 299
Hayes, Lee **6:** 667
Hayes, Michael *see* Most, Mickie
Hayward, Justin **10:** 1194-6, *1195-6*
Hayward, Louis 'Deke' **3:** 349
Hayward, Philip **5:** 600
Hayward, Richard **16:** 1858, *1858*
Hazan **20:** *2362*
Hazelwood, Lee **1:** 112-13, **2:** 198, **3:** *342,* 343, **4:** 394-5, **5:** *502,* 503, 507
Head **9:** 990
Head, Roy **10:** 1163
Headon, Nicky 'Topper' **18:** 2066-7, *2068,* 2069
Heartbeats **6:** 685
Heartbreakers **17:** *2001,* 2002, 2003, 2004, 2012, 2046, 2058
Heart Of A Man **4:** 430
Hearts and Flowers **15:** 1773
Heaven **19:** 2269, **20:** *2309,* 2309
Hebler, Dave **12:** 1321
Heckstall-Smith, Dick **5:** *583,* 586-7, **6:** *642,* **9:** 1032, **10:** 1114
Hedgehog Pie **13:** 1462
Hedgehoppers Anonymous **6:** *676,* 677, 659-60
Heilbut, Tony **2:** 158
Heintje **6:** *698,* 700
Heinz **4:** 437, **17:** 1928
Heinz, Charles **8:** 921
Hell, Richard **9:** 1003, **16:** 1863, **17:** *2001,* *2004,* 2007, *2008,* 2012-13, **18:** 2045

Hellerman, Lee **6:** 667
Hellions, The **4:** 430
Helliwell, John **15:** 1758-9, *1759, 1760*
Hello **15:** *1745*
Helm, Levon **3:** 251, **11:** 1209, **13:** *1546,* 1547, 1549
Helmore, Lucy **16:** 1810, *1810*
Helms, Bobby **2:** 234
Helms, Chet **8:** *919,* 920, **10:** 1170, **11:** 1225, **12:** 1389
Help! **8:** 847, 855, *856,* **10:** 1146-7
Hemmings, Courteney **19:** 2216
Hemmings, David **8:** *847,* **15:** 1691, 1697
Henderson, Dougie **8:** *948,* 949
Henderson, Jocko **3:** 343
Henderson, Luther **3:** 354
Henderson, Mike **3:** *246*
Henderson, Wayne **19:** 2173, *2174,* 2175
Henderson, Willie **3:** 332
Hendricks, Bobby **3:** 254, 290, 291
Hendrix, Jimi **1:** *1,* 8, 9, 16, **2:** 150, 195, **6:** *642,* **7:** *805,* **8:** 842, 850-1, 864, *941-2,* 942, 949, **9:** 966, 989-90, 1017, 1022, 1028, 1032, 1054-5, 1061-9, 1070, 1074, 1079, **10:** 1092, 1099, *1099-1100,* 1100, 1107, *1133,* 1173, **11:** 1220, 1245, 1250, 1253, 1299, 1300, *1300,* **12:** 1361, 1372, 1401, 1403, **13:** 1523, **14:** 1562, 1614-15, **15:** 1686, 1687, 1726, 1762, 1765, **16:** *1845,* 1857, 1862, **18:** *2137*
Hendryx, Nona (Wynona) **12:** 1402, *1415,* 1416
Heneker, David **4:** 428
Henley, Don **15:** 1772, *1773,* 1774, 1775
Henri, Adrian **10:** 1103
Henrit, Bob **4:** 372
Henry, Clarence **2:** 145, **4:** 458
Henry, Kent **9:** 1072
Henry, Pierre **15:** 1683
Henry, Stuart **7:** 745, *745*
Henry Cow **14:** 1568-9
Henshaw, Michael **11:** 1305
Hensley, Harold **3:** 245
Hensley, Ken **15:** 1728, 1729
Hentschel, David **16:** 1917
Hentzell, Perry **9:** 979
Hep Cat, Dr **19:** 2177
Hep Stars **6:** 700, **17:** 1944
Hepburn, Kenny **4:** 395
Hepstones **16:** *1882,* 1886, *1886,* 1887, 1894
Herbert, Victor **4:** 460
Herd **1:** *6-7,* 7, **8:** 942, *954-5,* **10:** 1085, **17:** 2038-40
Here, Kool **19:** 2177
Here Comes The Nelsons **3:** 302
Here We Go Round The Mulberry Bush **8:** 847
Herman, Gary **12:** 1324
Herman's Hermits **4:** 423, 447, **5:** 537, **6:** 602-3, 681, *681,* 684-7, 693, **7:** 749, 753, 757, **8:** 847, **9:** 1047, 1074, **10:** 1159, **16:** 1822, 1826, *1833,* 1834
Hernandez, Andy **20:** *2297*
Herold, Ted **3:** *249,* 250

Heron, Mike **13:** 1468-70, *1469-70,* **15:** 1717
Herring, Scooter **14:** 1605
Herrold, 'Doc' **1:** 55, *56*
Hess, Derek **16:** 1844
Hester, Carolyn **6:** 662, *665,* **11:** 1204
Hewlett, John **7:** 820
Hewson, Paul *see* Bono Vox
Heyman, Preston **18:** 2147
Heyward, Nick **20:** 2381, *2384,* 2384-5, *2385*
Hiatt, John **13:** 1560, *1560*
Hibbert, Toots **9:** 962-3, 970-1, **16:** 1886, *1887,* 1894
Hicks, Colin **3:** 251, *251,* **4:** 435
Hicks, Tony **6:** *604,* 605-8, *606*
Hideki Matsotake **20:** 2365
Hideo Inoura **20:** 2365
Hi Fis **6:** 683
Higgins, Monk **9:** 1060
Higgs, Joe **16:** 1889-90, 1892
High Numbers **7:** 816, **11:** 1264, *1264,* 1273, 1275-6, *see also* Who
Highlights **15:** 1732
High School Confidential **2:** *208,* 209
High Time **3:** 353
Highwaymen **6:** 669
Hill, Andy **20:** *2395,* 2396
Hill, Benny **10:** 1138-9
Hill, Big Bill **1:** 56
Hill, Carl **9:** 1031
Hill, Dave **12:** 1422, 1427-8, 1429
Hill, Dusty **16:** 1854, 1855
Hill, Ian **17:** 1999
Hill, Wally **5:** 522, 523
Hillage, Steve **20:** 2368
Hilliard, Bob **5:** 577, 579
Hillman, Chris **7:** *827,* 828-30, *829-30,* 831 **13:** 1556, **15:** 1765, 1773
Hilltoppers **2:** 235
Hilton, Ripton **20:** 2374
Hinch, John **17:** 1999
Hines, Ian **5:** 538
Hini, Akonidi **12:** 1372
Hinsley, Harvey **16:** 1826
Hipgnosis **11:** 1292-3
Hiroshi Min **20:** 2364
Hirsch, Chicken **10:** 1097
Hirt, Al **2:** 231, 234
Hiseman, Jon **6:** 642, **9:** 1032, **10:** 1114, **14:** 1620
Hite, Bob **10:** 1116-17, *1116*
Hit Parader **12:** 1329, 1331
Hitchcock, Russell **20:** *2371*
Hobbs, Elsbeary **3:** 291
Hobbs, Randy **11:** 1235
Hodder, Jim **16:** 1919-20, *1919*
Hodge, Alex **3:** 299
Hodge, Keith **16:** 1830, 1831
Hodgkinson, Colin 'Bomber' **17:** 1984
Hodgkinson, Tim **14:** 1569
Hodgson, Roger **15:** 1758, 1759, *1759,* 1760, *1760*
Hoenig, Michael **20:** *2369*
Hoffman, Abbie **11:** 1251, **12:** *1382*

Hoggart, Richard **12:** 1322
Hoh, Eddie **11:** 1221, 1240
Holden, Randy **14:** 1601
Holden, Ron **5:** *502*
Holder, Noddy **12:** 1422, 1427-8, *1428*
Hold On! **8:** 847
Holdsworth, Allan **14:** *1580*
Holiday, Billie **4:** *461,* **9:** 1042, **14:** 1590, 1592
Holiday, Jennifer **19:** 2164
Holland, Brian and Eddie **6:** *714,* 715, **9:** 1041, *1045,* 1046-9, 1054, 1057, **18:** 2102, 2107
Holland, Dozier and Holland **4:** 477, 478, **5:** 577, **6:** 702, 708, 710, 712-13, *714,* 714-19, 720, **9:** 1041, *1045,* 1046-7, 1048, 1049, 1051, 1054, 1057
Holland, Jools **19:** 2256-7, *2257*
Holland, W. S. **1:** 109
Holley, Major 'Mule' **15:** 1788
Hollies **2:** 182, **4:** 447, **6:** 602-3, 604-8, **7:** 741, 759, **10:** 1085, 1167, **12:** 1323, *1323,* **15:** 1702, 1764
Holloway, Brenda **4:** 478, **6:** 716, 719
Holloway, Loreatta **15:** 1783
Holly, Buddy **1:** 12, *80,* 113, 118, **2:** *162,* 163, 164, 165, 176, 177, 181, *181,* 182-3, *182, 183,* 184-9, 190, 191, 192, 193, 194, *194,* 195, *195,* 197, 200, 204, 205, 221, *229,* **3:** 245, 248, 254, 259, *284,* 309, 345, **4:** 456-7, **5:** 552, 561, 574, **9:** 1021, **10:** 1118, 1126, **12:** 1358, **13:** 1442, **14:** 1654, 1662, 1664, 1679, **17:** 1941, 1966
Holmes, Alan **7:** 756, **8:** 949
Holmes, Christine **5:** *526*
Holmes, Freddie **7:** 788
Holmes, Malcolm **20:** 2317
Holmes, Winston **16:** 1894
Holy Modal Rounders **9:** 1015, **10:** 1123
Holzman, Jack **9:** 1010, 1016, **10:** 1124-5, **12:** 1349, **13:** 1554, **15:** 1710
Hondells **7:** 765
Honeycombs **4:** 437, **8:** 950
Honeyman-Scott, James **19:** 2253, *2253*
Honeys **7:** 778
Honeysuckle Rose **14:** 1647, *1647*
Hoochie Coochie Men **15:** 1724
Hood, David **10:** 1189
Hoogenboom, Andy **5:** 587
Hook, Peter **19:** *2266,* 2266-7, *2268*
Hooker, John Lee **1:** 31, *31,* **2:** 158, **3:** 322, *322,* 339, **4:** 473, **6:** 679-80, **10:** *1116,* 1117, 1181, **18:** 2095
Hooper, Nesbert 'Stix' **19:** 2173, *2174,* 2175
Hoopii, Sol **14:** 1656
Hootenanny Singers **6:** 700, **17:** 1944-5
Hopkin, Mary **10:** 1139, 1150, 1158, **14:** 1632, 1679, **17:** 1955
Hopkins, Jerry **12:** 1324-5
Hopkins, John 'Hoppy' **11:** *1303,* 1304-5
Hopkins, Lightnin' **3:** 339, **5:** 582, **6:** 680, **10:** 1104-5, **11:** 1234
Hopkins, Nicky **7:** *757,* 758, 759-60, *759,* **11:** 1226

Hopkins, Thelma **4**: 459
Hopper, Brian **14**: 1579
Hopper, Dennis **8**: *843, 848*
Hopper, Hugh **14**: 1578-9, *1580*
Hopwood, Keith **6**: 685
Horn, Bob **3**: 357, 358
Horn, Jim **11**: 1237, **12**: 1345
Horn, Lawrence **9**: 1046
Horn, Trevor **15**: *1692,* 1695, **20**: 2348, 2396-7, *2397,* 2415
Horne, Nicky **17**: *1960*
Horono, Haroumi **20**: 2364-5
Horton, Gladys **6**: 719
Horton, Johnny **2**: 194, 234, **3**: *285*
Hossack, Michael **16**: 1851
Hot Band **17**: 2025
Hot Chocolate **12**: *1422,* **16**: *1822,* 1826-8, 1834
Hotlegs **16**: 1913
Hot Toddys **4**: 391
Hot Tuna **8**: 912-13, *912*
Houghton, Dave **19**: 2254
Hound Dog Man **3**: 353, *353*
Hounsome, Terry **12**: 1325
Hourglass **14**: 1603
House, Simon **17**: 1997
House Rockers **2**: 122
Houseshakers **1**: 118-19
Houston, Cissy **5**: 576
Houston, Joe **3**: 300, **4**: 389
Houston, Thelma **9**: 1043
Houston, Whitney **20**: 2413
Howard, Ken **13**: 1511
Howard, Pete **18**: 2069
Howarth, 'Bandsman' **17**: 1928
Howe, Bones **18**: 2095
Howe, Steve **14**: 1634, **15**: 1688, 1691, 1692-5, 1742
Howells, Johnny **12**: 1427
How I Won The War **8**: 847, 856, *856,* **10**: 1149
'How It Is' **8**: *852,* 852-3
Howard, Alan **6**: 615, 616
Howard, Barry **9**: 973
Howard, Don **3**: *341*
Howard, Jack **1**: 24-5
Howard, Ken **8**: 859, 950, *951,* 954-5, **10**: 1085
Howe, Steve **1**: 10, **9**: 1022
Howlett, Mike **16**: 1902, **19**: 2184, **20**: 2397
Howlin' Wolf **1**: 43, 44, 68, **3**: *339,* **4**: 465, 466-7, *467,* **9**: 1059, 1065, **10**: 1103, 1108, **11**: 1221, 1234, 1239, **13**: 1484
HP Lovecraft **8**: 914
Howson, Dave **11**: 1306
Hubbard, Freddie **13**: 1523
Hubbard, Joe **20**: 2315
Hubbard, Neil **14**: 1665
Hudson, Garth **11**: 1209, **13**: 1546, *1547*
Hudson, Harold **18**: 2117
Huff, Leon **3**: 266, *343,* **5**: 489, **7**: 795, **8**: 940, **9**: 1043, **14**: 1581, 1584, 1596-1600, **18**: 2102
Hugg, Mike **6**: 644-9

Hughes, Chris **20**: 2323, *2324*
Hughes, Dave **20**: 2317
Hughes, Finola **20**: *2337*
Hughes, Glen **12**: *1376,* 1379-80, **17**: 1984
Hughes, Leon **3**: *294,* 295
Hughes-Thrall **12**: 1380
Hugo and Luigi **14**: 1595
Hulin, T. K. **13**: 1445
Hull, Alan **13**: *1474-5,* 1475
Hulston, Leroy **7**: 795
Human Be-In, San Franssico **1**: 15, **8**: 920, **11**: 1242, *1242*
Human League **13**: 1519, **16**: 1902, **19**: 2168-9, 2261-2, **20**: 2301-2, 2306-9, 2343, 2359-60, 2395
Humble Pie **7**: 809, *809,* **8**: 955, **15**: 1721, 1725, **17**: 2038, *2039,* 2040
Humblebums **17**: 2028
Hummel, Andy **10**: 1175
Humperdinck, Engelbert **7**: 722, 740, **8**: *942,* **9**: 984, *985,* **17**: 1958
Humphreys, Paul **20**: 2316-17, *2316-17*
100 Club **18**: 2043, 2047, 2058, *2058,* 2060
Hunger, The **14**: 1631
Hunt, Bill **10**: 1185, **15**: 1747
Hunt, John **3**: 325
Hunt, Patrick **20**: 2384
Hunte, Gordon **9**: 969
Hunter, Clifford **14**: 1586
Hunter, George **11**: 1292, **12**: 1388, *1389*
Hunter, Ian **12**: 1325, **15**: *1699,* **16**: 1818, *1818-9,* 1819, 1820, **20**: 2133
Hunter, Ivory Joe **1**: 30, **3**: *273,* 274, 339
Hunter, Ivy **6**: 713, 716, 719, **9**: 1054
Hunter, Joe **3**: *272-3,* 274
Hunter, Meredith **11**: 1258, 1260, **20**: 2326
Hunter, Ray **2**: 135
Hunter, Robert **8**: *905,* 905-6, 908, **10**: 1192
Hunter, Steve **10**: 1178, **16**: 1866
Hunter, Tab, **3**: 306
Hunters **4**: 363
Hurricanes **3**: 243, *243,* 249, **4**: 381, 382, 395, 396-7, 402, 404, *404,* **5**: 522, 538, 540, 548, *548,* 550
Hurst, Mike **7**: 730, **10**: 1140, **12**: 1353
Hurt, 'Mississippi' John **2**: 159
Hutch, Willie **4**: 479, **9**: 1057, **12**: 1403
Hutchings, Ashley **13**: 1462, *1465,* 1466, *1471,* 1472
Hutchinson, Johnny **5**: 534
Hulston, Leroy **12**: 1414
Huth, Angela **8**: 852
Hütter, Ralf **20**: *2310,* 2310-11
Hutto, J. B. **4**: 465
Huxley, Aldous **12**: 1382
Huxley, Rick **6**: 609, *610*
Hyland, Brian **4**: 401, *401,* 418, 419
Hyman, Dick **3**: 268
Hyman, Jerry **13**: 1539
Hyman, Phyllis **14**: 1595
Hyman, Walter **8**: 875
Hymas, Tony **9**: 1033
Hynde, Chrissie **7**: 756, **18**: *2041*

I

Ian, Janis **15**: *1702*
Ian and the Zodiacs **5**: 523
Icehouse **20**: *2372*
Idle, Eric **17**: 1968, 1980
Idle On Parade **4**: 430, *430*
Idle Race **1**: 6, **6**: 603, **10**: 1185
Idol, Billy **18**: 2061, *2063,* 2148, **20**: 2405, *2406*
Idolmaker, The **3**: 265, 349
Ienner, Jimmy **14**: 1611
Ifield, Frank **4**: 374, **7**: 721, *721*
Iggy Pop **9**: 1002-3, **13**: *1481,* 1483, 1497-1500, **14**: 1623, 1626, 1632, **18**: 2042
Iggy and the Stooges **13**: *1481, 1482,* 1497-1500
Iguanas **13**: 1498
Ilka, Mick **6**: *620*
Illegal Records **18**: 2156
Illsley, John **19**: 2199, *2199*
Illuminated Records **18**: 2160
Illusion **6**: 653
Immagination **20**: 2392, *2392,* 2397
Immediate **7**: 758, *758,* 760, 807-8, 809, 815, 817, **8**: 952-3
Imoalas **2**: 237
Imperial Records **1**: 95, **3**: *261,* 262, 264, 271, 303, 304, **5**: 502, 507
Impressions **7**: 782, 793-5, **9**: 1059, **10**: 1099, **12**: 1402-3, 1412-14, **16**: 1885, 1887
'In Concert' **15**: 1703
Incredible String Band **1**: 8, **13**: 1461-2, 1468-70
In the Dark **16**: 1902
Indeep **18**: 2103
Indios Tabajaros, Los **3**: 270
Infante, Frank **20**: *2290, 2291,* 2293
Inferno, The **15**: 1688
Ingber, Elliott **7**: 734
Ingle, Doug **9**: 1071
Ingvars, Sven **6**: 700
Ink Spots **1**: 31, 61, 69, *69,* **3**: 290
Innes, Neil **17**: 1935, 1980
Instant Action Jug Band **10**: 1096
International Rhythm Band **11**: 1237
International Submarine Band **13**: 1556
International Times **13**: 1469, **14**: 1580
Intruders **14**: 1596-7
Invaders **2**: *128,* 129
Iommi, Tony **12**: 1369-70, *1370,* 1371
Iovine, Jimmy **18**: 2123
Iron Butterfly **9**: 1070, 1071-2, *1071,* **12**: 1365, **14**: 1601
Iron Maiden **11**: 1298, *1298-9,* **17**: 2000, **19**: *2223,* 2230-2
Isaacs, Bud **14**: 1656
Isaacs, Gregory **16**: 1896, *1896,* **20**: 2373
Island Records **9**: 961-2, *963,* 963-4, 971, 978-9
Isle of Wight Pop Festival (1969) **8**: *943,* **11**: 1242, *1242,* 1246-7, 1253, 1259
Isle of Wight Pop Festival (1970) **9**: *1068,*

1069, **11:** *1241,* 1243, 1247-8, 1286, **15:** 1687, 1716, 1739
Isles, Bill **14:** 1600
Isley Brothers **5:** 483, 489, **9:** 1053-5, *1065,* **14:** 1581
Israel, Yackov Ben **19:** 2163
Israel Vibration **20:** 2374
It Happened At The World's Fair **2:** 213
I-Threes **16:** *1892, 1893*
It's A Beautiful Day **11:** 1256, 1292
It's Trad Dad! **4:** 431, 433, 440
It's Your Thing **9:** 1055
I've Got A Horse **4:** 427-8, **8:** 844
Ives, Burl **10:** 1139
Ivory Coasters **17:** 1925

J

Jack, 'Wolfman' **1:** 43, 58, **18:** 2036
'Jack the Cat' **1:** 56
Jack the Lad **13:** 1462, 1475
'Jack Jackson Record Show' **8:** 842
Jackson, Al **7:** 784-5, *784,* **8:** 925, 929, *929* 937
Jackson, Bullmoose **1:** 30, **3:** 338
Jackson, Jackie **14:** *1583,* 1584
Jackson, Jermaine **14:** *1583,* 1583-5
Jackson, Joe **1:** 35, **19:** 2254-5, *2254-5,* **20:** 2360
Jackson, Lee **5:** 1685-7, *1687*
Jackson, Mahalia **2:** 151, 159, *159,* **15:** 1788, 1797
Jackson, Marlon **14:** *1583,* 1585
Jackson, Mel **7:** 800
Jackson, Michael **13:** 1504, **14:** 1582-5, 1587, 1593, 1679, **17:** 1966, **18:** 2103, **19:** 2161, *2161,* **20:** *2359,* 2360
Jackson, Millie **12:** 1410, **15:** *1781,* 1782, 1783
Jackson, Milt **3:** 327, **4:** 390
Jackson, Randy **14:** *1582,* 1584
Jackson, Ray **13:** 1475, *1475*
Jackson, Shot **14:** 1657
Jackson, Tito **14:** *1583*
Jackson, Tony **3:** 528-30, *529*
Jackson, Walter **9:** 1060
Jackson, Wanda **1:** 113, *113* **3:** 311
Jackson, Wayne **15:** 1785, 1786
Jackson, Willis **3:** 273
Jackson Five **9:** 1042-3, *1042,* **12:** *1420,* **13:** 1504, **14:** 1581, 1582-5, **15:** 1763, 1779, **18:** 2116-17
Jackson Heights **15:** 1687
Jacobs, Adolph **3:** *294*
Jacobs, David **4:** 377, *379,* 380, **8:** 841, 849, *849*
Jacobs, Dick **2:** 187, **3:** 331, **4:** 471
Jacobs, Ron **17:** 2037, *2037*
Jacobs, Wes **17:** 1949
Jacobsen, Erik **7:** 821-2, **8:** *866,* **9:** 967
Jacques, Mick **14:** 1576

Jacquet, Illinois **2:** 173
Jagger, Bianca **8:** *892,* 894
Jagger, Mick **1:** *3,* 8, *19,* **2:** 150, 194, **5:** 551, 582, *583,* 588, **6:** 622, *624,* 654, *655,* **7:** 722, 729, 760, *805,* 815, **8:** *847,* 848, 850, 880, *880,* 881-900, 922, **9:** 1017, 1022, 1065, *1073,* 1074, **11:** 1260, **12:** 1334, 1335, *1335,* 1387, *1403,* **13:** 1452, 1556, **14:** 1652, 1679-80, **15:** 1709, 1710, 1716, 1797, **16:** 1810, **17:** 1972-3, **20:** 2326, *2329,* 2360, *2417,* 2419
Jags **19:** *2242*
Jah Wobble **18:** 2048
Jailhouse Rock **1:** 90, **2:** 201, *202,* 208, 211-12, *212*
Jaimae **14:** 1604-5
Jamal, Ahmad **4:** 467, **9:** 1043
Jam **11:** 1261, *1261,* **12:** 1357, **18:** 2058, *2059,* 2062, 2063, 2073, **19:** 2188, 2241-2, 2244-8, *2245,* **20:** 2359
Jamboree **2:** 169, **3:** 316, 317
Jamerson, James **4:** 472, **6:** 717, **9:** 1039, 1057
James, Billy **9:** 1010
James, Brian **18:** 2078-80, *2079-80*
James, Dick **5:** 527, 537, *537,* 550, 555, **14:** 1665, 1667, 1668
James, Elmore **3:** 273, 339, **11:** 1221
James, Etta **5:** 495, **9:** 1059, **10:** 1181
James, Glodean **14:** 1589
James, Jimmy **7:** 812-13, 816, **11:** 1277
James, Linda **14:** 1589
James, Rick **9:** 1043, 1052, **15:** 1768, **19:** 2168, *2169*
James, Skip **2:** 159
James, Sonny **2:** 231, **4:** *412*
James, Tommy **1:** 13, **9:** 981-2, *981,* 994-5, *995,* 999
James, Tony **18:** 2063, 2078-9
James Gang **14:** 1601, 1612-13, **15:** 1775
Jameson, Peter **10:** 1187
Jamie and Jane **7:** 727
Jamie Records **3:** 341, *342,* 343, 360, **4:** 394, 395
Jam Today **18:** 2071
Jan and Arnie **7:** *766*
Jan and Dean **5:** 502, 503, 575, **7:** 764, 765, 766-7, 771, 775, 778, **10:** 1087, 1098
Janis **10:** 1170
Jankel, Annabel **20:** 2360
Jankel, Chaz **17:** 1931-2, *1933*
Jankowski, Horst **6:** 700
Jansch, Bert **1:** 8, **13:** 1461, 1462, 1476, *1477,* 1478
Jansen, Steve **20:** 2355-6, *2357*
Japan **11:** *1281,* **16:** 1803, 1806, 1863, **20:** 2355-6
Jarsine, Al **7:** *763,* 770, *770,* 772, 778
Jarrett, Hugh **1:** 94
Jarrett, Keith **13:** 1531
Jasper, Chris **9:** 1055
Jayettes **2:** *187*
Jaynettes **5:** 569

Jaywalkers **6:** *602*
Jazzboat **4:** 430
Jazz Crusaders *see* Crusaders
Jazz On A Summer's Day **2:** 209-10, **11:** 1209-12, 1252
J. B. and the Playboys **6:** 682
JBs **7:** *790,* 791
Jeff Beck Group **6:** 640, 653, **11:** 1228-32, **17:** 1982
Jefferson, Blind Lemon **2:** 159, **6:** *678,* 679-80
Jefferson Airplane **1:** *14,* 15, **6:** 678, **8:** 903, *903,* 905, 909-13, *912,* 913, 914-15, 917, 942, **9:** *984, 1019,* 1039, **10:** 1083, 1090, 1094, 1097, 1100, 1123, 1134, 1170, **11:** 1223, 1257, 1297, 1301, 1306, **12:** 1387, **13:** 1462, **15:** 1761, **18:** 2077
Jefferson Starship **2:** *192,* 193
Jeffery, Mike **9:** 1063
Jefferys, Paul Avron **16:** 1839, *1839*
Jelly Beans **5:** 567
Jenkins, Barry **6:** 660
Jenkins, Billy **9:** 1031
Jenkins, Gordon **6:** 667
Jenkins, Johnny **8:** 924-5
Jenkins, Karl **14:** *1580*
Jenner, Peter **11:** 1304, 1306, 1320, **13:** 1479
Jennings, Waylon **1:** 103, **2:** 177, 188, *189,* 234, **14:** 1641, 1647, 1652, 1653-5, 1659, *1660,* **17:** 2025
Jennings, Will **10:** 1192, **19:** 2175
Jensen, David 'Kid' **17:** *1959,* 1992
Jerks **19:** 2261
Jesus Christ Superstar **16:** 1876, **20:** 2321, *2329,* 2336, *2337, 2338*
Jethro Tull **10:** 1088, 1102, 1140, **12:** 1400, 1467, 1472, 1473, **14:** *1562,* 1563, 1570-4, **15:** 1692, 1742, **17:** 1921
Jet Records **7:** 817
Jets **5:** 538, **19:** *2258,* 2260
Jet Set **7:** 822, 828
Jets of Air **18:** 2073
Jet Storm, The **4:** 430
Jett, Joan **9:** 983, **17:** *1927,* 2011
Jim Kweskin Jug Band **7:** 822, *822-3,* **10:** 1123
Jimi Hendrix Experience **7:** 804, *805,* **9:** 989-90, 1063, *1063,* 1065-8, *1068,* 1069, **11:** 1253, 1277, **17:** 1981
Jiminez, Falco **13:** 1560
Jirous, Ivan **20:** 2376
Jivin' Gene **13:** 1455
J & M Studios, New Orleans **2:** 142, 145, 149, 154, 155, *155,* 200, *200*
Joan and the Demons **5:** 523
Jo Ann and Troy **10:** 1162-3
JoBoxers **18:** 2062
Jobraith **16:** 1863
Jobson, Eddie **14:** 1576, **16:** 1808, 1810
Jobson, Richard **19:** 2275, *2275*
Joe Jammer **11:** 1256
Joel, Billy **8:** 863, **17:** *2021,* 2035, *2035*
Joe Perry Project **16:** 1849
Johansen, David **16:** 1869, *1878,* 1879,

1880, *1880,* **18:** 2046
Johanson, Jai Johanny **14:** 1604, 1605
John, Dr **11:** *1220,* 1240, 1257, **18:** 2097
John, Elton **1:** 6, **2:** 163, *163,* 187, **3:** 337, **6:** 608, 645, **12:** 1336, 1422, *1424,* 1435, *1435,* **14:** 1632, 1661-2, *1661,* 1663-9, 1675, 1679-80, *1680,* **15:** 1779, **16:** 1802, 1866, *1912,* **17:** 1942, 1955, 1961, 1973, 1980, 2021,2035, **18:** 2099, 2124, **20:** 2402, 2409
John, Mabel **3:** 337, **8:** 930
John, Mertis **3:** 337
John, Prakash **16:** 1866
John Barry Seven **4:** 371, 372
Johnny and the Hurricanes **4:** 381, 382, 395, 396-7, 402, 404, *404,* **7:** 764, **9:** 1021
Johnny and the Self Abusers **19:** 2273
Johnny Mann Singers **3:** 248, **5:** 502
Johns, Andy **17:** 2007
Johns, Glyn **5:** 597, **6:** 640, **7:** *757,* 759, **10:** 1199, **11:** 1225-6, 1239, 1277, **15:** 1773, 1774, **19:** 2196-7
Johns, Jasper **5:** 498
John's Children **7:** 760, *818-19,* 820, **10:** 1085, **12:** 1438
Johnson, Alphonso **13:** 1532
Johnson, Ann and Enotris **2:** 149
Johnson, Bill **7:** 788
Johnson, Bob **13:** 1472-3
Johnson, Brian **19:** 2227-8, *2228*
Johnson, Bryan **17:** 1955
Johnson, Budd **3:** 273
Johnson, Curtis **1:** 112
Johnson, Dwight J. **14:** 1598
Johnson, Gerald **11:** 1227
Johnson, Holly **20:** *2414,* 2415
Johnson, James P. **2:** 179
Johnson, J. J. **11:** 1237
Johnson, Jimmy **16:** 1843
Johnson, Johnny **1:** 66
Johnson, Linton Kwesi **19:** 2216
Johnson, Lonnie **2:** 125, **5:** 585
Johnson, Louis **9:** 1039
Johnson, Mary **4:** *470,* 472, 477, **9:** 1045
Johnson, Pete, **1:** 39, **3:** 273
Johnson, Plas **2:** 198, 248, **4:** 389, 394, **11:** 1237
Johnson, Ralph **7:** 795, **19:** 2163
Johnson, Robert **5:** 582, **6:** 679-80, **12:** 1372, **18:** 2103
Johnson, Skip **8:** 913
Johnson, Teddy **17:** 1955
Johnson, Wild Willie **2:** 159
Johnson, Wilko **4:** 435, **17:** *1923,* 1928-9, *1929,* 1933
Johnston, Bob **10:** 1128, **11:** 1207, 1209, **13:** 1475
Johnston, Bruce **7:** *763,* 766, 772, 778-9, *779,* 780
Johnston, Tom **16:** *1825,* **17:** 1951, *1951,* 1952
Johnstone, Davey **14:** 1667, *1668,* **18:** 2124
Jo Jo Gunne **14:** 1615

Jolley, Steve **16:** 1902
Jon and the Nightriders **4:** 392
Jones, Allen **8:** 952-3
Jones, Brian **1:** *17,* **2:** 194, **6:** 645, 680, **8:** 881-900, **10:** 1099, **12:** 1335
Jones, Davey **1:** 12, **6:** 686, **9:** 983, *987-91*
Jones, David *see* Bowie, David
Jones, Eddie **3:** 325
Jones, Floyd **4:** 465
Jones, George **2:** 234, **15:** 1649, 1659, **17:** 2025
Jones, Gloria **12:** 1440
Jones, Grace **20:** 2281, *2298-2300,* 2156
Jones, Graham **20:** 2384
Jones, Hoppy **1:** 69, 70
Jones, Howard **20:** 2301, 2405
Jones, Jimmy **5:** 501
Jones, John Paul **6:** *642,* 653, **7:** 760, **11:** 1230, **12:** 1364, *1366-7,* 1368, **15:** 1724
Jones, Kenney **7:** 806-9, *806,* **11:** *1267, 1269,* 1277, **15:** 1725
Jones, LeRoy **7:** 782, **12:** 1322
Jones, Linda **15:** 1782-3
Jones, Max **5:** 584
Jones, Mick (Clash) **18:** 2066-8, *2067,* 2069, 2078
Jones, Mick (Foreigner) **18:** 2121, 2132-3, *2132*
Jones, Mickey **11:** 1209, **14:** 1647
Jones, Morgan **4:** 423
Jones, Nat **7:** 791
Jones, Neil **8:** 952-3
Jones, Palmer **15:** 1785
Jones, Paul **5:** *565,* 582, *589,* **6:** *625, 627-8, 641,* 643, 644-7, *644-5, 649,* 654-5, **8:** *846,* 847-8, **9:** 1022, **10:** 1188, **20:** 2338
Jones, Quincy **3:** 324, 328, **14:** 1584-5, **15:** 1791, **19:** 2167
Jones, Ray **5:** 583
Jones, Rickie Lee **18:** 2096-7
Jones, Rob **19:** 2219
Jones, Ronnie **5:** 588
Jones, Sammy **9:** 973
Jones, Shirley **3:** 301, **8:** *843,* **13:** 1502, 1517
Jones, Steve **11:** 1280, **18:** *2041,* 2045, 2048, 2145, 2151
Jones, Tom **5:** 599, **7:** *721-2,* 722-3, 735, 736-7, 740, **8:** 847, **9:** 984, **10:** 1194-5
Jones, Uriel **6:** 716, **9:** 1057
Jones, Will 'Dub' **3:** *294, 295,* 296
Jones, Wornell **16:** *1846,* 1847
Jonzun Crew **20:** 2303
Joplin, Janis **1:** 15-16, *17,* **3:** 312, **8:** 848, 909, 915, 919, **9:** 1002, 1020, **10:** 1083, 1093, 1099-1100, *1100,* 1170-3, **11:** 1251, **14:** 1650, **18:** 2096, 2158
Joplin, Scott **2:** 178
Jopling, Norman **12:** 1327, *1328*
Jordan **18:** *2041, 2052,* 2054, **20:** 2323, *2328*
Jordan, Cyril **20:** 2288, *2288*
Jordan, Fred **15:** 1786
Jordan, Louis **1:** 22, *22,* 33-5, **3:** 322, *322,* 338

Jordan, Peter **16:** 1879
Jordanaires **1:** 87, 94, *94,* **4:** 406, 415
Josef K **19:** 2273
Joseph And The Amazing Technicolor Dreamcoat **20:** 2337, 2338
Journey **13:** 1535, **18:** 2121, *2121,* 2128
Journeymen **7:** *823,* 838
Journey Through The Past **15:** 1770
'Journey To The Centre Of The Earth' **15:** 1697
Joy Of Cooking **8:** 914
Joy Division **18:** 2060, 2141, **20:** *2266,* 2266-9, *2268*
Joye, Col **18:** 2105
Jubilee **20:** 2321, 2323, 2328, *2328,* 2334
Judas Jump **8:** 953, 955
Judas Priest **17:** 1982-3, 1988-2000, *2000*
Juice on the Loose **17:** 1925
'Juke Box Jury' **4:** *379,* 380, **8:** 849, *849*
Julian, Ivan **17:** 2012, *2013*
Jumping Jacks **6:** 708
June Sultans **9:** 975
Junior *see* Giscombe, Junior
Junior, Bobby **19:** 2218
'Juno and Avas' **20:** *2377*
Jurgens, Udo **9:** 1055
Just A Gigolo **14:** 1629
Just For Fun **5:** 497, **8:** 844
Juste, Samantha **8:** 850, *850*
Justice, Jimmy **4:** 423
Justis, Bill **2:** 147

K

Kabaka, Remi **9:** 1031, **10:** 1189
Kabassele **20:** 2378
Kaegi, Adriana **20:** 2295, *2297*
Kaempfert, Bert **6:** 700
Kagan, Harvey **7:** 835
Kahl, Phil **2:** 192
Kahn, Steve **12:** 1322
Kajagoogoo **20:** 2325, *2381*
Kakoulli, Harry **19:** 2256, *2256*
Kalb, Danny **8:** 864
Kale, James **14:** 1616-17, *1616*
Kaleidoscope **8:** 903, **12:** 1390
Kalin, Twins **2:** 237, 240, **3:** 270, **4:** 385, **7:** 727
Kaminski, Mick **15:** 1747, 1748, 1749, *1749*
Kane, Arthur **16:** 1863, 1879, *1879, 1880*
Kane, Eden **2:** 139, **4:** 362, 372, 423, 427, **7:** 721
Kant, Rip **10:** 1114
Kantner, Paul **8:** 909-13, *910*
Kapp, Paul **5:** 570
Kapner, Mark **10:** 1097
Kapralik, David **12:** 1406
Karen, Kenny **4:** 444
Karn, Mick **11:** 1280, 1296, *1297, 1280,* **20:** 2342, 2355-6, 2357

Karoli, Michael **20:** 2367
Karpin, Peter **20:** 2372
Karstein, Jim **9:** 1036
Kasenetz, Jerry **9:** 981, 983, 995, 997-1000, *999*
Kashif **18:** 2103
Kath, Terry **13:** 1526-8, *1528*
Katz, Jeff **9:** 981, 983, 995, 997-1000, *999*
Katzman, Sam **2:** 207, 210, **13:** *1538,* **16:** 1901, 1919
Katz, Gary **16:** 1919
Katz, Steve **13:** 1539
Katzenjammer **17:** 1922
Kaufman, Phil **13:** 1557
Kaukonen, Jorma **8:** 909-13, *910-12*
Kavanaugh, Kevin **18:** 2092
Kay, John **10:** 1072, *1072*
Kaye, Carol **4:** 472, **5:** 520, 574, **6:** 717, **9:** 1039, *1039,* **18:** 2071
Kaye, Lenny **17:** 2019
Kaye, Sydney M. **4:** 460
Kaye, Tony **4:** 396, *396,* **15:** *1690,* 1691, 1692, 1697
Kaylan, Howard **8:** 992-3, *992-3,* **12:** 1439, **13:** 1495, *1496*
Kozohiko, Katoh **20:** 2364
Kazohiko, Mike **20:** 2365
Kazumi Watanabe **20:** 2365
KC and the Sunshine Band **16:** 1894
Keating, Johnny **4:** 362, 423
Keeble, John **20:** *2346,* 2347
Keef Hartley Band **10:** 1102, **11:** 1256
Keefe, Barry **20:** 2340
Keele Folk Festival **11:** 1245
Keen **5:** 502
Keen Records **3:** 334, *334*
Keene, Bob **2:** 196, 197, **3:** 334, **5:** 502, *502*
Keep It Cool **3:** 308, 309
Keep, Theodore **5:** 502
Kefford, Chris ('Ace') **10:** 1183, 1185
Keister, Marion **1:** 52
Keita, Salif **20:** 2379
Keith, Bill **7:** 822
Keith, Gordon **14:** 1583
Kekuku, Joseph **14:** 1656
Keld and the Donkeys **6:** 700
Keller, Jack **9:** 988
Kelley, Alton **12:** 1389-90
Kelley, Kevin **7:** *827, 829,* 830, **11:** 1237, *1237*
Kellie, Mike **10:** 1168, **17:** 1981, **18:** 2133
Kelly, Betty **6:** 717
Kelly, Brian **5:** 522, 523
Kelly, Pat **16:** 1887
Kelly Four **3:** 248
Keltner, Jim **17:** 1973
Kemp, Gary **20:** 2343, *2346,* 2347-8
Kemp, Gibson **5:** 540
Kemp, Lindsay **14:** 1625, **20:** 2331, 2339
Kemp, Martin **11:** *1306,* **20:** *2346,* 2347
Kemp, Rick **13:** 1472-3
Ken Colyer Band **4:** 439, 440
Keni, Inoue **20:** 2365
Ken Jones Orchestra **4:** 366
Kendricks, Eddie **1:** 62, **4:** 478, **6:** *718,* 719,

9: 1045, *1050,* 1050-2, *1052*
Kenn, Sonny **18:** 2092
Kennedy, Jackie **5:** 498, *500*
Kennedy, John **2:** *130,* 131, **12:** *1381*
Kennelly, Jack **4:** 414
Kenner, Roy **14:** 1613
Kennibrew, Dee Dee **5:** 514
Kenny, Bill **1:** 69
Kent, Nick **12:** *1328*
Kenton, Rick **16:** *1804,* 1807
Kentucky Colonels **8:** 905
Keranen, Grey 'Curly' **17:** 2017
Kerouac, Jack **3:** 340, **8:** 919, *919,* **12:** 1357, **18:** 2094-5
Kerr, Jim **19:** 2274, *2274*
Kershaw, Nik **20:** 2405
Kershaw Brothers **13:** 1455
Kerslake, Lee **15:** 1729
Kesey, Ken **1:** 15 **8:** 906, 919, *919,* and his Merry Pranksters **12:** *1383*
Kesler, Stan **1:** 115
Kessel, Barney **5:** 520, *520*
Kestrels **5:** 492
Kevin Ayers Band **19:** 2184
Kevin Coyne Band **19:** 2184
Keys, Bobby **8:** 894, **17:** 1976
KGB **11:** 1240
Khan, Chaka **13:** 1560, **15:** 1791, **20:** 2405, 2413, 2419
Khan, Morgan **20:** 2394
Khouri, Ken **9:** 961, 973, 975-6, 978
Kid Creole and the Coconuts **18:** 2103, **20:** 2281, *2294,* 2295-7
Kidd, Johnny **2:** 194, **4:** 362, 367, 421, 424, 434-5, **12:** 1377
Kid Galahad **1:** *212,* 214
Kid Lightning **11:** 1227
Kids Are Alright, The **11:** 1273, 1275, **14:** 1680
Kids From Fame **13:** *1502*
Kid Stormy Weather **2:** 154
Kihn, Greg **15:** 1763
Kilburn and the High Roads **17:** 1922, 1924, *1925,* 1930
Kilgore, Jerry **3:** 355
Kilkenny, Giorgio **19:** 2220
Killen, Buddy **7:** 796-7
Killing Joke **12:** 1372, *1372*
Kill Me Tomorrow **4:** 430
Kilminster, Ian 'Lemmy' **17:** 1996-7, *1997,* **19:** 2238-9, *2239*
Kilm, Andy **9:** *999,* 1000
Kimberlys **14:** 1654
King **18:** 2080
King, Alan **7:** 818-19
King, Albert **8:** 930, **10:** *1101,* 1103, 1114, **11:** 1238, 1293, *1293*
King, Andrew **11:** 1304, 1308
King, B. B. **1:** *30,* 35, 45, **3:** 322, 337, 339, **4:** 446, **7:** 799-800, *800,* **9:** 1065, **10:** 1102, *1102,* 1107, 1108-11, **11:** 1221, 1253, **12:** *1346,* **17:** 1976, **19:** 2175
King, Bam **17:** 1925
King, Ben E. **1:** 72, **3:** 266, 281, 283, 288, 290, 291, *291,* 292, **4:** 446, 459, **5:** 488-

9, 507
King, Bill **10:** 1172
King, Bobby **13:** 1560
King, Carole **3:** 265, *266,* 288, 292, 312, **4:** 403, 441, 443, 444, 447, 449, 452, 453, 457, 458, 459, **5:** 481, 488, 489, 513, 514, 567, 579, **7:** 723, **8:** 879, **9:** 981, 982, 988, 990, **10:** 1109, 1153, **11:** 1220, **12:** 1341, *1360,* **14:** 1650, **15:** *1701,* 1702, 1708, 1710, 1713, 1714-15, 1789
King, Clydie **1:** 90, **2:** 201, 204, 208, 211, **3:** 255, 256
King, Curtis **3:** 254, 265, 274, 282, 288, 296, *297,* **4:** 389
King, Danny **10:** 1181
King, Earl **13:** 1455
King, Ed **16:** 1843, 1844
King, Freddie **10:** 1102-3, *1103,* 1114, **11:** 1221
King, Jack **11:** 1227
King, Jim **10:** 1198-9, *1198*
King, Jon **19:** *2262*
King, Jonathan **6:** *675,* 676-7, **8:** 958-60, **13:** 1511, 1515, **15:** 1752, **16:** 1822, 1914, 1915
King, Martin Luther **6:** *679,* **7:** *781,* 782, 783
King, Maurice **7:** 716
King, Reggie **7:** 818-19
King, Sid **4:** 414
King, Simon **17:** 1997
King, Solomon **17:** 1958
King, William **18:** 2117
King Bees **14:** 1625, *1625*
King Biscuit Entertainers **1:** *57*
King Crimson **12:** 1398, **14:** *1561,* 1563, 1564-7, 1633, 1639, **15:** 1687, 1692, 1729, 1737, 1740, 1742, 1757, **16:** 1802, **18:** 2121, 2133
King-Federal **3:** 330, 331
Kingfishers **6:** 613-14 *see also* Freddie and the Dreamers
Kingham, Lionel **7:** *810,* 811
King Kong **9:** 966
King Oliver's Jazz Band **2:** *141*
King Radio **7:** 744-5
King Records **3:** 337, **4:** 463
King, Tim III **19:** 2177
Kingston Trio **5:** 574, **6:** 661, 662, 667, 668-9
King, Tubby **16:** *1897,* 1898, 1900
Kinks **1:** 6, **6:** 603, 657, 658, **7:** 724, *724,* 742, 750-6, 757, 758, 802, **8:** *851,* 880, 941-2, 944, **9:** 1010, 1029, **10:** 1102
Kirby, Kathy **4:** 386, **17:** 1955, *1955*
Kircher, Pete **15:** *1733,* 1735
Kirchins **2:** 122
Kirk, Roland **14:** 1563
Kirke, Simon **15:** 1738, 1739, *1739,* 1740
Kirkland, James **3:** 303
Kirkland, Leroy **2:** 174
Kirkpatrick, John **13:** 1473
Kirshner, Don **1:** 13, **3:** 265, *265,* 266, *266,* 345, **4:** 441-4, 447, 448, 449, 450, 451, 457, 458, 459, **5:** 489, 501, 508, 509,

567, 569, **9:** 981-3, 988-9, 999, 1000, **10:** 1119-20, *1119,* **15:** 1714-5
Kirwan, Danny **10:** *1133*
Kiss **14:** 1601, **15:** 1720, **16:** *1861,* 1862, 1863, 1868-71, 1879, **17:** 2026
Klein, Allen **3:** 343, **5:** 555, 557, **6:** 694, **8:** 891, 893, 896-7, *896,* **10:** 1151, 1156, 1159-60, *1159*
Kleinbard, Annette **5:** 506, *506,* 567
Kleinow, Sneaky Pete **10:** 1168, **12:** 1346, **13:** 1556, **14:** 1657
'Kleptomania', Carnaby Street **7:** *748,* 749
Klimt, Gustav **11:** *1294*
Klingman, Mark 'Moogy' **16:** 1905
Klymaxx **19:** *2179,* 2180
KMA radio station **1:** 57
Knack **15:** 1763, **16:** 1823, **20:** 2289, *2289*
Knack, The **8:** 847, 855
Knape, Skip **16:** 1856
Knebworth Festival **11:** 1243, 1248, *1248,* 1260, **13:** *1478-9,* 1479
Knechtel, Larry **5:** 519, **6:** 675, **7:** 829
Knickerbockers **6:** 682, **8:** *871*
Knight, Baker **3:** 303, 304
Knight, Curtis **9:** 1065, 1069
Knight, Frederick **8:** 922, 933
Knight, Gladys **6:** 719, **7:** 740, **9:** 1042, 1043, 1057,14: 1581, *1581,* 1584, 1586-7, 1042-3, 1057
Knight, Graham **8:** 947, *947,* 949
Knight, Jean **8:** 933
Knight, Larry **14:** 1615
Knight, Peter **3:** 351, **6:** 632, **10:** 1195, **13:** 1472-3
Knight, Ritchie **6:** 682
Knight, Steve **14:** *1606,* 1606-7
Knight, Terry **8:** *871,* 872, **14:** 1601, 1609-11
Knight, Tony **5:** 588
Knights, David **10:** 1087-8
Knopfler, David **11:** *1218,* 1220, **19:** 2199, *2200*
Knopfler, Mark **11:** *1218,* 1220, **19:** 2182, *2198-9.* 2199-2000
Knox, Buddy **1:** 102, **2:** 183, *183,* 185, 186, 190, 192-3, 200
Knudsen, Keith **16:** 1851, *1853*
Kodomo Band **20:** 2365
Koerner, Spider John **6:** 662
Kohn, Phil **14:** 1576
Kojo **17:** *1956*
Kokomo **17:** 1924
Kolber, Larry **4:** 443
Komoritz, Ronnie **14:** 1601
Kong, Leslie **9:** 971, 973, 976-7, 978, **16:** 1886, 1889, 1890
Kool and the Gang **18:** 2103, *2108,* 2109, **20:** 2418
Kooper, Al **1:** 64-5, **6:** 690, **9:** 1068, **10:** 1188, **11:** 1221, 1223, *1238,* 1239-40, *1240,* **13:** 1509, 1539, *1539,* **15:** 1699, 1793, **16:** 1843, 1847, **17:** 1973
Koos, Lord **9:** 975
Koppelma, Charlie **8:** 867, **9:** 993

Kopter **14:** 1615
Korner, Alexis **2:** 128, **4:** 454, **5:** *583,* 584, *584,* 585-7, *586,* 588, 598, 600, **6:** 642, 655, **8:** 889, **9:** 1027, **10:** 1102, 1109, 1112, **12:** 1387, **13:** 1476, **15:** 1738-9
Kornfeld, Artie **11:** 1250-1
Kortchmar, Danny 'Kootch' **8:** 864, **15:** 1707, 1715
Korum, Bob **4:** 457
Koschmider, Bruno **5:** 538, 548
Kossoff, Paul **15:** 1738, 1739, *1739,* 1740
Kowalski, Ted **2:** 235
Kozmic Clues Band **10:** 1172
Kraftwerk **6:** 700, **20:** 2301, 2301-12, *2310, 2312,* 2362, 2367
Kral, Ivan **17:** 2019
Kramer, Barry **12:** 1330
Kramer, Billy J. **5:** 523, 527, 532-4, *532, 535,* 537, 538, 551, *565,* **6:** 639, **7:** 729
Kramer, Joeyn **16:** 1849
Kramer, Wayne **13:** *1487,* 1488-9, *1489*
Krantz, Dale **16:** 1844
Kraus, Peter **3:** *249,* 260
Krause, Dagmar **14:** 1569
Krause, David **16:** 1848, 1849
Kresnow, Bob **13:** 1484
Kreutzmann, Bill **8:** *904-5,* 905-6, 908
Krieger, Robby **1:** 19, **9:** 1010, *1012,* 1013
Kriss, Tom **14:** *1612,* 1613
Kristal, Hilly **17:** 2001, 2007, 2011, 2012
Kristina, Sonja **14:** 1575-6, *1575, 1577,* **18:** *2076,* **19:** 2184
Krisftofferson, Kris **1:** 18, **3:** 320, **14:** 1650-2, 1659-60, **17:** 2023, 2025
Krokus **19:** *2223*
KROQ-RM radio station **20:** 2281
Krugman, Murray **18:** 2126
Kubert, Joe **10:** 1178
Kubota **20:** 2365
Kunkel, Russ **15:** *1767,* **16:** 1857
Kunze, Michael **18:** 2120, *2120,* **20:** 2362
Kupferberg, Tuli **1:** 19, **8:** *864,* 865, **9:** *1014,* 1015
Kursaal Flyers **17:** 1924
Kustow, Danny **18:** 2146-7, **19:** 2248
Kuti, Fela Anikulapo **9:** *962,* 963-4, *964,* 965-6, 1031, **20:** 2378
Kweskin Jug Band **7:** *822*

L

Labat, Jaques-Yves **16:** 1905
LaBeef, Sleepy **1:** *102,* 103, 113, **2:** 160
Label Records **18:** 2156
LaBelle **12:** 1402, *1415-17, 1419*
LaBelle, Patti **12:** *1415, 1415-16,* 1416, 1417, **15:** 1786
Labelled With Love **19:** 2257, **20:** 2340
Labes, Jeff **13:** 1552, 1553
Lady Sings The Blues **4:** *461,* **9:** 1042, **14:**

1590, 1592, *1593*
LA Express **15:** 1763
La Farge, Peter **14:** 1644
Lagin, Ned **8:** 908
Laguna, Kenny **9:** 983, *983*
Laidlaw, Ray **13:** 1475, *1475*
Laine, Cleo **11:** 1245
Laine, Denny **9:** 1031, **10:** 1183, 1185, 1189, 1193-4, *1193,* **17:** 1963-4, *1964,* 1966
Laine, Frankie **1:** 37
Laing, Corky **14:** *1606,* 1606-8
Laing, Dave **2:** 195, **12:** 1324-5, **14:** 1622
Laird, Rick **13:** 1524-5
Lake, Greg **14:** 1546, *1565,* **15:** 1687-8, *1688,* 1728
Lamb, Bob **19:** 2214
Lambert, Dennis **6:** 713
Lambert, Kit **5:** 535, **7:** 758, 816, **9:** 1065-6, **11:** 1265-7, 1273, 1275-7, *1276,* 1279
Lamble, Martin **13:** *1464,* 1465
Lamm, Robert **13:** 1526-8, *1528*
Lampell, Willard **6:** 667
Lana Sisters **7:** 730
Lancaster, Alan **15:** *1730,* 1731, 1732, *1733*
Lance, Major **5:** 482, **9:** 1059-60
Landau, Jon **12:** 1325, 1335, **13:** 1488, **15:** 1780
Landlord, The **15:** 1793
Landray, Jeanette **18:** 2151
Landscape **20:** 2381
Landy, Dr Eugene **7:** 777
Lane, Brian **15:** 1691
Lane, Ronnie **7:** 760, 806-9, *806, 809,* **13:** 1479, **15:** *1724,* 1725, 1726, 1740
Lane, Steve **4:** 439
Lang, Don **2:** 134, *134,* 135, **4:** 378, 430
Lang, Michael **11:** 1250-51
Lange, Robert John 'Mutt' **18:** 2133, **19:** 2227, 2237
Langer, Clive **16:** 1902, *1902,* **19:** 2278
Langford, Bonnie **19:** *2237*
Langhorne, Bruce **11:** 1207
Langstaff, Malcolm **15:** 1686
Langton, Huw Lloyd **17:** 1997
Lanier, Allen **17:** 2019, **18:** 2125-6, *2126*
Lanier, Don **2:** 192, 193
Lansdowne Studio **4:** 436, 437
LaPraed, Ronald **18:** 2117
Larden, Denis **3:** *305*
Lardies **2:** 139
Larkey, Charles **9:** 1015, **15:** 1715
Larks **1:** 71, **5:** 483
Larson, Nicolette **15:** 1770, **16:** 1860
LaSalle, Denise **15:** 1783
Lasers **20:** 2314
Last, Bob **20:** 2307
Last, James **6:** 700, **17:** *1942*
Last Exit **19:** 2184
Last Heard **16:** 1856
Last Movie, The **14:** 1652
Last Waltz, The **13:** 1548-9
Lateef, Yusef **7:** 783
Latham, Laurie **19:** 2257

Lauderdale, Jack **3:** 324
Lauper, Cyndi **20:** *2401,* 2405
Laurence, Lynda **9:** 1049
Laurie, Annie **2:** 153, 154
Laurie, Steve **18:** 2147
Lavis, Gilson **19:** 2256, *2257*
Law, Don **2:** 234, *234*
Lawes, Henry 'Junjo' **20:** 2374
Lawrence, Derek **15:** 1737
Lawrence, Vicki **5:** 575
Lawrie, Marie **8:** 947
Laws, Hubert **19:** 2173
Laws, Ronnie **19:** 2163, 2175
Lawton, John **15:** 1729
Lay, Sam **13:** 1498
Lea, Jimmy **12:** 1427-8
Leacox, Willie **15:** 1777
Leadbelly (Huddie Ledbetter) **2:** 125, 127, 159, **6:** 661, *662,* 667, 678, **11:** 1237
Leadbitter, Mike **12:** 1338
Leadon, Bernie **15:** 1772, 1773, 1774
League of Gentlemen **14:** 1567
Leahy, Dick **13:** 1510-11
Leander, Mike **3:** 292, **12:** 1430-1, **16:** 1822
Leandros, Vicky **17:** 1955, 1956
Leaner, George **9:** 1060
Lear, Amanda **16:** *1806,* 1810
Leary, Timothy **12:** 1382, *1382,* 1399
Leary, Vinny **8:** 865, **9:** 1015
Leavell, Chuck **14:** 1604-5
Leaves **8:** 872, *873,* **9:** 993, 1017
LeBon, Simon **20:** *2388,* 2389, *2390,* 2391, *2391*
Leber, Steve **16:** 1848, 1849
Leckenby, Derek **6:** 685
Led Zeppelin **1:** 16, **3:** 261, *271,* **5:** 582, **6:** *642,* 653, **7:** 760, **9:** *1023,* 1071, **10:** 1164, **11:** *1248, 1253, 1255,* 1257, 1266, *1284,* 1295, **12:** 1341, 1361, 1362-8, 1369, 1373, **13:** 1467, 1479, **15:** 1742, 1749, **17:** 1981, 1982, 1999, **18:** 2133, 2221-2, **20:** 2321, 2364
Lee, Adrian **20:** 2335
Lee, Albert **2:** *229,* **6:** 642, **7:** 814, 815, **9:** 1036, *1037,* **10:** 1168, **13:** 1560, **15:** 1779, **17:** 2025
Lee, Alvin **10:** 1102, 1107, **11:** *1253,* **12:** 1374-5, *1374-5,* **15:** 1721
Lee, Arthur **9:** 1010, 1016-17
Lee, Brenda **2:** 234, 240, **3:** *253,* 301, 311, 312, *312,* 318, 319-20, **4:** *454,* **6:** *619,* **8:** 879
Lee, Bunny **16:** 1898
Lee, Byron **9:** 962, *962,* 971, 978
Lee, Curtis **5:** 507
Lee, Dee C. **20:** 2405, 2419, *2420*
Lee, Dickey **5:** 575
Lee, Geddy **9:** 2234, 2235, *2236*
Lee, Julia **1:** 30
Lee, Laura **15:** 1782
Lee, Ric **12:** 1374-5
Leeds, Gary **8:** *942,* 956-7
Leeds, Peter **20:** 2293
Leek, Andde **19:** 2219

LeFevre, Mylon **10:** 1162, **12:** 1375
Leffler, Ed **16:** 1836
Legacy, The **11:** 1275
Le Gaire, Rich **9:** 1031
Legon, Freddy **2:** 125
Le Graff, Jack **2:** 218
Leib, Marshall **5:** 506, *506,* **7:** 734
Leiber, Jerry **1:** 71, **2:** 200, **3:** 265-6, 269, 272, 275, 280, 292, 295, **4:** 401, **9:** 982, 1000, 1054, **10:** 1089, 1107
Leiber, Jerry and Stoller, Mike **2:** 200, **3:** 265, 269, 272, 275, 280, 282, *282-3,* 286-9, 291, 292, 293, 294-6, *296,* **4:** 444, 447, 449, 459, 462, **5:** 507-8, 567, 578-9, **6:** 605, **10:** 1107, **12:** 1357
Leibovitz, Annie **12:** 1333
Leigh, Geoff **14:** *1568,* 1569
LeMaistre, Malcolm **13:** 1470
Lemmy **16:** *1824,* **18:** 2080, **19:** 2238-9, *2239-40,*
Lennon, Cynthia **10:** *1148*
Lennon, John **1:** 4-5, 8, 110, **2:** 127, *128,* 156, 195, 249-50, **4:** 416, 418, 433, **5:** 512, 533, 534, 536, 538, 541-60, **6:** 637, 640, **8:** 847, 854-7, 859, 891, 893, **9:** 1020, 1035, 1074, 1077, **10:** 1141-60, **11:** 1201, 1218, 1245, *1292,* 1297, *1298,* **12:** 1325, 1332, 1333, *1333,* 1335, 1358, 1397, 1398, 1399, 1400, **13:** 1495, **14:** 1628, 1633, 1679, **15:** 1681, 1692, 1703, 1710, 1718, 1737, 1748, 1479, **16:** 1810, **17:** 1961, 1963, 1964, 1967, 1968, 1969, 1970-4, 1980, **19:** 2265
Lennon, Sean **17:** *1974*
Lennox, Annie **14:** *1623,* **20:** *2359,* 2360, 2381, *2386,* 2386-7, *2387*
Lenny and the Thundertones **4:** 390, **20:** 2413, 2419
Lenoir, J. B. **4:** 465
Leon, Craig **7:** 835, **17:** 2011
Leonard, Glen **9:** 1052
Leone, Dave **16:** 1830
Lesh, Phil **8:** *904-5,* 905-6, 908, **9:** 1039
Leslei Ewst Band **18:** 2133
Leslie, Peter **4:** 440
Lester, Bobby **1:** 73
Lester, Richard **4:** 431, 433, 440, **8:** 844, 845, 847, 854-6, *856,* **9:** 982, 987, **10:** 1149
Let It Be **8:** *856,* 857, **10:** 1158, 1160, **15:** 1797
'Let It Rock **13:** 1515
Let's Do It Again **15:** 1793
Let The Good Times Roll In **2:** 207, **5:** 587
Letitt, Peter **2:** 235
Letts, Don **13:** 1502, **18:** *2060,* 2061, **20:** 2359
Levan, Larry **19:** 2169
Level '42 **19:** 2164, **20:** 2392-3, *2394*
Levene, Gary **10:** 1193
Levert, Eddie **14:** 1600, *1600*
Levin, Drake 'The Kid' **7:** 832-3
Levin, Tony **14:** 1567, *1567,* **15:** 1757
Levine, Joey **9:** 983, 997-8, *998,* 999
Levine, Keith **18:** 2048, 2067

Levine, Steve **20:** 2397
Levine, Stewart **10:** 1110
Levy, Jacques **7:** 831, **11:** 1211
Levy, Leeds **5:** *563*
Levy, Len **9:** 1060
Levy, Marcy **9:** 1036, *1037,* **16:** 1856
Levy, Michael **13:** 1514
Levy, Morris **2:** 192, **17:** 1973
Lewis, Bunny **4:** *362,* 363, 374, 375, 421
Lewis, Danny **14:** 1655
Lewis, Frankie Jean **2:** 166, *168*
Lewis, Gary **13:** 1444
Lewis, Jack **3:** 246
Lewis, Jerry Lee **1:** 2, 12, 35, *41, 46,* 47, *54,* 110, 118, **2:** 149, 156, 160, 161, *161, 162,* 163, 164, 165, 166-72, 178, 179, 180, 184, 202, 204, 205, *205,* 209, 217, **3:** 242, 247, 250, 252, 254, **7:** 739, **8:** 887, **9:** 990, 1021, **10:** 1116, 1162, 1168, **11:** 1300, **12:** 1335, 1384, 1434, **13:** 1444, **15:** 1698
Lewis, Ken **10:** 1085
Lewis, Kenny Lee **11:** 1227
Lewis, Lew **6:** 655
Lewis, Meade 'Lux' **2:** 179, *180*
Lewis, Mingo **13:** *1537*
Lewis, Myra Gale **2:** *168,* 169, 171
Lewis, Ramsey **4:** 467, **13:** 1521, **19:** 2162, 2164
Lewis, Rudy **3:** 290, 292, *293*
Lewis, Sir Edward **8:** 960
Lewis, Smiley **2:** 149, 154, **3:** 339
Lewis, Vic **1:** *27* **5:** 557
Ley Rochareau, Tabu **20:** 2378, 2379
Leyen, Klaas **18:** 2118
Leyton, John **4:** 427, 437, 440, **7:** 721, **8:** 844
Liberty Records **3:** 247, 248, **4:** 418, **5:** 502-3, **7:** 734-5, 766
Lichtenstein, Roy **5:** 498
Lidyard, Jess **20:** 2314
Lieberzeit, Jackie **20:** 2367, 2386
Lifeson, Alex **19:** 2234, *2236*
Lifetime **9:** 1032, *1032,* **13:** 1523
Lifehouse **11:** 1275, 1279
Ligertwood, Alex **13:** *1537*
Liggins, Jimmy & Joe **1:** 30
Lightfoot, Gordon **10:** 1124, *1124*
Lijadu Sisters **20:** *2379*
Lillywhite, Steve **16:** 1902, *1902,* **18:** 2151
Limahl **20:** *2381*
Limeliters **6:** 662
Lincoln, Paul **2:** 135
Lind, Bob **6:** *676,* 677, **10:** 1124
Lindes, Hal **19:** *2199,* 2200
Lindisfarne **13:** 1462, *1462-3,* 1474-5
Lindley, David **15:** 1779, 1780
Lindo, Earl 'Wia' **16:** 1893
Lindsay, Mark **7:** *832,* 832-3
Lindsay-Hogg, Michael **8:** 857, **10:** 1158
Lindsey, Steve **19:** 2278
Linn County **8:** 915
Linson, Art **16:** 1847
Linx **20:** *2392,* 2393
Lipsius, Fred **13:** 1539, *1539*

LiPuma, Tommy **19:** 2167
Liquorice **12:** *1340*
Lisberg, Harvey **16:** 1914, 1915
Lissauer, John **12:** 1351
Lissitzsky, Lazar El **11:** 1294, *1294*
Lisztomania **11:** 1275, **15:** 1697
Litter **14:** 1601
Little Anthony and the Imperials **4:** 452
Little Eva **2:** 240, **3:** *266,* 269, **4:** 447, **5:** 483, 488-9, 567
Little Fauss And Big Halsy **2:** 111
Little Feat **16:** 1841, 1858-60
Little Gerhard **3:** 251
Little Glimsted **3:** 251
Little John **8:** 914
Little Milton **9:** 1059
Little Richard **1:** 27, 30, 35, 81, 100, **2:** 141, 142, 145, 146, 148-52, 153, 154-5, 156, 161, 163,164, 165, 178, 179, *179,* 180, *180,* 184, 205, 207, 208, *209,* 217, 222, 225, 240, **3:** 242, 249, 251, 262, *263,* 327, 338, **5:** 502, **8:** 924, **9:** 978, 990, 1021, 1058, 1065, 1069, **11:** 1203, **12:** 1433, **13:** 1449, **15:** 1698, 1797, **16:** 1863
Little River Band **20:** 2371, *2371*
Little Sophus **3:** 251
Little Tony **3:** 243, *250,* 251
Little Walter **3:** 339, **4:** 464, *465,* 466, 467, **5:** 593, 595, **6:** 654, *654*
Little Willie John **3:** 322, 336-7
Little Wilton **9:** 1059
Littlefield, Little Willie **1:** 30, **2:** 145, **3:** 287
Littlejohn, Johnny **2:** 168, 169
Live Aid **19:** 2248, 2251, **20:** 2402-3, *2412- 13, 2418*
Live At Pompeii **11:** 1316-17, *1317,* **20:** 2326
Liverbirds **5:** 523, *540*
Liverpool Scene **10:** 1103
Livingstone, Bunny & Dandy **1:** 10 *see also* Wailer, Bunny
Lizard **20:** *2365*
Llewellyn, Barry **16:** 1886
Lloyd, Richard **17:** *2005-6,* 2007-8
Lloyd Webber, Andrew **15:** 1742 **20:** *2336,* 2336-7
Loading Zone **8:** 914
Lobo **13:** 1556
Locke, John **14:** 1614-15, *1615,* **17:** *1988,* 1989
Locking, Brian 'Liquorice' **4:** 387, *387,* 388, **17:** 1953
Lockwood, Robert Jr **1:** 56
Locomotion **5:** 483, 488-9
Lodge, John **10:** 1193-4, 1195-6, *1195-6*
Loewenstein, Prince Rupert **8:** 897, 900
Lofgren, Nils **16:** 1841, 1845-7, **18:** 2086
Lofgren, Tom **16:** *1846,* 1847
Logan, Harold **2:** 156, *156,* 157
Logan, Johnny **17:** 1957
Logan, Nick **12:** 1325, **19:** 2258, 2259, 2260
Loggins, Kenny **16:** 1852, **20:** 2420
Loggins and Messina **13:** *1544*

Logic, Laura **18:** 2061, *2071,* 2072
Logic, Lory **18:** 2061, *2070,* 2071
Lomax, Alan **2:** 124, 125, 127, **5:** 585, 592, **6:** 667, 678, *679,* 680, **11:** 1207
Lomax, Jackie **10:** 1151, 1158
Lomax, John and Alan **6:** 661, 667, 678-9, *679,* 680
London, Julie **2:** 208
London, Laurie **2:** 134, 204, *204,* **3:** 269, **4:** 433
London SS **18:** 2078
London Symphony Orchestra **15:** 1683, 1687, 1742
Lonesome Sundown **3:** 339
Lone Star **6:** 683
Long, Jerry **9:** 1057
Long, Joe **5:** 572-3
Long, Shortly **4:** 473
Longbrand, Pennywhistle **15:** 1772
Longest Day, The **3:** *308,* 309, *353,* **7:** *739*
Long Good Friday, The **15:** 1679
Longhair, Professor (Roy Byrd) **2:** 145, 154, *154,* **3:** 272, 339
Longmuir, Alan **13:** 1510, *1510*
Longmuir, Derek **13:** *1510,* 1510-11, 1513
Long Riders, The **13:** 1560
'Look Back In Anger' **12:** 1386
Look In Any Window **3:** 308
Looking For Love **3:** *316*
Lopez, Trini **2:** 182, 196, **17:** *2037*
Lorber, Alan **9:** 1074
Lord, Bobbie **2:** 231
Lord, John **12:** 1377, *1377,* 1379-80, *1380,* **15:** *1682,* 1683, 1697, **17:** 1984, 1987, 1989
Lord, Jon **5:** 531, **7:** 758, 760
Lord, Rockingham's XI **4:** 379
Lordan, Jerry **4:** 362, 386, *422,* 423
Loren, Donna **8:** 879
Lorenz, George 'Hound Dog' **3:** 253, *262, 263*
Lory, Al de **5:** 519
Lost Horizon **5:** 580
Loughnane, Lee **13:** 1527, *1528*
'Louisiana Hayride' **1:** 54
'Louis, Joe Hill **8:** 932
Louvin Brothers **2:** 225
Love **8:** 903, **9:** 1010, 1016-17, **10:** 1099, 1124, **15:** 1761
Love, Airrion **14:** *1589,* 1594-5, *1595*
Love, Darlene **5:** 509, 514, 569
Love, Mike **6:** *695,* **7:** 762, *763, 766,* 770, 772, *773,* 778, *779,* 780
Love, Steve **3:** 304, **7:** 770
Love Affair **8:** 960, **10:** 1132, *1133*
Lovelady, Dave **5:** 534, *535*
Love Me Tender **1:** 89, 92, **2:** 208, 211, *211*
Lovers' Rock **19:** 2216
Love Sculpture **10:** *1164,* **15:** 1683, **17:** 1934, *1935*
Love-Tones **6:** 716
Love Unlimited **14:** 1589, *1589*
Lovich, Lene **17:** 1939-40, *1940,* **18:** 2072
Lovin' Spoonful **1:** 18, **2:** 232, **6:** 654, 677, **7:** 821-2, **8:** 847, 863, 866-9, 880, 882.

914, **8:** 982, **10:** 1085, 1099, 1110, 1121, 1123
Loving You **1:** 90, **2:** 208, 211
Low, Andy Fairweather **8:** 952-3
Lowe, Bernie **2:** 220, **3:** 341-2, 343, *343,* 350-51, 355, 358, 360, **5:** 485
Lowe, Nick **17:** 1925, 1929, 1931, *1934,* 1934-5, 1937, 1939, **18:** 2156, **19:** 2241-3, 2182, 2193, 2241, 2242, 2253
Lowery, Bill **10:** 1176
Lowery, Elvis **11:** 1290
Lowry, Ray **11:** 1290
Lowther, Henry **6:** 647, **10:** 1102, 1114
Lucas, Carrie **19:** 2178
Lucas, Trevor **13:** 1466, *1467*
Lulu **6:** 621, *623,* 635-6, **8:** 842, 845, 847, 850, **18:** 2105
Luman, Bob **1:** 51, *113,* **3:** *253*
Lunch, Lydia **18:** 2151
Lustig, Joe **13:** 1472, 1473, 1476, 1477
Luvvers **6:** *635*
Lwin, Annabella **18:** 2050, **19:** *2264,* **20:** 2399
Lydon, John **18:** 2041, 2045, 2048, **20:** 2381 *see also* Rotten, Johnny
Lyles, Florence **6:** *702*
Lyman, Arthur **3:** 269
Lymon, Frankie **1:** 76-7, **2:** 164, *236,* **3:** *258,* 260, 269
Lynch, David **3:** 299, 300
Lyngstad, Anni-Frid 'Frida' **17:** *1943,* 1944, 1945, 1946, 1947
Lynn, Bonnie *see* Delaney and Bonnie
Lynn, Jimmy **19:** 2214
Lynn, Loretta **2:** 234, **14:** 1659, 1660, **17:** 2024
Lynne, Jeff **1:** 6, **4:** 393, 419, **10:** 1181, *1185,* **15:** 1746, 1747, *1748,* 1749
Lynott, Phil **17:** 1990-3, *2417*
Lyon, Johnny *see* Southside Johnny
Lyons, Leo **12:** 1374, 1375
Lyttelton, Humphrey **4:** 430, 437, 438, 440

M

Mabel Greer's Toyshop *see* Yes
Maben, Adrian **11:** 1317
Mabey, Richard **12:** 1324
Mabon, Willie **4:** 465
Maby, Graham **19:** 2254
MacArthur, Neil **6:** 691
MacDermot, Galt **8:** 860, **14:** 1576
MacDonald, Joe **9:** 1015, 1075, **10:** 1091, 1092, 1096-7, 1123
Macdonald, Robin **5:** 533
MacInnes, Colin **2:** 134
Mackay, Al **19:** 2163, 2165
Mackay, Andy **14:** 1639, **16:** *1804,* 1805, 1807, 1808, 1810, *1811*
Mackay, Dennis **16:** 1902
Mackay, Duncan **16:** 1839, 1915

Maclean, Bryan 9: 1016
Mackenzie, Billy 19: *2272, 2275*
Macauley, Tony 3: 293
Machuki, Count 9: 975, 16: 1882, 1883, *1884,* 19: 2177
Mack, Bill 1: *80*
Mack, Lonnie 10: 1124, *1163*
Mack, Ted 1: 114, 14: 1586
Mackleduff, Gerry 19: 2253
Maclaise, Angus 8: 865, 9: 1005
Macon, Uncle Dave 1: 39, 14: 1645
Mad Dogs and Englishmen 13: 1444-5, *1446,* 1449, 15: 1763
Mad Dogs and Englishmen 13: 1445, 20: 2326
Mad Lads 8: 929-30, *932*
Mad River 8: 914
Maddox Brothers 1: 32
Made 13: 1479
Madness 9: 973, 11: 1295, 15: 1700, 16: 1902, 17: 1940, *1940,* 19: 2202, 2203-5, 2210-12, *2210-13,* 2214, 20: 2329
Madonna 20: 2401, 2410-13, 2418
Mael, Ron 13: *1518,* 1519-20, *1520*
Mael, Russell 13: *1518,* 1519-20, *1520*
Maestro, Johnny 2: 236, 237
Magazine 11: 1294, *1294,* 20: 2301
Magic Band 13: 1481, 1483-4, *1483,* 1484-7, 1559
Magic Bus (Ken Kesey and His Merry Pranksters) 12: *1382-3*
Magic Christian, The 10: 1150
Magic Dick 6: 655
Magic Sam 1: 113, 10: 1102
Magic Tramps 17: 2001
'Magical Mystery Tour' 10: *1142,* 1143, 1149-51, 1158
Magicians 8: *862,* 864
Magma 20: *2367*
Magnificent Men 10: 1163
Magnolia Jazz 4: 439
Magnum 17: 1983
Magoogan, Wesley 19: 2209
Maguire, Les 5: 524-7
Maharishi Mahesh Yogi 10: *1143,* 1149-50, 12: *1397,* 1398-9
Mahavishnu Orchestra 13: 1523, 1524-5, 1537, 15: 1742
Maher, John 18: *2073,* 2074
Mahogany 14: 1590, 1592-3
Mainieri, Mike 15: 1711
Maison Rouge see Jethro Tull
Majestic Theatre, Birkenhead 10: *1142-3*
Majewski, Hank 5: 570, 571, *571*
Major, Ray 16: 1820
Makassy 9: 965
Makeba, Myriam 9: 966
'Make-Believe Ballroom' 1: 55
Makins, Ted 5: 596
Malanga, Gerard 9: 1006
Malaria 18: 2070, 2072
Malcolm 7: *782,* 783
Malcolm X 7: *783*
Malherbe, Didier 20: 2368
Mallaber, Gary 11: 1227, 13: 1552

Mallaber, Guy 11: 1227
Mallard 13: 1486
Malone, Marcus 13: 1535
Mamas and the Papas 1: 13, 15, *16,* 6: 677, 7: 822, *823,* 838-40, 8: 902, *902,* 9: 987, 10: 1081-2, *1083,* 1098, 1100, *1100,* 1123, 12: 1359, 15: 1761
Mammarella, Tony 3: 342, 355, 358, 360
Mammoth 18: 2130
Manasa, Rick 16: 1859
Manassas 15: 1765, 1766
Mandel, Harvey 9: 1017, 10: *1114,* 1115, 1117, 11: 1221, 1223, *1223*
Mandel, Mike 9: 1032
Mandrell, Barbara 14: 1659
Maness, Jaydee 14: 1657
Manfred Mann 5: 530, *565,* 583, 588, 600, 6: 603, *625,* 641, 642-3, 644-9, *645,* 654, 677, 7: 740, *740,* 759, 9: 982, 1022, *1024-5,* 1025, 1027, 10: 1102, 15: 1682, 1728
Mangeri, Rudy 2: 235
Mangione, Chuck 13: 1523
Manhattan Transfer 1: 63, *63,* 7: 740, *740*
Manhattans 1: 62
Manieri, Mike 19: 2200
Manilow, Barry 5: 577, 7: 740, *740,* 14: 1662, 16: *1824,* 17: 1942, 2021, *2033,* 2034-5
Man in the Moon 18: 2060
Mankey, Earle 13: 1519
Mankey, Jim 13: 1519
Man Who Fell To Earth, The 14: *1622, 1629,* 20: *2327*
Mann, Barry 3: 288, 292, 4: 403, 5: 509, 514-15, 12: 1357, 17: 2023
Mann, Barry, and Weil, Cynthia 3: 265, 288, 292, 4: *443,* 444, 447, 448, *448,* 452, 459, 5: 489, 509, 514, 517
Mann, Kal 3: 341, 342, 350, 355, 5: 485
Mann-Hugg Blues Brothers 6: 644, *644*
Manning, Donald 16: 1887
Manning, Lyndords 16: 1807
Mansfield, Jayne 2: 208, *208,* 3: 312
Mansfield, John 5: 600
Mansfield, Mike 20: 2324, 2360
Mansfield, Tony 5: 533
Manson, Charles 7: *779,* 780, 12: *1342*
Manuel, Bobby 7: 785
Manuel, Richard 11: 1209, 13: *1546,* 1547
Manyika, Zeke 19: 2273
Manzanera, Phil 14: 1639, 16: *1804,* 1805, 1807, 1808, 1810, *1811*
Manzarek, Jim 10: 1009
Manzarek, Ray 10: 1009-13, *1012* 15: 1700
Manzarek, Rick 9: 1009
Marascako, John 2: 150
Marc and the Manbas 18: 2151
Marcels 5: 487
Marconi, Premiata Formera 20: 2367
Marcucci, Bob 3: 265, 342, 348-9, 352, 353, 358
Marcus, Greil 12: 1321, 1325, 1330, *1331,* 1339, 13: 1547

Mardas, Alexis 'Magic Alex' 10: 1158-9 *1158*
Mardi Gras 2: 134, 8: 859
Mardin, Arif 7: 732, 8: 876-7
Maresca, Ernie 4: 409
Margen, David 13: *1537*
Margouleff, Robert 14: 1673
Marillion 15: 1755, 20: 2420
Marylin 20: 2394, 2418
Marimba, Ed 13: 1484, 1486
Marine Broadcasting (Offences) Act (1967) 7: 746
Marine Girls 18: *2157*
Marini, Lon 13: *1538*
Mark, Jon 10: 1115
Markee, Dave 9: 1036, 19: 2196
Mar-Kets 7: 757, 765
Mar-Keys 4: 390, 392, 7: 785, 8: 921, 928-9, *929,* 930
Markowitz, Ron 10: 1172
Marks, David 7: *763,* 770
Marley, Bob 1: 10, 4: 390-1, 9: 973, 977, 979, 1036, 12: 1372, 1402-3, 14: 1676, 16: *1881,* 1883, 1885-6, 1888-93, *1890, 1891, 1892,* 18: 2061, 19: 2216, 20: *2305,* 2373-4, 2375
Marley, Rita 16: 1892, 1893 see also Anderson, Rita
Marmalade 8: 947-9
Marmalade Records 7: 816
Marquee Club 5: 583, 586-7, 588, 598-9, 600, 7: 802, 812-13, 8: 887, *886-7,* 11: 1303-4, 1308, 18: 2058, 20: *2363*
Marotta, Jerry 15: 1757
Marr, Archie 13: 1511
Marriott, Steve 6: 697, 7: 760, 806-9, *806, 807, 808,* 9: 1022, 10: 1109, 12: 1398, 15: 1721, 1725, 17: 2038-9, *2039*
Marsden, Bernie 12: 1380, 17: 1984
Marsden, Beryl 5: *522,* 523, *538*
Marsden, Freddie 5: 524-7
Marsden, Gerry 6: 614, *682,* 8: *844,* 859
Marsh, Billy 4: 397
Marsh, Dave 12: 1330
Marsh, Ian Craig 20: 2306, 2308, *2308,* 2309
Marshall, Jim 18: 2139
Marshall, John 14: *1580*
Martell, Vince 9: 1070-71
Martha and the Vandellas 4: 462, 6: 715, 717, 718-19, 7: *724,* 782, 9: *1041,* 1046
Martin, Barbara 4: 478, 9: 1045-6
Martin, Bill 13: 1511, 16: 1821 and Coulter, Bill 6: 626-7, 628
Martin, Charlie Allen 16: 1856, 1857
Martin, Dean 1: 52, 3: 303, *304,* 17: 1942
Martin, Dewey 7: 825, *826*
Martin, Doug 5: 522, 523
Martin, George 1: 4, *5,* 2: 130, 5: 524, 525, 527, 529, 532, 533, 534, 542, *542,* 550, 551, 555, 6: 622, 630, 637-40, 7: 757, 759, 8: 856, 10: *1145,* 1160, 1182, 11: 1232, 12: 1325, 13: 1525, 15: 1682, *1777* 16: 1901, 1902, 1908, 1909, 17: 1966, 1980

Martin, Grady **1:** 112, **2:** 185, **4:** 406
Martin, Janis **1:** 113, **3:** 311
Martin, Luci **18:** 2114
Martin, Mel **7:** 835
Martin, Roamer John 'the Big Figure' **17:** 1928-9, *1929*
Martin, Rob **14:** 1576
Martin, Sara **2:** 159
Martindale, Wink **3:** 267
Martinez, Paul **12:** 1380
Martinez, Rudy **8:** 872
Martini, Jerry **12:** *1405,* 1406-7
Martyn, John **13:** 1462, 1477, **15:** 1740
Marvalettes **1:** 10, **2:** 240, **4:** 478, **5:** 567, *568-9,* **6:** 714-15, 718, *719,* **9:** 1046, 1057
Marvelows **9:** 1060
Marvin, Hank **2:** 127, 186, **4:** *367,* 368, 369, 384-8, 422, **9:** 1021, 1065, 1078, 1079, **16:** 1832, **17:** 1953
Marvin, Junior **16:** 1893
Mar Y Sol Festival, Puerto Rico **11:** 1243
Mascara Snake **13:** 1484
Mascots *see* O'Jays
Masekela, Hugh **9:** 964, *966,* **10:** 1099, 1100 **20:** 2380
Maskell, Albie **18:** *2144,* 2145
Mason, Barry **3:** 293
Mason, Dave **6:** 603, **7:** 840, **9:** 1035, **10:** 1188-9, *1190-1,* 1198
Mason, Lawrie **6:** 694-5
Mason, Melvin **9:** 1060
Mason, Nick **11:** 1307, *1307, 1310,* 1313, **18:** 2079
Mason, Terry **19:** 2266
Massaro, John **11:** 1227
Masser, Michael **14:** 1593
Massey, Bobby **14:** 1600
Massey, Marian **6:** 635
Massi, Nick **5:** 571-2
Mastrangelo, Carlo **4:** 409
Matadors **4:** 475
Matassa, Cosimo **2:** 142, 145, 149, 154, 155, 200, *200,* **3:** *264,* 265, 272
Matchbox **1:** 103, 118, *118,* 120
Matching Mole **14:** 1580, **18:** 2077
Mathis, Joe **3:** 303
Matlock, Glen **18:** 2045, 2047, *2047,* **19:** *2241,* 2242, **20:** 2351, 2353
Matrix Club, San Francisco **8:** 909, 914
Mattacks, Dave **13:** 1465, *1465,* 1466, *1466,* 1467, **19:** 2196
Matthew, Brian **4:** *376,* 377, 380, *380,* **8:** *851*
Matthews, Bob **8:** 905
Matthews, 'Count' Otis **5:** 590
Matthews, Ian **13:** *1464,* 1465, *1465,* **15:** 1707
Matthews, Neal **1:** 94
Matthews, Winston 'Pipe' **16:** 1886, 1887
Matthews Southern Comfort **13:** 1464, 1465
Matthias, Nathaniel 'Jerry' **9:** 970-1
Mattice, Butch **4:** 396, *396,* 397
Matumbi **19:** 2216

Matz, Peter **5:** 578
Mauds **8:** 872
Maudlin, Joe B. **2:** *162,* 185, *185,186,* 187, 188, *189,* 193, 227
Maughan, Susan **3:** 312, **6:** 629
Maupin, Bennie **13:** 1531
Mauriat, Paul **17:** 1956
Maurice, Brian **19:** 2220
Maus, John Joseph **8:** 956-7
Mavericks **12:** 1427
Maxfield, Mike **5:** 533
Maxim, Arnold **2:** 174
Maxwell, Larry **14:** 1587
Maxwell, Demon **14:** 1638
May, Billy **5:** 501
May, Brian **16:** 1812, *1812-13,* 1814-15, 1817
Mayall, John **4:** 382, 454, **5:** 588, **6:** 643, 648, 652, **7:** 817, **9:** 1022, 1027, 1033, **10:** 1102-3, 1112-15, 1118, 1132, *1132,* **11:** 1253, 1256, **15:** 1721
Mayfair Set **10:** 1181
Mayfield, Curtis **1:** 10, **3:** 266, 297, **5:** 562, **6:** 704, **7:** *781,* 782, 793-5, *793-5,* **9:** 1059-60, *1059,* **12:** 1402-3, 1412-14, 1420, **15:** 1791, 1792, **16:** 1885
Mayhew, John **15:** 1752
Maynard Ferguson Big Band **11:** 1256
Mayo, John 'Gypie' **17:** 1929, *1929*
Mayorga, Lincoln **6:** 716
Maytals **9:** 962-3, 970-1, 977, 979, **16:** 1885-6, *1887,* 1890, 1894
Maxda, Richard **18:** 2147
Maxur, Mark **20:** 2297
McAlister, Maurice **9:** 1059
McAuliffe, Leon **14:** 1656, 1657
McAvoy, Michael **17:** 1933
McBrian, Nick **19:** 2232
McCafferty, Dan **17:** *1988,* 1989
McCann, Les **15:** 1799
McCartney, Linda **10:** *1150,* 1159, **14:** *1679,* 1680, **17:** 1961, 1963, *1963-5,* 1973
McCartney, Paul **1:** 4-5, 16, **2:** *128,* 150, 191, **3:** 250, 293, **4:** *403,* 416, 418, 433, **5:** 537, 538, 541-60, 599, **6:** 637, 640, 693, **7:** 815, **8:** 847, 854-7, 859, 891, 893, **9:** 988, 1039, *1039,* 1066, **10:** 1099, 1141-60, 1194, **11:** 1304, **12:** 1335, **13:** 1480, **14:** 1585, 1661-2, *1662, 1676,* 1679-80, *1689,* **15:** 1681, 1703, 1718, 1748, **16:** 1901, **17:** 1961, *1962-5,* 1962-6, 1973, 1979, 1980 **18:** 2099, **19:** *2265,* **20:** 2360
McCarty, Jim **5:** 600, **6:** 650, *650,* 652-3, **10:** 1178
McClary, Thomas **18:** 2117
McClure, Bobby **9:** 1059
McClure, Michael **1:** 15, **8:** 919-20
McCluskey, Andy **20:** 2316-17, *2316-17*
McClymont, Davie **19:** 2273
McCormick, Galye **4:** 418
McCoy, Charlie **6:** 655, **11:** 1209, **17:** 2023
McCoy, John **17:** 1984, *1985*
McCoy, Van **3:** 332, **14:** 1587, 1595, **18:**

2102, 2103
McCracken, Charlie **10:** 1187
McCracken, Chet **16:** 1852
McCracken, Hugh **18:** 2133
McCrae, Josh **10:** 1138-9
McCrea, Earl-Jean **5:** 489
McCreery, Mary **13:** 1446
McCullin, Don **12:** 1436
McCulloch, Danny **6:** 660
McCulloch, Ian **19:** 2276-9, *2276-7,* 2280
McCulloch, Jimmy **7:** 809, **17:** 1964, *1964*
McCullom, Hazel **5:** 495
McCullough, Andy **14:** 1565
McCullough, Henry **10:** 1168, **17:** 1963
McDaniel, Luke **1:** *50*
McDaniels, Gene **4:** 446, **5:** *491,* 492, 579, **15:** 1799, 1800
McDaniels, Pete **7:** 819
McDermot, Jack **3:** 342, **5:** 496
McDevitt, Chas **2:** 125, 134, *165,* **4:** 384, 430
McDonald, Ian **14:** 1564, 1567, **18:** 2121, 2132, 2133
McDonald, Mike **15:** 1711, **16:** 1852, *1853*
McDonald, Joe **11:** 1250
McDonnell, Jim **19:** 2260
McDowell, Fred **6:** 678, *678,* 680
McDowell, Hugh **10:** 1185, **15:** 1747, 1748, 1749
McDowell, Paul **4:** 439
McDuff, Brother Jack **19:** 2167
McElhiney, Bill **4:** 406
McEnery, David **5:** 574
McFadden, Gene **14:** *1598,* 1600
McFadden and Whitehead **14:** 1600
McFall, Ray **5:** 522, 523, 540
McFarland, J. Leslie **1:** 27
McFarlane, Spanky **7:** *839,* 840
McFee, John **16:** 1852
McGarrigle, Kate and Anna **16:** 1857
McGee, Brian **19:** 2274
McGeoch, John **18:** *2150,* 2151, **20:** 2351
McGhee, Brownie **1:** 25, **3:** 338, **5:** *584, 585,* **6:** 654-5, 679, *679*
McGhee, Gosardy **3:** 324
McGhee, 'Stick' **1:** 31, **3:** 272
McGlynn, Pat **13:** 1513
McGowan, Cathy **7:** *743,* **8:** 849, *851*
McGuinn, Roger **5:** 543, **6:** 661-2, 682, **7:** 827-31, 836, **8:** 880, *880,* **9:** 1077, **10:** 1121, *1121,* **11:** 1211, *1211*
McGuinness-Flint Emsemble **6:** 648
McGuinness, Tom **5:** *589,* **6:** 644-5, *645-6,* 647-8
McGuire, Barry **6:** 676, *677,* **7:** 724, 822, *823,* **8:** 902, **10:** 1081-2, 1121, **12:** 1358
McGuire Sisters **2:** 235, **3:** 310, *311*
McHale, Dave **19:** 2251
McIntosh, Ken **2:** 122, 129
McIntosh, Peter **1:** 10
McIntosh, Robbie **1:** 68, **19:** 2253
McIntyre, Onnie **1:** 68
McJohn, Goldy **9:** 1072
McKay, Al **19:** 2163, 2165
McKay, John **18:** 2149, *2150,* 2151

McKechnie, Licorice 13: *1469,* 1470
McKellar, Kenneth 17: 1955, *1955*
McKennas, Hugh and Ted 17: 1995
McKenzie, Alastair 16: 1831
McKenzie, Ali 7: 819
McKenzie, Scott 1: 15, 7: 808, *822,* 838-9, 10: 1082, *1082,* 1085, 1090, 1098, 1123-4, 11: *1253*
McKeown, Les 13: *1510,* 1511, 1513, *1513*
McKernan, Ron 'Pigpen' 8: 905-6, *905, 907,* 908, 919
McKinnie, Dee 10: 1115
McLaglan, Ian 7: 806-9, 15: *1699,* 1725
McLain, Michael 6: 716
McLain, Tommy 13: 1455
McLaren, Malcolm 13: 1503, 16: 1863, 1866, 1879, 1890, 18: 2041, *2041,* *2043,* 2045-8, 2049-51, 2053, 2055, 2062, 2063, 2067, 2074, 2149, 19: 2252, 20: 2323, 2399, 2415
McLaughlin, John 6: 640, 642, 9: 1032, *1032,* 13: *1522,* 1523, 1524-5, 1531, 1537, 17: 1981
McLaughlin, Ollie 4: 417
McLean, Don 15: 1712-13, 1800
McLean Ernest 2: 146, 154
McLelland, Geoff 7: 820
McLouney, Vince 18: 2105, *2105*
McLuhan, Marshall 12: 1334
McManus, Gary 'Roobish' 19: 2207
McMasters, Andy 17: *1922,* 19: 2242
McNair, Barbara 4: 478
McNair, Harold 10: 1135
McNally, John 5: 528-31
McNeely, Big Jay 4: 389
McNeil, David 1: 71
McNeill, Michael 19: 2274
McNenery, Steve 19: 2242
McPhail, Richard 15: 1752
McPhatter, Clyde 1: 72, 74-5, 2: 160, 3: 273, *273,* 281, 290, *291,* 322, 330, 4: 452, 475
McPherson, Graham 'Suggs' 19: 2210, *2210, 2212*
McShee, Jacqui 13: 1462, 1476-7, *1477*
McSon Trio 3: 324
McTell, Ralph 10: 1124, *1125,* 13: 1461, *1462,* 1478
McVay, Ray 2: 139
McVicar 4: 372, 11: 1275, 14: 1680
McVie, Christine 10: 1119-20, *1120,* 17: 2031-2, *2031-2*
McVie, John 10: 1102, 1112-14, *1113-14,* 1118-20, *1118,* 17: 2030-1, *2031*
McVoy, Carl 4: 392
McWilliams, David 1: 5·
MC5 8: 872, 9: 1015, 10: 1124, 13: 1481, 1482, 1483, *1483,* 1487-8, 1489, 16: 1830, 1865
Meadon, Peter 7: 801, 806, 812, 816-17, 11: 1264-5, 1273, 1276-7, *1277,* 1279
Meat Loaf 16: 1863, 1905, 18: 2122-3
Meaux, Huey P. 7: 821, 834-5, 10: 1145, 13: 1445
Medal For The General, A 6: 632

Meddows-Taylor, Roger 16: 1812, *1812,* 1814, 1817, *1817*
Meditation Singers 15: 1782
Meditations 16: 1887
Medress, Hank 4: 459, 5: 567
Meehan, Patrick 12: 1370
Meehan, Tony 4: 362, 368, *384,* 385, 386, 387, 398, *398,* 400, 423
Meek, Joe 4: 362, 363, 393, 421, 435, *436-7,* 5: 562, *563,* 7: 737
Meeks, Johnny 1: 106, *107*
Meher Baba 11: 1279-80
Meisner, Ben 15: 1698
Meisner, Randy 3: 304, 15: 1772-3, *1773,* 1775
Mekons 19: 2261
Melanie 14: 1679, 15: 1716-17
Melcher, Marty 7: 766
Melcher, Terry 7: 833, 13: 1444
Mellows 2: *216*
Melly, George 11: 1297, 12: *1323,* 1324, 17: 1922
Melody Maker 12: 1326, *1326,* 1328, 14: 1573
Melson, Joe 4: 415, 416
Melting Pot 8: 914
Melton, Barry 10: 1096-7
Meltzer, Richard 12: 1330, 1339
Melvin, Harold 14: 1597-8, *1598,* 1600
Melvin, Rod 17: 1931
Memphis 8: 921-2, 928-33, 937, *939*
Memphis Horns 16: 1851
Memphis Jug Band 6: 678, 11: 1221
Memphis Slim 5: *581*
Men At Work 11: *1261,* 20: *2372*
Mencken, Robin 10: 1097
Mensi 18: *2153,* 2154
Mento 9: 975
Mercer, Chris 10: 1103, 1114
Mercer, Johnny 5: 501, 7: 739
Mercury, Freddie 16: 1812, *1812,* 1814, *1814,* 1815, *1815,* 1817, 1863, 18: *2099*
Mercury Records 1: 68, 3: 262, *262, 283,* 299-300, *300*
Meredith, James 7: 783, *783*
Merrick 20: *2324*
Merrill, B. B. 14: 1592
Merry Christmas Mr Lawrence 14: 1631
Merry Pranksters 8: 919
Mersey Beat 5: *521,* 522, 523, 524, 533, 536-7, 549, 550, 554, 555, 6: 601, 602
Merseybeats 5: *522,* 532, 534, *536,* 6: 601
Merseysippi Jazzband 4: 439
Merton Parkas 19: 2248
Mesner, Leo 3: 289
Mess Around 5: 483
Messner, Eddie 2: 155
Metal Urbain 18: 2157
Meteors 1: 120
Meyer, Angie 7: 834-5
Mezur, Mark 20: 2297
Mezzoforte 19: 2167
MFSB 14: 1598, 1600
MGM 3: 316-17, 4: 406, 407, 416, 5: 501
MGs 7: 782, 784-5, 8: 921-2, 929-30, 932,

10: 1099, 12: *1402-3*
MI5 8: 947
Mial, Terry Lee 20: 2323, *2323*
Mi Amigo 7: *746*
Micahnik, Irving 4: 396, 397, 417, 419, *419*
Michael, George 20: 2381, 2408-9, 2418
Michael Kohlhass 8: 893
Mickens, Robert 'Spike' 18: 2109
Mickey Most and his Playboys 16: 1832
Mickleburgh, Bob 4: *440*
Middle Earth Club 11: *1303,* 1306, 1309
Middleton, Max 11: 1232
Mid-Knights 6: 682
Midler, Bette 16: 1863, *1863,* 17: 2034, 18: 2095
'Midnight Special' 3: *341,* 8: *940,* 16: *1859*
Midnighters 3: 247, 330, 5: 494-5, *495,* 538-9, 15: 1749
Midnight Star 19: 2180
Midsummer Night's Dream Festival, Hull (1968) 11: 1242
Miesegaes, Sam 15: 1758
Miessner, Ben 15: 1698
Mighty Clouds of Joy 15: *1783*
Mighty Diamonds 16: 1884
Mighty Mighty Men 3: 338, 4: 463
Mighty Panthers 8: 924
Mik, Dik 17: 1996
Mike Cotton Sound 7: 729
Mike Westwood Orchestra 14: 1569
Milano, Fred 4: 409
Milander, Colin 5: 538
Milburn, Amos 1: 30, 2: 145, 3: 272, 339, *339*
Miles 11: 1304
Miles, Buddy 9: 1063, 1068, 11: 1239-40
Milk and Honey 17: 1956, *1956*
Millar, Bill 1: 119, 12: 1324, 1338
Miller, Bob 15: 1758
Miller, Bobby 9: 1059
Miller, Count Prince 7: 812-13, *813*
Miller, Daniel 18: 2156, 20: 2397
Miller, Dave 1: 24-6, 3: 341, *341*
Miller, Jay 2: 176, 13: 1455
Miller, Jim 11: 1225, 1227
Miller, Jimmy 8: 893, 10: 1198
Miller, Larry 8: 841
Miller, Mitch 1: 26, 2: 230, 6: 672
Miller, Roger 2: 234, 14: 1650
Miller, Stanley 'Mouse' 12: 1389-90
Miller, Steve 1: 15, 68, 10: 1100, 11: 1221, 1223, *1223.* 1224-7
Miller, Tom *see* Verlaine, Tom
Millie 6: 635
Millionaires 19: 2257
Million Dollar Quarter 1: *54,* 88
Mills, Don 2: 192
Mills, Freddie 4: 378
Mills, Gordon 2: 140, 7: 722, *722,* 737
Mills, Hayley 3: 312
Mills, Howard 11: 1251
Mills, Pat 8: 944
Mills Brothers 1: 31, 61, 3: 290
Millward, Mike 5: 534, *535*

Milos **4:** 458
Milsap, Ronnie **10:** 1163, **17:** 2025
Milton, Roy **1:** 30
Mimms, Garnet **8:** 934
Min, Hiroshi **20:** 2364
Mindbenders **6:** 602-3, 695, **16:** 1913
Mingus, Charlie **3:** 322, **12:** 1347
Minimoog **20:** 2301, *2318,* 2319
Minit **3:** 264
Minott, Sugar **16:** *1897,* 1897, **20:** 2374
Mintz, Leo **2:** 215
Miracles **4:** 472, 473, 475-80, **5:** 482, 483,
    6: 714-15, **9:** *1041,* 1042, 1045-6, 1048,
    1051, **14:** 1672
Mirren, Helen **20:** *2339*
Misfits, The **5:** 498, *499*
Missing Links **6:** 682
Missionary, The **15:** 1679
Mister Rock 'n' Roll **2:** 151, 174
Misty in Roots **19:** 2216
Mitchell, Blue **10:** *1114,* 1115
Mitchell, Chuch **12:** 1345
Mitchell, Eddie **3:** 250
Mitchell, Ian **13:** 1513, *1513*
Mitchell, Jeffrey **16:** 1830
Mitchell, Joni **1:** 18, **6:** 665, **7:** 822, **10:**
    1124, **11:** 1211, 1220, *1220,* 1247, 1258,
    12: 1341, 1345-7, 1349, 1359, *1360,* **13:**
    1462, 1465, **15:** 1703, 1708, 1710,
    1718, 1763, 1766, 1779, **17:** 1989, **18:**
    2096, *2097, 2100*
Mitchell, Julian **7:** 754
Mitchell, Mitch **9:** 1032, 1063, *1063,* 1065-
    8, *1068,* **14:** 1620, **15:** 1687, **17:** 1981
Mitchell, Willie **4:** 390, **10:** 1109, **12:**
    1410, **15:** 1780, 1781, 1782, 1785, 1786
Mittoo, Jackie **9:** 976, **16:** 1894
Mixing consoles **18:** 2139
Mix Me A Person **4:** 372, 431
Mizarolli, John **9:** 1031
Moby Grape **1:** 15, **8:** 915, *915,* **10:** 1100,
    11: 1240
Models, The **20:** *2371*
Model Shot, The **14:** 1614
Modern **3:** 307, **5:** 502
Modern Jazz Quartet **3:** 327
Modern Lovers **17:** 2004, 2016-17, *2017,*
    20: 2283
Modern Romance **19:** 2260
Mo-Dettes **18:** 2071
Modes, The **20:** 2365
Modugno, Domenico **3:** 269, 350
Moebius **14:** 1640
Moelis, Herb **9:** 988-9
Moerlen, Pierre **20:** 2368
Mohammad, Elijah **7:** 743, 797
Mojo **6:** 601
Mojo Navigator **12:** 1339, *1339*
Mojos **5:** *523*
Molina, Ralph **15:** 1768, *1770*
Moller, Kari-Ann **16:** 1810
Molloy, Jim **2:** *233*
Moman, Chips **8:** 928, **10:** 1174, **15:** 1789
Monarch, Michael **9:** 1072
Monarchs **13:** 1551, **14:** 1594

Monardo, Meco **18:** 2102
Monck, Jack **11:** 1320
Mondo Hollywood **13:** 1493
Money, Zoot **5:** 588, *588, 598,* **7:** 817, **10:**
    1085, 1087
Mongrel **10:** 1185
Monkees **1:** *12,* 13, 16, **4:** 441, 444, 447, **6:**
    683, 686-7, **7:** 804, **8:** *842,* 843, **9:** 981-2,
    981-2, 983, 984, 986-91, 1066, **10:** 1085,
    1092, *1100,* 1123, **11:** 1274, **12:** 1324,
    1354, **13:** 1502, 1515, 1517
Monkey **5:** 482, 483
Monkeys Uncle, The **8:** 845, *845*
Monkman, Francis **14:** 1562, *1563,*
    1575-6, *1577,* **15:** 1741
Monoton **20:** 2368
Monro, Mat **17:** 1955
Monroe, Bill **1:** 39, *39,* **2:** 225 and Charles
    12: 1401
Montana Jr., Vincent **18:** 2103
Mont de Marsan Punk Festivals
    (1976/77) **11:** 1243, *1243*
Monterey **8:** 848, 911, **10:** 1100, **11:** 1274
Monterey Pop Festival (1967) **1:** 15-17,
    16-17, **6:** 665, **7:** 826, 839, **8:** 903, *904-5,*
    909, 926, **9:** 1055, **10:** 1081-2, 1091,
    1092, *1092,* 1094, *1094,* 1098-1100,
    1116, **11:** 1242, 1252-3, *1253*
Montez, Chris **2:** 182, 196
Montgomery, Bob **2:** 185, *186,* 193, **3:** 245
Montgomery, Monk **1:** 79-80
Montgomery, Wes **19:** 2167
Monty Python's Life of Brian **14:** 1679
Monument **4:** 415, 416
Moody, James **2:** 173
Moody, Micky **15:** 1738, **17:** 1984
Moody Blues **6:** 603, 690, 713, **10:** 1167,
    1181, 1183, 1193-7, **12:** 1359, **15:** 1679-
    80, 1683, 1742, **16:** 1910, 1912
Moog, Dr Robert A. **20:** *2318,* 2319
Moon, Keith **11:** 1261-77, **12:** 1365, **13:**
    1479, **14:** 1620, **17:** 1972, 1976, 1981,
    18: *2134 see also* Who
Moondog Coronation Ball (1952) **2:** 215
Moondogs **7:** 743
'Moondog's Rock 'n' Roll Party' **1:** 57, 60,
    3: 252
Mooney, Kevin **20:** 2324
Mooney, Malcolm **20:** 2367
Mooney, Ralph **14:** *1655*
Mooney, Thom **16:** 1903, *1904*
Moonglows (Moonlighters) **1:** 73, *73,* **2:**
    209, 215, 216, 217, **4:** 465, **6:** 702
Moontrekkers **4:** 393
Moorcock, Michael **17:** 1997, **18:** 2127
Moore, Alan **17:** 1999
Moore, Bob **2:** 231, 233
Moore, Dorothy **8:** 931
Moore, Gary **17:** 1990, 1992-3, *1993*
Moore, Johnny **1:** *29,* 30, **3:** 281, 290, 292-
    3, *292,* 324
Moore, Lattie **3:** 337
Moore, Mary Tyler **2:** *213*
Moore, Merrill **1:** 32, 40
Moore, Pete **4:** 475, 477, 478, 479

Moore, Richard **8:** 946
Moore, Sam *see* Sam and Dave
Moore, Scotty **1:** 46-7, *52-3,* 52-4, 80, 94-5,
    95, **2:** 211, **9:** 1021, *1023*
Moore, Tommy **5:** 547-8, 549
Moorman, Charlotte **5:** 500
Moorshead, John **10:** 1107
Moran, Gayle **13:** 1525
Moraz, Patrick **10:** 1196, **15:** 1692, 1693,
    1694, 1699
More **11:** 1310, 1316, *1316*
'More Furious Madness From The
    Massed Gadgets of Auximenes' **11:**
    1309-10
Moreira, Airto **13:** 1532
Morgan, Dave **15:** 1749
Morgan, Derrick **9:** 976-7
Morgan, Hite **7:** 770
Morgan, John Russell **9:** 1072
Morgus and the Three Ghouls *see* Dr John
Morin, Frank **7:** 835
Morley, Paul **20:** 2415
Morning Glory **8:** 915
Moroder, Giorgio **13:** 1520, **18:** 2103,
    2110-11, *2118,* 2120, **20:** 2293, 2303,
    2356, 2362
Morris, Doug **10:** 1094
Morris, Eric **9:** 977
Morris, Kenny **18:** 2149, *2150,* 2151
Morris, Sonny **4:** *438,* 439
Morris, Steve **19:** *2266,* 2267
Morris, Sylvan **16:** 1894, 1900
Morrison, Jim **1:** 19, **8:** 902, **9:** *985,* 1002,
    1002, 1009-13, **10:** 1173, **15:** 1761
Morrison, Sterling **1:** *20,* **8:** *864,* 865, **9:**
    1004, 1005
Morrison, Van **3:** 332, **4:** *444,* **10:** 1090, **11:**
    1220, *1220,* **13:** 1541-3, *1541,* 1550-3,
    15: 1703
Morrissey, Mick **20:** 2315
Morrow, 'Cousin Brucie' **5:** 499, **17:** 2036
Morrow, James **4:** 414
Morse, Ella Mae **3:** 310, **10:** 1161
Morton, Everett **19:** 2208-9 *2209*
Morton, George 'Shadow' **4:** 402, **5:** 567,
    569
Morton, Jelly Roll **2:** 179, *179,* **4:** 438
Morton, Rockette **13:** 1484, 1486
Morton, Rocky **20:** 2360
Moscoso, Victor **11:** *1291,* 1292, **12:** 1389-
    90
Moss, Jerry **5:** 503, *503*
Moss, John **18:** 2079, **20:** *2399*
Moss, Ralph **14:** 1587
Moss, Wayne **11:** 1209, **17:** 2023
Most, Mickie **1:** 8, **4:** 437, **6:** 622, 635-6,
    635, 640, 653, 658-60, 685, *686,* 687, **7:**
    757, *758,* 759, 760, **10:** 1124, 1134-6,
    1136, **11:** 1228, 1230, **12:** 1422, **16:**
    1822, *1822,* 1823, 1826, 1830, 1831,
    1832-4, 1836
Most Brothers **16:** 1832
Mother Earth **8:** 914
Mother McCree's Uptown Jug
    Champions **8:** *905*

Mothers *see* Mothers of Invention

Mothers of Invention **1**: 18-19, **8**: 902, 917, **9**: 1035, **10**: 1114, **11**: 1253, 1257, **13**: 1481, 1482-4, *1481*, 1493, 1496, **16**: 1858, **18**: 2071

Mothersbaugh, Mark & Bob **17**: 2014, *2014*, **19**: 2252

Motion Picture **1**: 96

Motola, George **12**: 1405

Motor City Five *see* MC5

Motorhead **19**: *2221*, 2223, 2238-40, *2239-40*

Motors **19**: 2242, *2242*

Motortown Revue **4**: 477, **6**: 702, 706, **9**: 1046-7

Motown **1**: 62, **3**: 265, *265*, 266, **4**: 461-3, 472-3, 475, 477-9, **5**: 542, 562, 572-3, **6**: 701-20, **7**: 782-3, **9**: 1041-3, 1045-9, 1050, 1052, 1054-5, 1057, **12**: 1419, *1420*, **14**: 1581, 1583-5, 1587, 1590, 1593, 1672-3, 1675-6, **18**: 2102, 2116-17

Motown Revue **7**: *724*

Motown Spinners *see* Detroit Spinners

Mott *see* Mott the Hoople

Mott the Hoople **14**: 1623, 1626, **15**: *1699*, 1740, **16**: 1802, 1803, 1814, 1818-20

Moulten, Victor 'Moulty' **6**: 681

Moulton, Tom **18**: 2102

Mountain **14**: 1601, 1606-8, **18**: 2121

Mount Lebanon Spiritualist Singers **1**: 74, *74*, **2**: 160

Mount Rushmore **8**: 915

Mouse and the Traps **8**: 872, *873*

Mouzon, Alphonse **13**: 1532, **14**: 1620

Move **1**: 6, **6**: 603, **7**: 820, *820*, **10**: 1085, 1181, 1182-5, **15**: 1746, **16**: 1803

Moving Sidewalks **8**: 872, **16**: 1855

Mowatt, Judy **16**: 1892, *1893*

Moy, Sylvia **14**: 1672

Moyet, Alison 'Alf' **20**: 2405, *2407*, 2413, 2419

Moss *see* Mods

Mud **15**: *1745*, **16**: 1803, *1821*, 1822-3, 1834

Mudcrutch **18**: 2085

Muddy Waters **5**: 585, 586, *592-3*, **8**: *886-7*, 887, 889, **9**: 1059, 1065

Muddy Waters Band **5**: 593

Mudlarks **4**: 363, 366

Mugwumps **7**: 822, 828, **8**: 867

Muhammad Ali **6**: *693*

Muir, Jamie **14**: 1565

Muldaur, Maria and Geoff **7**: 822, **11**: *1240* **17**: 2023

Mullen, Larry **19**: 2270-1, *2271*

Mullican, Moon **1**: 40, *40*, 118, **2**: 181

Mulligan, Mick **4**: 439

Mumford, Eugene **1**: 71

Munden, Dave **6**: 615, 616

Mundi, Billy **13**: *1491*, 1493, 1554

Munroe, Tony **7**: 819

Murmaids **5**: 567

Murphy, Joaquin 'Poot' **14**: 1656

Murphy, John **19**: 2275

Murphy, Matt 'Guitar' **5**: *581*

Murray, Alex **11**: 1194, **16**: 1832

Murray, Dave **19**: 2230, *2230*

Murray, Dee **10**: 1187, **14**: 1667, *1668*

Murray, Don **9**: 992-3

Murray, Mitch **5**: 525, 534, **6**: 614, 616

Murray, Neil **17**: 1984

Murray, Pauline **18**: 2061

Murray, Pete **4**: *376*, 378, **8**: 849, **17**: *1958*

Murray, Ruby **3**: 310

Murray, Tony **8**: 946, *946*

Murray the K **5**: 498

Murrel, Chris **18**: 2154

Murrell, Herbie **14**: 1594, *1595*

Murcia, Billy **16**: 1863, 1879

Muscle Beach Party **3**: 317, **14**: 1672

Muscle Schoals, Alabama **8**: 940

Mushrooms **15**: 1772

Music Echo **12**: 1327

Music Explosion **9**: 999

Music Machine **8**: 872, **18**: 2060, **20**: 2350

Music students **17**: 1933

Music Television (MTV) **20**: 2281, 2360, 2392

Musical Youth **20**: 2396

Musselwhite, Charlie **10**: 1163, **11**: 1221, 1223, 1238

Mutabaruka **20**: 2375

Mute **18**: 2156

'Mutiny On The Bounty' **13**: 1509

Mutrix, Floyd **2**: 215

Myddle Class **4**: 447

Mydland, Brent **8**: 908

Myers, Alan **17**: 2014-15

Myers, Dave **1**: 24, 25, 26

Myers, Dr Elman B. **1**: 55

Myers, Richard *see* Hell, Richard

Mynah Birds **15**: 1768

Myriam, Marie **17**: 1957

Myrick, Don **19**: 2163

Mysterians **8**: 872, *873*

'Myths And Legends Of King Arthur And The Knights Of The Round Table, The' **15**: *1681*, *1696*, 1697

Myton, Cedric **19**: 2209

N

NAB **4**: 460

Naftalin, Mark **11**: 1239

Nahan, Irv **2**: 174

Napier, Alex **15**: 1728

Napier-Bell, Simon **6**: 653, **7**: 759-60, *760*, 820, **10**: 1085, **12**: 1436-7, 1440, **20**: 2356, 2408

Narell, Andy **11**: 1237

Nash, Brian **20**: 2415

Nash, Graham **6**: *604*, 605-7, *606*, *607*, 608, *608*, **7**: 826, **11**: *1251*, **12**: 1345, **15**: 1764, *1764*, 1766, *1766*

Nash, Johnny **16**: 1891

Nash and Young **17**: 2022

Nashville **14**: 1660

'Nashville notation' **2**: 233

'Nashville Sound' **2**: *222*, 223, 232-4

Nashville Teens **6**: *601*, 603, 695, **7**: 757

Nat King Cole Trio **5**: 501

Nathan, Syd **1**: 43, **3**: 299, 337, **4**: 463, **5**: 494-5, **7**: 789, **14**: 1600

National **3**: 262

National Jazz and Blues Festival (1968) **14**: 1570

Naturals **6**: 603

Naughty Rhythms Tour **17**: 1924, 1928

Nauseef, Mark **17**: 1984, 1992

Nazareth **17**: 1985, *1988*, 1989

Nazz **8**: 872, **16**: 1865, 1903, 1905

N'Dour, Yssou **20**: 2379, *2379*

Neal, Bob **1**: 54, **2**: 169

Neal, Dave **16**: 1831

Ned Kelly **8**: 893, **20**: 2326

Neeley, Ted **18**: 2124

Nektar **20**: 2367

Nelki, Gordon **17**: 1930

Nelson, Bill **20**: 2302, 2365

Nelson, David **3**: 302

Nelson, Earl **14**: 1589

Nelson, Jack **16**: 1814, 1817

Nelson, Keen **1**: 105-6, **2**: 199, 200

Nelson, Ozzie **3**: 302, *302*

Nelson, Paul **16**: 1879

Nelson, Phyllis **20**: 2413

Nelson, Ricky **1**: 102, 110, 114, **2**: 234, 239, 240, **3**: 242, 259, 301, 302-5, 307, 351, **4**: 404, *405*, **5**: 502, **7**: 728, **15**: 1773

Nelson, Sandy **3**: 269, **4**: 389, 400, *400*, **5**: 502, 506, **7**: 766

Nelson, Walter **2**: 146, **13**: 1451

Nelson, Willie **2**: 234, **11**: *1219*, 1220, **13**: 1446, **14**: 1641, 1646-7, 1649, 1650, 1652, 1659, *1660*, 1680, **17**: 2025, **18**: 2100

Nemes, Les **20**: 2384

NEMS **5**: 524, 525, 527, *532*, 532-5, 537, 554, 555, 556, 557, **6**: 630, 639, **10**: 1149, 1156, 1159

Neon Boys **17**: 2007, 2012

Nero and the Gladiators **4**: 393, **18**: 2133

Nervous Norvus **5**: 574

Nessmith, Mike **1**: 13, **7**: 753, **9**: 983, 987-91, **20**: 2360

Nestor, Pam **19**: 2196

'Neue Deutsche Welle' **20**: 2368

Neuwirth, Bob **11**: *1212*

Never Let Go **4**: 372

Neville, Art **2**: 145

Neville, Richard **8**: 852, *852*, **9**: 1015, **13**: 1482

Nevins, Al **3**: *266*, **4**: 441, *443*, 450, 451, 452, 458, 459, **5**: 489, **15**: 1714-15

New, Steve **19**: *2241*

Newbury, Mickey **10**: 1125

Newcastle Jazz Festival **11**: 1248

New Christy Minstrels **6**: 662, **7**: 828

New Hormones Records **18**: 2156

Newley, Anthony **3**: 306, **4**: 430, *430*, **7**: 739-40, **8**: *858*, 859, **14**: 1625

New Lost City Ramblers 6: 662
Newman, Andy 'Thunderclap' 11: 1279
Newman, Jeff 14: 1657
Newman, Jimmy 2: 234, 13: 1455, 14: 1655
Newman, Randy 10: 1125, 12: 1341, 1349, 15: 1700, 1703, 1718-20, 1763, 1795, 18: 2100, 20: 2326
Newman, Rick 18: 2134
Newman, Sandy 8: 949
Newman, Tony 11: 1231, 12: 1440
Newmark, Andy 10: 1192, 18: 2097
New Musical Express 1: 59, 67, 12: 1326, *1326-7*
New Order 19: 2269, 20: 2303 see also Joy Division
New Orleans 13: 1451-2
Newport Folk Festival (1965) 6: 662, *666*, 669, 672, 11: 1203, *1204*, 1205, 1207, 1207-8, *1214*, 1242, 1252, 12: 1351, *1360*
Newport Jazz Festival (1959) 3: 290-1, 11: 1242, 1252, 1253, *1253*
New Record Mirror 12: 1326, 1327, *1327*, 1328
New Riders of the Purple Sage 8: 912
News Beat 20: 2365
New Seekers 10: 1140, *1140*, 17: 1955
Newton, Egidio 19: 2207
Newton, John 2: 158
Newton-John, Olivia 7: *733*, 14: 1658, 17: *1941*, 1942, 1946, *1953*, 1955-7, 2025, *2025*, 18: 2106, 20: 2327, 2370, 2371
Newton, Juice 17: 2025
Newton, Paul 15: 1728
New World Rising 18: 2114
New York Dolls 9: 1002, 13: 1483, 16: 1862, 1869, *1878-80, 1905*, 17: *2001*, 2003, *2004*, 2012, 2017, 18: 2042, 2046, 2057, 2148
New York Rocker 12: 1331
Nice 1: 11, 11: 1247, 15: 1683, *1683*, 1684-9, 1691, 1692, 1697, 1699, 1700, 1742, 16: 1807
Nichol, Al 9: 992-3
Nichol, Simon 13: *1464*, 1465, 1466, *1466*, 1467
Nichol, Steve 19: 2247
Nicholas, Paul 13: *1509*
Nichols, Mike 10: 1129
Nichols, Paul 13: 1475
Nicholas, Paul 13: *1509*
Nicholson, Hughie 8: *948*, 949
Nicholson, Jack 8: *848*
Nick and the Jaguars 4: 473
Nicks, Stevie 10: 1120, *1120*, 17: *2021*, 2030-2, *2030-2*
Nico 1: 19, *20*, 8: *864*, 865, 9: *1006*, 1006-7, *1008*, 14: 1639, 15: 1778
Nicol, Jimmy 10: *1144*
Nicole 17: *1956*, 1957
Nieve, Steve 19: 2193, *2194*, 2195, 2213, 20: 2385
Nighthawk, Robert 1: 56
Nighthawks 15: 1688

Nightingale, Anne 12: 1323, *1323*, 17: 1959
Nightmares in Wax 19: 2262
Night Owl Cafe, New York 8: *862*, 863, 867
Nightriders 9: 992, 10: 1181, 1183, 1185
Night Timers 5: 588, 7: 818
Nilsson, Harry 7: 837, 9: 982, 17: 1972-3, 1976, 2039
1984 14: 1628, 20: 2387
1910 Fruitgum Company 9: 983, *997*, 997-8
Niney the Observer 16: 1898
Nitty Gritty Dirt Band 10: 1125, 15: *1762-3*, 1778, 16: 1801
Nitzsche, Jack 5: 509, *518*, 519, 520, *563*, 7: 765, 826, 8: 893, 956, 13: 1559, 15: 1768
Nix, Billy 'Sticks' 6: 708
Nix, Don 10: 1163
Nobles, Gene 1: 57
Nocentelli, Leo 12: 1416
Noel, Carl 7: 812
Nolan, Jerry 16: 1863, 1879, 1880, *1880*, 17: *2001*, 2002, 2004, 2012
Nolan, Larry 14: 1580
No Nukes Music 18: 2158, *2160*
Noone, Peter 6: 603, *681, 684*, 685-7, *686-7*, 880, 16: 1822
Norfolk Jazz Quartet 1: 61
Norman, Chris 16: 1823
Norman, Gene 3: 286
Norman Petty Trio 2: 190, *190*
Norma, Philip 12: 1325
Norman, Steve 20: *2346*, 2347
North London Invaders 19: 2210-11
North of Alaska 3: *352*, 353
Northern Songs 5: 537, 555, 10: 1159
Notes 8: 915
Noussel, Steve 15: 1799
Nova Express 16: 1807
Novi, Carlo 18: 2092
Nugent, Ted 14: *1601*
Numan, Gary 14: *1622*, 1623, 20: 2302, 2303, 2313-15, *2313, 2314*, 2351, 2353, 2356
Nunn, Bobby 1: 71, 3: 281, 294, *294*, 295, 296
Nyro, Laura 1: 16, 10: 1100, 12: 1341, 15: *1703*, 1710, 1779

O

Oakey, Phil 13: 1519, 20: 2306, *2308*, 2308-9, 2395
Oakley, Berry 14: 1603-4
Oasis 18: 2111
Oates, John 10: *1162*, 1163, 20: *2344*, 2355
Oban, George 19: 2216
Obey, Ebenezer 9: 967, 20: 2378, *2378*, *2380*
O'Brien, Denis 17: 1968

O'Brien, Richard 16: 1876, *1877*, 20: 2339
Ocean, Humphrey 17: 1964
Ochs, Phil 2: 195, 5: *503*, 6: 664, *664*, 680, 10: 1123-4, *1123*
O'Connor, Billy 20: 2292
O'Connor, Hazel 14: 1623
O'Daylie, Daddy 5: 489
Odetta and Peter 11: 1205
O'Dowd, George Alan see Boy George
Odyssey 18: 2103
Offord, Eddie 15: 1691, 1694, 16: 1901
Ogerman, Klaus 5: 489
'Oh Boy' 2: 123, 134, 137, 202, *205*, 4: 362, 366, 368, 372, 379, 380, 425, 8: 842, 849, 13: 1515
'Oh Calcutta!' 8: 859
O'Hara, Brian 5: 534, *535*
O'Hara, Helen 19: 2220
Ohio Express 9: 983, *996-7*, 997-8
Ohio Players 12: 1403
O'Horgan, Tom 8: 860
Oil Movement 18: 2141, 2154
Oily Records 19: 2274
O'Jay, Eddie 14: 1600
O'Jays 14: 1581, 1596, 1597, 1598, 1600, 19: 2182
O'Kaysions 10: 1163
O'Keefe, Johnny 3: *247*, 249, *249*
Okeh 9: 1059-60, 18: 2102
Oku Onuora 20: 2374
Ola and the Janglers 6: 682
Oldaker, Jamie 9: 1036, 16: 1856
Old And In The Way 8: 908, *908*
Old Dark House, The 16: 1877
'Old Grey Whistle Test' 8: 853, *853*, 16: 1801, 1807
Oldenburg, Claes 5: 498, 500
Oldfield, Mike 12: 1397, 15: 1742, 16: 1916-17, 17: *2026*, 2027, 20: 2301
Oldham, Andrew Loog 4: 418, 437, 5: 535, 557, 6: 640, 7: 758, *758*, 760, 807, 815, 816, *817*, 8: 881, 887, 891, 893, *896*, 896-7, 899, 952, 10: 1136, 13: 1503, 14: 1594, 15: 1685-6
Oldham, Spooner 10: 1174-5
Olenn, Johnny 3: 300
O'List, David 15: 1685-6, *1687*, 16: 1807
Olive, Patrick 16: 1826, 1828
'Oliver!' 8: 859
Oliver, Paul 2: 160, 5: 593
Ollis, Terry 17: 1996
Olsen, Keith 18: 2135
Olsson, Nigel 10: 1187, 14: 1667-8, *1668*
O'Malley, Tony 16: *1914*, 1915
Omartian, Michael 7: 800
Omega 20: *2377*
One-der-ful 9: 1058, 1060
101ers 17: 1925, 18: 2067
One From The Heart 18: 2095
One Plus One 8: 848
One PM 8: 911
One Trick Pony 10: *1128*, 1131
One Truth Band 13: 1525
O'Neil, Jimmy 5: *502*
O'Neil, Mike 5: *563*

Only Lovers Left Alive **8:** 893
Ono, Yoko **8:** 857, **10:** 1151, *1151, 1158-9,* **11:** *1298,* 1306, **12:** 1332, **13:** 1495, **14:** 1679, **15:** 1692, 1710, **17:** 1961, *1971, 1972-3, 1974*
On The Road To Freedom **12:** 1375
Onuora, Oku **20:** 2375
Open Road **10:** 1135
O'Rahilly, Ronan **7:** 744, *744,* 816-17
Orange, Watter **19:** 2217
Orange Juice **19:** 2273
Orbison, Roy **1:** 40, 46, 103, 118, **2:** 231, 238, 240, **4:** 401-2, 403, *403,* 412-16, **7:** 723, **8:** 847
Orbits **4:** 396
Orchestral Manoeuvres In The Dark **16:** 1902, **18:** 2070, 2158, **20:** 2302, 2316-17, *2317*
Orchids **7:** 758
Orejob **13:** 1486, *1491,* 1493
Organ Trio **19:** 2167
Original Hillbillies **1:** 39
Original London Blue Blowers **2:** 125
O'Riley, Tony **15:** 1691
Orioles **1:** 31-2, 70, **2:** 216, 236, **12:** *1418,* 1419
Ork, Terry **17:** 2007
Orlando, Tony **3:** 309, **4:** 426, 441,443 *443,* 447, 448, 458-9, 448
Orlona **5:** 483, 489
O'Rourke, Steve **17:**1924
Ory, Kid **2:** 179
Osborne, Gary **14:** 1668
Osborne, Joe **5:** 519
Osborne, Ozzy **12:** 1361, 1369-70, *1369-70,* **17:** 1982
Oscar's Hot Icebergs **2:** 122
Osei, Teddy **9:** 969
Osibisa **9:** 963-4, 965, 967, 968-9, **15:** 1728, 1740, **20:** 2362
Oskar, Lee **6:** 655
Osmond, Donny **3:** 309, **13:** *1501,* 1502, 1504-6, *1505-6, 1544*
Osmond, Jimmy **13:** 1502, 1504, 1506
Osmond, Marie **13:** 1504, 1506, *1506*
Osmonds **13:** 1502, 1504-6, **14:** 1583
Osterberg, Jim **9:** 1002
O'Sullivan, Gilbert **6:** 722, **14:** 1662, *1662,* **17:** 2034, 2035
Other Half **8:** 914
Otis, Johnny **1:** 30, *70-1,* **2:** 149, 236, **3:** 245, 286, 287, *287,* 289, 294, 330, 337, **4:** 462, **5:** 494, 495, 590, **10:** 1161-2
Otis, Shuggie **13:** 1495
O'Toole, Mark **20:** 2415
'Our World' **10:** 1149
Outlaws **4:** 363, 392, 437, **17:** 2025
Ovenall, Harry **10:** 1198, *1198*
Overlanders **6:** 694-5
Owen, Alan **8:** 854
Owen, Butch **2:** 171
Owen, Malcolm **18:** 2141
Owens, Campbell **19:** 2273
Owens, Charles 'Fizzy' **14:** 1648
Owens, Rick **9:** 1052

Oxford, Jumpin' George **1:** 56
Oxtoby, David **11:** 1296, *1296,* 1299-1300, *1300*
Oz **12:** *1382,* 1391

P

Pablo, Augustus **20:** 2374
Pacemakers **5:** 523, 524-7, 532, 537, 538
Pack, The **8:** *871,* 872
Paddy, Klaus and Gibson **5:** 540, **11:** 1266
Padovani, Henry **19:** 2184
Page, Gene **5:** 520, **14:** 1589, **18:** 2102
Page, Jimmy **1:** 2, *3,* **2:** 228, **4:** 383, **6:** 642, 651, 652-3, *652,* 685, **7:** 758-9, 760, 815, 819, **9:** 1021-2, *1022-3,* 1074, 1079, **10:** 1168, **11:** 1228, 1230, **12:** 1361, 1364-7, *1366-7,* 1368, 1373, **13:** *1478,* 1479, **14:** 1680, **15:** 1685, **17:** 1981
Page, Larry **7:** 760, *760,* **8:** 944, 946
Page, Patti **1:** 37
Paice, Ashton and Lord **12:** 1380
Paice, Ian **12:** 1377, *1377,* 1379-80, **17:** 1981, 1984, 1987
Paich, Marty **14:** 1614
Paige, Elaine **20:** *2337*
Paiva, John **5:** *571,* **8:** 894
Palin, Michael **17:** 1968
Pallenberg, Anita **8:** *893,* 894
Palma, Brian de **5:** 575
Palmer, Ben **9:** 1022, **10:** 1188
Palmer, Bruce **7:** 825, **15:** 1765, 1768
Palmer, Carl **6:** 603, 642, **7:** 815, **14:** 1620, **15:** 1687-8, *1688*
Palmer, Clive **13:** 1468-9
Palmer, David **14:** 1571, 1572, **16:** 1919
Palmer, Earl **2:** 149, 151, 154, *155,* 197, **3:** 248, **4:** 399, **5:** 510, 519, **6:** 717
Palmer, Poli **10:** 1199-1200
Palmer, Robert **9:** 973, *973*
Palmer, Tony **8:** 848, 851-2, **9:** 1022, 1032, **12:** 1351
Palmolive **18:** 2062
Pang, May **17:** *1971,* 1972, 1973
Pankow, James **13:** 1527-8, *1528*
Panozzo, Chuck **18:** 2128, *2128*
Panter, 'Sir Horace' Gentleman **19:** 2204, 2207
Papa Du Run Da Run **7:** 767
Papathanassiou, Vangelis **15:** 1692, 1695
Paper Lace **6:** 687
Pappalardi, Felix **9:** 1029, 1032, **14:** 1606, *1606,* 1607, 1608
Paradise Theater **18:** 2129
Paragons **16:** 1887
Paramor, Norrie **4:** *362, 365,* 366, 368, 386, 387, *387,* 421, *421,* 433, *433,* 434, **8:** 947, **17:** 1953, **20:** 2336, 2337
Paramount Jazz Band **4:** 440
Paramounts **5:** 583, **6:** *602,* 603, **10:** *1086,* 1086-7
Parazaider, Walter **13:** 1527, *1528*

Parfitt, Rick **15:** *1730,* 1731, 1732, 1733, *1733,* 1735
Paris, Johnny **4:** 396, *396,* 397, *397*
Paris, Jon **11:** 1235
Paris Sisters **5:** 508, 567
Pariser, Alan **10:** 1098
Parker, Alan **11:** 1313, 1317
Parker, Charlie **3:** 321, *321,* **12:** 1418, **13:** 1529, *1530,* **18:** 2095
Parker, Colonel Tom **1:** 15, 50, 54, 83, 86-90, 91-3, 96, **2:** 214, **3:** 255, 256, 304, **13:** 1503
Parker, Graham **17:** 1922, 1924, 1935, 1936-7, 1939, **19:** 2257
Parker, Ian **18:** 2147
Parker, Little Junior **1:** 45, **7:** *798,* 799-800
Parker, Maceo **7:** 791, **19:** 2171
Parker, Ray **20:** 2420
Parkes, Lloyd **14:** 1598
Parks, Gordon **12:** 1410
Parks, Lloyd **16:** 1887
Parks, Van Dyke **1:** 13, **5:** 502, 520, **7:** 772, 776, 779-80, **10:** *1092,* 1093, **16:** 1859
Parliament **12:** 1402, 1407, *1418,* **18:** 2103, **19:** *2170,* 2171-2
Parnes, Larry **2:** 122-3, 130-1, *131,* 136, 136-7, 138, 140, **4:** 361, 425, *425,* **5:** 547, 596, **13:** 1502-3
Parra, Fito de la **10:** 1116
Parson, Dave **18:** *2144,* 2145
Parsons, Gene **7:** 830
Parsons, Gram **7:** *827,* 829-30, **13:** 1443, 1541, 1543, 1556-7, 1559, **14:** 1652, **17:** 2022-3, 2025
Parton, Dolly **2:** *231,* **14:** 1659, *1659,* **17:** 2021, *2022,* 2023, 2024
Partridge Family **8:** 843, *843,* **13:** 1502, *1516,* 1517
Passions **18:** 2071
Pastorius, Jaco **9:** 1039, **12:** 1347, **13:** 1533, *1533*
Pate, Johnny **7:** 795, **9:** 1059
Pat Garrett And Billy The Kid **11:** 1210, **14:** 1650, *1651,* 1652
Paterson, Big Jim **19:** 2218, 2220
Paton, Dave **13:** 1511
Paton, Tam **13:** 1510-13, *1512*
Patience and Prudence **3:** 259
Patterson, Alvin 'Seeco' **16:** 1893
Pattison, Lee **19:** 2276, *2276, 2277*
Patto, Johnny **4:** 435
Patton, Charlie **2:** 159
Paul, Billy **14:** 1581, 1596, 1597, **18:** 2102
Paul, Clarence **6:** 716, *718,* 719, **9:** 1046, **14:** 1672-3
Paul, Les **1:** 78-9, *80,* **6:** *653,* **11:** 1225, *1229,* **16:** 1909-10
Paul, Steve **10:** 1094, **11:** 1234-5
Paul Butterfield Band **10:** 1103, 1116, **11:** 1207, *1207, 1238,* 1239, **13:** 1498-9
Paul Dowell and the Dolphins **16:** 1846
Paul Revere and the Raiders **4:** 391, **5:** 503, **7:** 821, 821-3, 872, **10:** 1092
Paulson, Kenny **5:** 496

Paupers **10**: 1099
Paxton, Tom **6**: 662, 664, *664*, 680, **10**: *1122*, 1123-4
Paycheck, Johnny **5**: 492
Payne, Bill **16**: 1858, 1860
Payne, Chris **20**: 2314
Payne, Davey **17**: 1921, 1931, 1933, *1933*
Payne, Freda **18**: 2102, *2102*
Payne, Scherrie **9**: 1049, *1049*
payola scandal **2**: *202*, 203, 217, 218-20, **3**: 353, 355, 360, **4**: 395, 460
Payton, Denis **6**: *610*, 610-11
Payton, Lawrence **4**: 472, **6**: 710-13
Peace **15**: 1740
Peacock, Trevor **4**: *422*, 423
Peanut Butter Conspiracy **10**: 1083
Pearl, Jack **4**: 463
Pearlman, Sandy **12**: 1339, 1371, **18**: 2126, 2127
Pearson, Ken **10**: 1172
Peart, Neil **19**: 2234-5
Peebles, Andy **17**: 1959, *1959*
Peek, Dan **15**: 1776, 1777, *1777*
Peel, John **1**: 7, *7*: 745, 824, **8**: 852, *852*, **12**: 1396-7, 1422, 1438, 1440, **14**: 1622, **17**: 1958, *1959*, **18**: 2076-7, *2076-7*, 2149, *2157*
Peellaert, Guy **11**: 1298, *1299*, **14**: 1628
Pegg, Dave **13**: 1466-7, *1467*
Peggy Sue **2**: *183*
Pegrum, Nigel **13**: 1472-3
Peloquin, Jerry **8**: 909
Pender, Mike **5**: 528-31
Pendergrass, Teddy **1**: 62, **14**: *1597*, 1597-8, 1600, **15**: 1787
Penetration **16**: 1902
Penguins **1**: *70-1*, 71, **3**: 299, 300, **13**: 1490, 1492
Penn, Dan **10**: 1174-5
Pennebaker, D. A. **10**: 1099
Penrod, Jerry **9**: 1071
Pentangle **1**: 8, **13**: 1461-2, 1465, 1476-7
Pentelow, Nick **10**: 1185
Pentifalla, Kenny **18**: 2092
People's Choice **14**: 1600
Peppermint Lounge, New York **8**: 862, *863*
Peppermint Trolley Company **9**: *996*, 998
Peraza, Armando **13**: 1537
Percussions **14**: 1594
Perez, John **7**: 834-5
Performance **8**: *847*, 848, 893, 900, **13**: 1559, **15**: 1719, **20**: 2326
'performance art' **20**: 2339
Perkins **16**: 1891
Perkins, Karl **1**: 35, 46, *46, 54*, 80, 81, *101*, 101-3, 109-11, 112-13, 116, 118, **2**: 184, **3**: *253*, 254, **5**: 552, **7**: 739, **14**: 1643
Perkins, Clayton **1**: *109*, 110
Perkins, George **15**: 1783
Perkins, Jay **1**: *109*, 110, **2**: 194
Perkins, John **2**: 235
Perkins, Luther **1**: 47, **14**: 1643, 1645
Perkins, Ray **2**: 235
Perren **18**: 2103

Perrin, Leslie **8**: 897
Perry, David **14**: 1607
Perry, Fred **7**: 732
Perry, Joe **16**: 1848, 1849
Perry, Jeffrey **3**: 332
Perry, Lee 'Scratch' **16**: *1882*, 1883, 1886, 1890, 1893, *1898*, 1899
Perry, Richard **13**: 1484, **14**: 1592, **15**: 1710, 1711, **17**: 1976, 2035
Perry, Willie **17**: 1928
'Perry Como TV Show' **1**: 110
Persuasions **1**: 63
Peter and Gordon **4**: 418, **6**: 693-4, 695, *695*, **8**: 880, **10**: 1149, **15**: 1707
Peter B's Looners **7**: 817
Peter, Paul and Mary **6**: 664, *664*, 667, 669, 675, **10**: 1082, 1121, 1127, 1139, **11**: *1204*, 1205, 1218, **12**: 1358, **14**: 1672-3
Peterman, Jim **11**: *1225*, 1225-6
Peters, Dale **14**: 1613
Petersen, Paul **5**: 502, 509
Petersen, Robert **8**: 905
Peterson, Big Jim **19**: 2218, 2219, 2220
Peterson, Colin **18**: 2105, *2105*
Peterson, Garry **14**: 1616 *1616*
Peterson, Ray **5**: 507, 575, *575*
Petty, Norman **1**: 43, **2**: 182-3, 185, 186-7, 190-1, *190-1*, 192, 200, **4**: 414, 457, **16**: 1901
Petty, Tom **4**: 420, *420*, **9**: 1079, **18**: 2081-2, *2083-6*, 2084-6
Petty, Vi **2**: 190, *190*, 193
Peverett, 'Lonesome' Dave **10**: 1102
Pfisterer, 'Snoopy' **9**: 1017
Phantom Of The Paradise **16**: 1863
Philadelphia Folk Festival (1980) **11**: *1254*
Philadelphia Jazz Festival **11**: 1253
Philles **3**: 265, **5**: 509-12, *509*, 514-15, 517, *517*
Phillips, Anthony **15**: 1752
Phillips, Dewey **1**: 43, *52*, 53, 56, 58
Phillips, Earl **5**: 595
Phillips, Eddie **7**: 759, 819
Phillips, Harry **10**: 1178
Phillips, John **1**: 15, **7**: *823*, 838-40, *838*, **10**: 1081-2, *1082, 1084*, 1098, 1100, **11**: 1252
Phillips, Little Esther **10**: 1161-2
Phillips, Mackenzie **7**: *839*, 840
Phillips, Michelle **7**: *838*, 838-40, *840*, **11**: *1253*
Phillips, Phil **13**: 1445
Phillips, Popeye **13**: 1556
Phillips, Sam **1**: *41*, 42-7, *44, 47*, 51-4, *52*, 58, 86, 94, 109-10, 112, 114, **2**: 168, 169, 182, 200, **3**: *261*, 262, 271, 276, **4**: 414, 462, 465, 472, **6**: 701, **7**: 785, 799, **8**: 921, 932, **9**: 1001, **11**: 1281, **14**: 1643, **16**: 1901
Phillips, Simon **9**: 1033, **17**: 1999
Phipps, Pete **20**: 2387
Phlorescent Leech and Eddie **9**: 993
Phoenix **5**: 507

Photoplay **1**: 96
Piano Red **1**: 31
Pichon, Walter 'Fats' **2**: 145
Pickett, Phil **20**: 2400
Pickett, Wilson **1**: *11*, **2**: 157, **7**: 782, 785, 796-7, 815, **8**: 922, 929-30, 937, 938-40, **9**: 966, **10**: 1176, **12**: 1401, 1420, **14**: 1603, **15**: 1789
Pickney, Fayette **14**: 1597, 1600
'Pick Of The Pops' **4**: 377, **8**: 841
Pied Piper, The **10**: 1135
Piepe, Judity **10**: 1128
Pierson, Clark **10**: 1172
Pierson, Kate **20**: *2286*, 2286-7
Piggee, Mutt **7**: 799
Pilgrim Travellers **2**: 160, **3**: 333
Pilkington-Mikso, Florian **14**: 1576, *1577*
Pilnick, Paul **5**: 534
Pinder, Mike **10**: 1193-4, *1195*, 1196, *1197*
Pine, Kenny **9**: 1015
Pinera, Mike **9**: 1071
Pingatore, Marshall **1**: 26
Pink Fairies **11**: 1257
Pink Floyd **1**: *8*, 8-9, 10, **6**: 619, 643, 647, **7**: 817, **8**: 847-8, **9**: *984*, **10**: 1085, **11**: 1247, 1257, 1293, *1294-5*, 1295, 1297-8: *1301-2*, 1303-4, *1303, 1307-17, 1319-20*, **12**: 1383, **14**: 1562, 1680, **15**: 1741-2, **17**: 1921, **18**: 2098, 2100, **20**: 2326, 2329, 2330
Pinkerton's Assorted Colours **6**: 603
Pink Military **19**: 2280
Pinkney, Bill **3**: 290
Pinnick, Chris **13**: 1528
Pioneer Company **9**: 961
Pioneers **9**: 978, **16**: *1885*, 1887
Pipe and the Pipers **16**: 1887
Pip Simmons Theatre Group **8**: 860
Pips **6**: 719, **9**: 1042-3, 1057
Piranhas **19**: 2260
pirate radio **7**: 743, 744-7, **8**: 841-2
Pirates **4**: 421, 434-5
Pirates Of Penzance, The **20**: 2339
Pirroni, Marco **18**: 2148, **20**: 2323, *2324*, 2325
Pitney, Gene **3**: 303, 309, **5**: 504, *505*, 507, 514, 579, **7**: 723, *723*, 726-9, **8**: 891, **13**: 1517, **15**: 1718
Pitt, Ken **14**: 1625
Pittman, Barbara **1**: *112*
Pittman, Bill **2**: 197
Plainsong **13**: 1464, 1465
Planet Patrol **19**: 2169, **20**: 2303
Planet Records **7**: 759
Planets **19**: 2280
Plank, Conny **20**: 2310-11, 2386
Planno, Mortimer **16**: 1890-1
Plant, Robert **6**: *642*, 653, **12**: 1364-6, *1366-7*, 1368, **17**: 1982, **18**: 2133, 2135
Planzty **20**: 2333
Plaster Casters Of Chicago **9**: 1075
Plastic Ono Band **9**: 1035, **15**: 1692, **17**: 1972, 1976
Plastic People Of The Universe **20**: *2376*
Plastics, The **20**: *2363*, 2365

Platters **1:** *62, 70,* 71-2, *84,* **3:** 252, 281, 283, *283,* 298-300, **5:** 495, **7:** 761
Play It Cool **4:** 426, *426,* 433, **13:** 1514
Playboys **1:** 73, **6:** 682, **7:** *736*
Playmates **2:** 237
Play Misty For Me **15:** 1799
Pleasers **19:** *2242,* 2242-3
Pleasure Seekers **16:** 1830, 1831
Plummet Airlines **17:** 1924
Plumpton Pop Festival (1970) **11:** 1243
Poco **7:** 826, *826* **14:** 1657, **15:** 1773, 1775
Poets **6:** 603, **8:** 949
Pointer Sisters **20:** 2419
Poison Girls **18:** 2160, *2160*
Poitier, Sidney **2:** *207*
Polci, Gerry **5:** *570,* 573
Polecats **1:** *102, 116,* 120
Poliakoff, Stephen **20:** 2340
Police **14:** 1576, **15:** 1737, **19:** 2182-3, *2182,* 2184-6, *2186-7,* 2205, **20:** 2281, 2292
Pollitt, Tessa **18:** 2062
Polymoog **20:** 2319
Poly Styrene **18:** 2053, 2061
Pompilli, Rudy **1:** 28
Pomus, Doc **3:** 292, 342, 350, 352
Pomus, Don and Shuman, Mort **4:** 444, 445, 446, *446*
Ponica, Vinnie **5:** 509, 514
Pons, Jim **9:** 993
Ponty, Jean-Luc **13:** 1495, 1525
Pony **5:** 483, 485
Poole, Brian **5:** 537, **6:** 615-17
Pooler, Frank **17:** 1949
Poor **15:** 1772
Pop, Iggy **5:** 500, **13:** *1481,* 1481-3, 1497-1500, **14:** 1626, *1632*
Pop, The **20:** *2288*
Pop Art **5:** 498-500, **7:** *818,* 820, **11:** 1296-1300
Popcorn Blizzard **18:** 2122
Pop Gear **6:** 659-60, **8:** 845
'Poppa Stoppa' **1:** 56
Popul Vuh **11:** 1316
Pop Weekly **12:** 1327
Popwell, Robert 'Pops' **8:** 877, **19:** *2174,* 2175
Porcaro, Jeffrey **18:** 2097
Porter, David **8:** 932-3, *933,* 936-7, **12:** 1408-9, *1410*
Porter, Hubert **9:** 975-6
Porter, John **10:** 1192
Porter, Shirley **14:** 1597
Porter, Tiran **16:** 1851, *1853*
Portsmouth Sinfonia **14:** 1638
Portz, Chuck **9:** 992-3
Posey, Sandy **1:** 16
Postcard Records **19:** 2273-4
Potger, Keith **10:** 1140
Potter, Brian **6:** 713
Potter, John **17:** 1928
Pottinger, Sonia **16:** *1882*
Potts, Jr., Wardell **19:** 2179
Powell, Andy **15:** 1736, *1736,* **20:** 2330, 2331

Powell, Billy **16:** 1843, 1844
Powell, Cozy **11:** 1232, **16:** *1822,* **17:** 1982, 1984, 1986
Powell, Don **12:** 1427
Powell, Jimmy **15:** 1724
Powell, Nick **19:** 2242
Powell, Peter **17:** *1959*
Powell, Roger **7:** 818-19, **16:** 1905, **20:** 2318, *2319*
Powell, William **14:** 1600, *1600*
Power, Duffy **2:** 137, *137,* 138, **4:** 427
Power, Duffy **2:** 137, *137* 138, **4:** 427
Powers, Ralph **1:** 55
Powers, Tony **4:** 449 **5:** 509
Power Station **20:** 2391, 2418
Prager, Bud **18:** 2133
Prater, Dave *see* Sam and Dave
Pratt, Michael **4:** 421, 422, *423*
Pratt, Mike **8:** 859
Premiers **1:** 76
Presley, Elvis **1:** 3, 12, 27, *28,* 41, 41-3, *43, 44,* 45-7, 48-54, 61, 75, 80, 81-3, 86-90, 103, 105, 109-10, 112-14, 116, 118, **2:** 122, 129, 135, *136,* 146, 148, 153, 155, 156, 158, 161, 163, 164, 165, *165,* 166, 168, 169, 183, 184, 200, 201, 202, *202,* 204, 205, 208-9, 210-14, 220, 230, 232, 234, 238, 239, 240, **3:** 241, 243, 245, 247, 249, *249,* 250, 254, 255-7, 258, 259, 262, 274, *285,* 288-9, *289,* 304, 306, 308, 310, 311, 313, 314, 332, 337, 355, **4:** 392, 401, 402, 406, 422, 445, 446, 454, 456, **5:** 551-2, **6:** 683, **7:** 722, 735, 739-40, **8:** 843-4, **9:** 1001, 1021, *1023,* 1045, **10:** 1098, 1110, 1118-19, 1143, 1162, **11:** 1281, 1289-90, 1296-7, *1296-7,* 1300 **12:** 1321, 1325, 1387, 1401, 1434, **13:** 1442, 1457, 1503, 1515, 1556, **14:** 1643, 1647, 1652, **16:** 1834, **17:** 1941, **18:** *2064,* 2084, 2087, **20:** 2340
Presley, Reg **8:** 944-6
Pressure Point **3:** *347*
Prestridge, Herbert **7:** *810,* 811
Preston, Billy **2:** 150, 179, *180,* **3:** 334, **9:** 1043, **10:** 1158, **14:** 1679, **15:** 1790, 1796-7, **17:** 1976
Preston, Don **13:** *1491,* 1493
Preston, Johnny **5:** 575
Preston, Mike **4:** 362
Pretenders **7:** 756, **19:** 2242, 2252-3, *2253*
Pretty Things **6:** 603, 657, 658, **7:** 742, 758, 803, 817, **8:** 848, **9:** 1065, **10:** 1101, **11:** 1247, **12:** 1366
Preuss, Oscar **6:** 637-8
Price, Alan **5:** 597, **6:** 643, *657-8,* 657-60, **7:** *817,* **15:** 1692, 1700
Price, Jim **8:** 894
Price, Leo **2:** 150, 156
Price, Lloyd **1:** 42, **2:** 142, 149, 154, 156-7, **8:** 939, **13:** 1452
Price, Louis **9:** 1052
Price, Ray **14:** 1647
Price, Red **4:** *379*
Price, Rick **10:** 1185, **15:** 1747

Priest, Steve **16:** 1835, *1836-7,* 1837
Prime Movers **13:** 1498
Primes **9:** 1045, 1050
Primettes **9:** 1045-6
Primitives **9:** 1005
Prince **12:** 1407, **19:** 2168, 2172, **20:** 2303, 2418, *2419*
Prince, Graham **3:** 354
Prince, John **3:** 309
Prince, Prairie **16:** 1873, *1873*
Prince, Viv **11:** 1228, 1230
Princess **20:** 2419
Prine, John **11:** 1220
Prior, Maddy **13:** *1471,* 1472-3
Prisonaires **1:** 45, *45*
Privilege **6:** 647, **8:** *846,* 847
Proby, P. J. **7:** 723, *722-3,* 734-5, **14:** 1680, **15:** 1718, **20:** *2338,* 2340
Procol Harum **1:** 7, **10:** 1085, 1086-9, 1167, **11:** 1305, **12:** *1383,* **15:** 1682, 1683
Professor Longhair **13:** 1451, 1452
Promises **5:** 580, **8:** 859
Propaganda **20:** 2415
Prosen, Sid **10:** 1126
Pruett, Sammy **2:** 225, 228
Pryor, Snooky **4:** 465
Prystock, Arthur **7:** 796
Psychedelic Furs **16:** 1905
Psychedelic Rangers **9:** 1009
Psycho **5:** 498
Psych-Out **8:** 848
public address (PA) systems **19:** 2137-40
Public Image Ltd **11:** 1292, **18:** 2048, **20:** 2381
Pukwana, Dudu **9:** 964, 966, *967,* 971
Punter, John **20:** 2356
Pure Garbage **16:** 1863
Purple Gang **11:** 1305
Purple Rain **20:** 2418, *2419*
Pursey, Jimmy **15:** 1757, **18:** 2061, 2141, *2142, 2144,* 2145, 2146
Pursuit Of Happiness **15:** 1719
Pussycat **17:** *1926*
Putnam, Norbert **6:** 673, **10:** 1136
Putney (EMS) VCS-3 (synthesizer) **20:** 2301
Pye **5:** 528, 530-1, 536, **7:** 750, 753-4, 758
Pyle, Artimus **16:** 1844
Pyle, Pip **20:** 2368
Pyramids **7:** 765

Q

Quad City Wranglers **9:** 993
Quadrophenia **11:** 1261, 1273, *1273-4,* 1275, 1277, **12:** *1393,* **20:** 2328, 2334
Quaife, Peter **7:** 750, *750,* 754
Quarrymen **2:** 127, *128,* **5:** 532, 534, *535,*

546-7, *547 see also* Beatles
Quatro, Suzi **8:** 872, **16:** 1821, 1822, *1823,* 1829-31, **18:** 2071, 2099
Quaye, Caleb **14:** 1634
Quaye, Russell **2:** *123*
Queen **11:** *1245, 1284,* **12:** 1423, **14:** 1633, **15:** 1698, 1728, **16:** 1812-17, 1819, 1863, **18:** 2098, *2099,* **20:** 2420
Quickly, Tommy **5:** *532,* 534, *535,* 551
Quicksilver Messenger Service **1:** 15, **7:** 760, **8:** 905, *914,* 915, 917, **10:** 1100, 1170, **11:** 1223, *1290,* 1292
Quiet Sun **17:** 1807, 1810
Quine, Richard **17:** 2012-13, *2013*
Quine, Robert **14:** *1636-7,* 1637
Quinn, Derek **6:** *612-13,* 613-14
Quinn, Freddy **6:** 700
Quinn, Patricia **16:** *1877*
Quinteros, Eddie **2:** 196
Quintessence **12:** *1398,* 1399
Quinton, Derek **18:** 2147
Quiver **17:** 1922

R

Rabbit Foot Minstrels **1:** 33
Rabbitt, Eddie **14:** 1659, **18:** *2055*
Rabid Records **17:** 1925
Race, Steve **1:** 98
Radar Records **19:** 2182
Radcliffe, Leroy **17:** 2017
Radha Krishna Temple **12:** 1396
Radiants **9:** 1059
Radio Atlanta **7:** 744, 746
Radio Caroline **4:** *434,* **7:** 744-5, *744,* 746-7, *747,* 758, **8:** 841
Radio City **7:** 744, *746,* 746-7
Radio England **7:** 745
Radio Essex **7:** 745
Radio 5 **19:** 2262
Radio Invista **7:** 744
Radio London **7:** 745, 747
Radio Luxembourg **4:** 376, *376,* 377, *377,* **7:** 744, 745, **8:** 841
Radio On **20:** 2328, *2329*
Radio One **17:** 1958-60
Radio 1 DJs **1:** 19
Radio Scotland **7:** 745
Radio Sutch **7:** 744
Radle, Carl **9:** 1035-6, **13:** 1444, 1449
Rado, James **2:** 228
Raelettes **3:** *325,* 327, 328, 337
Rafelson, Bob **9:** 982, 987, *987,* **20:** 2360
Rafferty, Gerry **17:** 2021, 2028-9, *2028-9*
Ragtime **15:** 1720
Rainbow **12:** 1380, **17:** 1983-7, 2000, **18:** 2060
Rainbow Bridge **9:** 1068
Rainbows **6:** 702
Raincoats **18:** 2072
Raindrops **4:** 423, 449, **5:** 569

Rainey, Chuck **13:** 1555, **19:** 2173
Rainey, Gertrude 'Ma' **1:** 33
Rains, George **7:** 835
Rainwater, Marvin **1:** 113, **3:** 316, 317, **5:** 501
Raitt, Bonnie **15:** 1780, **16:** *1859*
RAK Records **16:** 1822, 1834
Ralphs, Mick **15:** 1740, **16:** 1818, 1819, *1820*
Ram, Buck **1:** 71-2, **2:** 217, **3:** 281, *283,* 298-9, 300, *300*
Ram Jam Band **19:** 2216, 2218, 2219
Ram Jet Band **7:** 810-11, 820
Ramblers **4:** 393
Ramone, Phil **13:** 1528
Ramones **9:** 1002, **17:** 2002, 2003, 2007, 2008, 2009-11, 2012, **18:** 2053, 2058, 2086, **20:** 2328
Ramrods **4:** 391
Rance Allen Group **15:** 1783
Randazzo, Teddy **2:** 236, **14:** 1595, *1595*
Randi, Don **5:** 520
Randle, Bill **1:** 57, **2:** 235, *235*
Randolph, 'Boots' **1:** 94, 95, **2:** 185, 233, *233*
Range Drifters **1:** *25*
Rangers **13:** 1460
Ranglin, Alvin **16:** 1896
Ranglin, Ernest **9:** *975*
Rankin, Billy **17:** 1989
Rankine, Alan **19:** *2272,* 2275
Ranking. Roger **19:** 2208, *2209,* 2214
Rare Earth **9:** 1042, 1052, 1057
Raspberries **15:** 1721, **20:** 2288-9
Rathbone, Don **6:** 605
Rationals **8:** 872
Ratledge, Mike **12:** 1397, **14:** 1562, 1578-80, *1578-80* **15:** 1700, **18:** *2076*
Rats **14:** 1633
Rat Scabies **18:** 2062, *2078,* 2079, *2080*
Rattles **3:** 250, **6:** *682,* 683
Rauschenberg, Robert **5:** 498
Raven, Genya **18:** 2127
Raven, Mike **10:** 1101-2, **17:** 1958
Raven, Paul *see* Glitter, Gary
Ravens **1:** *69,* 70
Ravenscroft, Raphael **17:** 2028
Rawls, Lou **2:** 160, **3:** 334, **10:** 1099, **14:** 1600, **15:** *1799,* **18:** 2102
Raw Records **17:** 1925
Ray, Johnnie **1:** 45, 98, **2:** 122, **3:** 307
Rayber Voices **4:** 472-3
Raymonde, Ivor **4:** 362
Rays **3:** 342
'Razzmatazz' **20:** *2385*
Reaction **11:** 1266, 1276
Read, Mike **12:** *1325,* **20:** 2415
'Ready Steady Go!' **1:** 110, **4:** *380,* **6:** *689,* **7:** 737, 743, *743,* 803, 818, **8:** 842, 849-50, 851, *851,* **10:** 1124, 1134, *1134*
RCA Records **1:** 89-90, **3:** 262, 294, 309, *333,* 334, 335, **8:** 909, 911-12, 913, **11:** 1265, 1273, **12:** 1436
Real Kids **20:** *2289*
Reame-James, Milton **16:** 1839, *1839*

Rebel Rousers **5:** 534
Rebel Without A Cause **1:** 23, 90, **2:** 207, 211, **12:** 1385
Rebennack, Mac *see* Dr John
Recommended Records **18:** 2159
Record Exchanger **12:** 1339
Records **19:** 2243
Records World **1:** 59
Red Bird Records **3:** 266, 289, 292, *300,* **4:** 449, **5:** 567, 569
Redbrass **20:** 2386
Redcaps **7:** 758, **10:** 1183
Red Crayola **8:** 872
Redd, Gene **7:** 789
Redding, Noel **9:** *1063,* 1065-8, *1068*
Redding, Otis **1:** 10, *11,* 16, **2:** 149, 150, **3:** 296, 327, 335, **7:** 782-3, 785, 795, 796-7, 811, 815, **8:** 848, 887, 921-2, 923-7, 929-30, 932-3, 934, 937, 939, **9:** 971, **10:** 1099, 1100, **11:** 1300, **12:** 1401, 1409, 1420, **15:** 1781, 1789, **16:** 1881
Redding, Zelma **8:** 924, 926
'Red Hot 'n' Blue Show' **1:** 56
Red Squares **6:** 682-3
Red Wedge **20:** 2401
Reebop Kwaku-Baah **9:** 1036, **10:** 1189, 1192, *1192,* **20:** 2367
Reece, Red **2:** 139, **5:** 596
Reed, Alto **16:** 1856
Reed, Bill **2:** 235
Reed, Ernest 'Pepper' **19:** 2179
Reed, Herbert **3:** 299, 300
Reed, Jimmy **3:** 339, **5:** 582, **8:** *864,* 865, **9:** 1002-3, 1004-8, 1020
Reed, Lou **14:** 1623, 1626, 1632, 1634-7, **16:** 1802, 1806, 1808, 1866, **17:** 2019, **18:** 2042
Reefer Madness **9:** 1019
Rees, John **20:** 2372
Reeves, Greg **15:** 1765
Reeves, Jim **2:** 194, 195, *222,* 232, 234, **9:** 966, **10:** 1139
Reeves, Lois **6:** 717
Reeves, Martha *see* Martha and the Vandellas
Reeves, Tony **10:** 1114, **14:** 1576
Regents **1:** 63, **2:** 237, *237*
Reich, Charles A. **12:** 1323
Reid, Duke **9:** 961, 975-6, 977, **16:** *1883,* 1884, 1889
Reid, John **14:** 1667, **16:** 1817
Reid, Keith **10:** 1086-9, *1088*
Reid, Neil **13:** *1544*
Reid, Terry **12:** 1364
Reiley, Jack **7:** 772, 780
Reilly, Maggie **16:** 1917
Reinhardt, Django **2:** 121
Reinhardt, Larry **9:** 1071
Relf, Keith **6:** 650, *650-1,* 652-3, 654, **11:** 1228
Rel Yea's **4:** 390
Remains **8:** 872
Remington, Herb **14:** 1656
Renaissance **6:** 653
Renaldo and Clare **11:** 1211

Renbourn, John **13:** 1462, *1476,* 1476-7, 1478
Renegades **6:** 683
Renwick, Tim **14:** 1668
REO Speedwagon **17:** 2021, **18:** 2121
Republic **17:** 1925
Resnick, Artie **3:** 292, **5:** 562, **9:** 983, 998, *998*
Revers, Paul *see* Paul Revere and the Raiders
Rexroth, Kenneth **11:** 1301
Reynolds, Allen **14:** 1658
Reynolds, Debbie **3:** 312
Reynolds, Jody **4:** 402
Reynolds, Malvina **10:** 1139
Reynolds, Nick **6:** 662, *668-9,* 669
Rezillos **20:** 2307
RGM Sound **4:** 437
Rhodes, Bernie **18:** 2041, 2046, 2067-8
Rhodes, Harold **15:** 1698
Rhodes, Nick **20:** *2320, 2388,* 2389, *2390, 2391*
Rhythm 'n' Greens **8:** 844
Rhythm Orchids **2:** 183, 185, 190, 192-3, *193*
Rhythm Rockers **1:** 118
Rice, Jo **12:** *1325*
Rice, Mack **8:** 939-40
Rice, Tim **12:** *1325,* **13:** 1509, **15:** 1697, 1742, **20:** 2336-7
Rich, Charlie **1:** 44, *46-7,* 47, 103, **14:** 1658, *1659,* **17:** 2024
Rich Kids **8:** 863, **19:** 2242-3, **20:** 2351, 2353
Richard, Cliff **2:** 131, 134, 136, 137, 204, 205, *205,* 239, **3:** 249, 251, **4:** 361, 362, *362,* 363, *363,* 364-9, 379, 384, 385, 386, *387,* 388, 392, 404, 418, 422, 424, *429,* 430-1, *431,* 433, **5:** 504, *504,* 542, **7:** 722, 759, **8:** 844, 847, 850, 854, **12:** 1322, **14:** 1667, **17:** *1950-3,* 1950-3, 1955, *1955,* 2003
Richards, Keith **1:** 2, 8, 67, **2:** 175, **5:** *508, 551,* **6:** 680, **7:** 815, **8:** 881-90, 992, *943,* **11:** 1297, **12:** 1335, **13:** 1556, **15:** 1716, **16:** 1847, **20:** 2360
Richards, Ricky **5:** 538
Richards, Ron **6:** 640, **7:** 759
Richardson, Barry **17:** 1921
Richardson, Del **9:** 969
Richardson, Jack **14:** 1617
Richardson, Karl **18:** 2106-7
Richardson, Wendell **15:** 1740
Richbourg, 'John R.' **1:** 57, **8:** 926
Richie, Lionel **9:** 1043, **14:** 1593, *1675,* **20:** 2360, *2418*
Richman, Jonathan **9:** 1007, **15:** 1763, **17:** 2016-17, *2026-17,* **20:** 2283
Richmond, Dave **6:** 644-5
Rick and the Ravens **9:** 1009-10
Rickfors, Mikael **6:** *607,* 608
Rico **19:** 2203-5, 2216
Riddle, Nelson **1:** 34
Ridgeley, Andrew **20:** 2408-9, 2418
Ridgio, Gene **3:** *246*

'Riding The Rails' **14:** *1644*
Ridley, Greg **17:** 2039, **18:** *2133*
Rieley, Jack **7:** 722, 780
Righteous Brothers **4:** 459, **5:** 510-11, 516-17, 574, **9:** 981, **10:** 1161, 1163, 1173, **13:** 1449
Riley, Billy Lee **1:** 46, *112,* 118
Riley, Martin **16:** 1887
Riley, Michael **19:** 2216
Riley, Winston **16:** 1887
Riordan, Vince **18:** *2153,* 2154
Riot On Sunset Strip **8:** 847
Riot Squad **7:** 760, *819,* 820, **9:** 1065
Rip Chords **7:** 765
Ripperton, Minnie **15:** 1783
Riser, Paul **9:** 1057, **18:** 2102
Rising Sons **11:** 1237, **13:** 1559, *1559*
Ritter, Tex **1:** 37, 38, *39*
Rivera, Scarlet **11:** 1211
Rivers, Dick **2:** 243, 250
Rivers, Johnny **5:** 502, **10:** 1099, 1177
Rivets **6:** 683
Riviera, Jake **17:** 1925, 1934, 1935, 1939, *1939,* **18:** 2042, 2049, 2062, 2079, **19:** 2182, 2193, 2195, 2239, 2257
Rivieras **10:** 1178
Robb Brothers **4:** 419
Robbins, Hargus **11:** 1209
Robbins, Marty **2:** 234, **5:** 578, **14:** 1641
Robbins, Robyn **16:** 1856, 1857
Roberts, Chris **5:** 587
Roberts, Elliott **12:** 1345, **15:** 1762, 1763, 1766
Roberts, John **7:** 811, **11:** 1250-1
Roberts, Paul **11:** 1296
Roberts, Rick **13:** 1556
Robertson, Brian **17:** 1986, 1992, *1993,* **19:** 2239, *2239*
Robertson, Eck **1:** 39
Robertson, Ker **4:** 378
Robertson, Phil **5:** 586
Robertson, Robbie **3:** 251, **11:** 1209, **13:** 1546, 1547-9, *1549,* **14:** 1680, **17:** 1976
Robertson, Sandy **13:** 1472
Robert Stigwood organisation **20:** 2327, 2328, 2337
Robey, Don **7:** 799
Robi, Paul **3:** 299, 300
Robie, John **19:** 2169
Robivc, Ivo **3:** 269
Robins **1:** 71, **3:** 287-8, 294-5, *295*
Robinson, Bobby **14:** 1586-7, **19:** 2177
Robinson, Claudette **4:** 475, 477, 479
Robinson, Cynthia **12:** *1405,* 1406-7, **19:** 2171
Robinson, Danny **19:** 2177
Robinson, Dave **17:** 1922, 1931, 1936, 1937, 1939-40, 2016, **19:** 2182, 2212-13
Robinson, Freddie **10:** 1115
Robinson, Guy **4:** 434
Robinson, Harry **4:** 379
Robinson, Sandi **10:** 1083
Robinson, Smokey **1:** 10, 62, 75, **4:** *470,* 472, 473, 475-80, **6:** 702, 706-7, 713, 714, 717, **8:** 941, **9:** *1041,* 1042-3, 1045-

6, 1048, 1050-1, 1052, 1055, 1057, **10:** 1099, **14:** 1584, 1594, **15:** 1757
Robinson, Sylvia **19:** 2177, *2177*
Robinson, Tom **15:** 1757, **18:** *2146,* 2146-7, 2158, 2159, **20:** 2381
Rocca, John **20:** 2392
Rocco and the Saints **3:** 350
Rochereau, Tabu Ley **20:** 2378
Rock against Racism **18:** 2158, *2159*
Rock and Roll Dubble Bubble Trading Card Company, of Philadelphia **9:** 998
Rock Around The Clock **2:** 207, 210, 216, **3:** *243,* 251, 299, **4:** 429, **12:** 1385
Rock-a-Teens **4:** 381
Rock-Boris **3:** 251
Rockestra **17:** *1966*
Rockets **15:** 1768
'Rock Follies' **16:** 1810
Rock Goddess **18:** 2072
Rockin' Berries **6:** 603, **7:** 741, **10:** 1181, *1181,* 1183
Rockin' Devils, Los **6:** 683
Rockin' Dopsie **17:** 1925
Rocking Russian **11:** 1294, *1294*
Rockin' Rebels **4:** 391
Rockin' R's **4:** 391
Rock in Rio Festival (1985) **19:** 2228
Rockin' Sinners **2:** 122
Rockin' Vickers **19:** 2238
Rock-Jerry **3:** 251
Rock-Lenne **3:** 251
Rock-Love **3:** 251
Rock Market Place **12:** 1339
Rockpile **17:** 1934-5, *1934*
Rock Pretty Baby **2:** 208, *208*
Rock Rock Rock **1:** 114, **2:** 201, *209,* 210, *215,* 216
Rockshow **14:** 1680
'Rock 'n' Roll Circus' **8:** 848, 893, 897
'Rock 'n' Roll Dance Party' **2:** 217
Rock 'n' Roll Trio **1:** 114, *115*
Rock-Olga **2:** 251
Rock-Ragge **2:** 251
Rocky Horror Show **12:** 1433, **16:** 1863, *1876,* 1876-7, **20:** 2339
Rock You Sinners **2:** 122
Roddam, Frank **11:** 1275
Roden, Jess **7:** *820,* **9:** 1013
Rodgers, Billy **19:** *2174,* 2175
Rodgers, Clodagh **17:** 1955
Rodgers, Curtis **15:** 1785
Rodgers, Jimmy **1:** 39, **12:** 1401, **14:** 1649
Rodgers, Nile **14:** 1593, 1631-3, 1633, **15:** 1791, **18:** 2103, *2113,* 2114-5
Rodgers, Paul **15:** 1738, *1738,* 1739, *1739,* 1740, **16:** 1819, **18:** 2133
Rodgers, Rick **19:** 2204
Rodhe, Jan **3:** 251
Rodney, Winston **16:** *1882,* 1886 *see also* Burning Spear
Rodriguez, Paul **19:** 2169
Rodriguez, Rico **9:** 971
Roe, Tommy **2:** 240, **3:** 309, **10:** 1176, *1176*
Roeder, Kaus **20:** 2311-12
Roeg, Nicolas **20:** 2321, 2326-7

Roeser, Donald *see* Dharma, Buck
Rogers, Bobby **4:** 475, 477, 478, 479
Rogers, Claudette **4:** 475, 477, 479
Rogers, Jimmy **1:** 37, 39, **4:** 464, 466, **5:** 593
Rogers, Kenny **5:** 575, *575,* **14:** 1658, *1659,* **17:** 2021, 2024, *2025,* **18:** 2117
Rogers, Roy **1:** 37
Rogers, Sonny **4:** 475
Rokes **6:** 699
Roli, Gregg **13:** 1535, **18:** 2121
Rollicks **6:** 683
Rolling Stone **1:** 68, **12:** *1329,* 1330, 1332-3, **13:** 1478, 1482
Rolling Stones **1:** 3, 8, 67, **2:** 123, 128, 137, 149, 150, 194, **5:** *508,* 514, 551, 555, 557, 559, 564, *565,* 582, 583, 586, 588, *588-9,* 595, 599-600, **6:** 603, 619, 642, 643, 644, 650, 654, 657, 658, 682, 690, 693, *695,* **7:** 721-2, 724, *725,* 742, 749, 757, 802-3, 815, 816-17, **8:** 845, 847-8, 850, 851, *852-3,* 880, *880,* 881-900, 922, 941-2, 944, 959, **9:** 1001, 1026, 1027, 1029, 1042, 1074-5, **10:** 1085, 1091, 1099, 1101, 1109, 1115, 1143, 1153, 1159, 1167, **11:** 1243, *1244-5,* 1247-8, 1259-60, 1289, 1292, 1298, **12:** 1335, 1358, *1386-7,* 1396, **13:** 1477, 1503, 1556, 1559, **14:** 1564, 1661, 1673, 1679-80, **15:** 1685, 1726, 1761, *1796,* 1797, **16:** 1803, 1828, 1829, 1832, 1834, 1845, 1862, 1863, **20:** 2321, 2326, 2327, 2340, 2341, 2360
Rolling Thunder Revue **11:** 1211, *1212*
Roll Over **14:** 1652
Rollo, Zoot Horn **13:** 1484, 1486
Romao, Dom Um **13:** 1532
Romeos **14:** 1596
Romero, Chan **2:** 196
Rondinelli, Bobby **17:** 1986
Ronettes **1:** 12, **5:** 508-9, *510,* 513-15, *513-14,* 566, 567, **6:** 621, **7:** *733,* **12:** 1381, **15:** 1682
Ronny and the Daytonas **7:** 765
Ronson, Mick **11:** 1211, *1212,* **14:** 1622, 1626, 1632-3, 1634, **16:** 1802, *1819,* 1820
Ronstadt, Linda **6:** 694, **9:** 1059, **10:** 1125, **13:** 1560, **15:** 1763, 1772, 1773, 1780, **17:** 2021, 2023-5, *2024*
Roosters **5:** 588, *589,* **6:** 645, 650, **7:** 793, **9:** 1022, 1026
Rootie Tootie **7:** 796
Rose, Biff **10:** 1085
Rose, Fred **1:** 35, **2:** 230
Rose, Tim **11:** 1245
Rose, Wesley **2:** 225, 227, 228, 231, **4:** 414, 415
Rosenberg, Richie 'La Bamba' **18:** 2092
Rosenburg, Lee **4:** 406
Rosenman, Joel **11:** 1250-1
Rosenthal, David **17:** 1987
Rose Royce **9:** 1057
Rosko, Emperor **7:** 745, **8:** 842, *842,* **17:** 1958

Rosman, Ronnie **9:** 994-5
Ross, Diana **1:** 10, **4:** 447, *461, 472,* 478, **6:** 704-5, 706, 715, **7:** *738,* 740, 782, **9:** 1041-2, *1042-3,* 1043, *1044-5,* 1045-9, **12:** *1420, 1425,* **14:** 1581, 1583-5, *1584,* 1590-3, **18:** 2103, 2111, 2114, 2115, 2117, **20:** 2360
Ross, Malcolm **19:** 2273
Rossi, Francis **15:** *1730,* 1731, 1732, 1733, *1733,* 1735
Rossi, Ken **3:** 360
Rossington, Gary **16:** 1843, 1844
Rossington/Collins Band **16:** 1844
Rostill, John **4:** *382, 386,* 388
Rotchelle, Dave **19:** 2242
Roth, Dave Lee **18:** 2121, 2130, *2131*
Rothbard, Bernie **3:** 355
Rothchild, Paul **9:** 1002, 1010, 1017
Rotolo, Suze **11:** 1201, 1204-5, *1208-9,* 1216
Rotten, Johnny **9:** 1002-3, **16:** 1866, **18:** 2042, *2044,* 2045, *2047,* 2048, 2049, 2053, *2054,* 2063, *2098,* 2158
Rough Trade Records **18:** *2155,* 2157, **20:** 2378
Roulette Records **9:** 994
Roulettes **4:** 372, *372,* 392, 393
Roundabout **5:** 531
Rovell, Diane **7:** 778 *778*
Rovell, Marilyn **7:** 778, *778*
Rovers **5:** 574
Rowberry, Dave **6:** *658,* 660
Rowe, Dick **4:** 362, *362,* 440
Rowland, Bruce **10:** 1168, **13:** 1467
Rowland, Kevin **13:** 1463, **19:** 2218-20, *2218,* 2220
Rowland, Steve **8:** 950
Rowles, Gary **9:** 1017
Rowles, John **17:** 1958
Rowse, Dick **4:** *426*
Roxon, Lillian **12:** 1323, 1351, **13:** 1554
Roxy Music **9:** 1005, 1008, **11:** 1293, *1293,* **14:** 1623, 1629, 1634, 1638, 1639, **15:** 1721, 1729, **16:** 1801, 1802, 1803, 1804-11, **20:** 2354, 2356, 2364, 2365
Royal, Billy Joe **10:** 1176, *1176*
Royal Guardsmen **9:** *997,* 999
Royal Philharmonic Orchestra **15:** *1682*
Royal Rasses **20:** 2374
Royals **5:** 494-5
Royaltones **4:** 381, 390, 396
Royer, Ray **10:** 1087
Royer, Robb **5:** *518,* 519
Royster, Joe **5:** 491, 492
Rubber Soul **8:** 850
Rubettes **6:** 687
Rubin, Barbara **8:** 865
Rubin, Don **8:** 867
Rubin, Jerry **1:** 14, **12:** *1382*
Rubin, Nathan **13:** 1553
Ruby **13:** 1458
Rudd, Phil **19:** *2226,* 2227-8
Rude Boy **20:** 2329
Rudge, Peter **11:** 1277, **16:** 1844
Rudolph, Paul **17:** 1997

Ruffin, Bruce **16:** 1887
Ruffin, David **1:** 62, **4:** 464, 473, 478, **6:** 719, **9:** 1050-2, *1050,* 1057
Ruffin, Jimmy **1:** *10,* 11, **4:** 478
Rumblers **7:** 765
Rum Rummer Club **20:** 2389
Rumour **17:** 1937
Runaways **17:** *1927,* **18:** 2071, 2156
Run Home Slow **8:** 847, **13:** 1492
Rundgren, Todd **8:** 872, **13:** 1519, 1611, **16:** 1879, 1901, 1903-5, **17:** 2020, **19:** 2123
Running, Jumping and Standing Still Film, The **8:** 844, 854
Rupe, Art **2:** 149, 155, 156, **3:** 333, 334, **4:** 462
Rush **19:** 2223, 2234-5, *2235*
Rush, Billy **18:** 2092, *2092*
Rush, Otis **10:** 1102, 1114, **11:** 1221, *1221* 1238
Rush, Tom **12:** 1345
Rushent, Martin **16:** 1902, **18:** 2074-5, **19:** 2182, **20:** 2309, 2395, *2396*
Ruskies **5:** 534
Ruskin, Mickey **8:** 865
Russell, Brenda **18:** 2103, **19:** 2163
Russell, Graham **20:** *2371*
Russell, Jim **14:** 1576, **18:** 2075
Russell, John **12:** 1430, 1432
Russell, Ken **11:** 1275, **20:** 2327
Russell, Leon: **5:** *518,* 519, 520, **6:** 675, **7:** 829, **9:** 1035, **10:** 1109, 1163, 1168-9, *1168,* **13:** 1443, 1444-7, 1449, **14:** 1647, **15:** 1763, 1797
Russell, Willy **17:** 1980
Russian rock scene **20:** 2376-7
Russley, Bill **5:** 534
Rustiks **5:** *535*
Rutherford, Mike **15:** *1751,* 1752, 1754, 1755
Rutles **17:** *1980*
Rutley, Tom **13:** 1535
Ruts **18:** 2141
Rutsey, John **19:** 2234
Rydell, Bobby **3:** 260, *260,* 311, 341, 342, *342,* 343, *343,* 344, 348, 349, 350-1, *358,* 359, **4:** 401, 487
Ryder, Mitch **8:** 872, **10:** 1178-80

S

Sad Cafe **16:** 1915
Saddlemen **1:** 22, 25, **3:** 341, 354
Sade **20:** *2404,* 2405, 2413, 2418-19
Sadistic Mika Band **20:** *2364,* 2364-5
Sadler, Sergeant Barry **6:** 677
Sahm, Doug **7:** 834-5, 872, **13:** 1455
Sailor Who Fell From Grace With The Sea, The **14:** 1652
Sainte-Marie, Buffy **6:** 662, *665*
Saints **4:** 392, **16:** 1854

Sakamoto, Riuichi **20:** 2356, *2364,* 2365
Sakkarin **8:** 960
Salty Peppers **19:** 2163
Salvation **8:** 914, *915,* **20:** 2338
Sam and Dave **1:** 10 **7:** 782, 785, **8:** 921, *921-2,* 930, 932, 936-7, **12:** 1409
Sam and the Goodtimers **9:** 990
Sam Gopal Band **19:** 2238
Samla Mammas Manna **20:** 2367
Sampedro, Frank **15** *1771*
Sample, Joe **19:** 2173, *2174,* 2175
Sampson, Doug **19:** 2230-1
Sampson, Wallace **9:** 1059
Samuels, Calvin 'Fizzy' **12:** 1375, **15:** 1765
Samuels, Julie **8:** *844*
Samwell, Ian 'Sammy' **4:** 366, 368, 422, *423,* 424, 450, **5:** 596-7, **6:** 650, *650,* 652, **7:** 759, 806, **15:** 1777
Sanwell-Smith, Paul **9:** 1022, **12:** 1355, **15:** 1710
San Francisco **8:** 847
San Francisco Mimi Troupe **11:** 1223
Sancious, David **9:** 1033
Sander, Ellen **1:** 98
Sanders, Alex **12:** 1373
Sanders, Ed **1:** 19, **8:** *864,* 865, **19:** 1014, 1015
Sanders, Sonny **3:** 332
Sanderson, David **4:** 396
Sandii And The Sunsetz **20:** 2365, *2365*
Sandon, Johnny **5:** 528
Sandford, Gary **19:** 2254, *2255*
Sands, Jodie **3:** 342, 343
Sands, Tommy **3:** 307
Santana **10:** 1093, *1095,* **11:** 1257, **13:** 1534-7, **15:** 1742, 1761, 1766
Santana, Carlos **12:** 1400
Santieno, Edward **2:** 145
Santo and Johnny **4:** 391
Saperstein, Hank **1:** 92
SAR Records **3:** 334
Sardo, Frankie **2:** *187,* 197 **3:** 254
Sarne, Mike **8:** 844
Sarnoff, David **12:** 1392
Sarstedt, Peter **10:** 1139 *1165*
Satellite **8:** 928-9, 932-3 *see also* Stax
Satintones **4:** 473
'Saturday Club' **4:** *376,* 377, *377,* **8:** 841
Saturday Night Fever **5:** *481,* 483
Saturday Night Out **5:** 529
Saunders, Pete **19:** 2218
Saunders, Richard **10:** 1096
Savage, Rick **19:** 2236-7, *2237*
Savage Resurrection **8:** 915
Savile, Jimmy **4:** *376,* 377, **6:** *682,* **8:** 849-50, *850*
Saville, Peter **19:** 2269, *2269*
Savoy **3:** 262, 271
Savoy Brown **10:** 1102, *1102*
Sawyer, Phil **10:** 1187
Saxa **19:** 2208-9, *2209*
Saxon **19:** 2222, *2223,* 2231
Saxon, Sky **8:** 872
Saxons *see* Bay City Rollers

Sayer, Leo **4:** 372, **14:** 1662, *1662,* **17:** 2035, *2035*
Scabies, Rat **18:** 2062
Scaduto, Tony **12:** 1324
Scaffold **10:** *1164*
Scaggs, Boz **11:** 1221, 1223, *1225,* 1225-6, **14:** 1603, **17:** 2021
Scarfe, Gerald **11:** 1317
Scarlet Party **19:** 2243
'Scene' **8:** 852-3
Scene club **7:** 802, 816
Schacher, Mel **14:** 1609, 1611, *1611*
Schaeffer Music Festival, New York (1974) **8:** *936*
Scheck, George **3:** 316, 345, **6:** 706
Schekeryk, Peter **15:** 1716
Schilling, Jerry **7:** 772
Schloser, Jack **11:** 1251
Schmidt, Irmin **19:** 2367
Schmit, Timothy B. **15:** 1775
Schmoelling, Johannes **20:** 2369
Schneider, Abraham **9:** 989
Schneider, Bert **9:** 982, 987-8
Schneider, Florian **20:** *2310,* 2310-11
Schneider, Fred **20:** *2286,* 2286-7
Schnitzler, Conrad **20:** 2369
Schofield, Willie **8:** 939
Schon, Neal **13:** 1535, **18:** 2121
Schreiber, Dave **3:** *246*
Schroeder, Aaron **7:** 728
Schroeder, Barbet **11:** 1310, 1312, 1316-17
Schroeder, John **4:** 422, *432,* 433, **15:** 1732
Schroer, Jack **13:** 1552, 1553
Schultz, Arnold **2:** 224
Schulze, Klaus **20:** 2369
Schwall, Jim **11:** 1223
Schwartz, Andy **12:** 1331
Schwartz, Professor Bernard **2:** 219
Schwartz, Gene and Bob **4:** 409
Schwartz, Glenn **14:** 1613
Schwarz, Brinsley **17:** 1921, 1922, 1924, 1925, 1928, 1935, *1935,* 1936, 1937, 1939
Scorpions **20:** 2362
Scott, Andy **16:** 1835, *1835,* 1837, *1837,* **18:** 2154
Scott, Bon **19:** *2226-7,* 2227
Scott, Frankie **1:** 28
Scott, Jack **4:** 468-9
Scott, Joe **7:** 799-800
Scott, Keith **5:** 587
Scott, Ken **14:** 1632, **15:** 1758, 1759
Scott, Roger **17:** *1960*
Scott, Ronnie **2:** 122, 130
Scott, Sherry **19:** 2163
Scott, Simon **7:** 817
Scott, Tom **12:** 1346, *1347,* **15:** 1763, **17:** 1976, **18:** 2097
Scott, Tony **7:** 759
Scottsville Squirrel Barkers **15:** 1773
Screen Gems **4:** 444, 459, **5:** 501, **9:** 981, 982, 987-8, 989-90
Scritti Politti **18:** 2157
Seaga, Edward **9:** 976

Sea Level **14:** 1605
Seaman, Phil **9:** 1031, **10:** 1189
Searchers **2:** 183, **5:** 523, 528-31, 532, 536-7, 538, **6:** 601, 693, **9:** 1054, **10:** 1153, **17:** 1925
Sears, Pete **8:** 913
Sears, Zenas **1:** 56, **3:** 275
Sebastian, John **1:** 18, **6:** 654, **7:** 822, *823,* **8:** 863, 866-9, **10:** 1121, *1122,* 1182-3, 1185, 1194, **15:** 1702-3
Sebastian, Tom 'The Great' **9:** 975
Second Coming **8:** 914
Secret Affair **19:** *2225*
Sector 27 **18:** 2147
Secunda, Tony **10:** 1087, 1181, *1182,* 1182-3, 1185, 1194, **13:** 1473, **19:** 2239
Sedaka, Neil **2:** 205, 210, **3:** 265, 307, 308, 311, 317, **4:** 441, 442, *442,* 443, *443,* 447, 450-53, **6:** 640, **7:** 723, **9:** 982, 988, **13:** 1517, **15:** 1702, 1714, 1715, **16:** 1914, **17:** 1942
Sedrone, Danny **1:** 27
Seeds **8:** *870,* 872, **10:** 1081, 1085
Seeger, Pete **6:** 662, 663, 666-7, 675, **10:** *1121,* 1124, 1139, **11:** *1204,* 1205, 1207, **15:** 1799
Seekers **10:** 1138-9, 1140, *1140*
Seger, Bob **8:** 872, **15:** 1772, **16:** 1856-7, **18:** *2081,* 2082
Sehorn, Marshall **5:** 562
Seiwell, Denny **17:** 1963
Selecter **9:** 973, **19:** *2201,* 2203-5, 2207-8, 2212, 2215, 2218
Selico, Ron **10:** 1115
Sellers, Peter **6:** 638, 639, 640
Semens, Antennae Jimmy **13:** 1484
Senators **7:** 737
Seneca, Joe **3:** 337
Seniors **5:** 538
Sensational Alex Harvey Band **17:** 1994-5
Sensational Nightingales **15:** 1781
Sequencers **20:** 2302
Seraphine, Dan **13:** 1527, *1528*
Sergeant, Will **19:** 2276, *2276*
Serious Charge **4:** 430
Serpent Power **8:** 915
Seto, Chica **20:** *2363*
Setzer, Brian **1:** *101,* 116, **19:** *2259,* 2260 747 **17:** 1922
'Seven Little Joys, The' **13:** 1504
Severin, Steve **18:** 2148-51, *2150*
Seville, David (*alias* Ross Bagdasarian) **3:** 269
Sex Gang Children **8:** 863, **14:** 1623, **16:** 1863, **18:** *2054,* **20:** 2399
Sex Pistols **8:** 883, **9:** 1002, *1003,* 1075, **11:** 1261, 1280, *1294,* 1295, **12:** 1336, *1358,* **13:** 1483, 1498, 1503, **16:** 1863, 1879, 1880, **17:** *1927,* 1998, 2026, 2031, **18:** *2041,* 2043, *2043-4,* 2044-8, *2046-7,* 2049-50, 2053, *2059,* 2061, 2063, 2066, 2072, 2073, 2074, 2080, 2145, 2146, 2148, 2151, 2152, 2160, **19:** 2188, 2241, 2249, 2251, 2261, 2266, **20:**

2321, 2329, 2341, 2351, 2352
Seymour, Phil **20:** 2288
Sgt Pepper's Lonely Hearts Club Band **6:** 639, **13:** 1528, **19:** 1849
Shaar Dahaud **13:** 1553
Shadettes **17:** 1989
Shadows **4:** 362, 363, *364-5, 366-7,* 368, 369, 381, 383, *382-3,* 384-5, 393, 395, 400, 404, *422,* 423, 429, **7:** 722, **8:** 844, 847, 850, **9:** 1021, 1039, 1077-8, **10:** 1086, **17:** 1953, 1955
Shadows (USA) **4:** 457
Shadows of Knight **8:** *870,* 872, **9:** *997,* 998-9
Shaft **12:** 1410, 1414
Shake, Rattle and Roll **2:** 208
Shakedown Sound *see* Mott the Hoople
Shakespeare, Robbie **16:** 1884, 1887, 1894, **17:** 1933, **20:** 2300, 2374, *2375*
Shakin' Pyramids **19:** 2275
Shakin' Stevens **1:** 120, **13:** 1515, **19:** 2260, **20:** *2338,* 2340
Shakti **13:** 1525
Shalamar **18:** 2103, *2179,* **20:** 2394, *2394*
Sham 69 **18:** 2060, 2061, 2141, 2144-5, 2146
Shamblin, Eldon **1:** 38, *39*
Sha-Na-Na **1:** 63
Shane, Bob **6:** 662, 669, *668-9*
'Shang-A-Lang' **13:** 1512, *1512*
Shanghai Surprise **20:** 2413
Shangri-Las **4:** 449, **5:** 566, *566,* 567, 569, 575, **6:** 621, **9:** 1074, **12:** 1357, **16:** 1879, **17:** 1942
Shankar, Ravi **1:** 16, **9:** 963, **10:** 1099, 1100, 1149, **12:** 1396-7, *1398,* **15:** 1716, **17:** 1968
Shannon, Del **2:** 239, **4:** 401, 402-3, *403,* 409, 417-20, 454, *454,* 462, **16:** 1857
Shannon, Tommy **18:** 1234-5
Shapiro, Ben **10:** 1098
Shapiro, Brad **8:** 937, 940
Shapiro, Helen **2:** 240, **3:** 269, *269,* 312, *313,* **4:** 421, 422, 432-3, 440, **6:** 621, 622, 629, **7:** 721, **9:** 1079, **12:** 1436
Shapiro, Lee **5:** *570,* 573
Sharkey, Feargal **20:** 2405, *2406,* 2413
Sharks **15:** 1740
Sharman, Jim **16:** 1876
Sharp, Dee Dee **5:** 487, 489, **14:** 1600
Sharp, Martha **4:** 457
Sharp, Martin **9:** 1029, **12:** 1391
Sharpe, D **17:** 2017
Sharpe, Ray **1:** 113, *113*
Sharpley, Ced **20:** 2314, 2315
Shaw, Adrian **17:** 1997
Shaw, Arnold **12:** 1323
Shaw, Gred **12:** 1329, 1330, 1338-9, *1339*
Shaw, Sandie **1:** 16, **4:** 372, **6:** *621,* 621-2, 624, 626-8, 631, 635, **7:** 723, **8:** 880, **12:** 1434, **17:** 1953, *1955,* 1956
Shaw, Tommy **18:** 2128, *2129*
Shears, Stevie **20:** 2352
Sheeley, Sharon **2:** 197, **3:** 248
Sheets, Scott St Clair **18:** 2135

Sheila and B. Devotion **18:** *2114,* 2115, 2120
Sheila E. **20:** 2405
Sheldon, Doug **7:** 757
Shelley, Pete **7:** 815, **18:** *2073,* 2073-5
Shelley, Peter **13:** 1514
Shelton, Anne **3:** 310, *310,* 311
Shelton, Gilbert **12:** 1391
Shelton, Seb **19:** 2220
Shenson, Walker **8:** 854
Shepherd, Bill **18:** 2105
Sheridan, Mike **6:** 603, **10:** 1181, 1183, 1185
Sheridan, Tony **5:** 538, 540
Sherman, Gary **4:** 444
Shermon, Bobby **8:** 879
Sherrill, Billy **2:** 234, **14:** 1658, **17:** 2024-5, **19:** 2195
Sherrys **3:** *342,* 343, **5:** 567
Sherwood, Jim 'Motorhead' **13:** 1492, 1493
Shields **2:** 237
Shiels, Brendan **17:** 1990
Shiloh **15:** 1772
Shiloahs **13:** 1556
'Shindig' **8:** 880, **11:** 1273, **13:** 1449, **15:** 1797
Shindogs **13:** 1449
Shines, Johnny **4:** 466
Shipley, John **19:** 2207
Shirelles **2:** 240, **4:** *442,* 443, 447, 452, 459, **5:** 513, 566-7, *567,* 579
Shirley, Jerry **11:** 1320, **17:** 2039
Shirley and Lee **2:** 154
Shiva **12:** 1399
Shocking Blue **6:** *698,* 700, **20:** 2362
Shockley, Stephen **19:** 2179
Shogren, Dave **16:** 1851, *1851*
Sholes, Steve **1:** 26, 86, 88, 110, **2:** 233, **4:** 453
Shondells **9:** 981-2, *981,* 994-5, 999
Shorrock, Glen **20:** 2371
Shorter, Wayne **12:** 1347, **13:** 1523, 1530, 1531, 1532, 1533, *1533*
Shotgun Express **6:** 642, **15:** 1725
Shotton, Peter **5:** 546, 557, **10:** 1158
Shout, **12:** 1338, *1338*
Showaddywaddy **1:** 63
Shrager, Carl **10:** 1096
Shrimpton, Jean **6:** 683, **7:** *741*
Shrieve, Mike **13:** 1535, *1535,* 1537
Shuman, Mort *see* Pomus and Shuman
Sibbles, Leroy **16:** 1886, 1894
Sidran, Ben **11:** 1226-7
Siegel, Corky **11:** 1223
Siegel/Schwall Band **11:** 1223
Sigler, Bunny **14:** 1598
Silhouettes **2:** 196
Silkie **5:** 534
Sill, Lester **3:** *282,* 283, 286, 287, 295, *342,* 343, **5:** 503, 507, 508-9
Sils, Leslie **9:** 988
Silva, Kathy **12:** 1407
Silva-Tones **2:** 236
Silver, Horace **3:** 321

Silver, John **15:** 1752
Silver Bullet Band **16:** 1856, 1857, **17:** *1957*
Silver Convention **18:** 2103, 2120, *2120*
Silver Dream Racer **13:** 1508, 1509
Silver Records **3:** 246, 247-8
Silverstein, Shel **3:** 297
Simenon, Paul **11:** *1243*
Simmonds, Kim **10:** 1102
Simmons, Gene **16:** *1868,* 1869, *1869, 1871,* **18:** 2130
Simmons, Jeff **13:** 1493
Simmons, Pat **16:** *1850,* 1851, *1851,* 1852, *1853*
Simms, Speedo **8:** 926
Simon, Carly **10:** *1124,* 1125, **12:** 1341, **15:** 1703, 1708, 1709-11, 1763, 1773, 1780
Simon, Paul **2:** 182, **4:** 447, **5:** 562, **6:** 665, **7:** 822, **10:** 1098-9, *1121,* 1123, 1125, 1126-31, 1139, **11:** 1220, *1238,* 1252, **12:** 1359-60, **13:** 1559, **14:** 1675, **15:** 1705, 1714, **17:** 1941
Simon, Robin **20:** *2352*
Simon and Garfunkel **1:** 16, **6:** 661, 665, 667, **7:** 804, 822, *823,* **8:** 847, **10:** 1099, 1124-5, 1126-31, **11:** 1288
Simon Sisters **15:** 1709
Simone, Nick **14:** 1575-6
Simone, Nina **7:** *782,* 783, **15:** 1794-5, 1799
Simonon, Paul **18:** 2066-7, *2067,* 2069, *2143*
Simper, Nicky **12:** 1377, *1377,* 1379, **17:** 1984
Simple Minds **19:** 2273, 2274, *2274,* **20:** 2420
Simpson, Graham **16:** 1807
Simpson, Jim **12:** 1369-70
Simpson, Rose **13:** *1469,* 1470
Simpson, Valerie **9:** 1041, 1043 **14:** 1587, 1590, 1592, 1593
Sims, Danny **16:** 1891
Sims, Dick **9:** 1036, **16:** 1856
Sinatra, Frank **1:** 82, *82,* 89, **3:** 308, 309, **5:** 501, **7:** *738,* 739, **17:** 1942, 2021, *2034,* 2035, 2037
Sinclair, John **9:** 1015, **13:** 1482, 1488-9, **15:** 1729
Sinclair, Richard **14:** 1579
Sinfield, Peter **14:** 1564-5, **16:** *1802*
Singer, Artie **2:** 236
Singer, Ray **20:** 2356
Singing Nun **3:** 269, *269*
Singing Orchestra Circus **9:** *998,* 999
Singing Postman **10:** 1139
Singleton, Shelby S. **1:** *47*
Siomos, John **17:** 2040
Siouxsie and the Banshees **11:** *1294,* **18:** 2046, *2053,* 2054, *2059,* 2060, 2061, 2072, 2074, 2077, 2141, 2148-51, *2148-9,* **20:** 2307, 2323, 2381
Sir Coxsone the Downbeat *see* Dodd, Clement
Sir Douglas Quintet **2:** 182, 196, **7:** 821, 834-5, **8:** 872, 880, 914

Sir Lord Comic **9:** 977
Sire Records **17:** 2002, *2003*
Sirens **16:** *1809*
Sister Sledge **18:** *2114,* 2115, **20:** 2419
Sisterhood of Spit Big Band **18:** 2072
Sisters of Mercy **19:** *2261,* 2262
'6.5 Special' **2:** 123, 126, *134,* 134-5, 202, **4:** 366, 371, 374, 378-80, *378,* 429-30, *429,* 430
16 **12:** 1329
Skaggs, Ricky **17:** 2025
Skatalites **9:** 962, 977, **16:** 1890
Skellern, Peter **2:** 139
Sketch **20:** *2392, 2393*
Skids **19:** 2275, *2275*
skiffle **2:** 123, *123,* 124-8, *132,* 134, 145, **3:** 267, 268, **4:** 392, **5:** 582, 585, **6:** 601, 613, **12:** 1322, **13:** 1461, 1478
Skolimowsky, Jerzy **11:** 1316
Sky **14:** 1576
Sky Saxon's Blue Band **10:** 1085
Skyliners **2:** 235, *236,* 237
Slade **6:** *620* **12:** 1422, *1422,* 1426-9, **15:** 1721, **19:** 2239, **20:** 2420
Slade in Flame **12:** 1428
Slades **2:** 237
Slagg, Paul **18:** *2154*
Slapp Happy **14:** 1569
Slattery, Mick **17:** 1996
Slaughter, Todd **1:** 97
Slay, Frank and Crewe, Bob **3:** 342, **5:** 496-7
Sledge, Percy **15:** 1789
Slick, Darby **8:** 914
Slick, Grace **1:** *14,* 16, **8:** 909-13, *910,* 914, **9:** 984, **10:** 1083, 1170, **18:** 2158
Slik **17:** *1927*
Slim, Guitar **3:** 325
Slim, Lightnin' **3:** 339
Slim, Sunnyland **4:** 464
Slim and the Boys **14:** 1594
Slim Smith **16:** 1887
Slingerland, Bud **4:** 399, 400
Slits **18:** 2058, 2062, *2063, 2070-1,* 2072
Sloan, P. F. **3:** 266, *274,* 275, 277, **6:** *675,* 677, **10:** 1121
Sly and Robbie **7:** 788, 791
Sly and the Family Stone **1:** *63,* **3:** 327, **9:** 1039, 1057, *1095,* **10:** 1110, **11:** 1249, **12:** *1401,* 1402, 1404-7, 1413, 1420, **13:** 1555, **15:** 1691
Small Faces **6:** 603, 683, **7:** 725, 759-60, *802,* 806-9, 816-17, 818, **8:** 845, 942, **11:** 1245, 1281, *1292,* 1293, **15:** *1699,* 1721, 1725, **17:** 2038, 2039
Small Wonder Records **18:** 2157
Smart, Keith **10:** 1185
Smart, Norman **14:** 1606
Smart, Terry **4:** 366, 368
Smash, Chas **19:** 2210-11, *2211,* 2213
Smash Hits **12:** *1327,* 1328, **19:** 2258
Smedley, Major Oliver **7:** 746
Smilin' Joe (Joseph Pleasant) **2:** 145
Smirks **19:** 2242, *2243*
Smith, **4:** 418-19

Smith, Arlene **5:** 566
Smith, Arthur **1:** 32, 40
Smith, Bessie **2:** 159, **5:** 483
Smith, Bill **3:** 254, **4:** 390
Smith, Bob **2:** 216, 217
Smith, Carl **2:** 225
Smith, Cherry **16:** 1889
Smith, Clarence 'Pine Top' **1:** 39
Smith, Claydes 'Clay' **18:** 2109
Smith, Connie 'Guybo' **3:** 245, 247
Smith, Fred **17:** *2006,* 2007-8, **20:** 2292
Smith, Fred 'Sonic' **13:** *1488,* **20:** 2292
Smith, Huey 'Piano' **2:** 145, 165, 179
Smith, James **14:** 1594, *1595*
Smith, Judi **7:** 758
Smith, Lawson **5:** 494
Smith, Melvin **2:** 149
Smith, Michael **20:** 2375
Smith, Mike **5:** 549, 555, **6:** 609-11, *610,* **7:** 759, **8:** 952-3
Smith, Mike 'Smitty' **7:** 832-3
Smith, Neal **16:** 1865
Smith, Norman **11:** 1308
Smith, O. C. **11:** 1253
Smith, Ocie **2:** 231
Smith, Patti **9:** 1002, **11:** 1295, *1295,* **12:** *1330,* **17:** 2001, 2003, 2004, *2004,* 2011, 2012, *2018-20, 2028-30,* **18:** 2062, 2072, 2089, 2090, 2127, 2135
Smith, Phil **20:** 2384
Smith, Robert **18:** *2150,* 2151
Smith, Slim **16:** 1887
Smith, Tony **15:** 1753
Smith, Warren **1:** 46, 118
Smith Brothers **2:** 122
Smiths, The **20:** 2381, *2416*
Smokey and the Bandit **14:** 1641, 1660
Smokie **16:** 1821, *1822,* 1823, *1833,* 1834
Smyth, Gill **20:** 2368
Smythe, Danny **10:** 1174-5
Sniffin' Glue **12:** 1340
Snow, Don **19:** 2257
Snow, Hank **1:** 54, 91, **2:** 234
Snyder, Gary **1:** 15
Sobelles **5:** 523
Society Bag **9:** 975
Soft Boys **11:** 1318, **17:** 1925
Soft Cell **16:** 1862, 1863, **19:** 2262, **20:** 2302, 2343
Soft Machine **1:** 9, 10, **7:** 816, **11:** 1297, 1301, *1303,* 1304-5, **12:** 1397, **14:** 1563, *1563,* 1578-80, **15:** 1681, 1700, **18:** *2076,* 2077, 2078
Soft White Underbelly **18:** 2125-6
Sohl, Richard **17:** 2019
Soileau, Floyd **13:** 1455, *1455*
Solar **19:** 2178-80
Solley, Pete **10:** 1089, **17:** 1984
Soloff, Lew **13:** *1538,* 1539
Solomon, Clifford **10:** *1114,* 1115
Solomon, Clive **12:** 1325
Somerville, David **2:** 235
Somerville, Jimmy **20:** *2419*
Sommerville, Brian **5:** 557
Sonday Records **5:** 577

Sondheim, Stephen **12:** 1349
Song And Dance **20:** 2337
Song Hits **12:** 1329
Song Remains The Same, The **12:** 1368
Sonics **8:** 872, *873*
Sonics Rendezvous **13:** 1489
Sonny and Cher **6:** 676, *676,* 677, **7:** 821-2, 825, 836-7, **8:** 847, 880, 902, **15:** *1745,* 1761
Sonny Kenn Blues Band **18:** 2092
Sons of Champlin **8:** 914
Sopwith Camel **8:** 914
Sorrows **6:** 603
SOS **19:** 2261
Soul, David **17:** *2034*
Soul Band **17:** *1994*
Soul Children **8:** 933, **15:** 1782
Soul Clan **7:** 796
Soul Giants **13:** 1493
Soul Mates **15:** 1785
Soul Sonic Force **19:** 2168, *2169,* 2177
Soul Stirrers **2:** 160, **3:** 322, 333, 334, **8:** 930, **9:** 1052
Soul To Soul **15:** 1793
Soule, Mickey Lee **17:** 1985
Sounds **12:** *1326,* 1328, **18:** 2141, **19:** 2223, 2236
Sounds Incorporated **4:** 388, 393, **5:** 534, *535*
'Sounds Of The Seventies' **16:** 1807
South, Joe **9:** 1079, **10:** 1176-7, **13:** 1443
Souther, J. D. **15:** 1772
Souther-Hillman-Furay Band **16:** 1841
Southern Comfort **15:** 1560
Southern Death Cult **14:** 1623, **16:** 1863, **19:** 2262, *2262*
Southern Stompers **4:** 439
Southside Johnny and the Asbury Jukes **5:** 515, *515,* **17:** 1936, **18:** 2089, 2092-3, *2093*
Spalding, Phil **20:** 2335
Spandau Ballet **9:** 1075, **16:** *1801,* 1806, **20:** 2341, *2341,* 2343, *2346,* 2347-9, 2397, 2420
Spaniels **5:** 595
Spanky and Our Gang **8:** 902, *902,* **9:** 993, **10:** 1123
Sparks **13:** 1518-20, **16:** 1903
Sparks, John B. 'Sparko' **17:** 1928-9, *1929*
Sparks, Speedy **7:** 835
Sparrow **9:** 1072
Spartacus **9:** 969
Speare, Paul **19:** 2220
Special AKA **18:** 2160, **19:** 2201, 2203, 2204, *2206,* 2207, 2208, 2211, 2212, 2215, 2218, **20:** 2387
Specials **1:** 10, **9:** 983
Specialty Records **2:** 149, 150, 151, 156, **3:** 262, 264, 271, 333, 334, **5:** 502
Spector, Phil **1:** 12-13, 63, **2:** 127, 240, **3:** 265, 288, 289, **4:** 401, 402, 403, **5:** 501, 503, 506-12, 513-15, 517, *518,* 519-20 562, *563,* 564, 566-7, 569, **6:** 640, **7:** 727-8, 762, 765, 775, 836-7, **8:** 891, 893, **9:** 981-2, 1057, **10:** 1155, 1160, **12:**

1351, 1381, **15:** 1682, 1761, **16:** 1901, 1909, 1912, **17:** 1963, *1967,* 1972-3, *1967,* 2011, **18** 2102
Spector, Ronnie **5:** 514, *515,* **18:** 2093
Spectres **15:** 1731, *1733*
Spectrum **17:** 1949
Spedding, Chris **9:** 1032, **13:** 1479, **15:** 1740
Speight, Ted **17:** 1933
Speiser, Jerry **20:** 2372
Spence, Alexander 'Skip' **8:** 909-10
Spence, Mervyn **15:** 1737
Spencer, Bobby **1:** 77
Spencer, Kevin **19:** 2179
Spencer, Jeremy **10:** 1118-19, *1119*
Spencer Davies Group **6:** 603, **7:** *758,* 759, 804, **9:** 978, **10:** 1181, 1183, 1186-7, 1188
Spenner, Alan **10:** 1168
Spiders from Mars **14:** 1626, 1628, 1632-3
Spinetti, Henry **8:** 955, **9:** 1036, **19:** 2196
Spinetti, Victor **8:** 854, *855*
Spinners, **3:** 332, **4:** 473
Spirit **14:** 1614-15
'Spontaneous Underground' **11:** 1303, 1308
Spooky Tooth **15:** 1683, **17:** 1981-2, 2028, **18:** 2133
Spooner, Bill **16:** 1873, *1873*
Spooner, Steve **19:** 2218
Spotnicks **3:** 251, **4:** 381, *389,* 393, **6:** 700
'Sport Alive' **19:** 2239
Spratley, Bill **14:** 1598
Spring **7:** 778, *778*
Springfield, Dusty **5:** 599, **6:** 621-2, *623, 626, 682, 684,* **7:** 723, 740-3, **10:** 1140, *1140*
Springfield, Rick **20:** 2371
Springfield, Tom **7:** 730, **10:** 1140, *1140*
Springfields **7:** 723, 730, *733,* **10:** 1138-40, *1139*
Springsteen, Bruce **1:** 16, **2:** 238, **5:** 491, *492,* 492-3, 515, **6:** 608, **11:** 1220, 1300, **12:** 1335, *1336,* **15:** 1688, 1703, 1780, **17:** 2020, **18:** *2081,* 2081-2, *2087-9,* 2087-90, *2091,* 2092, 2093, *2100,* 2124
Spungen, Nancy **9:** 1075, *1075,* **16:** 1863, **18:** *2047,* 2048, *2143*
Square, Lester **20:** 2323
Squares **19:** 2261
Squeeze **19:** 2182, 2256-7, *2257,* **20:** 2281, 2340
Squire, Chris **9:** *1039,* 1040, **15:** *1690,* 1691, 1692, *1695*
Squires, Douglas **4:** 378
Sri Chinmoy **13:** 1524, 1535, 1537
SRO Artists **3:** 360
St Claire, Alex **13:** 1484
St Louis Blues **15:** 1797
St Louis Union **6:** 603
St Nicholas, Nick **9:** 1072
St Winifred's School Choir **19:** 2265, *2265*
Staccatos **6:** 682
Stacia **17:** *1996*

Staehely, Al **14:** 1615
Staehely, John Christian **14:** 1615
Stafford, Jo **1:** 37
'Stage Show' **1:** 87, *95*
Stainton, Chris **9:** 1036, **10:** 1167-8, **13:** 1445, 1446
Stairsteps **15:** 1797
Stalk-Forest Group **18:** 2126
Stallone, Frank **18:** 2107
Stamp, Chris **11:** 1265, 1273, 1275-7
Stampfel, Peter **9:** 1015
Standells **8:** 872, *873,* **16:** 1858
Stanley, Paul **16:** 1869, *1869*
Stannard, Terry **10:** 1192
Stanshall, Viv **10:** 1189, 1192
Staple Singers **8:** 922, *922,* 933, **15:** 1783, *1783,* 1792-3
Staples, Cleotha **15:** 1792, 1793
Staples, Mavis **3:** 334, **15:** 1783, 1792, 1793
Staples, Neville **19:** 2203, 2204, *2206,* 2207
Staples, Pete **8:** 944, 946
Staples, Roebuck 'Pop' **15:** *1792,* 1793
Staples, Yvonne **15:** 1792, 1793
Star Club, Hamburg **5:** 523, 528, 539-40, *539-40,* 549, 550
Star Crazy **20:** 2365
Stardust **2:** 212, **4:** 372, **11:** 1275, **13:** 1508, *1509*
Stardust, Alvin **2:** 139, **13:** 1507, 1514-15
Star Is Born, A **14:** 1650, 1652, *1652*
Starlighters **8:** 874-5, *875*
Starr, Edwin **9:** 1057
Starr, Freddie **5:** 538-9
Starr, Kay **1:** 32, **3:** 310, *310*
Starr, Maureen **10:** *1148,* 1149
Starr, Ringo **4:** *399, 403,* **5:** 483, 541-60, **6:** *629,* 639, **8:** 844, 848, 854-7, **10:** 1109, 1141-60, **12:** 1440, **13:** 1445, 1508, **14:** 1659, 1679, **17:** 1961, 1966, 1968, 1972, 1975-7, *1975-7,* 2039
Stars **11:** 1320
Staton, Candi **15:** 1782
Statton, Alison **18:** 2157, *2157*
Status Quo **8:** 955, **13:** 1460, **15:** 1721, *1721,* 1730-5, 1747, **17:** 1982
Stavers, Gloria **12:** 1329
Stax Records **1:** 10, **3:** 266, 275, **7:** 782, *784,* 784-5, **8:** 921-2, *921-2,* 925-6, 928-33, 936-7, *939,* **12:** 1401, 1409-10
Stax/Volt Revue **8:** 926, 932
Stealers Wheel **17:** *2028*
Steampacket **6:** 682, **8:** 816, **15:** *1723,* 1724
Steel, John **6:** 657, *657,* 660
Steel Pulse **10:** 1181, **19:** 2216, *2217*
Steele, Andrew **8:** 954-5, *955,* **17:** 2038, *2038*
Steele, Bob **10:** 1096
Steele, David **19:** 2208, 2209, *2209*
Steele, Tommy **1:** 85, **2:** 122, *122,* 129-31, 134, *134,* 135, 136, 164, *165,* **3:** 249, 251, **4:** 371, *379,* 422, *423,* 428, 430, *430,* 437, **5:** 497, **6:** 639, **7:** 739-40, **8:** *858,* 859, **12:** 1322, **13:** 1502

Steeleye Span **10:** 1125, **13:** 1462-3, 1464, 1466, 1471-3, 1477
Steelmen **2:** *122,* 130, *130*
Steely Dan **16:** 1841, 1851, 1901, *1918,* 1918-20, *1920*
Steen, Roger **16:** 1873, *1873*
Stein, Chris **13:** 1499, **17:** 2001, 2003, 2012, **20:** *2290, 2291,* 2292
Stein, Jeff **11:** 1275
Stein, Mark **9:** 1070-1
Stein, Seymour **17:** 2003, 2011
Steinberg, Lewis **7:** 784, 785
Steinman, Jim **18:** 2122-4, *2123*
Stensby, Roald **3:** 251
Stephens, Barbara **8:** 929
Stepney, Charles **9:** 1059, **19:** 2163
Steppenwolf **9:** 1070, *1070-2,* 1072, **11:** 1256
Sterling, Annette **6:** 717
Stern, Jack **14:** 1589
Steve Allen TV Show **2:** 161
Steve Gibbons Band **7:** 817, **11:** 1277
Steve Miller Band **7:** 757, **11:** 1223, 1225-7 *1225-7*
Steve Miller Blues Band **8:** 914-15
Stevens, Cat **1:** 11, **8:** *942,* **9:** 978, **12:** 1341, 1353-5, 1359, 1400
Stevens, Connie **3:** 312, *312*
Stevens, Guy **7:** 802, 816, *817,* **8:** 881, 887, **10:** 1087, **15:** 1739, **16:** 1818, **18:** 2068
Stevens, Stella **2:** *212,* **3:** 346
Stevenson, Mickey **6:** *718,* 719
Stevenson, Nils **18:** 2149, 2151
Stevenson, William **6:** 702, 717, 719
Stewart, Al **18:** 2145, **13:** 1462, *1463* 1478
Stewart, Billy **6:** 702, **9:** 1059
Stewart, Chris **15:** 1752
Stewart, Dave **6:** 691, **20:** *2359, 2386,* 2386-7, *2387*
Stewart, Ed **7:** 745, **17:** 1958, *1958,* 1960
Stewart, Eric **6:** 602, **16:** *1913,* 1913-15
Stewart, Freddie **12:** *1405,* 1405-7
Stewart, Ian **8:** 889, 891
Stewart, Jim **3:** 275, **7:** 784-5, **8:** 921, *921,* 925-6, 928-33, 937, **12:** 1409
Stewart, John **1:** 13, **6:** *668,* 669
Stewart, Lee **3:** 357
Stewart, Rod **1:** 6, **5:** 582, **6:** 642, 653, 655, **7:** *733,* 783, 809, **9:** 1027, 1028, 1033, *1070,* 1071, **10:** 1156, **11:** *1229,* 1230-1, *1243,* 1248, **12:** 1336, 1354, **14:** *1668,* **15:** 1721, 1722-7, **16:** 1802, 1840, **17:** 1924, 1942, 1980, **18:** 2099, *2099,* 2124, and the Faces **11:** 1248
Stewart, Rose **12:** *1405,* 1406, 1407, **17:** 2071
Stewart, Sylvester *see* Stone, Sly
Stewart, Wynn **14:** 1648
Stewart Brothers **12:** 1405
Stiff Little Fingers **18:** *2156,* 2157
Stiff Records **13:** 1515, **17:** *1921,* 1922, 1925, 1931, 1934, 1938-40, 2003, 2013, 2014, **18:** 2042, 2062, 2079, 2156, **19:** 2182, 2193, 2213
Stigwood, Robert **1:** 18, **4:** 437, **5:** 555, **7:**

817, *817*, **9**: 1027-8, **10**: 1156, **11**: 1266, 1275-6, **13**: 1449, **18**: 2105-6, *2107*, **20**: 2327, 2328, 2337
Stilettoes **16**: 1863, **20**: *2290, 2291*, 2292
Stillman, Jim **4**: 457
Stills, Stephen **1**: 12, 13, **7**: 821, *823, 824, 825-6, 826*, **9**: 1035, **10**: 1123, **11**: 1240, **12**: 1346, 1349, **15**: 1702, 1703, 1764, *1764*, 1765-6, *1766*, 1768, *1770*, **19**: 2195
Sting **11**: *1243*, 1284-5, **19**: 2187, **20**: 2328, *2328, 2402*, 2405, *2407*
Stirling, Leon 'Peaches' **2**: 176
Stix Nix Band **6**: 708
Stoker, Gordon **1**: 94, **12**: 1321
Stoller, Mike *see* Leiber and Stoller
Stoller, Rhet **4**: 392
Stollman, Steve **11**: 1303
Stone, Asst. District Attorney Joseph **2**: 219
Stone, Brian **7**: 825
Stone, David **17**: 1986
Stone, Jesse (*alias* Charles Calhoun) **3**: 272-3, 325
Stone, Rose *see* Stewart, Rose
Stone, Sly **1**: 16, 62
Stone, Vanetta **12**: 1407
Stone and Santana **10**: *1095*
Stone Canyon Band **3**: 304, *305*, **15**: 1773
Stoner, Rob **11**: *1212*
'Stones In The Park' **8**: 851, *852-3*
Stooges **8**: 872, **9**: 1002, *1002*, 1003, **13**: 1482, 1498-9
Stookley, Paul **6**: 664, *664*
Stop The World, I Want To Get Off **7**: 740, **8**: *858-9*
Storer, George **2**: 219
Stories **16**: 1828
Storm, Rory **3**: 243, *243*, 249, **5**: 522, 538, 550, 548, *548*, 550, **6**: 630
Storm, Tempest **1**: *82*
Storm, Warren **13**: *1454*, 1455
Stormsville Shakers **5**: *600*
Stormy Six **20**: 2367
Storz, Todd **8**: 841, **17**: 2036
Strain, Sammy **14**: 1600
Straits **19**: 2261
Strange, Billy **5**: 519, *520*
Strange, Steve **11**: 1306, *1306*, **14**: *1622-3*, 1623, **18**: 2055, **20**: *2342, 2343, 2347*, 2350-1, *2350-1*
Strangers **13**: 1444, **14**: 1648-9, *1649*
Stranglers **18**: 2042, 2058, 2063, 2074, **19**: 2182, *2188*, 2188-90, *2190-1*
Stratton, Dennis **19**: 2231-2
Stratton-Smith, Tony **13**: 1475, **15**: 1686, 1752, 1753
Stravinsky, Igor **13**: 1492
Strawberry Alarm Clock **1**: 13, **10**: 1083, *1083*
Strawbs **8**: 953, **13**: 1465, 1466, **15**: 1692, *1696*, 1697
Stray Cats **1**: 116, *118-19*, 120, **19**: 2260, 2275
Street, Richard **9**: 1050, 1052

Streisand, Barbra **14**: *1652*, **17**: 1942, *1942*, **18**: 2107, 2112
Strickland, Keith **20**: 2286, *2286*
String-a-Longs **2**: 191, **4**: 390
Strong, Barrett **4**: 473, 477, **6**: *718*, **9**: 1051-2, 1057, **14**: 1651-2, 1657
Strontium 90 **19**: 2184
Strummer, Joe **1**: *2*, **17**: 1925, **18**: 2042, 2062, 2066-7, *2067*, 2069, 2158, **19**: 2204, **20**: *2345*, 2373
Strykert, Ron **20**: 2372
Stuart, Chad **6**: 694
Stuart, Michael **9**: 1017
Stuermer, Daryl **15**: 1754
Stubbs, Joe **8**: 939
Stubbs, Levi **5**: 494, **6**: 710-13, 715-16, 718
Style Council **19**: 2219, 2248, *2248*, **20**: 2394
Stylistics **14**: 1581, 1594-5
Styrene, Poly **18**: 2061, *2063*, 2070, *2070*
Styx **18**: 2121, 2128-9, *2128-9*, 2133
Subway Sect **18**: 2058, 2062, 2148
Sue Records **4**: 462, **7**: 816
Sugarhill Gang **19**: *2176*, 2177
Sulley, Susanne **20**: 2308, *2308*
Sullivan, Arlene **3**: *356*, 360
Sullivan, Big Jim **2**: 139, **5**: 597, **9**: 1021
Sullivan, Ed **1**: 90-2, **2**: *192*, 202, *203*, **5**: *542*, 560, **6**: *610*, 692
Sullivan, Niki **2**: 185, *186*
Sullivan, Peter **6**: 640, **7**: 759
Sulton, Kasim **16**: 1905
Sumlin, Hubert **4**: 466
Summer, Donna **18**: 2103, 2110-12, *2110-12, 2118-19*, 2119, 2120, **20**: 2362
Summer Holiday **4**: *368*, 369, 431
Summers, Andy **5**: *598*, **19**: 2184-5
Summers, Gene **1**: *103*, 120, **3**: 254
Sumner, Bernard **19**: 2267
Sumner, Gordon *see* Sting
Sun Records **1**: 41-2, 44-7, 51, 52, 53, 54, 109-11, *110*, 119, **3**: *261*, 262, 264, 271, **4**: 414, **14**: 1643-4
'Sunday Night At The London Palladium' **5**: 559, **8**: 850
Sunny and the Sunglows **2**: 196
Sunnyland Slim **4**: 464, 465
Sunshine, Monty **4**: *438*, 439, 440
Superfly **12**: 1403, 1414
Super K **9**: 981, 983, 997, 999
'Supersonic' **12**: *1438-9*, 1440, **13**: 1512
Supertramp **15**: 1698, 1758-60
Supremes **1**: *10*, 11, **4**: *472*, 473, 478, **6**: 624, *625*, 710, 713, 714-15, *714-15*, 717-18, **7**: 724, **9**: *1041*, 1041-2, 1044-9, 1057, 1070, **10**: 1085, **12**: *1420*, 1434-5, **14**: 1581, 1583, 1590, 1592
Surfaris **4**: *381*, 392, 395, 400, **7**: *764*, 765, **9**: 1017
Sutch, David 'Screaming Lord' **4**: 393, **5**: 587, 588, **7**: 744
Sutcliffe, Stu **2**: 194, **5**: 540, *544*, 547-9
Susuki, Kenji 'Damo' **20**: 2367
SVT **8**: *912*

Swaggart, Jimmy Lee **2**: 166
Swain, Hamp **8**: 924
Swain, Tony **16**: 1902, **20**: 2348
Swain and Jolley **20**: 2397
Swan Records **3**: 341, 342-3, 360, **5**: 496-7
Swan Silvertones **3**: 324, **7**: 795
Swanee Quintet **7**: 788
Swapo Singers **20**: 2380
Swarbrick, Dave **13**: 1462, *1463, 1465*, 1465-7, *1467*, 1472
Sweeney's Men **13**: 1465
Sweet **6**: *619*, **12**: *1422*, 1423, **15**: *1704*, **16**: 1821, 1822, 1823, 1829, 1835-7, 1863
Sweet, Darrell **17**: *1988*, 1989
Sweet, Rachel **17**: 1939
Sweet Inspiration **1**: 95
Swing Time **3**: 324, 325
Swinging Blue Jeans **5**: 538, **7**: 729
Swingin' Tigers **4**: 473
Swinging U.K. **8**: 844
Swingsters **19**: 2173
Switch **18**: 2103
Sykes, John **17**: 1993
Sylvain, Sylvain **16**: 1879, 1880, *1880*
Sylva, Buddy de **5**: 501
Sylvers, Leon **14**: 1587, **19**: 2178-9, *2180*
Sylvester **12**: *1402*, 1403
Sylvester, Terry **6**: 607
Sylvester, Tony **18**: 2103
Sylvian, David **14**: *1622*, **20**: 2355-6, *2357*
Symphony Sid **2**: 201
Syndicate of Sound **8**: 872
Syracuse, Russ The Moose **8**: 841, **17**: 2037
Syreeta **2**: 180, **9**: 1043, **14**: 1673, **15**: 1797, *1797*
System, The **8**: 844
Sytner, Alan **5**: 522
Szymczyk, Bill **14**: 1613, **15**: 1774, 1775

T

Tages **6**: 682
Taj Mahal **11**: *1223*, 1236-7, **13**: 1559
Takahashi, Yukihiro **20**: 2365
Talbert, Wayne **7**: 835
Talbot, Billy **15**: 1768, *1771*
Talbot, Mick **19**: 2219, 2248, *2248*, **20**: 2360
Talisman **19**: 2216
Talking Heads **9**: 966, 1002, **14**: 1638, 1640, **15**: 1763, **17**: *2003*, 2004-5, 2011, 2016, **18**: 2072, 2086, 2103, 2115, **20**: 2281, 2283-5, 2356
Tallent, Garry **18**: *2089*
Talley, Gary **10**: 1174-5
Talley, Lewis **14**: 1648-9
Talley, Nerda **5**: 514
Talmy, Shel **4**: 437, **6**: 697, **7**: 750, 754, 757-9, *757*, 758, *759*, 819, **8**: 952, **11**: 1265, 1266, 1276, 1277, **13**: 1477

TAMI Show, The **8:** 845
Tams **10:** 1176, **16:** 1885
Tandy, Richard **15:** 1747, 1748, 1749, *1749*
Tangerine Dream **20:** *2319,* 2367, 2369, *2369*
Tangerine Peel **16:** 1822
Tangerine Records **3:** 328
Tannen, Paul **4:** 406, 407
Tanz Der Youth **18:** 2080
Tarheel Slim **1:** 71
Tarney, Alan **17:** 1953
Tarnopol, Nat **3:** 331
Tarplin, Marv **4:** 477, 479
Tarsavallan Presidentii **20:** 2367
Taste **11:** 1245, **15:** 1721
Tate, Bruce **3:** 300
Tate, Sharon **7:** 780
Taupin, Bernie **14:** *1665,* 1665-6, 1668, **16:** 1866, **18:** 2099
Taurog, Norman **2:** 208
Taylor, Alex **15:** 1707, *1708*
Taylor, Andy **20:** *2388,* 2389, *2390, 2391*
Taylor, Alistair **5:** 557, **10:** 1159
Taylor, Bobby **7:** 814-15
Taylor, Cecil **3:** 321, *321,* 322
Taylor, Clive **8:** 952-3
Taylor, Dallas **15:** 1765
Taylor, Derek **1:** 15, 17, 83, **5:** 557, **7:** 775, **8:** 889, **10:** 1098-9, 1158-9, **12:** 1322, 1325
Taylor, Diane **14:** 1589
Taylor, Dick **8:** 887, *889*
Taylor, Dolphin **18:** 2146-7
Taylor, Eddie **5:** 595
Taylor, Eve **4:** *371,* **6:** 622, 626, *627,* 628
Taylor, Felice **14:** 1589
Taylor, Gary **8:** 954-5, *955,* **18:** 2038, *2038*
Taylor, Glen **8:** 949
Taylor, Hugh **15:** *1780*
Taylor, James **2:** 182, **6:** 694, **7:** 822, **8:** 864, **10:** 1124, 1158, **11:** 1220, **12:** 1341, 1346, 1359, *1360,* **13:** 1483, **14:** 1650, 1679, **15:** 1701, 1702, 1703, 1707-8, *1710,* 1715, 1718, 1780, **18:** *2108,* 2109
Taylor, John **9:** *1040,* **20:** *2388,* 2389, *2389, 2390, 2391*
Taylor, Johnnie **8:** 922, 930, 932-3
Taylor, Kate **15:** 1702, 1707, *1708*
Taylor, Kingsize **5:** 522, 523, 534, 538, 540
Taylor, Larry **7:** 734, **10:** *1114,* 1115, 1116-17
Taylor, Liningston **15:** 1702, 1707, *1708*
Taylor, Mick **8:** *882,* 883, 884, 885, 887, 889, *889,* 893-4, 898, 900, **9:** 1033, *1033,* **10:** 1102, 1114, 1115, **15:** 1728
Taylor, Paul **19:** 2219
Taylor, Phil 'Philthy Animal' **19:** 2239, *2239*
Taylor, R. Dean **9:** 1048
Taylor, Roger **16:** *1812,* 1817, **20:** *2388,* 2389, *2389, 2390, 2391*
Taylor, Sam 'The Man' **2:** 174, **3:** 273, 274, **4:** 389, **5:** 576

Taylor, Vince **3:** 250
Taylor, Zola **3:** *299,* 300
T-Bones **7:** *759,* 816, **15:** 1685
Tear Gas **17:** 1995
Teardrop Explodes **18:** 2060, **19:** 2262, 2276, 2277, 2278, *2278,* 2279-80, **20:** 2316
Tears for Fears **19:** 2266, **20:** 2418, *2420*
Techniques **9:** 977, **16:** 1882, 1887
Teddy Bears **2:** 237, **5:** 506, *506,* 507, 567
Tedesco, Tommy **5:** 519
Teegarden, Dave **16:** 1856, 1857
Teenage Lust **17:** 2001
Teen Kings **4:** *413,* 414
Teen Queens **3:** 300
Tee Set **6:** *698,* 699
Television **17:** 2003, *2004,* 2006-8, 2012, 2019, **18:** 2045, 2086, **20:** 2281, *2283,* 2292, 2293
Temperance Seven **3:** 268, *268,* **4:** 439, *439,* 440, **6:** 637, 638, 639
Temperance Ted **10:** 1093, 1125, **13:** 1486, **15:** 1711, **16:** 1851, 1860
Temple, Julien **20:** 2359
Templeman, Ted **10:** 1093, 1125, **13:** 1486, **16:** 1851, 1860, **18:** 2103
Tempo Toppers **2:** 149
Temprees **8:** 933
Temptations **1:** 10, 62, **4:** 478, **6:** 714, 718-19, **7:** 783, **9:** *1041,* 1042-3, 1045, 1048, 1050-2, *1056,* 1057, **12:** *1420,* **16:** 1885, **18:** 2102
10cc **4:** 453, **6:** 602, **8:** 960, **14:** 1680, **16:** 1901, 1913-15
Ten Years After **10:** 1102, 1107, **11:** 1253, *1253,* **12:** 1361, 1374-5, **15:** 1721
Tench, Benmont **18:** 2085, 2086
Tench, Bob **11:** 1232
Tennessee Three **14:** 1645
Tepper, Jeff Morris **13:** 1486
Tepper, Sid **4:** 363, 422
Terrell, Jean **9:** 1049
Terrell, Tammi **6:** *703,* 704, 718-19, **7:** 783, **9:** 1042, 1043
Terry, George **9:** 1036, *1036*
Terry, Helen **20:** 2400, *2400*
Terry, Sonny **2:** 125, **5:** 584, 585, **6:** 654-5, 679, *679*
Terry and the Blue Jeans **4:** 393
Tesluk, Paul **4:** 396, *396,* 397
Tex, Joe **7:** 782-3, *796-7,* **12:** 1409, **15:** 1781
Texas Longhorns **14:** 1654
Texas Playboys **1:** *23, 38,* 56, **2:** 181, **14:** 1649, *1657*
Thain, Gary **15:** 1728, 1729
'Thamesbeat' **19:** 2242
'Thank Your Lucky Stars' **4:** 380, *380,* **8:** 849-50, *851*
Tharpe, Sister Rosetta **2:** 158, *158,* 160, **5:** 585, **10:** 1162
That'll Be The Day **4:** 372, 428, **13:** 1508, **20:** 2327
Thau, Marty **16:** 1879
Theaker, Drachen **9:** 1017

Them **4:** 381, **13:** *1551,* 1553
These Dangerous Years **4:** 430
Thiele, Bob **2:** 186, *190*
Thin Lizzy **15:** 1737, **17:** 1981, 1990-3
Third Ear Band **11:** 1247
Third World **20:** *2374*
Thirteenth Floor Elevators **8:** 872, *919,* 920, **11:** *1291,* 1292
31st of February **14:** 1603
'33⅓ Revolutions Per Monkee' **9:** 990
This Is Elvis **2:** 214
Thomas, Alex **19:** 2163
Thomas, B. J. **5:** 575, 580
Thomas, Bruce **15:** 1738, **17:** 1925, **19:** 2193, *2194*
Thomas, Carla **6:** 706, **8:** 921-2, 928, 930, 923, 933
Thomas, Charles **3:** 291
Thomas, Chris **10:** 1089
Thomas, Irma **15:** *1782*
Thomas, Jeff **20:** 2389
Thomas, Keith **19:** 2247
Thomas, Leon **13:** 1537
Thomas, Mary **5:** 514
Thomas, Mickey **8:** 913
Thomas, Pete **17:** 1925, **19:** 2193, *2194,* 2195
Thomas, Ray **10:** 1193-6, *1195*
Thomas, Rufus **1:** *42,* 43, 45, **5:** 483, **8:** 921-2, 928-9, 932
Thomas, Victor **6:** 708
Thompkins, Russel Jr. **14:** 1594-5, *1595*
Thompson, Chester **15:** 1754
Thompson, Danny **10:** 1135, **13:** 1462, 1476-7
Thompson, Dennis **13:** 1487, **17:** 2109
Thompson, Dicky **11:** 1227
Thompson, Dougie **15:** 1758, *1758,* 1760
Thompson, Errol **16:** *1900*
Thompson, Hunter S. **12:** 1323
Thompson, Kix **19:** 2205
Thompson, Lee **19:** 2210-11, *2211,* 2213
Thompson, Paul **16:** *1804,* 1807, 1808, 1810
Thompson, Richard **13:** *1461,* 1462, *1464,* 1465-7, 1560
Thompson, Richard and Linda **12:** 1400
Thompson, Stephen **10:** 1114-15
Thompson, Tony **18:** 2114
Thompson, Wayne Carson **10:** 1174-5
Thompson Twins **20:** 2303, 2381, 2394
Thor, Marc **17:** 2005
Thorne, Tracy **18:** *2157*
Thornton, Big Mama **3:** 286-7
Thorogood, George **10:** 1163
Thorup, Peter **5:** 586
Thrasher, Andrew **3:** 290
Thrasher, Gerhart **3:** 290, 291
Three Blazers **1:** *29,* 30
Three Chuckles **2:** 236
Three Degrees **14:** 1581, 1596, 1597, 1598, 1600, **18:** 2102
Three Suns **3:** 298
Three Tons of Joy **3:** *287*
Threshold Records **10:** 1195-6

Thrillers **3:** 330
Thunderbirds **5:** 588, **6:** 642, 814, *814,* 815, *815*
Thunderbrain **17:** 2004
Thunderbyrd **7:** *830*
Thunderclap Newman **11:** 1279
Thunders, Johnny **16:** 1863, *1878,* 1879, *1880,* **17:** *2001,* 2002, 2012
Thundertones **4:** 390
Thurston, Colin **20:** 2397
Thurston, Scott **13:** 1499
Tibbs, Gary **20:** 2324, *2324*
Tiger Beat **12:** *1329*
Tight Fit **13:** *1503*
Tijuana Brass **5:** 503, *503*
Til, Sonny **1:** 70
Til, Sonny and the Orioles **12:** *1418,* 1419
Tilbrook, Glenn **19:** 2256, *2256-7,* **20:** 2340
Till, Emmett **1:** 83
Tilley, Sandra **6:** 717
Tillman, Georgeanna **6:** 719
Tillotson, Johnny **4:** 401, *402,* 403, 406-7, 418
Time Machine **20:** 2376
Timmons, Bobby **3:** 321
'Tin Pan Alley' **4:** 421
Tiny Tim **10:** *1165*
Tippet, Keith **14:** 1564-5
Tipton, Glen **17:** *1998,* 1999, *2000*
Titelman, Russ **5:** 502, 519, **16:** 1838
T-Neck **9:** 1055
Tobin, George **4:** 479
Toby **15:** 1740
Together **6:** 653
Tokens **4:** 450, 459
Tom, Georgia **2:** 159
Tomita, Isao **20:** 2301, *2301*
Tommy **11:** 1269, 1273-4, *1274,* 1275, 1277, **14:** 1664, 1667, **15:** 1742, **20:** 2327
Tommy Steele Story **2:** 131
Tommy The Toreador **4:** 430, *430*
Tomorrow **9:** 1022, 1085, **11:** 1301, 1305
Tom Robinson Band **11:** 1220, **16:** 1905, **18:** *2146,* 2146-7, 2158-9
Tom Tom Club **20:** 2285, 2360
Tonight **19:** 2242
Tonite Let's All Make Love In London **8:** 847
Tontoh, Mac **9:** 963
Tonto's Expanding Headband **14:** 1673
Took, Steve Peregrine **12:** 1422, *1436,* 1438, 1440
Too Late Blues **3:** *346*
Toomey, Jim **20:** 2386, *2386*
Toots and the Maytals **9:** 962-3, 970-1, 977, 979
'Top Of The Pops' **8:** 842, 849-50, *850,* **11:** 1265, 1319, **12:** 1422-3, 1428, **13:** 1519, **16:** *1826,* 1866
Topham, Tony 'Top' **6:** 650
Torello, Bobby **11:** 1235
Torian, Reggie **7:** *793,* 795
Tork, Peter **1:** 13, **9:** 983, 987-91, **10:** *1100,* 1123
Torme, Bernie **17:** 1984, *1985*

Tornados **4:** 363, 383, 388, 392, *393, 435,* 437, **7:** 765
Tosh, Peter **9:** *976,* 977, 1051, **12:** *1403,* **16:** 1885, 1886, 1887, 1889, 1892, 1894, *1914,* 1915, **20:** 2373, 2374, 2375
Toto **18:** 2121
Tourists **20:** 2386, *2386*
Toussaint, Allen **2:** 145, 154, **5:** *561,* 562, **10:** 1115, **12:** 1416, **13:** 1451, 1452, **16:** 1859
Tower of Power **8:** 914
Towns, Colin **17:** 1984, *1985*
Townsend, Rob **10:** 1198
Townshend, Pete **1:** 6-7, *7,* **7:** 721, *749,* 803, 806, **8:** 845, 856, **9:** *1003, 1035,* 1035-6, 1063, 1065, 1079, **10:** 1100, **11:** 1261, 1264, 1265, 1266, 1267, *1269,* 1273, 1274, 1275, *1277,* 1278-80, 1297, **12:** 1400, **14:** 1633, 1680, **19:** 2244, *2247,* **20:** 2327, *see also* Who
T.P.O.K. Jazz Band **20:** *2378*
Track Records **11:** 1277
Traffic **1:** 8, 9, **6:** 603, 647, **9:** 1031, 1035, **10:** 1187, 1188-9, 1189-91, *1192,* **11:** 1247, **14:** 1562, **17:** 1981
Traffic Jam **15:** 1732
Train **11:** 1251
Trans-Oceanic Trouser Press **12:** 1339, *1340*
Trapeze **17:** 1984
Trashmen **4:** 392
Travers, Brian **19:** 2214, *2214*
Travers, Mary **6:** 664, *664*
Travers, Pat **19:** 2232
Travis, Dave Lee **7:** 745
Travis, Merle **1:** 40
Travolta, John **5:** *481,* 482, **18:** 2103, 2106, 2107, 2109, **20:** 2327, *2328*
Treadwell, George **1:** 72, **3:** *282,* 283, 291, 292
Treganna, Dave 'Kermit' **18:** 2145
Tremblers **6:** 687
Tremeloes **5:** 537, **8:** 844, *851,* **12:** 1354
Tribe, Tony **19:** 2215
Tridents **11:** 1228
Trigger **13:** *1478-9,* 1479
Trimmer, Ian **9:** 1031
Trinity **13:** 1524
Trip, The **8:** *846,* 847, 902, **11:** 1239
Tripp, Peter **2:** 220
Trips Festival, San Francisco (1967) **8:** 917, 920
Tritsch, Christian **20:** 2368
Triumph **4:** 437
Troggs **6:** 603, 695, **7:** 760, *760,* **8:** *941,* 942, 944-6, **10:** *1084,* 1085
Troiano, Dom **14:** 1613
Trotman, Lloyd **3:** 273
Troubador Club, Los Angeles **15:** 1761-2, *1762-3,* 1763
Trower, Robin **9:** 1062, **10:** 1086-7, *1087,* 1089
Troy, Doris **5:** 576, 579
Trucks, Butch **14:** 1603-4
Tubb, Ernest **1:** 39

Tubby, King **16:** 1898, *1898*
Tubes **16:** *1862,* 1863, 1872-5, 1879, 1905, 1913, **17:** 2015
Tubeway Army **20:** 2314
Tucker, Ira **2:** 160, **3:** 322
Tucker, Jim **9:** 992-3
Tucker, Maureen 'Mo' **1:** *20,* **8:** *864,* 865, **9:** *1004,* 1005, 1007-8
Tucker, Mick **16:** 1835, *1835,* 1837
Tucker, Tanya **2:** *172*
Tuckey, Len **16:** 1830, 1831, *1831*
Tune Rockers **4:** 382
Tunesmiths **2:** 225
Turbans **1:** 62
Turco, Art **12:** 1339
Turkey Trot **5:** 482, *488,* 489
Turnbull, John **17:** *1930,* 1931, *1933*
Turner, Fred **14:** 1617
Turner, Ian **8:** *853*
Turner, Ike **1:** 30, 44, **7:** 799, **10:** 1109
Turner, Ike and Tina **1:** *11,* 12, **4:** 462, **5:** *511,* 511-12, 517, **9:** 982, 996, 1065, **10:** 1109
Turner, Jefferson 'Stinky' **18:** *2153,* 2153-4
Turner, Joe **1:** 31, 39, 43, **2:** 155, 221, *222,* **3:** 273, *273*
Turner, Joe Lynn **17:** 1986
Turner, John **11:** 1234-5
Turner, Linda **14:** 1597
Turner, Lonny **11:** *1225-6,* 1225-7
Turner, Martin **15:** 1736, 1737
Turner, Nik **17:** 1996, *1996*
Turner, Simon **8:** 960
Turner, Sonny **1:** 72, **3:** 300
Turner, Ted **15:** 1736, *1736,* 1737
Turner, Tina **12:** 1435, **15:** 1782, **20:** 2309, 2381, 2405, *2405,* 2413, 2419
Turtles **6:** 682, **8:** *864-5,* 902, **9:** 982, 992-3, 1017, **10:** 1081, 1082-3, 1121, 1123, **15:** 1761
Tuten, Randy **12:** 1390, *1391*
Tutt, Ron **13:** 1557
TV Smith **18:** *2061*
TV21 **19:** 2274-5
Twiggy **8:** 880, *880*
Twilley, Dwight **20:** 2288, *2288*
Twink **11:** 1320
Twinkle **5:** *574*
Twist Around The Clock **2:** 210, *210,* **3:** 269, *270,* **5:** 487, *487,* 504, *505,* 514
Twisted Sister **19:** *2221*
200 Motels **11:** 1275, **13:** 1495
Two Little Bears, The **3:** 320
2-Tone **18:** 2159-60, **19:** 2201-3, *2203,* 2204
Tyler, Alvin **2:** 154, **4:** 389
Tyler, Bonnie **20:** 2405, 2419
Tyler, Steven **16:** *1848,* 1849
Tympany Five **1:** 34, **3:** 338
Tyner, Rob **13:** 1487, 1488
Tyrannosaurus Rex **1:** 6, **11:** 1247, 1248, **12:** 1422, 1423, 1436-40, **13:** 1507, 1514, **18:** 2077

U

UB40 **11:** *1294,* **19:** 2214-15, *2214-15,* **20:** 2373
Ubu, Pere **17:** 2003
UFO **6:** 640, **17:** 1982
UFO Club, London **11:** 1301, *1301,* 1303, *1304,* 1305, 1306, 1308, 1309
Ugly Ducklings **8:** 872
UK Subs **18:** 2152-3, 2154, *2154*
UK Swings Again **8:** 844
Ullman, Tracey **19:** 2260, **20:** 2381, 2392, 2396
Ultimate Spinach **12:** 1335
Ultravox **16:** 1902, **20:** 2301, 2302, 2313, *2342,* 2343, 2347, 2348, 2351, 2352-4
Ulvaeus, Bjorn **6:** 700, **17:** *1943,* 1944, *1944,* 1946-7
Um Romas, Dom **13:** 1532
Uncle Dog **17:** 1922
Undertakers **5:** *523*
Undertones **19:** *2225*
Underwood, Ian **13:** 1495
Underwood, Lee **13:** 1554
Underwood, Mick **17:** 1984, *1985*
Undisputed Truth **9:** 1042, 1052, 1057
Uniques **16:** 1887
Unit Four Plus Two **6:** 603
Universal Attractions **4:** 463, **7:** 789
Unrelated Segments **13:** 1488
Untamed Youth **2:** *208,* 209, **3:** 248
Unwin, Stanley **7:** 808
Up, Arri **18:** 2062, *2062*
Upsetters **2:** 151, **16:** *1882,* 1890
Uptights **14:** 1589
Upton, Steve **15:** 1736, 1737
Urban Cowboy **16:** 1857
Ure, Midge **11:** *1280,* **17:** *1927,* 1993, **19:** 2241, 2242, 2273, **20:** 2302, *2342,* 2351, 2353-4, *2353, 2354,* 2360, 2403, 2405
Uriah Heep **15:** 1728-9, 1737, **17:** 1982, **19:** 2239
U-Roy **16:** 1882-4, *1884,* 1898
Usher, Gary **7:** 778, **10:** 1083
Utopia **16:** 1905, *1905*
U2 **19:** 2266, 2270-1, *2271,* **20:** 2303, 2381, 2420

V

Vagabonds **7:** 812-13, 816, **11:** 1277
Vagrants **8:** 863, **14:** 1606
Valance, Ricky **2:** 240, **3:** 270, *270,* **4:** 402, **5:** 575
Vale, Mike **9:** 994-5
Valens, Ritchie **2:** 176, 181, *182,* 183, 188, 194, 195, *195,* 196-7, **3:** 254, 259, *259,* 334, **5:** 502
Valentine, Gary **20:** 2292, 2293
Valentine, Hilton **6:** 643, 657, *657, 659,* 659-60

Valentino **7:** 840
Valentinos **3:** 334
Vallet, Gary **4:** 391
Valley, Jim **7:** 833
Valli, Franki **5:** 562, 570-3
Vallory, Ross **11:** 1227
Van Defitte, David **9:** 1057
Van Der Graaf Generator **14:** *1562*
Van Dyke, Earl **6:** 701, 716, *717,* **9:** 1057
Van Halen, Alex **18:** 2121, *2130,* 2131, *2140*
Van Halen, Eddie **18:** 2121, 2130-1, *2130-1, 2140,* 2161, **19:** 2223
Van Leer, Thijs **20:** *2361,* 2367
Van Leeuwen, Roberts **18:** 2119
Van Leuman, Robby **6:** 700
Van Osten, Carson **16:** 1903, *1904*
Van Ronk, Dave **6:** 662, *664,* **11:** 1204, 1218
Van Walls, Harry **3:** 273
Van Zandt, Steve **16:** *1843, 1844,* **18:** *2089,* 2092, 2093, **20:** 2401
Van Zant, Donnie **16:** 1844
Van Zant, Ronnie **16:** *1842,* 1843, *1843,* 1844, *1844*
Vance, Tommy **7:** 745, **8:** 853
Vanda, Harry **6:** 696, 697, **19:** 2227
Vandellas **9:** 1046
Vander, Christian **20:** *2367*
Vandross, Luther **14:** *1629,* 1633, **15:** 1791, **18:** 2103
Vangelis **15:** 1692, 1695, **20:** 2301, *2303*
Vanguard Records **6:** 672
Vanian, Dave **18:** 2054, 2078-80, *2079-80*
Vanilla Fudge **8:** 863, **9:** 1070-1, *1072,* **12:** 1365, **15:** 1691
Varese, Edgae **13:** 1492
Variety **1:** 59
Varnals, Wendy **1:** 8, **8:** *853*
Vaughan, Frankie **4:** 430, 436
Vaughan, Ivan **5:** 557
Vaughan, Sarah **16:** 1915, **17:** 1941
Vaughn, Jack **2:** 190, *190*
Vaughn, Stevie Ray **14:** *1633*
Vee, Bobby **2:** 239, 240, **3:** 308, **4:** 452, 456-7, 458, 459, **5:** 502
Vee-Jay Records **3:** 262, 264, 266, **5:** 571, 572, 595, **9:** 1058-9, 1060
Veltones **8:** 921
Velvet Underground **1:** 2, 19-20, *20,* **8:** *864,* 865, **9:** *1001,* 1002-3, *1002,* 1004-8, **11:** 1297, **13:** 1481, 1498, **14:** 1634, 1637, 1638-9, **16:** 1802, 1862, 1863, 1879, **17:** 2001, 2005, 2006, 2016, 2017, 2019, **18:** 2072, 2073, 2077, 2148, 2151
Velvettes **5:** *584,* 588, **6:** 718, **9:** 1057
Venet, Nik **7:** 757
Ventures **3:** 251, **4:** 383, 391, 392, 393, 395, 404, *405,* **7:** 765
Veres, Mariska **6:** 700
Verlaine, Tom **17:** 2001, 2004, 2005, 2006, 2007-8, *2007,* 2012, 2019
Vernon, Mike **17:** 1929
Vernon, Mike & Richard **10:** *1102,* 1102-

3, 1113, 1118-19, *1119*
Vernons Girls **4:** 379, 380
Verrett, Harrison **2:** 145, *145,* 154
Verve Records **3:** 302-3, **5:** 517
Vestine, Henry **10:** 1116-17
Vibrations **5:** 483, 530
Vibrators **17:** 1929, **18:** 2058, 2061
Vicious, Sid **9:** 1020, 1075, *1075,* **16:** 1863, **18:** *2043, 2046,* 2047-8, *2048,* 2050, 2054-5, *2054,* 2058, 2063, *2143,* 2148
Vickers, Mike **6:** 664-5, *645,* 647
Vikings **6:** 603, **9:** 970, **10:** 1181, 1183
Village People **9:** *982-3,* 983, **18:** *2103*
Vincent, Gene **1:** 12, 80, *84,* 102, *103,* 104-8, 116, 118-19, **2:** 138, 140, *140,* 163, **3:** 243, 247, 248, 283, **4:** 367, *379,* 380, **11:** 1281, 1300, **13:** 1442
Vincent, Robbie **20:** 2394
Vinton, Bobby **2:** 239
Vipers **2:** 125, *125,* 127, 134, 135, **4:** 371, 385, **6:** 639
VIPs **7:** 816
Virgin Records **9:** 964-5, **17:** 2027
Virtue, Mickey **19:** 2214, *2214*
Virtues **4:** 391
Visage **20:** 2347, 2348, 2351, 2354
Visconti, Tony **12:** 1438, 1440, **14:** 1625, 1632-3, *1632*
Viscounts **2:** 138, *139,* 140, **4:** 382, 391, **7:** 737
Vitous, Miroslav **13:** 1532
Viva Las Vegas **2:** *213*
Vogue Records **6:** 632, 633
Voidoids **17:** *2003,* 2011, *2012*
Volk, Philip 'Fang' **7:** 832, 833
Volman, Mark **6:** 682, **9:** 992-3, *992-3,* **12:** 1439, **13:** 1495, *1496*
Voormann, Klaus **5:** 540, 548, **6:** *646,* 647, 649, **13:** 1445, **15:** 1710, **17:** 1972

W

Wace, Robert **7:** 750
Wachtel, Waddy **16:** 1857
Wadleigh, Mike **11:** *1250-1*
Waganfeald, Eddie **4:** 397
Wagner, Dick **16:** 1866
Wagoner, Porter **17:** 2023
Wah! Heat **19:** 2262, 2276, 2277, 2278, 2279
Waifs **16:** 1845
Wailer, Bunny **16:** 1885, 1886, 1889, 1892, 1894
Wailers **1:** 10, **4:** 390-1, **9:** 973, 977, **11:** 1293, **12:** 1403, **16:** 1883-4, 1885-6, 1889-91, *1890,* 1893, **19:** 2216
Wailing Souls **10:** *1186,* **16:** 1886-7
Wainman, Phil **13:** 1512, **16:** 1822, 1835, 1836
Wainwright III, Loudon **11:** 1220, **12:** 1400

Wainwright's Gentlemen *see* Sweet
Waits, Tom **18:** 2094-5, *2094-5,* 2096, 2098, 2100
Wakefield, Frank **15:** 1713
Wakefield, Ron **4:** 477
Wakeling, Dave **9:** *1078,* **19:** 2208, 2209
Wakeman, Rick **1:** 2, **12:** 1355, **14:** 1633, 1680, **15:** *1681,* 1682, 1691, 1692, 1693, 1694, *1694,* 1695, 1696-7, 1699, 1741, 1742, **16:** 1912, **20:** 2301
Wald, Jeff **13:** 1528
Walden, Michael Narader **13:** 1525, **14:** 1604, 1620, **18:** 2103
Walden, Phil **8:** 924-5, 926, **13:** 1443
Walicki, Franciszek **3:** 251
Walker Brothers **8:** *942,* 956-7
Walker, Charley **1:** *43*
Walker, Colin **15:** 1747
Walker, Dave **12:** 1370
Walker, Jimmy **5:** 517
Walker, Johnnie **7:** 745, **8:** 842, *842*
Walker, Junior **2:** 150, **4:** 473, **6:** 708-9, 719, *720,* **9:** 1057, **18:** 2133
Walker, T-Bone **1:** *29,* 30, 78, **3:** 340, **4:** 390, **10:** 1106-7, 1108
Wall, The **11:** 1313, 1316-17, *1316-17,* **14:** 1680
Wallace, Ian **14:** 1565, *1566*
Wallace, Leroy 'Horsemouth' **14:** 1620
Walldoff, Sven-Olaf **17:** *1944,* 1946
Waller, Dave **10:** 1120, **12:** 1370, **16:** 1836, **19:** 2173, 2244
Waller, Fats **2:** *178,* 179
Waller, Gordon **6:** 693-4
Waller, Mickey **11:** *1229,* 1230-1
Wallis, Larry **19:** 2238-9
Walsh, Ed **19:** 2200
Walsh, Joe **10:** 1109, **14:** *1612,* 1613, **15:** *1773,* 1774-5, 1777, **18:** *2099,* 2100
Walters, John **18:** 2077
Walton, Kent **4:** 378
Wammack, Travis **4:** 382, 392
War **6:** *660*
Ward, Algy **18:** 2080
Ward, Bill **12:** 1369-70, *1370*
Ward, Billy **1:** 74, **3:** 281, 330, 331, *331*
Ward, Clara **15:** 1788
Ward, Del **5:** 538
Ward, Ed **12:** 1330, **13:** 1482
Ward, Peter **10:** 1112, *1113*
Ward, Sammy **4:** 477
Ware, Martyn **20:** 2306, 2308, *2308,* 2309, *2309*
Warhol, Andy **1:** 2, 19-20, *20,* **5:** 498, *498,* 500, *500,* **8:** *864,* 865, **9:** 1002, 1005-6, 1007, **11:** 1296-7, *1297,* 1300, **14:** 1625, 1626, 1634, **16:** 1863, **20:** *2320*
Warlocks **8:** *904,* 906, **10:** 1123
Warm Sound **10:** 1085
Warner, Frank **6:** 669
Warner Brothers Records **2:** 227, 228, 231, **5:** 501-2
Warnes, Jennifer **10:** 1169, *1169,* **17:** 2025
Waronker, Lenny **2:** 193, **10:** 1125, **15:** 1718, 1719, **16:** 1851, **18:** 2096

Waronker, Sy **3:** 247, **5:** 502
Warren, Andy **20:** 2323
Warriors **15:** 1691
Warsaw **19:** 2266-7
Warwick, Clint **10:** 1193-4
Warwick, Delia 'Dee Dee' **5:** 576, 577, 578, 579
Warwick, Dionne **3:** 292, **5:** 562, *562,* 576-7, 579, 580, **9:** 1054, **10:** 1099, **18:** 2107
Washington, Chet **19:** 2163
Washington, Geno **7:** 810-11, 817, 820, **19:** 2216, 2218, 2219
Washington, Grover, Jr. **9:** 1043, **13:** 1523, **15:** 1800, **18:** 2103, **19:** 2175
Washington, Tony **6:** 708
Waterboys **20:** 2420
Waters, Muddy **1:** 31, *32,* 65, *65,* 66, **3:** 339, *339,* **4:** 464, *464,* 465, *465,* 466, 467, **5:** 582, 585, 586, 588, *592-3,* **6:** 654, **9:** 1028, **10:** 1102, 1103, 1105, **11:** 1221, 1225, 1228, 1234-5, *1235,* 1238, 1252
Waters, Roger **11:** *1301,* 1304-5, 1307, *1307,* 1308, 1309, *1310,* 1312-13, 1317, 1318-19
Watkins, Charlie **18:** *2137,* 2139
Watson, Bernie **10:** 1112, *1113*
Watson, Deek **1:** 69
Watson, Peter **7:** 818-19
Watt-Roy, Norman **17:** *1930,* 1931, *1933*
Watts, Alan **12:** 1382
Watts, Charlie **5:** *583,* 587, *587,* **8:** 880, *881, 883,* 889-90, 893, 897-8, **13:** 1445
Watts, Ernie **18:** 2097
Watts, Dr Isaac **2:** 158
Watts, Pete 'Overend' **16:** 1818, *1819,* 1820
Wattstax **15:** 1793
Wattstax Festival **12:** 1410
Way, Darryl **14:** 1575-6, *1577*
Way, Pete **18:** 2154
Waybill, Fee **16:** 1863, *1863, 1872,* 1873, *1873,* 1874
Waylors **14:** 1654, *1655*
Waymon, Sam **15:** 1795
Wayne, Carl **6:** 603, **10:** 1181, *1182-3,* 1183
Wayne, Dig **18:** 2062
Wayne, Jeff **6:** 1822
Wayne County **17:** 2003, 2004, 2012, 2017, **18:** 2058
Weathermen **8:** 960
Weather Report **12:** 1347, **13:** 1523, 1530, 1532-3
Weatherly, Jim **14:** 1581, 1587
Weaver, Blue **8:** 952-3
Weaver, Ken **8:** *864,* 865, **9:** *1014,* 1015
Weavers **6:** 662, *663,* 667, *667*
Web, Chick **1:** 33, *33*
Webb, George **4:** 438, 439, *439*
Webb, John **20:** 2315
Webb, Jimmy **6:** 640, **9:** 1049
Webb, Russell **19:** 2275
Webb, Stan **10:** *1101,* 1102, 1107
Webber, Andrew Lloyd **15:** 1742, **20:** *2336,* 2336-7

Weber, Joan **3:** 310
Weber, Steve **9:** 1015
Wedgewood, Mike **14:** 1576
Weedon, Bert **4:** 386, 392, *393*
Weeds **7:** 794, **8:** 931
Weekend **18:** *2157*
Weeks, Willie **10:** 1192, **14:** 1628, **18:** 2097
Weider, John **6:** 660, **10:** 1199-1200, *1199*
Weil, Cynthia **3:** 288, 292, **12:** 1357
Weinberg, Max **18:** 2089
Weir, Bob **8:** *904-5,* 905-6
Weisbart, David **1:** 90, **2:** 211
Weiss, Church E. **18:** 2096
Weiss, Danny **9:** 1071
Weiss, Jerry **13:** 1539, *1539*
Weiss, Mary and Betty **5:** 569
Weissleder, Manfred **5:** *539,* 539-40
Welborn, Larry **2:** 185, *186*
Welch, Bob **10:** 1119-20, **17:** 2031
Welch, Bruce **4:** *367,* 368, 384-8, 422, **16:** 1832, **17:** 1953
Weld, Tuesday **2:** 209, 210, 212
Weller, Fred **7:** 833
Weller, Paul **9:** *1077,* **19:** 2219, 2244-8, **20:** 2360
Wells, Junior **10:** 1102, *1102*
Wells, Mary **4:** 462, *472,* 473, 478, **6:** 704, 706-7, 714-15, 716, **9:** 1043, 1046, 1060
Welnick, Vince **16:** 1873, *1873*
Welsh, David **6:** 694-5
Wenner, Jan **1:** 15, **12:** 1330, *1332,* 1333, 1338
Werber, Frank **6:** 662
Werman, Tom **18:** 2127
Wesley, Fred **19:** 2171
West, Bruce and Laing **9:** 1032, **14:** 1607, *1608*
West, Leslie **9:** 1032, *1033,* **14:** *1606,* 1607, 1608
West, Red and Sonny **12:** 1321
West, Ricky **6:** 615-16, *617,* **18:** 2109
West, Speedy **14:** 1656
West Bay Singers **17:** 1944
Weston, Bob **10:** 1120
Weston, Jonathan **10:** 1087
Weston, Kim **6:** *703,* 704, *718,* 719, **9:** 1043, 1046, 1057
Westwood, Vivienne **18:** *2041,* 2045, 2050, *2051,* 2053, 2055
Wetton, John **10:** 1200, *1200,* **14:** *1564,* 1565, 1566, 1567, **15:** 1688, 1729, 1737
Wexler, Jerry **1:** *43,* 57, *59,* 75, **2:** 216, **3:** 262, *270, 272, 273,* 274, *274,* 275, 282, *282,* 290, 291, 292, 293, **7:** 732, 785, **8:** *922,* 923, 926, 929, 935, *935,* 937, 939-40, **11:** 1220, **14:** 1647, **15:** 1715, 1789, 1790, **19:** 2199
Weymouth, Nigel **7:** 816, **12:** *1391*
Weymouth, Tina **18:** 2072, **20:** 2283-4, *2283-4*
Wham! **19:** 2260, **20:** 2325, 2350, 2401, 2408-9, 2418
Wharton, Darren **17:** 1993
Wharton, Pete **5:** 538

What A Crazy World **4:** 430, 431, **6:** 614, **8:** 844

What A Whopper! **4:** 372, 431

Wheatstraw, Peetie **12:** 1372

When The Boys Meet The Girls **3:** 317

Where The Boys Are **2:** 210, *210*, **3:** 317

Whiskey, Nancy **2:** 125, 134, *165*

Whiskeyhill Singers **6:** 669

Whispers **6:** 682, **19:** 2179, *2179*

Whitcomb, Ian **6:** 693, 695, *695*, **8:** 853, *853*, **12:** 1324, *1324*

White, Alan **14:** 1619, **15:** 1692, 1693, *1694*

White, Barry **3:** 332, **9:** 973, **12:** 1410, **14:** 1581, 1588-9, **18:** 2102, 2118

White, Bukka **10:** 1108

White, Butch **3:** 303

White, Carol **7:** *797*

White, Chris **6:** 688-9, 691

White, Clarence **7:** 830, **10:** 1168, **13:** 1556, **14:** 1657, **15:** 1719

White, Fred **19:** 2163

White, Jay **3:** *305*

White, Josh **2:** 159, **5:** 585

White, Judi **9:** 1055

White, Lenny **14:** 1620

White, Maurice **12:** 1408, **19:** 2162-4, *2163-4*

White, Norman **1:** 10

White, Robert **6:** 716, **9:** 1057

White, Ronald **4:** 473, 475, 477, 478, 479, **9:** 1051

White, Roy **9:** 975

White, Snowy **17:** 1993

White, Ted **15:** 1789

White, Tony Joe **10:** 1163, *1163*, 1177

White, Trevor **13:** 1519

White, Verdine **9:** *1038*, 1039, **19:** 2163-4, *2164*

White Rock **15:** 1697

White Whale Records **9:** 992-3

Whitehead, Alan **8:** *947*, 949

Whitehead, Annie **19:** 2207, **20:** 2413

Whitehead, Don **19:** 2163

Whitehead, Ian **7:** 819

Whitehead, John **14:** *1598*, 1600

Whitehead, Ralph **13:** 1542

Whitesnake **11:** 1293, *1293*, **12:** 1380, **17:** 1983, 1984, 1987, *1987*

Whitfield, Norman **1:** 62, **6:** 717, 718-19, *718*, **7:** 783, **9:** 1042-3, 1051-2, 1056-7, **12:** 1409, **14:** 1587, **18:** 2102, 2103, 2110

Whitford/St Holmes Band **16:** 1849

Whitlook, Bobby **9:** 1035

Whitman, Charles **5:** 574

Whitman, Slim **10:** 1139

Whitney, Charlie **10:** 1198-1200, *1198-1200*

Whitney, Marve **9:** 1055

Whitsett, Carson **7:** 785

Whitten, Danny **9:** 1020, **15:** 1768, 1770

Whitwam, Barry **6:** 685

Who **1:** 6-7, 16, **6:** 603, 683, **7:** 742, 749, 757, 758-9, 801-2, *801*, 806, 812, 816-17, 818-19, **8:** 942, **9:** 1001, 1022, 1035, **10:** 1085, 1092, *1098*, 1099, 1100, 1164, **11:** 1251, 1261-7, 1298, 1300, **12:** 1357-8, 1384-5, **14:** 1616, 1617, 1680, **15:** 1685, *1742*, **16:** 1834, **18:** *2143*, **20:** 2328

Whodini **20:** 2303

'Whole Scene Going On, A' **8:** 852, *853*

Whyton, Wally **2:** 125, *125,* 134, **4:** 371

Wickham, Steve **19:** 2271

Wicks, John **19:** 2243

Widlake, Terry **6:** 694-5

Wigwam **20:** 2367

Wilcox, John 'Willie' **16:** 1905

Wild Angels, The **8:** 847-8, *848*

Wild Cats **2:** 139

Wild In The Country **2:** 212

Wild In The Streets **8:** 847

Wild Man Fischer **13:** 1495

Wild One, The **1:** 23, **2:** 206-7, **12:** 1385

Wild Turkey **14:** 1571

Wilde, Kim **16:** *1833,* 1834

Wilde, Marty **2:** 122, 131, *135,* 136-7, *136,* 138, 139, **3:** *285,* **4:** 361, *361,* 368, 374, 379, 380, 387, 424, 425, 427, 430, 431, **8:** 859, **13:** 1503, 1515

Wilde, Ricky **8:** 960, **15:** *1704*

Wilkeson, Leon **16:** 1843, 1844

Wilkie, Derry **5:** 523

Willcox, Toyah **20:** 2321, *2321,* 2334-5, *2334,* 2340

Williams, Allan **5:** 538, *544,* 547, 548, 549

Williams, André **9:** 1060

Williams, Andy **7:** 739, **13:** 1504, **17:** 1941

Williams, Big Joe **6:** 680

Williams, Charles **2:** 154

Williams, Cliff **19:** 2228

Williams, Deniece **15:** 1783, **18:** 2103

Williams, Don **17:** 2025

Williams, Hank **1:** 18, 22, *23,* 36-7, 39, 118, **2:** 195, **3:** 245, 328, **5:** 501, **10:** 1161, **11:** 1203, 1298, *1299*

Williams, Hank Jr. **14:** 1641, 1649

Williams, Heathcote **11:** 1248

Williams, Kae **3:** 343

Williams, Lamar **14:** 1604, 1605

Williams, Larry **2:** 155, 156, 165, 179, **3:** 241, **7:** 836

Williams, Leona **14:** 1649

Williams, Maurice **6:** 605

Williams, Millan **18:** 2117

Williams, Otis **9:** 1050, *1051,* 1052

Williams, Paul **3:** 337, **9:** 990, 1045, 1050, *1050,* 1052, **10:** 1114, **12:** 1329, 1339

Williams, Robert **13:** 1486

Williams, Terry **17:** 1935, **19:** 2199

Williams, Tony **1:** 72, **3:** 281, 299, 300, **9:** 1032, *1032,* **13:** 1523, 1530-1

Williams, Walter **14:** 1600, *1600*

Williamson, Billy **1:** 26

Williamson, James **13:** 1498-9, *1499*

Williamson, Robin **12:** 1398, **13:** 1468-70, *1469, 1470*

Williamson, Sonny Boy **1:** 56, *57,* **4:** 465, *466,* 467, **5:** *581,* **6:** 654, 657, **10:** 1102, 1108, 1114, **11:** 1221

Willis, Chuck **1:** 30-1, **3:** 275, *275*

Willis, Edgar **3:** 325

Willis, Pete **19:** 2236

Wills, Bob **1:** *23, 38,* 56, **2:** 181, **12:** 1401, **14:** 1648, 1649

Wills, Rick **7:** 809, *809,* **17:** 2040, **18:** 2133

Wilson, Al **10:** *1116,* 1116-17

Wilson, Andree **7:** 778

Wilson, Andy **20:** *2286*

Wilson, B. J. **10:** 1086-7, *1089,* **12:** 1364

Wilson, Barbara **7:** *779*

Wilson, Bernard **14:** 1598

Wilson, Brian **1:** 12, 13, 16, 63, **3:** 283, **4:** 402, **5:** 563, **7:** 761-2, *761,* 763, 765, 767, 770-2, 774-7, *779,* 778-80, **9:** 987, **10:** 1099

Wilson, Carl **7:** 762, *763,* 770, *770,* 772, 778, 780, **10:** 1099

Wilson, Chris **20:** *2288*

Wilson, Cindy **20:** *2286,* 2286-7

Wilson, Dennis **7:** *763,* 770, 772, *773,* 778, *779,* 780, **8:** 901, **17:** 2032

Wilson, Don **4:** 391

Wilson, Frank **6:** 713

Wilson, Fred **9:** 975

Wilson, Jackie **1:** 30, 74, **2:** 209, 240, **3:** 281, 322, 330-2, **4:** *463,* 471-2, 475, 494, **6:** 710, 714, **9:** 1045, 1054, **10:** 1161, 1165, **12:** 1419, **15:** *1785*

Wilson, Johnny 'Peanuts' **4:** 414

Wilson, Mari **19:** 2260, *2260,* **20:** 2345, *2345*

Wilson, Mary **4:** 478, **6:** 715, **9:** *1044-5,* 1045-9, *1049*

Wilson, Mick **9:** 950

Wilson, Murry **7:** 770, 775, 778, *779*

Wilson, Ricky **20:** 2286, *2286*

Wilson, Teddy **15:** 1788

Wilson, Tom **6:** 660, **7:** 822, **10:** 1128, **13:** 1493

Wilson, Tony **16:** 1826, 1828, *1828*

Wilson, Vic **19:** 2233

Wilson, Wallace **7:** 812

Wilson, Wes **12:** *1389*

Winchester, Jesse **16:** *1859,* 1903

Winfield, Church **13:** *1538,* 1539

Wingfield, Pete **6:** 608

Wings **17:** 1961, 1962-6

Winkelman, Bobby **11:** 1227

Wink Westerners **4:** *412,* 413

Winston, Jimmy **7:** 806, *808*

Winston, Stanley **15:** 1783

Winter, Edgar **11:** 1234-5

Winter, Johnny **4:** 390, **5:** 593, **11:** 1221, *1222,* 1223, 1223-5, 1251, 1253, 1256

Winter, Kurt **14:** 1617

Winthrop, Dave **15:** 1758

Winwood, Mervyn 'Muff' **10:** *1186,* 1186-7, 1188, **13:** 1519, **19:** 2199

Winwood, Steve **1:** 8, **6:** 603, **9:** 971, 1031, 1035-6, **10:** 1168, 1181, 1186-7, 1188-92, 1199, **11:** *1243,* **14:** 1562

Wisefield, Laurie **15:** *1736,* 1737

Wishbone Ash **15:** 1736-7

Wissert, Joe **9:** 993, **19:** 2163

Withers, Bill **19:** 2175
Withers, Pick **19:** 2199
Wizzard **10:** 1181, *1185,* **12:** 1423, **15:** 1747, **16:** 1803
Woffinden, Bob **12:** 1325
Wogan, Terry **17:** *1958,* 1960
Wolfe, Tom **8:** 906, **12:** 1323, *1323*
Wolfert, David **6:** 713
Wolff, Claud **6:** 622, 632-3, *633*
Wolff, John **11:** 1277
Wolfman, Jack **1:** 43, *58*
Womack, Bobby **3:** 334, 335, **8:** 940, **12:** 1403, **19:** 2175
Womack, Cecil **6:** 707
Wonder, Stevie **1:** *10,* **3:** 327, **4:** 445, 473, 479, **6:** 655, *655,* 704, 714, 718, 719, **7:** 781, **9:** 1040, *1041,* 1042-3, *1043,* 1049, **12:** 1416, **14:** 1581, 1583, 1620, 1661-2, *1661,* 1668, 1670-7, **15:** 1699, *1700,* 1763, 1785, 1791, 1800, **17:** 1942, 1966, 1973, **20:** 2360, 2387, 2420
Wonderful Life **4:** *429,* **8:** 844
Wonderlove **3:** 327, **14:** 1673
Wood, Chris **9:** 1031, **10:** 1188-9, *1190*
Wood, Randy **1:** 57, **3:** 313
Wood, Ron **7:** 809, 819, **8:** 883, *883,* 885, *889,* 894, 898, **9:** 979, *1035,* 1036, **11:** *1228,* 1230-1, 1243, **15:** 1721, *1724,* 1725, 1726
Wood, Roy **1:** 6, **10:** 1181, 1182-3, *1182,* 1185, *1185,* **15:** 1746, 1747, *1747*
Wood, Stuart 'Woody' **13:** *1510,* 1511, 1513
Woodgate, Dan 'Woody' **19:** 2210, *2210*
Woodley, Bruce **10:** 1140
Woodhams, Danny **17:** 1949
Woodmansey, Mick 'Woody' **14:** 1633
Woods, Gay **13:** 1466, *1471,* 1472
Woods, Georgie **10:** 1161, *1161,* **19:** 2177
Woods, Sonny **3:** 330, **5:** 494
Woods, Terry **13:** 1466, *1471,* 1472
Woodstock Festival **6:** 665, 676, **8:** 868, 912, **9:** 1068, **10:** 1085, 1091, 1096, 1164, 1168, 1171, **11:** 1241-2, 1250-1, 1253-4, 1258-9, *1258,* **12:** 1341, 1375, **13:** 1535, 1542, **15:** 1716, 1765, **19:** 2221
Woodstock **8:** 843, **11:** 1250-1, 1275, **12:** 1375, **13:** 1535, **20:** 2326
Wooler, Bob **5:** 522, 523
Worried Men **2:** 134, **4**: 371
Worth, Johnny **4:** 362, 371, 372, 422-3, *422*
Wray, Link **4:** 390, *390*
Wreckless Eric **17:** 1931, *1939*
Wright, Adrian **20:** 2306, 2308, *2308*
Wright, Billy **1:** 30, **2:** 149, **3:** 332, 338
Wright, Chris **12:** 1375, **14:** 1570
Wright, Gary **17:** 1982, **18:** 2133
Wright, Jeff **7:** *810,* 811
Wright, Norma Jean **18:** 2114
Wright, O. V. **15:** 1781-2
Wright, Richard **11:** 1307, *1307,* 1310, 1312, 1313, 1319-20
Wright, Simon **19:** 2228

Wright, Stevie **6:** 697
Wright, Syreeta **14:** 1673
Wurzels **10:** *1138,* 1139
Wyatt, Robert **13:** 1478, **14:** *1568,* 1569, 1578-80, *1579,* **15:** 1681, *1705,* **19:** 2207
Wylie, Pete **19:** 2276, 2278-9, *2279*
Wyman, Bill **8:** *881,* 882, 884, 885, 887, 890, *890,* 894, 897-8, 900, **9:** *1040,* **13:** 1445
Wynette, Tammy **2:** 234, **14:** 1659, **16:** *1824,* **17:** 2021
Wynter, Mark **4:** 374, 427

X

Xanadu **15:** 1749
X-5, Los **6:** 683
Xmal Deutschland **18:** 2072, *2156,* 2157
X-Ray Spex **18:** 2053, 2058, *2059,* 2061, 2070, *2070*
XTC **6:** 655

Y

Yachts **19:** 2242
'Yakety Yak!' **12:** *1356-7*
Yamauchi, Tetsu **16:** 1726, 1740, **20:** 2364
Yamomoyo, Kyoji **20:** *2363*
Yanovsky, Zal **1:** 18, **7:** 822, 838, **8:** 863, *866,* 867-8, *868*
Yardbirds **1:** 16, 67, **2:** 123, **5:** 595, 599, 600, **6:** 642-3, 650-3, 654, **7:** 724, *725,* 742, 759, *759,* 802, 803, 816, 820, **8:** 847, *871,* **9:** 1021-2, *1025,* 1026, **10:** 1113, 1154
Yarrow, Peter **6:** 664, *664,* **11:** 1228, *1229,* 1230, 1274, **12:** 1364, 1388, **15:** 1685, 1710, 1724, **16:** 1822
Yasgur, Max **11:** 1250, 1251
Yates, Paula **19:** 2251
Yazoo **18:** 2157, **20:** 2303, *2383*
Yello **20:** 2303, 2368
Yellow Magic Orchestra **20:** 2302, *2303, 2363,* 2364-5
Yellowman **16:** 1883, **20:** 2374, *2374*
Yellow Submarine **8:** 856, *856-7*
Yes **9:** 1022, *1039,* 1040, **11:** *1294,* **14:** 1562, 1565, 1619, **15:** 1681-2, 1690-5, 1721, 1742, 1759, **16:** 1901, 1910, **20:** 2397
Yester, Jerry **8:** *869,* **13:** 1554
Yewington, Macolm **1:** 47, 53
York, John **7:** 830
York, Pete **10:** 1186-7, 1188
Yorko, Dave **4:** 396, *396,* 397
Young, Angus **19:** *2226,* 2227, *2228-9*
Young, Faron **14:** 1647

Young, George **6:** 696-7, **19:** 2227
Young, James **18:** 2128, *2128-9*
Young, Jessie **3:** 295, 296, **15:** *1702,* 1703
Young, Jimmy **17:** *1958,* 1958-9
Young, Kenny **3:** 292, **5:** 567
Young, LaMonte **9:** 1005
Young, Larry **9:** 1032, **13:** 1523
Young, Lester **12:** 1418
Young, Neil **1:** 12, **6:** 655, **7:** 824-6, *824, 826,* **9:** 1020, *1076,* 1078, **10:** 1123, **11:** 1220, *1220,* **12:** 1359, **13:** 1548, **14:** 1659, **15:** 1702, 1764, 1765, 1766, 1768-71, **16:** 1845, 1846, 1847
Young, Paul **14:** *1657,* **18:** 2257, **20:** *2383,* 2394, 2405, *2408-9*
Young, Rusty **14:** 1657, *1657*
Young, Wanda **6:** 719
Young Ones, The **4:** 369, 430, 431, **5:** *504*
Young Rascals **8:** 862-3, 874-7, **9:** 1066, **10:** 1099
Yssou, N'Dour **20:** 2379
Yukihiro Takahashi **20:** 2365

Z

Zacharias, Ernst **15:** 1698
Zachery, Leno (Zack) **14:** 1598
Zaentz, Saul **13:** 1457
Zappa, Frank **1:** 18-19, **2:** 197, **8:** 847, 902, **9:** 990, 1015, *1074,* 1074-5, 1079, **10:** 1116, **13:** 1481-4, *1482,* 1486, 1490-6, 1525, 1526, 1529, 1554, **14:** 1611, 1620, **15:** 1683, **16:** 1858, 1865, **20:** 2376
Zarjazz Records **19:** 2213
Zawinul, Josel **13:** 1523, 1530-3, *1532,* **15:** 1699
Zevon, Warren **15:** *1761,* 1778
Zildjian, Avedis **4:** 400
Zigzag **12:** 1340, *1340*
Zimmerman, Robert *see* Dylan, Bob
Zito, Richard **14:** 1668
Zodiacs **6:** 605
Zombies **6:** 603, 688-91, 692, *692,* 693, **8:** 847
Zoo Records **19:** 2262
Zoom Records **19:** 2273
Zoot Horn Rollo **13:** 1484, 1486
Zoot Money **19:** 2184
ZTT Records **20:** 2413
Zukie, Tapper **20:** 2373, *2375*
Zu Zu Blues Band **13:** 1452
ZZ Top **14:** 1601, **15:** 1721, 1735, **16:** 1841, 1854-5

PICTURE CREDITS

VOLUME 1

Cyrus Andrews 6(T); **Richard Burgess** 19(Tr); **Elektra** 8(L); **EMI Records** 5(C,B); **John Frost** 18(Inset); **London Features International** 2, 3, 6/7(B), 10(T), 11(Tr); **Pictorial Press** 8(C), 13, 14/15(Tc, C, B, Br); **Polygram/Record and Tape Exchange** 18(L), **Vinyl Solution** 20(T); **Popperfoto** 12(B), 19(Br); **Pye Records/Bill Millar** 11(Tl); **Rex Features** 4, 5(T), 7(Tl), 8(R), 9(T), 10(B), 11(B), 12(T), 13(Inset), 14(Tl), 16(Inset), 17(Tl, B); **Stephen Shore** 20(C, B); **Syndication International** 1, 9(B), 16(T), 17(Tr), 18(T), 19(Bl); **Tate Gallery** 19(Tl); **Country Music Foundation Library and Media Center** 23(T), 40(T and Bl); **Culver Pictures** 22(B), 30(T), 35; **Chris Gardner** 24(Inset), 25(T and B), 26(B), 27(T), 28; **Grand Ole Opry** 36, 40(Br); **Norbert Hess Collection** 33(B), 34; **Jazz Music Books** 22(T), 33(T); **Living Blues** 29(T), 31(B), 32; **Bill Millar** 36 (Inset); **Michael Ochs** 29(B), 30(B); **Old Time Music** 23(B), 38(T and B), 39(T); **Peter Newark's Western Americana** 31(T), 39(B); **Popperfoto** 26(Tr), 27(B); **Rex Features** 21, 24, 26(Tl); **Billboard** 60(B); **Broadcast Pioneers Library** 56(T); **Charly Records** 46(C), 47(Tl and r); **Elvis Presley Fan Club** 54(B); **Elvis Presley Museum, PO Box 16911, Memphis TN** 53; **Charlie Gillett** 43(L), 59; **Globe Photos** 49(B), 54(T); **Martin Hawkins** 41(R), 42(B), 45(T), 46(Tl and r, Bl and r), 47 (B); **Dick Horlick/Bill Millar** 45(C); **The Image Bank** 60(T); **Jerry Lee Lewis Fan Club/Bill Millar** 41(L); **Peter Kanze Collection** 55, 57(T), 58(T); **The Kobal Collection** 58(B); **Living Blues** 57(Bl); **Memphis Press-Scimitar** 44/45, 52(B); **Bill Millar** 44(Bl), 52(Tl); **Old Time Music** 57(Bl inset); **Bill Prosser** 50/51; **Randy's Record Shop, Nashville** 42(T), 57(Br); **Syndication International** 43(R); **UPI** 56(B); **WLAY AM-FM Radio, Muscle Shoals and WJBB AM-FM Radio, Haleyville, Alabama** 44 (Tl); **Atlantic Records/Honest Jon's** 70(T); **BBC copyright photograph** 80(Tr); **Capitol Records/Bill Millar** 70/71; **Chess Records** 66(T); **Simon de Courcy Wheeler** 78; **Culver Pictures** 69(B); **Federal Records/Honest Jon's** 70(B); **Charlie Gillet** 62(L); 71(T); 72, 73(B), 75; **Jazz Music Books** 79; **Jubilee Records/ Honest Jon's** 70(C); **Peter Kanze Collection** 73(T); **Dianne Kaslow** 80(B); **Keystone Press** 80(Tl); **London Features International** 63(T), 64, 67(Br), 68(T); **Bill Millar** 67(T), 74(B), 76, 77(T and B); **Michael Ochs** 69(B); **Peter Newark's Western Americana** 65(T); **Pictorial Press** 68(B); **Popperfoto** 62(R); **Pye Records/Bill Millar** 67(Bl); **David Redfern Photography** 61, 63(B), 64(inset); **Rex Features** 65(B), 74(T); **Steve Richards** 66(B); **Roulette Records** 77(C); **Associated Press** 99(Cl and r); **Phillip Castle/Arcade Records/Francis Kyle Gallery, London** 99(T); **Culver Pictures** 87; **Elvis Presley Fan Club** 97(B); **Rob Finnis** 84(C); **Chris Gardner** 84 (T); **Keystone Press** 92(B), 99(B); **Kobal Collection** 83(T); **London Features International/Paul Cox** 94(T); **Bill Millar** 84(B), 95(T), 98; **Pictorial Press** 90(T), 97(C and Cr); **Popperfoto** 82(T and B), 83(B), 85,(L and R), 97(Tl); **RCA Victor** 89(T); **Rex Features** 93(R); **Syndication International** 88(B), 90(B), 91, 92(T), 96(L); **UPI** 100; **Award Records** 113(Lt); **Graham Barker** 102(L), 117(Tr); **Paul Barrett** 119(T); **Big Beat Records** 120(C); **Capitol Records** 104(T and B); **Charly Records** 110(B); **Martin Hawkins** 101(R), 110(T); **Dianne Kaslow** 103(B), 106(T), 106/107, 107(T and B); **G. Lautrey, S. Schlawick, J. Merritt, D. A. Kaslow/Gene Vincent Story series** 105(T and B); **London Features International** 101(L), 109(T), 110/111, 118/119, /Simon Fowler 118, 120(Br),/ **Michael Putland** 102(R); **Menswear Magazine** 116/117; **Bill Millar** 113(R), 114(B), 116(T), 120(T); **New Kommotion** 103(T), 108(B) 109(B), 112(L and R); **Phonogram Ltd** 117(Tl); **Record Exchanger, Box 6144, Orange, California** 114(T), 115(T); **Rex Features** 108(T), 111; **Solid Smoke Records** 115(Bl); **Gene Vincent Fan Club** 106(B); **Warner Bros** 113(Lb).

VOLUME 2

BBC Hulton Picture Library 123, 124(B), 130(Bl), 133(B), 134(B); **John Beecher/Paul Pelletier** 127; **Hal Carter** 138(L); **Dash Music/Paul Pelletier** 125(C); **Decca Record Company** 126(B); **Ronald Grant Archive** 140(C); **Keystone Press** 132(T), 135; **Liverpool Daily Post and Echo** 132(B); **Larry Parnes** 138(R); **Paul Pelletier** 122(C); **Pictorial Press** 121, 136(Tc and Tr), 137(Tand B), 139(C and B), 140(T); **Popperfoto** 122(T), 124(T), 125(T), 126(T), 128, 130(T), 130(Bc), 132/133, 134(Tl), 139(T); **Michael Reine Music/Paul Pelletier** 134(Tr); **Rex Features** 129(L), 130(Br), 131, 135 (Inset); **Talent Artists** 129(Tr), 129; **Thames Television** 136(B); **John Topham Picture Library** 133(T); **ABC Paramount Records/Bill Millar** 157(L); **Blues Unlimited** 145(B); **John Broven** 145(C), 154(Bl), 155(Bl); **Charlie Gillett** 150/151, 151(L), 152; **Bill Greensmith** 154(Br); **G. D. Hackett** 142; **Paul Harris** 155(C and Br); **Jazz Music Books** 144(Inset), 146(B), 150(R), 154(C), 156(R); **Bill Millar** 156(L and C); **David Redfern Photography** 144, 146(C), 158(L); **Rex Features** 143(Tr and B), 147, 148, 149, 150(L), 157(R); **Steve Richards** 151(R); **Mike Rowe** 141(T), 153(L); **Doug Seroff** 159(C); **Specialty/Sonet Records** 152(Inset); **Syndication International** 146(T); **Times Picayune, New Orleans** 143(Tl); **UPI** 158(R); **Val Wilmer** 141(B), 153(R), 160(T and C); **Lloyd Yearwood** 159(B). **Jerry Allison/John Beecher** 162(T); **Associated Press** 168; **John Beecher** 162(B), 169(T); **Daily Express/Barrie Gamblin** 170(B); **Bob Erskine** 177(T); **Barrie Gamblin** 161, 167(Tl); **Jazz Music Books** 175, 178(T),179(B), 180(Br); **Peter Kanze Collection** 165(B), 173(B); **London Features International** 171(T), **Paul Cox** 180(T); **Mercury Records/Bob Jones** 176(C); **Bill Millar** 164(T), 167(Tr), 172(L), 173(T), 176(T), 177(B), 179(T), **Bill Prosser** 170/171; **RCA Victor** 165(Cr); **David Redfern Photography** 167(B); **Rex Features** 163(B), 165(T), 169(C)), 172(R); **William Russell** 180(B); **Specialty/Ember Records/Bob Erskine** 163(T); **Talent Artists** 165(Cl); **UPI** 166; **Paul Vernon** 174; **Lloyd Yearwood** 164(C); **Ampex Corp** 198; **Associated**

VOLUME 3

VOLUME 4

408(R), 409; **London Records** 405(Bl); **Bill Millar** 401(Inset), 403(T); **Michael Ochs** 405(C); **Mick Perry** 414(C); **Steve Petryszyn** 405(Br), 406, 408(L), 412(B); **Pictorial Press** 401, 404(T), 405(T); **Popperfoto** 415; **Rank Records** 402(B); **Rex Features** 402(T), 412/413, 416, 417, 420(T); **Sire Records** 418, 419; **Studio Briggs** 410/411; **Ian Tilbury** 407(Inset); **Warner Bros Records** 408(Inset); **Hal Carter** 424, 427(Tl); **Cinema Bookshop** 429(B); **Brian Gregg** 434(B); **Brian Innes** 439(Tr,B); **Jazz Journal International** 438(T); **Jazz Music Books** 439(Tl), 440(L); **Chris Knight/Alan Blackburn, Joe Meek Appreciation Soc, 22 Plane Tree Walk, London SE19** 436; **H. J. Sheryn** 437; **Kobal Collection** 430(B), 431(B); **London Features International** 423(Inset T), 427(Tr), 428(T), 434(T); **Jerry Lordan** 422(Inset B, Background B), 423(Background T); **Rare Pics** 422(Inset Tl), 432(Inset); **Pictorial Press** 421(L), 425(Lt), 426/427, 433, 435; **Popperfoto** 421(R), 426(T, B), 438(B); **Rex Features** 422(Inset Tr), 425(Lb), 428(B), 429(T), 430(T), 431(T), 432, 432/433, 440(R); **Talent Artists** 423(Insert B); **Thames Television** 425(R); **Charlie Gillett** 442/443, 443(Tr), 447, 448(T), 449(T), 454(B), 458, 460; **Peter Kanze Collection** 441(B), 444; **London Features International** 442(Tl), 450/451, 450/451(Inset), 454(Cr), 459; **LFI/Michael Putland** 453; **Melody Maker** 446(T), 449(B); **Bill Millar** 443(Tl); **Steve Petryszyn** 441(T), 442(Tr); **Pictorial Press** 450(Inset), 454(Cl), 455(C), 456(Inset B), 457; **Popperfoto** 455(T), 456; **Rare Pics** 448(B); **David Redfern Photography** 454/455; **Rex Features** 452, 452/453, 455(B), 456(Inset T); **Val Wilmer** 445, 446(B); **Al Abrams** 471, 476(Tr); **Associated Press** 463(B); **Graham Barker** 469; **Peter Benjaminson** 461(L), 473(B); **Blues and Soul** 476(Tl); **Blues Unlimited** 462(B); **De Luxe Records** 463(Tl); **Charlie Gillett** 465(B); **Norbert Hess** 464(T), 465(T, C, B); **Peter Kanze Collection** 470(Br); **London Features International** 476(Tc), 478(T); **Melody Maker** 473(T); **Bill Millar** 470(Bl), 472(T); **Motown Records** 479; **Michael Ochs** 468; **Steve Petryszyn** 464(T); **Rare Pics** 470(T); **David Redfern Photography** 463(Tr), 464(B), 466(B), 467(B), 472(Br), 478(B), 480; **DRP/Beryl Bryden** 461(R); **Rex Features** 472(Bl), 474/475, 476/477; **Tom Sheehan** 470/471; **Val Wilmer** 462(T).

VOLUME 5

Blues and Soul 486; **Leo Castelli Gallery** 498(R); **Andre Csillag** 490/491, 492/493; **Daily Telegraph Colour Library/D. Franklin** 498(L), 500(B); **Charlie Gillett** 491(B); **Keystone Press** 481(R), 500(T); **King Records** 494(L); **The Kobal Collection** 487, 499(Insets L, C); **London Features International** 496(L), 522(L), 524, 535(T); **LFI/Lynn McAfee** 497(R); **Mander and Mitchenson Theatre Collection** 481(C); **Melody Maker** 484; **Bill Millar** 491(T); **Steve Petryszyn** 496(R); **Pictorial Press** 485(Ct and B), 488(Insets), 489; **Rare Pics** 482/483, 485(L); **David Redfern Photography** 485(R); **Rex Features** 481(L), 482/483 (Background), 483(R), 497(L), 499, 499(Inset R); **Steve Richards** 494(R), 495; **Syndication International** 488; **John Topham Picture Library** 486(Inset); **Rob Finnis** 506(T); **Denis Gifford** 505(Tl); **Charlie Gillett** 503(B), 505(Tr), 509; **Peter Kanze Collection** 502(B), 513(B), 518(Tr); **London Features International** 504(Tl), 511(Inset R), 515(B), 517(B), 518(Tc), 519(T); **Melody Maker** 507(Tr); **Michael Ochs** 502(T), 503(C), 506(B), 512(T), 520(C); **Pictorial Press** 504(Tr), 508(Tl, B), 512(B), 517(T), 518/519, 518(Tl); **David Red-**fern Photography 503(T), 510/511, 515(T), 520(T); **Rex Features** 504(B), 507(Tl, B), 508(Tr), 513(T), 514(B), 516, 520(B); **Spectrum Colour Library** 501; **Syndication International** 502(C), 505(B), 511, 514(T); **Bill Harry** 521(Inset), 522(R), 523(C); **Keystone Press** 526(Inset L), 527(Inset), 536, 537; **LFI/Simon Fowler** 530/531; **Liverpool Daily Post and Echo** 533; **Pictorial Press** 525(T), 529(Inset), 535(Cb); **Popperfoto** 521, 528/529; **David Redfern Photography** 523(L), 526(Inset R), 528(Inset C), 535(Br); **Rex Features** 525(B), 526/527, 532, 534, 535(Cl, Bl), 537(Inset), 538(Inset), 539(InsetL), 540; **Syndication International** 522(C), 523(R), 535(Ct); **Zefa** 538/539; **Jurgen Vollmer** 539(Inset R); **Tony Barrow** 556(Tl, B); **EMI Records** 545(Tl); **Keystone Press** 544(T), 548(B), 551 (Inset), 555(B); **London Features International** 541, 545(B), 557(R); **Pictorial Press** 546, 551, 553(Tl and r, C), 557(L); **Popperfoto** 543(Tr), 545(Tr), 549(Inset), 550, 554(T), 558(Insets, 560(Ct); **David Redfern Photography** 553(B); **Rex Features** 542, 549, 552, 554(B), 555(T), 556(Tr), 559; **David J. Smith** 544(C, B); **Syndication International** 543(T), 558, 560(Cb); **Jurgen Vollmer** 548(T); **Blues Unlimited** 561(T); **Jeremy Fletcher** 565(C); **Charlie Gillett** 567(T), 568(Inset L), 571(Tl); **Peter Kanze Collection** 563(Tl, Cr, B), 569(Inset), 575(T), 579(Inset); **Chris Knight/Alan Blackburn** 563(Cl); **London Features International** 568/569, 572(B), 573(T), 574, 575(B), 576(Inset C), 577(B); **Michael Ochs** 566(L), 571(Tr, C); **Pictorial Press** 563(Tr), 566(Rt), 576; **David Redfern Photography** 561(B), 566(Rb), 572(T), 573(B), 579; **Rex Features** 564(T), 565(B), 567(B), 568(Inset C), 570, 580; **Sailor's Delight** 565(T); **Syndication International** 562, 564(B), 576(Inset T), 578; **John Topham Picture Library** 568(Inset R); **Cyrus Andrews** 589(Bl); **Jeremy Fletcher** 589(Tl), 598(Tl and R), 599(R); **Philip Goodhand-Tait** 600(R); **Peter Kanze Collection** 595; **London Features International** 584(Bl), 585, 586(T, C),587(B), 590, 591(L), 592(B), 597(L); **LFI/Paul Canty** 592(T), **LFI/Chris Walter** 582(B); **Tom McGuinness** 589(Tr); **Bill Millar** 591(C,R); **Pictorial Press** 594, 596, 597(R), 599(L), 600(L, B); **David Redfern Photography** 582(T), 584(T); **Rex Features** 588/589, 593, 596(Inset), 598(B); **Sailor's Delight** 581, 584(Br), 586(B).

VOLUME 6

Home Counties Newspapers 619(T); **Peter Kaye** 604(Cr); **London Features International** 602(B), 603, 607(L, Br), 608, 610/611, 611(B), 615, 616/617(Insets); **Mander and Mitchenson Theatre Collection** 618(B); **Pictorial Press** 602(Tl), 604(L, Br), 606, 607(Tr), 608, 610(B), 616/617, 618(T); **Rare Pics** 612/613; **Rex Features** 601, 602(Tr), 604(Tr), 612(B), 613(B), 614; **Syndication International** 612(T); **Thames TV** 605; **Turvey and Turvey** 619(B), 620; **BBC copyright photograph** 633(C), 634(Inset); **London Features International** 622/623(T), 623(T), 625(Bl), 628(T), 630(L), 630/631, 633(B), 636(Tr, C); **Melody Maker** 627, 639(C); **Chris Morris** 624(B); **Pictorial Press** 621, 622, 623(B), 626, 627(Inset L), 628(B), 630(R); **Popperfoto** 624(Tr); **David Redfern Photography** 629; **Rex Features** 622/623(B), 624(C), 625(Br), 627(Inset R), 628(C), 632, 633(T), 634, 634/635, 635(T), 636(Tl), 637(L), 638, 639(T, B), 640(T); **Thames TV** 625(T); **Cyrus Andrews** 653(C); **London Features International** 643(T), 652/653, 656, 658(T); **LFI/Paul Canty** 649(T), **LFI/Paul Cox** 648/649; **Tom McGuinness** 645 (Inset T); **Roger Morton** Inside back cover; **Pictorial Press** 642 (Inset B), 644 (Inset), 647 (L, R), 648(T), 650/651,

653(Bl), 655(Tl and B), 657(Tl and B); **Rare Pics** 646; **David Redfern Photography** 645 (Inset B), 654, 655(Tr); **Rex Features** 642/643, 642(Inset T), 648(C), 651, 652(Br), 657(Tr), 659, 660; **Syndication International** 641, 644/645, 652(Bl). **CBS Records** 675(Inset B); **Robert Ellis** 680(T); **Flicks Photo Library** 679(T); **Bob Gruen** 672/673; **Marjorie Guthrie/Karl Dallas** 674(Inset T); **Jazz Music Books** 661(L), 662, 663(T), 678(C); **Peter Kanze Collection** 664(Br); **London Features International** 674(Inset B), 675(Inset T), 676(Rb); **Melody Maker** 669, 678(B); **Michael Ochs** 663(Tr), 664(Tr,Bl), 677(B); **Pictorial Press** 664(Tl), 666(B), 671(Inset L); **Popperfoto** 662, 663(B); **Rare Pics** 663(C), 668(Inset R); **David Redfern Photography** 665(Tl), 666(T), 668, 671(Inset R); **Rex Features** 663(Inset), 665(Tr), 668(Inset L), 670, 671, 671(Inset C), 672, 674/675, 676(Rt), 677(T), 679(C), 680(B); **Vanguard Records** 667; **Cyrus Andrews** 689(T), 690/691, 692(Br); **Dezo Hoffman/Rex Features** 688, 689(B), 690(Tl), 691(Tr); **Peter Kanze Collection** 694(T), **London Features International** 682(L), 684, 685(T), 690(Tr), 691(Tl), 695(Cr), 698(T), 699; **Mills Music Ltd** 695(Tl); **Michael Ochs** 683(L), 695(Tr); **Pictorial Press** 683(R), 684(Inset), 687, 693(R), 696(Tl), 697, 698(B); **Barry Plummer** 686(T); **Popperfoto** 692(T); **David Redfern Photography** 686/687, 695(Cl), 700; **Rex Features** 681, 682(R), 685(B), 692(B), 696(Tr), 696(B); **Syndication International** 693(L), 694/695; **Cyrus Andrews** 716(Br), 719; **Peter Benjaminson** 716(T), 720(B); **Adrian Boot** 705, 713; **Charlie Gillett** 714; **Dezo Hoffman/Rex Features** 706, 717(T); **Peter Kanze Collection** 716(B); **London Features International** 708, 709(T), 711(Inset Rt), 720(T); **Melody Maker** 703(Inset Tr), 707(R); **Bill Millar** 718(Tl and r, B); **Motown Records** 701, 702, 703(Inset Tl), 712(B), 716/717; **Rare Pics** 709(B); **David Redfern Photography** 703, 704, 710/711, 714/715, 717(Bl), 718(Tc); **Rex Features** 703(Inset B), 712(T); **Syndication International** 711(Inset Rb).

VOLUME 7

Cyrus Andrews 725(T); **Graham Gardner** 723(T), 735(T); **London Features International** 721(T), 724(B), 725(C, B), 728(R), 736(B); **LFI/Simon Fowler** 730(B); **Melody Maker** 722/723, 724(T); **Michael Ochs** 726; **Pictorial Press** 721(B), 730(T), 735(B), 736 (Tr); **Popperfoto** 722(T), 735(C); **David Redfern Photography** 729(R), 732/733, 733(T), 740(T); **Rex Features** 727, 729(L), 730(C), 731, 732(Inset), 734, 736(Tl), 737, 738, 739, 740(B); **Cyrus Andrews** 758(Tl); **Barnaby's Picture Library** 748(T, Bl), 749(Br); **Elly Beintema** 757; **Colour Library International** 741(B), 748(Bc); **Bill Greensmith** 759(Tl); **Keystone Press** 743(Inset), 744(T); **David Lewis/Tight But Loose** 759(Tr); **London Features International** 751, 752(L), 754/755, 756; **Melody Maker** 755(Tl and r); **Pictorial Press** 742(R), 745(B), 749(Tl), 753(B); **Popperfoto** 747(T); **Press Association** 746(T); **Rare Pics** 758(Tr); **David Redfern Photography** 753(T); **Rex Features** 745(Tl and r), 746/747, 749(Tr), 752(R), 757(B), 758(B), 759(B), 760(B); **Syndication International** 741(T), 742(L), 743, 744(B), 748(Br), 749(Bl), 750, 755(Tc), 760(T); **Cyrus Andrews** 763(Tc); **Beachboys Stomp/Mike Grant 22 Avondale Rd, Wealdstone, Mx HA3 7RE** 776(B), 778; **Brothers Records** 774/775; **Rob Burt Collection** 761, 763(Tl), 764(T, C), 771(Inset); **Capitol Records Inc** 768, 769(Tl), 776(Inset R), **CRI/Mike Grant** 776(Inset 1); **CBS Records** 769(Tr); **EMI Records (UK)** 762/763, 777; **Peter Kanze Collection** 767(B), 770(Inset);

London Features International 763(Tr), 770/771; **LFI/Brad Elterman** 766(B); **LFI/Peter Mazel** 770(R); **LFI/Michael Putland** 770(L); **Alvan Meyerowitz** 780(B); **Michael Ochs** 765, 766(T); **Pictorial Press** 770(C), 774(Inset R); **David Redfern Photography** 780(T); **Peter Reum Archives** 774(Inset 1), 778(T); **Rex Features** 767(T), 773(R), 778(B); **Pete Still** 773(B); **Syndication International** 778(C,Br); **WEA Records** 769(Bl); **Zefa** Cover(T), 764/765; **Associated Press** 782(Tr); **Jill Furmanovsky/Cliff White** 792; **Charlie Gillett** 784(Background); **Paul Harris** 798/799(Inset B); **Norbert Hess** 798/799(Inset T); **Peter Kanze** 793(T); **London Features International** 795(L), 796; **Pictorial Press** 783(T); **Popperfoto** 782(B), 783(B); **Rare Pics** 797; **David Redfern Photography** 786/787, 787, 790(B), 798/799; **Rex Features** 781, 782(Tl), 788(B), 790/791, 793(B); **Steve Richards** 784, 795(R); **Paul Vernon** 788/789; **Chris Walter/Cliff White** 790(T); **Cliff White** 786, 788(T), 789, 790(T); **Val Wilmer** 800; **BBC Hulton Picture Library** 802(B); **Robert Ellis** 808/809; **Dezo Hoffman/Rex Features** 817(Tl); **Peter Kanze Collection** 804(Bl); **London Features International** 804(Br), 805(B), 809(R), 810/811, 815(Bl); **LFI/Adrian Boot** 809(L); **Pictorial Press** 802(T), 807, 808(T), 813, 815(T), 818, 819(Cb), 820(B); **Rare Pics** 817(Tr); **Rex Features** 801, 803, 804(T), 819(B); **Syndication International** 808(B), 817(Bl), 819(T and Ct); **Val Wilmer** 812; **John Blackmore** 835(Bl); **CBS Records** 821(B); **Charlie Gillett** 824/825; **Peter Kanze Collection** 823(C), 826(B), 834; **Kobal Collection** 823(Tl); **London Features International** 823(Tr), 829(T), 830(B), 831, 835(Br), 839, 840(Tl); **Melody Maker** 828(B); **Michael Ochs** 823(B), 838; **Pictorial Press** 821(T), 823(Tc), 824(T), 827(T), 832(B), 836, 837(B); **Rare Pics** 829(B), 835(Tl); **Rex Features** 828(T), 830(T and C), 832(T), 833, 837(T), 840(Tr); **Syndication International** 840(B).

VOLUME 8

BBC Copyright Photograph 842(Tl and Tr), 852(Tr), 853(B), 856(B); **Keystone Press** 852(Tl), 858(Inset), 860; **Kobal Collection** 843(T and B), 845(T and Bl), 846, 847, 848, 854(Tl and B), 855(Tl, Tr, C and B), 856(Ct), 857; **Pictorial Press** 842(B), 850(L); **Popperfoto** 841, 842(Tc), 849, 851(T), 853(Tl), 854(Tr), 855(Tc), 858(Bl); **Courtesy Radio Times** 850(R); **David Redfern Photography** 851(Br); **Rex Features** 843(C), 850/851, 850(C), 851(Bl), 856(T and Cb), 858(T and Br); **Syndication International** 844, 853(Tr), 859; **Walt Disney Productions** 845(Br); **Cyrus Andrews** 867; **Daily Telegraph** 864(T); **DT/David Redfern** 861(B); **Peter Kanze Collection** 862(R), 870/871, 873, 876(B), 878/879; **Kobal Collection** 869(T); **Michael Ochs** 862(L), 864(Inset L), 866(T), 868(T), 870(Cl), 873(Tr, Cr), 874(B), 875(L, T); **Pictorial Press** 866(B), 868(B), 869(B), 875(Ct, Cb, B), 877, 879(T); **Pop Op Corporation** 863(Bl); **Rex Features** 863 (Tl), 878(Tr), 879(Inset), 880(C, B); **Syndication International** 864(B), 878(Tl), 880(T); **UPI** 861(T), 863(Tr, Br); **Colour Library International** 888(Inset B), 899; **Decca Records** 884; **London Features International** 882(Tl), 883(T, C), 886(Inset Cl), 888(Inset Tl), 892(Insets T and C), 895(Inset); **LFI/Anton Corbijn** 900(B); **LFI/Michael Putland** 889(L), 894/895; **Melody Maker** 896; **Pictorial Press** 882(B), 886/887, 890/891, 892/893; **Popperfoto** 892(Inset B); **David Redfern Photography** 883(B), 886(Insets far L and R, and Cr), 898; **Rare Pics** 897; **Rex Features** 882(Tr), 888, 889(R), 892/893(Inset), 894(Inset), 896/897, 900(T); **Rolling Stone Records/EMI** 885; **Daily**

Telegraph Colour Library 918/919, 920(B); **Rick Griffin/John Platt** 920(T); **Peter Kanze Collection** 913, 915(T, C); **Kobal Collection** 910/911(Inset); **London Features International** 905(C); **LFI/Michael Putland** 912(T); **Jim Marshall** 903(B), 906(T), 916(B); **Melody Maker** 917(L); **Mouse Studios/John Platt** 903(Inset); **Michael Ochs** 903(T), 909(B), 914, 915(B), 917(R); **Pictorial Press** 901, 902, 909(T), 910/911, 910(Insets T and B), 911(Insets T and B), 916(T); **John Platt** 904, 908(T); **Popperfoto** 918(B); **Nick Ralph** 904(Tr), 907(Tr); **Rare Pics** 908(B); **Jonathan Reed** 912(B); **Steve Rennick/John Platt** 919(C); **Rex Features** 904/905, 906/907, 918(T), 919(Lb); **UPI** 919(Lt and c, R); **Tony Ziemba/Nick Ralph** 905(T); **Atlantic Records/Bill Millar** 924(Br); **Blues and Soul** 930, 933(T), 934; **Charlie Gillett** 921(T, C), 922(B), 928(B), 929(B), 935(B); **Peter Kanze Collection** 921(B), 922(C), 929(Tl and r); **London Features International** 925(T), 931(B), 932(Tl), 939(R); **J. P. Leloir** 923, 927(B); **Melody Maker** 940(B); **Michael Ochs** 924(Bl); **Pictorial Press** 926, 939(L); **David Redfern Photography** 922(T), 928(T), 936; **Rex Features** 935(T), 940(T); **Steve Richards** 924(T), 932(Tr); **Christian Rose** 931(T), 933(B), 938; **Stax/Bill Millar** 933(Inset), 937(T); **Wes Wilson/John Platt** 927(T) **ATV** 959(Tl); **Robert Ellis** 953(B); **Charlie Gillett** 951(Inset); **London Features International** 947, 948/949, 950, 952, 953(T), 954, 955, 958; **LFI/Simon Fowler** 960; **Melody Maker** 958/959; **Gary Merrin** 948(Insets); **Pictorial Press** 941, 942, 945(Tl); **Rare Pics** 945(B); **David Redfern Photography** 956, 959(Tr); **Rex Features** 943(C), 946(B), 951(T), 957; **Syndication International** 944, 945(Tr).

VOLUME 9

Arista Records 962(L); **Arista/Michael Putland** 964; **Robert Ellis** 972(Inset B); **Island Records** 963(R); **J. S. Library International** 965(T); **London Features International** 963(L), 970/971, 972, 972(Inset T), 977(C, Bl); **LFI/Adrian Boot** 974(main picture), 975(T), 976, 977(Tl); **LFI/Paul Cox** 980(Inset); **Melody Maker** 973; **David Redfern Photography** 966(L), 967(T), 968/969, 971, 980; **Rex Features** 961, 978, 979; **Val Wilmer** 965(B), 966(R), 967(B), 975(B); **Buddah Records/Tom Hibbert** 996(Br), 997(Bl and c); **Colour Library International** 991(R); **André Csillag** 992/993; **Dezo Hoffman** 990/991; **Peter Kanze Collection** 982, 986, 988(Rt), 989, 994, 997(Br), 998(T), 999(T, Bl), 1000(B); **London Features International** 981(B), 983, 985(Tl), 990, 993; **Barry Lazell** 995(T); **Melody Maker** 998(B); **Michael Ochs** 981(T), 988(L), 996(L), 997(C); **Pictorial Press** 982/983, 984(B); **Popperfoto** 985(B), 987, 988(Rb), 991(L); **Nick Ralph Collection** 984(T); **Rex Features/Globe** 995(B); **Roulette Records/Barry Lazell** 994(Insets); **WEA Records** 985(Tr); **Wes Wilson/John Platt Collection** 992; **Commerce Studio, Cleveland, Ohio** 1010/1011; **Daily Telegraph Colour Library** 1020; **Mick Gold** 1006(T); **London Features International** 1001, 1012; **David Morosoli** 1016/1017(Insets); **Martin Norris** 1002; **Michael Ochs** 1004, 1014(Tl), **Jan Persson** 1014(Tr), 1016/1017; **Pictorial Press** 1003(Tl), 1006(B), 1008(T); **David Redfern Photography** 1005, 1007; **Rex Features** 1003(B), 1018; **Rex/Globe** 1009, 1013; **Gus Stewart** 1008(B); **Cyrus Andrews** 1024(Inset); **Robert Ellis** 1022/1023, 1023(Inset T), 1034/1035, 1036/1037(Inset); **Jeremy Fletcher** 1027(T); **London Features International** 1024/1025, 1025(Inset), 1028, 1032(L), 1035(Inset L, T, B), 1036/1037, 1040(B); **LFI/Simon Fowler** 1038; **LFI/Michael Putland**

1033(Lb), 1039(C), 1040(T); **Jan Persson** 1027(B); **Pictorial Press** 1021, 1026, 1028/1029; **Polydor Records** 1028/1029(Insets); **David Redfern Photography** 1030/1031, 1032(R); **Rex Features** 1033(Lt), 1034(Inset), 1038/1039; **Peter Benjaminson** 1048(T); **Rob Burt Collection** 1044, 1047; **CBS Records** 1054/1055; **Robert Ellis** 1048(B); **London Features International** 1049; **Bill Millar** 1056(B); **Motown Records** 1045(T, B), 1056(T); **Pictorial Press** 1045(C), 1046; **Robert Pruter** 1058, 1059, 1060; **David Redfern Photography** 1050/1051, 1052, 1053; **Rex Features** 1042/1043; **Syndication International** 1041; **Tony Bacon** 1078(R); **Paul Day** 1078(L), 1080; **Joel Finler** 1073(T); **J. P. Leloir** 1064, 1066/1067, 1067(Tl), 1069; **London Features International** 1075, 1079(B); **LFI/Paul Canty** 1079(Tr); **LFI/Paul Cox** 1078(B), 1079(Tl); **LFI/Brad Elterman** 1077(Inset B); **LFI/Simon Fowler** 1077(Inset T); **LFI/Michael Putland** 1076/1077; **Jim Marshall** 1068(T); **Melody Maker** 1068(C); **Jan Persson** 1067(Tr); **Pictorial Press** 1062(T), 1063, 1072(L); **Rare Pic** 1071(B); **David Redfern Photography** 1062(B), 1070(B); **Rex Features** 1061, 1077(Inset) 1080; **Rex/Globe** 1068(B), 1070/1071, 1074; **Syndication International** 1072(R), 1073(B); **Val Wilmer** 1066(T).

VOLUME 10

Yoram Kahana 1100(Tr, B); **Peter Kanze** 1083(T), 1093(B), 1097; **London Features International** 1083(B), 1084/1085, 1084(Inset L, R), 1086(L), 1089(Inset), 1094(Inset T, B), 1095(Inset T, B); **Melody Maker** 1094/1095; **Jim Marshall** 1098, 1099, 1100(Tl); **Michael Ochs** 1092, 1093(C), 1094(B), 1098(Inset); **Pictorial Press** 1082, 1084(Inset C), 1086(R), 1088; **John Platt Collection** 1096(Inset); **Popperfoto** 1090/1091, 1091(Inset); **David Redfern Photography** 1088/1089, 1088(Inset); **Rex Features** 1081, 1090, 1093(T), 1094(T), 1096; **Decca Records** 1113(T, C); **Jazz Music Books** 1105(T); **J. P. Leloir** 1106/1107; **London Features International** 1102(Rc), 1103(R), 1120(L); **Philip Melnick** 1116(Inset); **Melody Maker** 1114(Inset T); **Jan Persson** 1114(Inset B); **Pictorial Press** 1114/1115, 1118/1119; **Rare Pics** 1108; **David Redfern Photography** 1101(Inset), 1102(Rb), 1104, 1110/1111, 1112; **Rex Features** 1109, 1116/1117; **Val Wilmer** 1102(Rt); © **1983 David Gahr** 1122, 1123; **Yoram Kahana/Shooting Star Photo Agency** 1126; **Peter Kanze Collection** 1124(Br); **Kobal Collection** 1128; **London Features International** 1122(Inset L), 1124(T, Bl), 1130(Inset L), 1136(Inset B), 1138(T, B), 1140; **LFI/Michael Putland** 1124(C); **Melody Maker** 1133(B); **Michael Ochs Archive** 1127(Inset); **Pictorial Press** 1136/1137, 1136(Inset T), 1139(L); **David Redfern Photography** 1121, 1127, 1130/1131, 1139(R); **Rex Features** 1130(Inset R), 1133(Tl, Tr), 1134/1135; **Syndication International** 1122(Inset R), 1125, 1133(Tc); **Fred Woods/Folk Review** 1121(Inset); **Colour Library International** 1142(Bl and c), 1146/1147(T), 1148(Br), 1150/1151, 1154/1155; **EMI Records** 1152(Insets); **Keystone Press** 1142/1143, 1147(Br), 1158(T); **Kobal Collection** 1151, 1160(T); **Melody Maker** 1141; **Pictorial Press** 1143, 1148(Tr), 1150; **Popperfoto** 1146/1147(B); **Rex Features** 1142(Br), 1144(Inset), 1146, 1148(Tl, Bl), 1149, 1152, 1155(Inset), 1156(T), 1157, 1158(B); **Syndication International** 1144/1145, 1159, 1160(B); **John Topham Library** 1156(B); **Cyrus Andrews** 1178; **Aura Records/Tom Hibbert** 1175(T); **Bell Records/Tom Hibbert** 1174(B); **Capitol Records** 1161; **Island Records** 1169(Inset); **Peter Kanze Collection** 1162(T); **Kobal Collection** 1166,

1170; **J. P. Leloir** 1167(B); **London Features International** 1162(B), 1163(T), 1164(T, B), 1165(T, C, B), 1166 (Inset), 1167(T), 1168(T), 1177, 1180(T); **LFI/Janet Macoska** 1180(B); **Michael Ochs** 1163(B), 1168(B), 1174(T), 1179; **Pictorial Press** 1176; **Rex Features** 1169; **Elliot Landy/Star File** 1172, 1173, 1173(Inset); **Bobby Davidson** 1182(L), 1183; **Island Records** 1188; **Alan Johnson** 1190/1191(T), 1191; **J. P. Leloir** 1194; **London Features International** 1181, 1182(R), 1183(Inset), 1184, 1185, 1189(T), 1192, 1195(Tl, Tr, Bl, Br); **Pictorial Press** 1186(T), 1187, 1189(B), 1190/1191(B), 1195(C), 1196(B), 1199(T); **David Redfern Photography** 1197; **Rex Features** 1193, 1196(T), 1198; **Sailor's Delight** 1186(B); **Ray Stevenson** 1199(T).

VOLUME 11

CBS Records 1215(L), 1216, 1217(T); **1983 David Gahr** 1204(Tl, Tr), 1206/1207(T), 1207, 1208/1209(B, Inset Br), 1214; **Bob Gruen** 1212; **Kobal Collection** 1219(Inset Tl); **Elliot Landy/Star File** 1217(B); **J. P. Leloir** 1218/1219; **London Features International** 1208/1209(Inset L); **LFI/Adrian Boot** 1218(Inset B); **LFI/Neal Preston** 1220; **LFI/Michael Putland** 1219(Inset Tr); **Michael Ochs** 1204(B); **Pictorial Press** 1204(C), 1210/1211; **David Redfern Photography** 1213; **Rex Features** 1201, 1202, 1205, 1206, 1206/1207(B), ·1208/1209(Inset Tr), 1215(R), 1218(Inset B); **CBS Records** 1230, 1232(B); **David Gahr** 1224(C); **Charlie Gillett** 1204(T); **Colin Hill** 1224(Tr); **J. P. Leloir** 1226(Inset), 1233(Inset B); **Living Blues/Amy O'Neal** 1221; **London Features International** 1223(B), 1224, 1228/1229, 1229(B), 1231, 1233(Inset T), 1237, 1240(B); **LFI/Adrian Boot** 1232(T); **Melody Maker** 1223(Tl), 1229(T); **Michael Ochs Archive** 1225, 1238(T); **Nick Ralph Collection/CBS Records** 1239(B); **David Redfern Photography** 1222/1223, 1234, 1235(B), 1239(Tl, Tr); **Rex Features** 1226(T), 1226/1227, 1229(C); **Dave Walters** 1238(B); **CBS Records** 1243(C); **Joel Finler** 1250; **1983 David Gahr** 1252, 1254(T); **Steve Hare** 1242(T); **Peter Kanze Collection** 1253(Lt); **Kobal Collection** 1249, 1249(Inset R); **London Features International** 1242(Bl), 1242(Br), 1248(T); **Melody Maker** 1257(T); **National Film Archive** 1258(T); **Michael Ochs** 1258(C, B); **John Platt Collection/Rick Griffin** 1242(Bc); **Barry Plummer** 1260(B); **Popperfoto** 1244(B), 1245(T); **David Redfern Photography** 1241, 1244(T), 1246/1247, 1246(Inset), 1247(Inset B), 1253(R); **Rex Features** 1243(Tr), 1245(B), 1247(Inset T), 1247, 1248(B), 1249(Inset L), 1251, 1254(B), 1255, 1256, 1257(B), 1259, 1260(T); **Val Wilmer** 1243(Tl); **Brad Elterman** 1277(T); **Flashbacks** 1274(T); **Charlie Gillett** 1266; **J. P. Leloir** 1278; **London Features International** 1267(T), 1268, 1272; **Pictorial Press** 1261(T), 1279; **Polydor Records** 1262/1263; **Rex Features** 1261(B), 1267(Br), 1269, 1270(Inset), 1270/1271, 1274(B), 1276, 1280(B); **T. Spencer/Colorific!** 1264; **Syndication International** 1267(Bl), 1273; **Trinifold** 1274(C), 1277(B); **Chris Morphet/Trinifold** 1265; **Virgin Records** 1202(L); **WEA/Atco Records** 1280(T); **Arista Records** 1295(Lb); **Atlantic Records** 1294(Tl); **Blue Note Records** 1290(Tr); **Adrian Boot** 1288(L); **Bridgeman Art Library** 1294(Bl); **CBS Records** 1291(Bl), 1293(Br); **Leo Castelli Gallery** 1297(T); **Colour Library International** 1298(B); **Duke Records/Phil Hardy** 1293(Bl); **Robert Ellis** 1284(B), 1285, 1286, 1287; **EMI Records** 1289(L), 1293(C), 1294(Tr, CRt), 1295(Lt); **EMI/Phil Hardy** 1290(Bl); **F Beat Records** 1291(Tl); **Jill Furmanovsky** 1297(B); **Graduate Records** 1294(Br);

Immediate Records/Phil Hardy 1292(T, C); **International Artists/Phil Hardy** 1291(Tr); **Peter Kanze Collection** 1283(Tl); **Keystone Press** 1288(R); **London Features International** 1281, 1283(Tr), 1284(T); **LFI/Adrian Boot** 1283(B); **Mercury Record Corp/Phil Hardy** 1292(B); **David Oxtoby/photo Miki Slingsby** 1296, 1300; **Guy Peellaert/Peter Schunemann** 1299(T); **Pictorial Press** 1298(T); **Polydor Records** 1290(Tl), 1294(Cl); **Polydor/Graham Fuller** 1293(T); **RCA Victor** 1290(Br); **RCA/Phil Hardy** 1295(R); **Rex Features** 1298/1299; **Rex/Dezo Hoffmann** 1282; **Stax/Phil Hardy** 1291(Br), 1293(Bc); **Virgin Records** 1294(C), 1294(CRb); **WEA Records/Phil Hardy** 1289(R); **Whitworth Art Gallery, University of Manchester** 1297(C); **BBC Hulton Picture Library** 1306(T); **EMI Records** 1314, 1318(Tr, Br); **Joel Finler** 1317(T); **Mick Gold** 1308; **Graham Keen** 1303(Tl, Bl, Bc); **J. P. Leloir** 1309, 1310/1311; **London Features International** 1303(Br), 1310(B), 1311(T, B), 1312/1313, 1319(B), 1320(T), Inside back cover; **Chris Morris** 1303(C), 1304; **John Platt** 1301(B), 1305(L); **Pictorial Press** 1303(Tr), 1305(R), 1318(L), 1319(T); **David Redfern Photography** 1310(T); **Rex Features** 1306(B), 1307; **United International Pictures** 1316(L), 1317(B); **Graham Wright** 1312/1313(T).

VOLUME 12

Creem 1331(Br); **Pete Frame/Geoffrey Tyrell** 1340(B); **John Frost** 1337; **Charlie Gillett** 1324(Tr); **Grrr Books/Guinness Superlatives Ltd** 1325; **London Features International** 1330(L); **Greil Marcus/Mark Sarfati** 1331(Bl); **New Musical Express** 1328(R); **Newsweek** 1336; **Popperfoto** 1323(Tr); **Rex Features** 1323(Tl, B), 1334, 1335; **Rex/Dezo Hoffman** 1328(L); **Greg Shaw/Bomp Enterprises** 1339(T); **Rolling Stone** 1332(Bl and r); Thanks to **Stephen Barnard, Charlie Gillett, Phil Hardy, John Platt** and **Bob Woffinden. CBS Records** 1350; **David Gahr** 1344(Inset), 1360; **John Haynes/Half Moon Theatre** 1356(Br); **J. P. Leloir** 1345, 1347(T), 1352(Inset); **London Features International** 1342(C, B), 1343(B), 1347(B), 1348(B), 1351, 1354(Inset L), 1358(Inset); **Melody Maker** 1346; **Michael Ochs** 1348(T); **Guy Peellaert/Peter Schünemann** 1360(Inset); **Barry Plummer** 1352(C); **David Redfern Photography** 1344, 1349, 1354, 1356(T); **Rex Features** 1342(T). 1343(T), 1354(Inset R), 1359(Inset); **Spectrum Colour Library** 1358/1359; **Elliot Landy/Star File** 1356(Bl); **Virgin Records** 1358(B); **George Wilkes** 1353; **Atlantex Music Ltd./MXR Innovations Inc.** 1620(Inset B); **Peter Kanze Collection** 1603(B), 1611(T), 1612; **J. P. Leloir** 1609; **London Features International** 1604(L), 1610, 1612(Insets), 1614, 1616, 1617, 1618, 1619; **Melody Maker** 1615; **Michael Ochs** 1603(T), 1612; **Barry Plummer** 1607, 1608(B); **Pictorial Press** 1601, 1611(B); **Pix International/Debbie Leavitt** 1614/1615; **David Redfern Photography** 1602; **Rex Features** 1604(R), 1606, 1608(T); **Simmons Electronics Ltd.** 1620(T); **Starfile/Bob Gruen** 1605, 1620; **Fin Costello** 1380(B); **Kurt Hanson** 1363; **Chris Horler** 1373; **J. P. Leloir** 1378/1379; **London Features International** 1372(C), 1375, 1378/1379(Inset); **LFI/George Bodnar** 1371(T); **LFI/Paul Canty** 1369(B); **LFI/Simon Fowler** 1365; **LFI/Gary Merrin** 1380(T); **LFI/Mike Putland** 1366/1367(Inset T), 1368; **Ilpo Musto** 1366/1367(Inset B), 1374/1375; **Pictorial Press** 1362/1363, 1372(R), 1374(T), 1377(B); **David Redfern Photography** 1369(T), 1376; **Rex Features** 1361, 1364/1365, 1366/1367, 1370/1371, 1372(L); **All Sport** 1394,

1394(Inset R); **BBC Hulton Picture Library** 1392(B), 1393(T); **CBS Records** 1392(T); **David Gahr** 1382/1383; **Mick Gold** 1383(B); **Grundig** 1394(Insert L); **Phil Hardy** 1382(C); **London Features International** 1386/1387, 1398, 1400(B); **John Platt Collection** 1388(L); **Wes Wilson** 1388(R); **Mouse Studios** 1389(L); **Victor Moscoso** 1389(R); **Rick Griffin** 1390(L); **Bob Fried** 1390(R); **Randy Tuten** 1391(L); **Michael English** 1391(R); **Pictorial Press** 1385(T, Ctr), 1397(T), 1399(B); **David Redfern Photography** 1398(Inset); **Rex Features** 1385(B), 1393(C, B), 1396, 1397(B), 1399(T), 1400(T); **Sony** 1395; **Elliott Landy/Star File** 1383(T); **Syndication International** 1385(Cbl, Cbr), 1386; **John Topham Picture Library** 1384, 1385(Ctl); ; **Blues and Soul** 1410; **Adrian Boot** 1403; **CBS Records** 1415, 1416, 1417(T); **André Csillag** 1401; **William Gottlieb/David Redfern Photography** 1419(Lt); **Jazz Journal International** 1418(Lb); **J. P. Leloir** 1411; **London Features International** 1412, 1413, 1414(B), 1418(R); **LFI/Mike Putland** 1409; **Melody Maker** 1405; **Motown Records** 1420(T); **Michael Ochs** 1418(Lt); **Pictorial Press** 1402(R), 1420(B); **Barry Plummer** 1406/1407; **Rare Pics** 1414(T); **David Redfern Photography** 1402(L), 1404; **Rex Features** 1419(R); **Val Wilmer** 1419(Lb).

VOLUME 13

Alan Ball/Keith Altham 1429(B); **Allan Ballard/Scope Features** 1423; **London Features International** 1422(T, Ct, Cb), 1424, 1425, 1427, 1433(C), 1437; **Pictorial Press** 1435(B); **Barry Plummer** 1421, 1432/1433, 1433(T, B), 1435(T), 1439(Inset); **Rex Features** 1422(B), 1429(T), 1430, 1431, 1432(Inset), 1440; **Syndication International** 1426, 1428, 1436(T), 1438/1439; **David Gahr** 1448(B), 1450; **Paul Harris** 1454(R), 1455; **J. P. Leloir** 1457; **London Features International** 1441, 1442(T), 1446(Inset L), 1452/1453, 1458/1459, 1458/1459(Inset R); **Melody Maker** 1449; **Michael Ochs** 1445, 1446(Inset R), 1451; **Pictorial Press** 1454(L), 1456, 1457(Insets), 1458/1459(Inset L), 1460(L); **Barry Plummer** 1458, 1460(R); **Rare Pics** 1443(T), 1444/1445; **David Redfern Photography** 1452; **Rex Features** 1446/1447; **Mick Gold** 1474; **Kobal Collection** 1475; **J. P. Leloir** 1473, 1478/1479(B), 1480(B); **London Features International** 1462/1463, 1463(Inset L), 1464/1465, 1467(B), 1470, 1477(Inset L), 1478/1479(T), 1480(T); **Melody Maker** 1462(Inset); **Pictorial Press** 1470(Inset); **Barry Plummer** 1463(Inset R); **Rare Pics** 1467(T); **David Redfern Photography** 1468/1469(T, B), 1474(Inset), 1476/1477, 1476(Inset), 1477(Inset R); **Rex Features** 1472; **Syndication International** 1465; **WEA Records** 1466(Inset L, R); **CBS Records** 1491, 1496; **CBS/Terry Lott** 1492(T); **CBS/Tom Sheehan** 1494; **David Gahr** 1493; **Peter Kanze Collection** 1483(T), 1488/1489; **J. P. Leloir** 1485, 1490; **London Features International** 1499(B); **LFI/Paul Canty** 1500(Tl); **LFI/Paul Cox** 1500(B); **Melody Maker** 1483(B), 1484; **Michael Ochs** 1491(Inset), 1499(T); **Pictorial Press** 1487(Inset L), 1496(Inset); **Barry Plummer** 1497, 1500(Tr); **Nick Ralph Collection** 1487(Inset R); **David Redfern Photography** 1481, 1492(B); **Rex Features** 1494/1495, 1495; **Star File/Bob Gruen** 1482; **André Csillag** 1508, 1514(B), 1519(B); **London Features International** 1501(T), 1502, 1503, 1504, 1506, 1507, 1509, 1510, 1511, 1512(T), 1513, 1514(T), 1517, 1520; **LFI/Mike Putland** 1515, 1519(T); **Barry Plummer** 1501(B), 1512(B); **Rex Features** 1516, 1518, 1519(B); **Star File/Bob Gruen** 1505(B); **CBS Records** 1524, 1525(B), 1532/1533, 1537; **Al Johnson** 1528(B); **Kobal Collection** 1536; **J. P. Leloir** 1522; **London Features International** 1521, 1522/1523(B); **Michael Ochs** 1539(B); **Pictorial Press** 1528(T), 1530; **Rare Pics** 1531, 1535; **David Redfern Photography** 1526/1527, 1529, 1530(Inset), 1534, 1539(T); **Rex Features** 1522/1523(T).

VOLUME 14

David Gahr 1543; **J. P. Leloir** 1553, 1558; **London Features International** 1544, 1545, 1548/1549, 1550, 1560(T); **Michael Ochs** 1550/1551, 1559; **Rare Pics** 1542(T), 1557; **Reprise Records** 1556; **Rex Features** 1560(B); **Chester Simpson** 1552; **Star File** 1546; **Elliott Landy/Star File** 1541, 1542(B); **Brian Cooke** 1568(Inset); **E.G./Polydor** 1565(Tl, Tr), 1567(Bl, Br); **J. P. Leloir** 1564, 1566(T), 1568, 1578(Inset); **London Features International** 1561, 1562, 1565(C, Bl), 1566(B), 1570/1571, 1575; **Melody Maker** 1569; **Gary Merrin** 1563; **Pictorial Press** 1563(Inset), 1579(Inset), 1580; **David Redfern Photography** 1572(Inset R); **Rex Features** 1567(T), 1572, 1572(Inset L), 1577(Inset R); **Syndication International** 1574, 1577; **Peter Benjaminson** 1593(T); **CBS Records** 1588; **Charlie Gillett** 1597(T); **Peter Kanze Collection** 1583, 1598(T, Br); **Wayne Léal** 1592/1593; **London Features International** 1582, 1584(B), 1585; **LFI/Paul Cox** 1581; **LFI/Simon Fowler** 1597(Bl); **Pictorial Press** 1597(Br); **David Redfern Photography** 1587(T), 1595, 1598(Bl), 1599; **Rex Features** 1584(T), 1586, 1587(B), 1589, 1590/1591, 1594, 1600; **Starfile/Bob Gruen** 1592(T); **Jill Furmanovsky** 1640; **J. P. Leloir** 1637(Inset); **London Features International** 1622, 1623, 1628, 1632, 1633(B), 1635, 1636/1637; **Michael Ochs** 1634(L); **Pictorial Press** 1621, 1624, 1625(B), 1639; **Rex Features** 1625(T), 1626/1627, 1630/1631, 1636(Inset), 1638; **Mick Rock** 1634(C, R); **Star File/Chuck Pulin** 1633(T); **CBS Records** 1642; **Stephanie Chernikowski** 1648; **Andre Csillag** 1645; **Henry Diltz** 1650/1651; **Peter Kanze Collection** 1655(B); **Kobal Collection** 1644, 1647, 1651(B), 1652; **J. P. Leloir** 1641, 1658(T,B), 1660(B); **London Features International** 1646, 1649, 1651(T), 1659; **Michael Ochs** 1643(T), 1646(Inset); **RCA Records** 1660(T); **David Redfern Photography** 1656, 1657(C); **Rex Features** 1643(B); **Star File/Bob Gruen** 1654; **Charlyn Zlotnik** 1655(T), 1657(T,B); **Joe Bangay** 1675(T), 1679; **J. P. Leloir** 1669, 1670, 1676(B); **London Features International** 1661, 1662(B, Inset L), 1663, 1668(Tl), 1671, 1672/1673, 1678; **Pictorial Press** 1664(Inset), 1665(Inset B); **David Redfern Photography** 1666; **Rex Features** 1662(Inset R), 1668(Tr, B), 1674, 1675(C, B), 1680; **Rocket Record Co. Ltd.** 1664/1665, 1665(Inset T), 1666(Insets); **Star File/Richard Aaron** 1677.

VOLUME 15

Chrysalis Records 1682(B); **J. P. Leloir** 1684(T), 1688/1689; **London Features International** 1688(T, B), 1694(L, R), 1695(R), 1694/1695, 1696(Inset R), 1699, 1700; **Melody Maker** 1682(T), 1683; **Pictorial Press** 1687, 1692, 1693; **Barry Plummer** 1693(Inset); **David Redom** 1686; **Rex Features** 1681, 1696, 1696(Inset L); **Paul Snelgrove** 1698; **Syndication International** 1695(L), 1697; **CBS Records** 1702(B), 1708(B); **André Csillag** 1707(T); **David Gahr** 1711; **Jak Kilby** 1705(B); **London Features International** 1701, 1702(T, C), 1704, 1705(T), 1708(T), 1710(C, R), 1716, 1717, 1718; **Michael Ochs** 1715; **Picto-**

rial Press 1706, 1712; **Rare Pics** 1703; **David Redfern Photography/Allyce Hibbert** 1720; **Rex Features** 1709, 1713; **Star File/Richard Aaron** 1719; **Bob Gruen** 1710(L); **André Csillag** 1739(Inset); **André Csillag/Steve Emberton** 1736(T); **Jill Furmanovsky** 1736(B); **Al Johnson** 1738, 1739; **J. P. Leloir** 1736(C); **London Features International** 1724(T), 1726(B), 1728/1729, 1729, 1730/1731; **Ilpo Musto** 1722/1723, 1732(Inset T), 1733(Inset B); **Pictorial Press** 1732/1733; **Barry Plummer** 1732(Inset B); **David Redfern Photography** 1727; **Rex Features** 1724(B), 1725, 1726(T), 1728, 1730(Inset), 1733(Inset T); **Syndication International** 1721, 1734/1735; **André Csillag** 1746(T), 1747(T), 1760(Br); **Armando Gallo** 1750/1751, 1750(T), 1751(T), 1752/1753, 1752(Bl), 1754(B), 1756 (video colourisation by Ken Rubin), 1757, 1760(T); **J. P. Leloir** 1752(Br); **London Features International** 1744, 1745, 1748/1749, 1749(T), 1750/1751(T), 1753, 1754(T), 1759, 1760(Bl, Bc); **Janet Macoska/Kaleyediscope** 1755; **Melody Maker** 1747(B); **Pictorial Press** 1743(Tr); **Barry Plummer** 1743(B); **David Redfern Photography** 1741; **Rex Features** 1742; **Syndication International** 1746(B); **CBS Records** 1771(Inset R); **Henry Diltz** 1761(Inset), 1762, 1764, 1768/1769, 1770/1771, 1772, 1774, 1776, 1778; **Brad Elterman** 1770; **David Gahr** 1779; **Gijsbert Hanekroot** 1767(T); **J. P. Leloir** 1767(B); **London Features International** 1771, 1773(T, B), 1775; **Michael Ochs** 1762(Inset); **David Redfern Photogrpahy** 1777; **Rex Features** Front cover, 1761, 1780, Back cover; **WEA Records** 1771(Inset L); **Blues and Soul** 1784(Tr), 1795(B); **David Gahr** 1784/1785, 1786(Inset L), 1788; **J. P. Leloir** 1789, 1794; **London Features International** 1793(B), 1796, 1797, 1798, 1800; **Janet Macoska/Kaleyediscope** 1787; **RCA Records** 1783; **David Redfern Photography** 1781, 1782(T), 1784(L), 1786(Inset R); **Rex Features** 1790/1791, 1793(T), 1795(T), 1799; **Star File/Vinnie Zuffante** 1782(B), 1786.

VOLUME 16

Brian Cooke 1804(Inset); **E. G. Records** 1806(Inset); **Kobal Collection/ABC/Allied Artists** 1802(L); **J. P. Leloir** 1811(Inset L, R), 1812/1813; **London Features International** 1801(Inset), 1804/1805, 1806, 1807, 1811, 1812, 1814, 1815, 1817, 1818/1819; **Barry Plummer** 1815(Inset), 1816(Inset); **Pictorial Press** 1820(T); **Rex Features** 1801, 1802(R), 1803(T, B), 1805(Inset), 1808/1809, 1810, 1816; **Adrian Boot** 1827; **André Csillag** 1840; **Alan Johnson** 1828(B); **London Features International** 1822(B), 1824(T), 1824(Br), 1825(T), 1826, 1832/1833, 1836(T), 1836/1837, 1839; **Alvan Meyerowitz** 1825(B); **Pictorial Press** 1838(Rt); **Barry Plummer** 1823; **David Redfern Photography** 1821, 1824(Bl), 1830/1831, 1838(Rb); **Rex Features** 1828(T), 1830, 1838(L); **Syndication International** 1822(T), 1829, 1834, 1835; **Suzan Carson** 1859(B); **Peter Kanze Collection** 1851(B); **J. P. Leloir** 1843(B), 1848(T), 1852, 1857, 1858; **London Features International** 1841, 1846(Inset), 1854, 1855, 1860(B); **MCA Records** 1844(B); **Pictorial Press** 1853, 1860(T); **Barry Plummer** 1842, 1851(T); **David Redfern Photography** 1845(Inset), 1846, 1848(B), 1850, 1856/1857; **Rex Features** 1844(T); **Starfile/Steve Joester** 1859(T); **David Staugas** 1843(T); **Chris Walter** 1845; **G. Amman** 1862; **Robert Knight** 1863(B); **London Features International** 1861, 1862(Inset), 1863(C), 1865(B), 1867(Tl, Cl and r), 1869, 1870/1871, 1871(Inset L), 1875(Inset); **Pictorial Press** 1867(Tr), 1874(Inset); **Barry Plummer** 1863(T); **David Redfern Photography** 1868,

1874/1875, 1878; **Rex Features** 1867(Bl), 1871(Inset Rt), 1872, 1876, 1877(B), 1878(Insets L and R), 1879; **Star File/Bob Gruen** 1867(Br), 1871(Inset Rb); **Bob Leafe** 1864; **Syndication International** 1880; **WEA Records** 1865(Tl and r)**Adrian Boot** 1886(R), 1897(Tr); **Fin Costello** 1895; **Island Records** 1881; **Island Records/Adrian Boot** 1893; **Howard Johnson** 1883(B), 1884(Inset L, C), 1896(L); **London Features International** 1885(Tl), 1895(Inset T), 1897(Br); **LFI/Adrian Boot** 1884, 1884(Inset R), 1887(L), 1890(Tl, B), 1890(B), 1896(R), 1899; **Phil McHugh** 1897(L); **Melody Maker** 1882; **Barry Plummer** 1891; **David Redfern Photography** 1886(L), 1887(R), 1894; **Rex Features** 1885(B), 1888, 1890(Tr), 1892; **Peter Simon** 1883(T, C), 1895(B), 1898(T), 1900; **Star File/Kate Simon** 1898(B); **Air Studios** 1909; **Adrian Boot** 1902(L); **André Csillag** 1913; **Gijsbert Hanekroot** 1918, 1920; **Peter Kanze Collection** 1904(Inset L); **J. P. Leloir** 1904; **London Features International** 1905(T), 1914(T), 1915, 1917; **Neve International Ltd** 1908(B), 1910/1911 (photograph); **Michael Ochs** 1919; **Pictorial Press** 1912; **David Redfern Photography** 1906; **Rex Features** 1901, 1908(T); **Star File/Bob Gruen** 1904(Inset R); **Steve Joester** 1903; **Elliott Landy** 1905(B); **David Street** 1910/1911 (artwork); **Syndication International** 1914(B).

VOLUME 17

John Blackmore/Nick Pawlak 1923(B); **Nigel Cross** 1922(L); **André Csillag** 1934(L), 1940(Br); **John Frost Newspaper Collection** 1927(Tr); **Mick Gold** 1925; **Chris Horler** 1928/1929; **London Features International** 1921, 1922(R), 1924, 1926(L, R), 1927(Tl), 1930(T, C), 1932, 1933(T, B), 1935(T), 1936, 1937(T, B), 1938, 1940(T, Bl); **Barry Plummer** 1929, 1931, 1939; **Pictorial Press** 1927(B), 1930(B), 1935(B); **Chris Walter** 1927(C); **A&M Records** 1942(B); **BBC Copyright Photograph** 1954(T), 1959(R); **Capital Radio** 1959(L), 1960(Tl); **André Csillag** 1949; **London Features International** 1943, 1944(T, B), 1948, 1952, 1954(B), 1955(T, B), 1957, 1958(R); **LFI/Warner Bros.** 1947(Inset); **Pictorial Press** 1955(C); **David Redfern Photography** 1950/1951; **Rex Features** 1941, 1942(T, C), 1945, 1946/1947, 1953(T, B), 1956(T, C, B), 1960(Tc, Tr); **Syndication International** 1952(Inset), 1958(L), 1958/1959; **Colour Library International** 1971(Inset L); **Apple/EMI Records** 1961(T, Ct, Cb); **MPL Communications/EMI Records** 1961(B); **David Gahr** 1972/1973; **Kobal Collection** 1967(B); **London Features International** 1964(Tl), 1969, 1976(Tl, Tr), 1977, 1980(T); **Pictorial Press** 1975, 1979(C, B); **Barry Plummer** 1966; **David Redfern Photography** 1964(Tr); **Rex Features** 1962, 1964(B), 1970/1971, 1971(Inset Tr, Br), 1974(B), 1978, 1979(T); **Starfile/Bob Gruen** 1964/1965; **Starfile/Vinnie Zuffante** 1974(T); **Syndication International** 1963, 1976(B); **UPI** 1967(T); **WEA Records** 1980(B); **Darren Crook** 1982/1983; **London Features International** 1982, 1985, 1986, 1987(T), 1988, 1991(Inset), 1993(L), 1994(T), 1995(T), 2000(T, C); **Pictorial Press** 1994(B), 1995(B); **Barry Plummer** 1981; **David Redfern Photography/Peter Cronin** 1990/1991; **Rex Features** 1983, 1987(B), 1992/1993, 1993(R), 1997(B); **Hannes Schmidt** 1988(Inset); **Star File/Steve Joester** 1998/1999, 2000(B); **Syndication International** 1985(T); **Stephanie Chernikowski** 2005(C, B), 2007; **Arnold Desser/Tom Hibbert** 2002/2003; **David Gahr** 2019; **Norma Wiggins** 2013(Inset); **London Features International** 2004(L), 2008(R), 2010(B), 2017(T, B),

2018; **Pictorial Press** 2009; **David Redfern Photography** 2006, 2020; **Rex Features** 2010(T), 2014, 2104/2015, 2015; **Starfile/Bob Gruen** 2001, 2004(R), 2004/2005, 2005(Tl, Tr), 2008(L), 2012, 2013; **André Csillag** 2035(B); **Drake-Chenault** 2037(Tl); **David Gahr** 2022(L), 2023; **Peter Kanze Collection** 2036(B), 2037(B, Tr); **J. P. Leloir** 2040(L); **London Features International** 2024, 2025(C, B), 2026, 2027(B), 2032(B), 2033, 2038(T), 2039; **Pictorial Press** 2028; **David Redfern Photography** 2025(T), 2031(B), 2035(T); **Rex Features** 2022(R), 2029, 2031(T), 2032(T), 2034/2035(T, C, B), 2038, 2040(R); **Star File/Richard Aaron** 2021, 2030; **UPI** 2036(T); **Virgin Records** 2026(Inset); **WEA Records** 2027(T, C).

VOLUME 18

André Csillag 2042(Inset B); **Walt Davidson** 2059(Cr); **Erica Echenberg** 2042/2043, 2043(Inset B), 2059(Bl), 2060; **John Frost** 2042(Inset); **London Features International** 2044(B), 2046/2047, 2054(C), 2055(L, R); **Barry Plummer** 2046, 2047(T), 2051(Tr), 2059(Br); **Rex Features** 2041, 2042(T), 2043(T) 2044(T), 2049, 2051(Tl, Bl, Br), 2053(T, Cr, Cl, Br), 2054(Bc, Br), 2059(Tl); **Star File/Bob Gruen** 2047(B), 2048, 2051(Cr), 2052, 2054(T), **Star File/Kate Simon** 2043(Inset T); **Gus Stewart** 2059(Cl); **CBS Records** , 2068(Inset), 2068/2069; **Kevin Cummins** 2074; **Erica Echenberg** 2070, 2075(B); **London Features International** 2064, 2065(T), 2070/2071, 2072, 2073(B), 2075(T), 2079(T, B); **Barry Plummer** 2062(L), 2063(T); **Rex Features** 2061, 2063(B), 2065(B), 2066, 2067(B), 2076(B), 2077, 2080(L, R); **Star File/Bob Gruen** 2067(T, C), 2078(B); **Gus Stewart** 2078(T); **CBS Records** 2081(T), 2087, 2088, 2089, 2091, 2100(B); **David Gahr** 2090(T, B), 2092(C), 2093; **London Features International** 2081(B), 2084, 2084/2085, 2085, 2086(L, R), 2092(T), 2095, 2099(B); **J. P. Leloir** 2097(T, B); **MCA Records** 2083; **Pictorial Press** 2099(T); **Barry Plummer** 2100(C); **David Redfern Photography** 2092(B), 2098(T), 2100(T); **Rex Features** 2094, 2096, 2098(B); **Star File/Bob Leafe** 2090(C); **Michael Kunze** 2120; **London Features International** 2101, 2102(B), 2103(L), 2107(T), 2108, 2113, 2114(B), 2116/2117, 2119(Inset); **Pictorial Press** 2105, 2111(Inset R), 2114(C), 2120(Inset); **David Redfern Photography** 2115; **Rex Features** 2102(T), 2103(R), 2104, 2106/2107, 2110/2111, 2111(Inset L), 2114(T), 2117(Inset), 2118; **Star File/Richard Aaron** 2112; **Star File/Barry King** 2110(Inset); **WEA Records** 2119; **A & M Records** 2129(L); **J. P. Leloir** 2126(Inset T), 2126/2127, 2130/2131; **London Features International** 2121, 2122, 2123(Tl), 2124(T, B), 2128(T, B), 2129(R), 2130(Inset T), 2132(Inset B), 2135, 2136(B), 2138(T), 2138/2139; **Jan Persson** 2123(B); **Barry Plummer** 2123(Tr), 2127(Inset T); **Pictorial Press** 2137(T); **David Redfern Photography** 2131(Inset); **Rex Features** 2125, 2130(Inset B), 2134, 2136(T), 2139(Inset), 2140(T); **Star File/Geoff Thomas** 2132/2133; **Star File/Bill Warren** 2140(B); **WEM** 2137(B); **Dave Crump/Ealing Gazette** 2141; **André Csillag** 2146(T); **Martin Dean** 2153(T); **Do It Records** 2155(B); **Erica Echenberg** 2144/2145(T); **John Frost** 2143(T); **Go-Feet Records** 2160(Tr); **Human Records** 2155(B); **Illuminated Records** 2160(Tl); **Alastair Indge** 2150(Tl), 2156(B), 2157; **The Label** 2155(B); **London Features International** 2143(C), 2148, 2149, 2150(Tr), 2156(T); **Raymond Morris** 2144(B); **No Nukes Music** 2160(B); **Pictorial Press** 2147; **Barry Plummer** 2146(B), 2159; **Rex Features** 2144(T), 2150(B);

Rough Trade 2155(T, B); **Virginia Turbett** 2144/2145(B); **Fernando Valverde** 2143(B); **Val Wilmer/Format** 2142.

VOLUME 19

CBS Records 2161, 2162, 2164(T); **Jill Furmanovsky** 2169; **J. P. Leloir** 2166, 2170, 2175(B); **London Features International** 2163, 2167, 2169(Inset), 2171(T), 2172, 2173, 2174(Tr), 2175(T), 2176(T); **Tony Mottram** 2164(L); **David Redfern Photography** 2164/2165, 2165(T), 2171(B), 2174(Tl); **Rex Features** 2179(B); **Vernon St. Hilaire** 2176(B); **Star File/Lydia Criss** 2168; **WEA/Solar Records** 2178, 2179(T, C), 2180; **Val Wilmer/Format Photography** 2177; **Keith Altham** 2186(T, B), 2187(T); **André Csillag** 2191; **Ralph Denyer** 2183; **Erica Echenberg** 2186(C); **F-Beat Records** 2192; **Jill Furmanovsky** 2182; **J. P. Leloir** 2198; **Liberty/United Artists** 2190(C); **London Features International** 2181, 2182, 2188, 2188/2189, 2193(B), 2194(Tr and l), 2196, 2197(T, B), 2199, 2200(T); **Pictorial Press** 2187(B), 2194(C); **Barry Plummer** 2200(B); **Rex Features** 2184/2185, 2186/2187(T, C), 2190/2191(B), 2194(B); **Star File/Bob Gruen** 2193(T, C); **Adrian Boot/Judy Totten** 2209; **CBS Records/Terry Lott** 2217(T); **J. P. Leloir** 2212/2213(Tc); **London Features International** 2202(Inset Tl, Tr), 2202, 2204/2205, 2205, 2206, 2212/2213(Bc,B), 2214/2215, 2217(R), 2218/2219, 2219(Inset L), 2220(B); **Dennis Morris** 2217(C); **David Redfern Photography** 2215(L); **Rex Features** 2201(T), 2206(Inset Tl), 2219(Inset R), 2220(T); **Vernon St. Hilaire** 2208, 2217(Bl); **Star File/Oliver Monroe** 2215(R); **Stiff Records** 2210/2211, 2212, 2212/2213(T); **2-Tone/Chrysalis Records** 2201(B), 2206(Inset Tr); **Atlantic Records** 2228; **André Csillag** 2232(T), 2235; **J. P. Leloir** 2228/2229; **London Features International** 2221, 2224(L), 2225, 2226, 2233, 2234, 2236/2237, 2238, 2239, 2240(Inset T); **Observer Magazine** 2223; **Pictorial Press** 2224(R), 2227, 2230, 2232(B); **Rex Features** 2226(Inset), 2230/2231, 2240(Main picture, inset bottom); **Paul Slattery** 2223;**Star File/Steve Joester** 2222, **Star File/Kaplan** 2228(Inset), **Star File/Bob Leafe** 2231; **Janette Beckman** 2247(B); **Fin Costello** 2249; **André Csillag** 2247(Tl); **Jill Furmanovsky** 2256, 2257(B); **Kobal Collection** 2259(Inset); **London Features International** 2241, 2242(T, C, B), 2245, 2246(B), 2248, 2250(Tl, Tr), 2250/2251, 2254, 2257(T), 2258(T, B), 2259, 2260(B); **Klad McNulty** 2243; **Pictorial Press** 2255(T); **Barry Plummer** 2255(B); **Rex Features** 2247(Tc), 2253, 2260(T); **Star File/Bob Gruen** 2252; **Star File/Steve Joester** 2246(T); **Star File/Laurie Paladino** 2247(Tr); **Peter Anderson** 2267(Tr); **David G. Bailey** 2279(C); **André Csillag** 2262(T), 2274(B); **Rob Doolaard** 2267(B); **Erica Echenberg** 2270(T); **Factory Records** 2269(Inset); **Trevor Key** 2269; **London Features International** 2261, 2262(B), 2263(T), 2264(B), 2265(Tr), 2286, 2270(B), 2272, 2273, 2274(T), 2275, 2276, 2277, 2279(T, B); **Gary Lornie** 2262(C); **Pictorial Press** 2278; **Barry Plummer** 2267(Tl); **Rex Features** 2264(T), 2265(Tl), 2271(R); **Paul Slattery** 2266; **Star File/Robert Bentchick** 2271(Lt); **Star File/Oliver Monroe** 2271(Lb).

VOLUME 20

Ross Halfin 2292/2293; **Island Records** 2286, 2294(T), 2295, 2296/2297, 2297(L, R), 2298(T), 2299(B); **J. P. Leloir**